SPEAKING TRUTH TO POWER

The Art and Craft of Policy Analysis

SPEAKING TRUTH TO POWER

The Art and Craft of Policy Analysis

Aaron Wildavsky

Little, Brown and Company

BOSTON   TORONTO

H
6 |
.W554
1979

CREDITS

Chapter One, "Policy Analysis Is What Information Systems Are Not." Reprinted by permission from *New York Affairs*, Vol. 4 (Spring 1977), pp. 10–23,
© 1977.

Page 2, T. S. Eliot. Lines from "The Naming of Cats" from *Collected Poems
1909–1962* by T. S. Eliot. Reprinted by permission of the publishers, Harcourt
Brace Jovanovich, Inc., and Faber and Faber Ltd.

Pages 21–22, Henry Aaron. Excerpted from a speech given to the Evaluation
Society. Reprinted by permission.

Pages 71–72, Phillippe C. Schmitter. Excerpts from "Still the Century of
Corporatism?" in F. B. Pike and T. Stritch, eds., *The New Corporatism: Social
Political Structures in the Iberian World.* Copyright © 1974 by University
of Notre Dame. Reprinted by permission of University of Notre Dame Press.

Pages 109–110, Charles E. Lindblom. Excerpted from *Politics and Markets:
The World's Political-Economic Systems,* by Charles E. Lindblom, pp. 249–
255, © 1977 by Basic Books, Inc., Publishers, New York.

Chapter Six, "A Bias Toward Federalism." Reprinted by permission from
Publius, Vol. 6, No. 2 (July 1976), pp. 95–120.

Chapter Eight, "Economy and Environment/Rationality and Ritual." Reprinted by permission from the *Stanford Law Review*, Vol. 29 (1976), p. 183.
Copyright 1976 by the Board of Trustees of the Leland Stanford Junior University.

(*continued on page 421*)

For Gale Gordon
M.V.M.F.R.J.D.

ACKNOWLEDGMENTS

This book recites lessons I have learned from my teachers: the students, staff, and faculty at the Graduate School of Public Policy of the University of California at Berkeley. Two chapters have been coauthored with students at the school: David Good on "A Tax by Any Other Name," and Bob Gamble, Presley Pang, Fritzie Reisner, and Glen Shor on "Coordination without a Coordinator." Presley Pang used his incisive understanding to help me tease out the craft aspects of policy analysis. The chapter "Distribution of Urban Services" originally appeared, in slightly different form, in *Urban Outcomes: Schools, Streets, and Libraries,* with Frank S. Levy, and Arnold J. Meltsner, co-authors who are also colleagues. My collaborators on two other chapters — Jack Knott on "Jimmy Carter's Theory of Governing," and Bruce Wallen on "Opportunity Costs and Merit Wants" — were then students in the Political Science Department. No one knows enough about the broad sweep of public policy to do it alone and I have not tried.

Like everyone else I have benefitted by reading classics in the field — Yehezkel Dror's *Public Policy Making Reexamined* (San Francisco: Chandler, 1968), Charles Hitch and Rowland McKean's *The Economics of Defense in the Nuclear Age* (Cambridge: Harvard University Press, 1960 for the Rand Corporation, Santa Monica, California), E. S. Quade's *Analysis for Military Decisions* (New York: Elsevier, 1970), Sir Geoffrey Vickers' *The Art of Judgment: A Study of Policy Making* (New York: Basic Books, 1965). Critical commentary has proved invaluable. Robert Merton has provided the best (and toughest) comments it has ever been my good fortune to receive. Gordon Wasserman helped me cut out as well as include in. Herman van Gunsteren, Elaine Spitz, and Paul Sneiderman improved the sections on citizenship and trust. Leroy Graymer and several commentators for Little, Brown gave me a useful teaching perspective. Harvard Williamson helped improve my expression. I mean this book to be widely accessible, so that special thanks are due to my citizen critics — Juliette Diller and Judith Polisar. William Siffin labored long for Little, Brown (but more for me) to bring out the potential of this volume. I alone am irresponsible.

CONTENTS

SPEAKING TRUTH TO POWER

The Art and Craft of Policy Analysis

ANALYSIS AS ART

"What is Policy Analysis?
Why do you ask?"
   Anonymous

It would be a disservice to suggest that my images of policy analysis sprang full blown from imagination, or with the exact order into which these ideas have been pressed here. These conceptions are shaped by what was happening to me — devising a curriculum for a school of public policy, as much in an effort to understand analysis as to teach it — and to the country — the social programs of the sixties, filtered through one to two hundred analyses a year done by students and colleagues. That I came to analysis via the study of budgeting, in which politics and economics are intertwined, may account for my refusal to dissolve one into the other and my preference for trying to keep them together as political economy. Though now I think of myself as a political economist, I was first a political scientist. The capacity to make decisions in the future, to mobilize support for substance — that is, political rationality — is as least as important as generating economic growth so that there will be resources to allocate. Since policy analysis is about people, a category in which I am forced to include myself, my experiences matter.

Having begun with modest expectations (politics discourages heroics) I have not been disillusioned by the difficulty of finding programs that work well. There was little reason to believe that speaking truth to power (if only we had either!) would be more successful now than in the past. Problem-solving may, however, give way to problem succession (cut one off and another sprouts). Instead of attending only to trouble (how far have we fallen short?), I have learned also to ask whether our current difficulties are better or worse for people than the ones we used to have. On this score, as I will try to show, modest optimism is justified. It is no mean accomplishment that the federal government has put its money where its mouth is by increasing both absolutely and proportionately the amounts devoted to social-welfare programs. It helps to learn what government is worse at doing (changing citizens' behavior) and what it is better at doing (moving money). Then we would be less surprised that citizens are better able to get government to change what it does than they are at getting government to change the way their fellow citizens behave.

In the beginning, however, were the words — attractive, elusive, frustrating. How can you teach (or write a book about) a subject if you can't say what it is?

At the Graduate School of Public Policy in Berkeley, I discouraged discussions on the meaning of policy analysis. Hundreds of conversations on this slippery subject had proven futile, even exasperating, possibly dangerous. For whenever my colleagues and I began our courses by asking "What is a policy analysis?" or, a choice that proved to be worse, "What is a problem?" student anxiety rose alarmingly. The classroom crackled with tension. It was as if students felt the faculty were withholding something vital — the strange and simple secret of analysis (which we must have known because students couldn't learn it). Perhaps analysis was like one of T. S. Eliot's creatures in *Old Possum's Book of Practical Cats.*

> When you notice a cat in profound meditation,
> The reason, I tell you, is always the same:
> His mind is engaged in rapt contemplation
> Of the thought, of the thought, of the thought of his name:
> His ineffable effable
> Effanineffable
> Deep and inscrutable singular Name.

Yet our promise of pie in the sky by-and-by, though designed of course, to soothe the raging beast, was proved by experience. Students did learn to do analysis; and if our observation and their job experience were any guide, students not only *felt* but *were* more competent. What was it, then, that could be learned but not explained, that all of us could sometimes do but that none of us could ever define (at least to anybody else's satisfaction)? Our inscrutable ineffable friend, policy analysis. Cold comfort; those who can't say what it is, teach, and those who can do policy analysis, still can't say how it was possible to do it.

A first clue came from an unusual aspect of our teaching experience:

policy analysis is better taught backward. Instead of beginning by formulating a problem, considering alternative solutions, developing criteria, applying criteria to data, and so on, students' work improved when exercises went the other way around. The best way to begin learning was to apply strong criteria to good data, go on to create criteria and discover alternatives, and, after numerous trials, formulate a problem at the very end. Why did anxiety decline and confidence rise when entering through the back door? Possibly, formulating the problem was more like the end than the beginning of analysis.

Reflection, accompanied by observation of research in public policy, revealed that creativity consists of finding a problem about which something can and ought to be done. In a word, the solution is part of defining the problem. Mike Teitz tells about a soldier in New Zealand who was ordered to build a bridge across a river without enough men or material. He stared along the bank looking glum when a Maori woman came along asking, "Why so sad, soldier?" He explained that he had been given a problem for which there was no solution. Immediately she brightened, saying, "Cheer up! No solution, no problem."

Problem-finding is analogous to inventing or theorizing. In invention the task is not to compile a list of all unfulfilled human needs (or even the shorter list of those which deserve fulfillment), but to connect what might be wanted with what can be provided. The prizes in science go to those who choose problems that turn out to be interesting and solvable. So, too, in policy analysis, the most creative calculations concern finding problems for which solutions might be attempted. No wonder, then, that students go into shock the first week if they are (in effect) asked to create original social inventions. Even their teachers usually can't do that on demand. Because policy analysis presumes creativity, a subject on which much is written but little is known, our inability to teach analysis directly is easy to understand. (The injunction "Be Creative!" is notoriously unhelpful.)

PROBLEMS OF IMPLEMENTATION

What tools does the policy analyst use? Qualitative political theory, for refining our picture of where we want to go; quantitative modeling, for systematizing guesswork on how to get there; microeconomics, for disciplining desire with limited resources, and macro-organization theory, for instilling the will to correct errors: each has its place. Policy analysis, however, is one activity for which there can be no fixed program, for policy analysis is synonymous with creativity, which may be stimulated by theory and sharpened by practice, which can be learned but not taught.

Creativity in policy analysis may have social roots. History is food for thought. All who have lived through the exalted promises and disappointed hopes fed by the social programs of the sixties, to come to our times, are seared by that experience. Much of the scholarship of the seventies, my own included, has been an effort to understand what went wrong and to learn how things might be made to work better, or whether government should take some actions at all. The more government attempts to do, the larger its difficulties. For in that greater attempt it must intervene further in personal behavior or extract more of personal income. Diogenes notwithstanding, it appeared easier to find an honest man than an effective program. Why?

Visiting Washington, I heard the plaintive cry that prospects which looked rosy there would dissipate in the hinterlands of this vast continent. In response I started an action-research project in Oakland, California. When Jeff Pressman told me that a program designed to create minority employment there was credited with stopping riots, I asked him to investigate. It turned out that little had happened. As simple as the project appeared, it had run into numerous detours, delays, and blind alleys. To discover why something that seemed simple actually was so convoluted, we wrote a book on *Implementation*[1] to show how the complexity of joint action — multitudes of agencies, innumerable regulations, stacked-up levels of government — made it difficult to move. The reforms of the past lay like benign booby traps, which could make one stumble even if they did not explode. Yet all this had been set up for reasons that once seemed good.

The more the nation attempted to control public policy, the less control there seemed to be. A troublesome parallel aspect of this expanding public sector was the feeling that unintended consequences were overwhelming the ability to cope. Vast changes were taking place amid suspicion that here was change for change's sake alone. Immobility and change appeared to be different sides of the same coin. Increasingly policies led lives of their own, independent of human volition. I wondered if policy could possibly be its own cause.

Indeed, it was possible. The larger each policy grows in its own sector, the more it insinuates itself into the man-made environment with which we must contend. More and more public policy is about coping with consequences of past policies — years of controversy over spending a billion dollars of federal money in New York City on highways or subways go on without a word about responding to its transportation needs but a million words about using other people's money — and less and less about events in society. The more we do, therefore, the more there is for us to do, as each program bumps into others and sets off consequences all down the line. In this way past solutions, if they are large enough, turn into future problems. And who is to deal with such problems? Naturally, those people paid to work at it full time, namely, the bureaucracy. That is how the bureaucratic sectors of policy become at once the strongest stokers and the most determined dampers of change. In the growing bureaucratization of public policy, we experience direct consequences of the good things we have done — in alleviating poverty, improving medicine, increasing safety, purifying the environment, and all the rest. Why then do we feel so bad about the good we have tried to do?

The title of Chapter 2, "Doing Better and Feeling Worse," expresses the contradiction: health rates for all sectors of the population have improved; access to medical facilities for the poor and elderly are more nearly equal; yet the feeling of crisis in health care grows. Unwilling to try either a market solution, abolishing insurance and subsidy, or a bureaucratic solution, abolishing private medicine, we keep funneling in more money and complaining about the inflation that comes out. Where does the fault lie, then — with policies that have undesirable side effects, or with people who want the policies, but not the resulting perils?

Comparing the social state of the nation before and after these social policies, however, I wonder if we would be willing to trade current problems for those we used to have. I would not. I don't consider the sixties a disastrous decade nor would I go back willingly to a time when race, poverty, environment, and a host of other difficulties were ignored. Perhaps, instead, we need to ask if present standards for judging public policies are appropriate.

Thinking that social ills are puzzles that can be solved (once and for all, as President Carter might say) instead of problems that may be alleviated or eventually superseded, can make us despondent when they do not yield to our ministrations. A good comparison is to do something, as opposed to nothing, and then evaluate the result. The rub there is that you don't know whether some other action might have been better or worse. A better comparison is to contrast the problems we have now with those we had before. Instead of thinking of permanent solutions we should think of permanent problems in the sense that one problem always succeeds and replaces another. Then we might ask whether today's answers are more moral or more effective than the solutions they succeeded or which they might replace. Are today's inflated medical costs preferable to yesterday's restricted access to medical care? The capacity of policies to generate more interesting successors and our ability better to learn from them what we ought to prefer, may be their most important quality.

But why don't public agencies seem to profit from mistakes? Is it because these institutions don't want to (the worse conditions get the higher their budget), or don't know how? Study of budgeting in federal recreation agencies pointed me in the right direction.[2] The traditional budget was attuned to its political environment but did not produce an evaluation that questioned fundamental assumptions behind programs. The new program budget, which was out of tune with politics but designed to do analysis, also failed to use evaluation that would challenge current programs. The important question, therefore, is why agencies, regardless of their techniques, do not use evaluation.

The easy answer is that organizations don't want to rock the boat;

they establish interests — benefits, careers, clientele — apart from any supposedly desirable objectives. The hard answer is that, in order to do good
things, organizations need sources of support that encourage stability as
well as change. Resistance to evaluation is part of self-protection. Skepticism clashes with dogma in organizations as well as in thought. Getting
organizations to act is the hardest part of policy analysis. Unless it is designed to be still born, analysis includes action. That is why efforts to
make organizational considerations an integral part of policy analysis
(rather than an afterthought) are essential.

My experience as an administrator reinforced a passion for correcting errors. Trying to avoid error stultifies; besides, no application of care
will avoid all mistakes. Expecting to make errors and pick up after oneself is much more satisfactory. John Wheeler wrote, "our whole problem
is to make errors fast enough." Yet, in a university where every colleague
is king and rationalization is high art, it is hard to convince people who
think they know better to recognize mistakes and persuade them (orders
are out of the question) to take corrective action. In teaching, if errors
are nobody's business except the instructors', other colleagues will pay no
attention and there will be no external and independent corrective. You
will find that in the appendix to this book on "Principles for a Graduate
School of Public Policy" I suggest a collective interest in correcting the
required courses. By making it clear that error was expected, correction
was considered commonplace and those corrected did not feel threatened.
Finding a new mistake became the thing to do. Unless recognition of errors is rewarded, they will not be corrected.

To recognize error is one thing: to become a side-show example of
error that cannot be corrected is quite another. If governmental agencies
are asked to change people's behavior (health habits, reading scores,
criminal activities) that no one can (or is willing to) control, agencies
will be guilty of failure even before being so charged. No one likes to
be dubbed a failure, so public agencies try to escape by transforming
what they can do into what they are supposed to do. If the change is
within the agency, controllable resources may become the agency's objectives; what agency would fail to seek salvation by spending? Or if the
change is in the client, an agency can find clientele (reading-ready children, employable adults, healthy elderly) who will be able to achieve
those objectives.

Making what one can do into what one is supposed to accomplish, or
choosing capable clients who are already accomplished, are means of constructing a benevolent environment. But escaping external censure is not
the same as an internal desire for self-correction.

The good organization evaluates its own activities, correcting error
as it goes along, and acknowledging mistakes as a way of improving performance. Because it goes against organizational nature, however, self-
evaluation must be reinforced by studies that are external, multiple, inde-

pendent, and continuous. Evaluation should be independent (and therefore external) to avoid self-serving behavior. Because more than one political perspective is involved, evaluation should be multiple. Multiplicity also facilitates generation of alternatives without which choice cannot be genuine. Because there is no one truth — indeed, because correcting error rather than establishing truth is the norm — evaluation should be continuous so that common understandings (not mere assertions) can grow. Evaluation fares well when a variety of organizations are motivated to conduct and use studies. Evaluation, therefore, is conceived best as a social procedure that is the cumulative result of many efforts rather than just one.

If evalution is social, correction of errors depends on how society is organized. The relative objectivity of analysis depends on people living together in reasonable trust within a common culture. The cultural conditions within which analysis takes place — the sort of social structure thought desirable, the values to be obtained — guide and shape what is done. If trust declines, the framework of facts that can be taken for granted declines with it. Without agreement on a starting place, there is no end to debate. Theories harden into dogma, and assertion replaces evidence. Policies then are judged not by their merits but by the motives of their proposers.

Evaluation of programs, to be sure, is not necessarily analysis of policy. Telling people they have not achieved intended objectives does not necessarily help them discover what should be done. Unfortunate program managers who need to know which activity deserves priority in the budget are not helped by blanket condemnation or the kind of proposals that only the president, Congress, the United Nations — anybody but someone at their level — can act upon.

Looking back at what we want from evaluation in political arenas — recognition and correction of errors, encouraged by social processes rich with varied reactions — we see something similar to decision-making in economic markets. For a market to qualify as relatively fair and functioning, it might have many buyers and sellers (not just one), repeatedly making independent bids (not just once), evaluating results compared to opportunities elsewhere (not just in this market). In a word, markets should be rife with redundancy. Each bid builds upon and succeeds the one before, and errors are corrected by historical comparison with the last previous interaction. Prices that reflect current conditions are retained and those which do not are rejected. Markets that function so as to recognize and correct error, therefore, fulfill norms for interaction (independence, multiplicity, continuity) that aid bureaucracies in evaluation.

Just as no man necessarily is good for all seasons, no institution's structure is equally appropriate under any and all conditions. Private markets have well-known imperfections, such as failing to take account of inequalities in distribution of income. Markets make dollars (not people) equal. The external effects of individual actions, when what one does imposes direct burdens on others who cannot be compensated, may demand nonmarket mechanisms. If markets were perfect, after all, there would be no need for governmental intervention. Suppose, however, we remove the distinction between economic markets and political arenas, by considering a problem — inflation of medical costs — for which contemporary history has ruled out a market solution. Is it better for government to exert cost control by monitoring every transaction in hospitals at the cost of being overwhelmed or should government give lump sums, not to be exceeded, leaving to hospitals the detailed allocation of resources? Even within a governmental structure, then, planning and politics — cogitation versus interaction — compete for our loyalties. It is not politics and economics that are at loggerheads, because both are forms of interaction, but rather orders that tell people what to do versus helping them figure things out for themselves.

If planning were judged by results, that is, by whether life followed the dictates of the plan, then planning has failed everywhere it has been tried. Nowhere are plans fulfilled. No one, it turns out, has the knowledge to predict sequences of actions and reactions across the realm of public policy, and no one has the power to compel obedience. So far so bad. Why, then, is planning so popular? Why, facing universally negative experience, is planning still pursued? Has mankind's desire to control its fate — on paper with a plan, if nowhere else — led to justification not by deeds but by faith? If so, planning is not so much an answer to a question about public policy (what should be done about polluted water or bad health or whatever?) but a question in the form of an answer: provide a plan.

Thinking about planning in poor countries,[3] I wondered whether following the forms of planning (specifying and ranking objectives, selecting alternatives, choosing the best one) was valued not for what planning did but for what it was — comprehensive, coordinated, consistent, above all, rational. Thus, planning led me to rationality. How could it be rational to fail? If planning led to failure, if it led to bad behavior instead of right action, then planning must be irrational, i.e., known to produce wrong results.

The method called the "rational paradigm" (order objectives, compare alternatives, choose the highest ranking) is mistaken as describing either how decisions are or ought to be made. This paradigm conveys the wrong-headed impression that all one has to do to answer a question is to ask it. Just how thoroughly available answers determine the kinds of questions asked (as solutions often search for problems[4] and resources affect objectives) remains unrecognized. Creativity is compromised by squeezing the peregrinations of the mind into one sequence.[5] The derivation of the word analysis itself, which comes from a Greek root meaning subdivide, is derogated by implying that everything was understood at once, not, as is far more likely, in steps through which, darting back and forth, difficulties are divided and decomposed until they are made manageable or abandoned. The hypothetical *Journal of Negative Results* is a nonstarter. Intellectual cogitation is treated as if all were done by a single mind while the contributions of countless others, whose social support is indispensable for past ideas and future criticism, is neglected. Meanwhile a passion for gaining power over nature by acting as if there had always been (and, therefore, always will be) an orderly universe overwhelms everyday observation to the contrary.

What could be rationally wrong with collectively considering where we want to go and what might be the best way of getting there? So much is wrong it is hard to know where to begin. The question itself is confusing. Does destination know no limitation? Do we first decide where and then how? This priority is perverse; it is no better than the reverse, as if the journey always mattered more than the destination. No, where one wishes to go depends on whether one is able to get there. Life is larger than our categories. When my grandfather lost the family fortune, comprised of fifty rubles, he went to see the local miracle Rabbi, Joseph of Slutsk, who consulted mystical works, and told him to collect ten kopecs apiece from his friends and relatives and take it to the train. "But where shall I go?" Grandpa cried. "As far as your money will take you," replied the Rabbi, who knew more about the relationship of resources to objectives than his seemingly scientific successors.

Error manifests itself as confusion between a mode of presenting results and a method of making choices. Having finished a study or made a decision, we find it economical of time and effort to present not the historical evolution, the short cuts, the blind alleys, the trial and error that led to a recommendation, but, by way of summary, the alternatives adopted with the evidence in favor of the winning one. Alas, the form has come to be identified as the substance of rationality. And so departures from this facile form of presentation are now labeled irrational both as description ("the crazy-quilt patterns of politics") or prescription ("man has been made into a machine by soulless market forces").

Here again interest in budgeting proved helpful. Originally I had seen that budgetary procedures based on comprehensive planning failed from the usual lack of knowledge and power. No one knew how to do program budgeting (comparing consequences horizontally across all major programs) or zero-base budgeting (comparing results vertically within each program by starting from scratch each year) because the required calculations boggled the mind. Both budgeting methods threatened to burden operating agencies with greater central control without enabling them to offer compensating gains; agencies thus lacked incentives to cooperate. The purpose of analysis is to connect knowledge with power, not ignorance with weakness.

When time and attention are scarce it cannot be rational to revive all past conflicts or reconsider all past solutions (those which work and those which don't). Simplification is essential to avoid being swamped. Sensitivity studies, the effort to determine which variables might (or, almost as important, might not) affect policy recommendations, are part and parcel of analysis. Only in this way can one learn which variables may be left out safely so that analysis can be converted into action. The analysis of analysis, so to speak — relating resources to objectives in the act of analysis, the knowledge, time, and assistance available to the analyst — demonstrates the need for simplification. Analyst, study thyself! One must decide how much intellectual as well as material resources are worth expending on each program. Feasibility is studied in order to learn whether and at what cost obstacles may be overcome. To sum up, because analysis of policy is supposed to be an applied discipline, it includes not only thinking up ideas but also facilitating their application.

There is a difference between including expected difficulties of implementation in analysis, which is part of good craftsmanship, and acting to implement the analysis, which is salesmanship. In my book, craftsmanship is mandatory but salesmanship is voluntary. The unarmed analyst rarely conquers. I appreciate the value of those analysts who have done their bit by doing good work. My personal preference, having gone that far, is to supplement knowledge with persuasion by actively helping policy ideas make their way in this world.

If analysis is about accomplishment, it should be useful to study that element in organizations which specializes in information about results. When I taught courses on information systems designed to improve decision-making (management by objectives, social indicators, the critical path method, PPBS, ZBB, national planning), a common pattern appeared: rationality was thought to inhere in objectives. Objectives are to be ranked, compared, discussed, imposed, accepted — everything, it seems, except realized. A moment's thought should convince anyone that objectives depend on resources, for what one might do depends in part on the resources one has for achieving goals. But, if the point is obvious, why is it so often missed? Just as every newly married couple hopes to avoid whatever led to the previous divorce, so a fixation on objectives is a reaction against a prior romance with resources. Where older modes of justification concentrated on resource inputs (effort, monies, personnel), new modes concentrate on objectives (reading scores, health rates, return to prison). Analysis of policy, by contrast, always considers resources and objectives, means and ends together, never separately. The proper comparison for the policy analyst is always between alternative programs, which combine resources and objectives, in different ways, but not the one or the other in isolation. By making it appear that rationality resided in the activity of ranking objectives, planning had become ineffective and therefore irrational.

Yet my own argument that rationality resides in results evidently was not convincing enough to planners, nor did it go deep enough. Why were planners so dead set against spontaneity and so insistent on control? I had missed the war of opposites close to the heart of disputes over planning. Two images began to grow in my mind. One was of social interaction, as in political arenas or economic markets, where people pursue their own interests, and the results of their reactions are summed up in decisions about office holders or prices without anyone necessarily controlling the sequences of individual actions or intending an outcome. The troublesome aspects of social interaction are its willfulness, messiness, and apparent disorder. Selfishness and chaos lack appeal as organizing principles. To remedy these defects, I drew from Lindblom the opposing image of intellectual cogitation* that orders social relations through mental processes as if they were taking place in one mind. Control is exercised by anticipation. Social actors are assigned positions, given motivations, and guided through the mind of the planner to that destination determined to be in the best interest of all. Intellectual cogitation imposes severe strains on cognitive capacities; central command is in danger of becoming remote or oppressive. The conflict between social interaction and intellectual cogitation involves different psychologies (expression versus control), cognitive styles (adaptation versus anticipation), political processes (bargaining versus hierarchy), and moral calculus (the individual versus the collective). With differences so fundamental that their full extent is often unrecognized, it is not surprising that apparent agreement on one direction breaks down on others, or that there is difficulty agreeing on facts — which in any event rarely appear decisive in designing or evaluating policies.

* These ideas (and the terms "social interaction" versus "intellectual cogitation") originated from dissatisfaction with my own previous work on planning. (See "If Planning Is Everything, Maybe It's Nothing," *Policy Sciences*, Vol. 4, No. 2 (June 1973), pp. 127–153. Readers would say "yes, yes," but not many minds were changed. Earlier, I had thought that more could be done with Charles E. Lindblom's "mutual partisan adjustment" as a mechanism for policy design. See his *The Intelligence of Democracy* (New York: Free Press, 1965). As I began writing this book, the necessity of connecting thought to action was uppermost in my mind, a connection that had to be made without sacrificing one to the other. The term "interaction" has been a staple of sociological thinking and discourse for generations, not least in the work of Georg Simmel, who devoted his monumental *Soziologie* (1908) in no small measure to *soziale Wechselwirkung*, writing that "Society is merely the name for a number of individuals connected by interaction." Translation by Kurt H. Wolff, *The Sociology of Georg Simmel* (New York: Free Press, 1950), p. 10. "Intellectual cogitation" came from thinking of a parallel to "social interaction." Later, when I sent a preliminary draft of chapter V to Lindblom, I received papers from him showing that his thought was far advanced on these matters. His main intent is to compare capitalism and communism; mine is to think about policy analysis. Nevertheless, these terms are used in a remarkably similar way and his come first. Many times I have acknowledged my debt to his thought before the fact and now I must do so during and afterward as well. For differences as well as similarities in our thought, see my review of his *Politics and Markets* (New York: Basic Books, 1977) in the *Yale Law Review*, Vol. 8, No. 1 (November 1978).

Comparing interaction among a multiplicity of units with planning by hierarchy in just one leads to renewed interest in centralization versus decentralization. Principles of federalism apply not merely to relations between central and state governments but also to relations within agencies and programs. Evidence is accumulating that in public policy economies of scale are illusory. For the most part, increasing size coupled with central direction is accompanied by declining performance in consolidated school districts, police forces, and a host of other services. My federal bias — when in doubt, a large number of small units are preferable to a small number of large ones — inclines to interaction so as to make government more accessible to citizens. Analysis is needed not to eliminate interaction by consolidation but to liberate it by different designs for decentralization.

Evidently, people interested in analyzing policy do not want to do away with intellect or to do without interaction. Analysts want to anticipate difficulties as well as to react to them. As much as they enjoy solving problems, analysts would like to have most difficulties dealt with by the relevant parties. Yet analysts also want to be able to suggest that ways other than those voiced may be preferable. Policy analysis, therefore, is about combining social interaction with intellectual cogitation.

My preference for interaction rather than cogitation, for more "asking" and less "telling," for politics over planning, is not meant to protect interaction from scrutiny as if it were a dogma. On the contrary, skepticism should extend especially to interaction — how it develops, what sustains it, why it produces outcomes, its class and ideological biases, when it should be changed — precisely because we begin by intending to rely on it. In a word, the main task of responsible intellectual cogitation is to monitor, appraise, modify, and otherwise strengthen social interaction.

And this requirement (a responsibility, really, for a democracy in which popular preferences should matter) holds true if one is an analyst acting as a citizen or a citizen doing analysis. Analysts act as citizens (see Chapter 15 on urban services) when they bring to light deviations of actual policy outcomes from accepted norms. Seek and ye shall find! Choice determines which discrepancies to bring to light. Citizens act as analysts when they take responsibility for policy performance by comparing what they receive for what they put in, by learning to refine their preferences, and by developing morally in connecting what they do to what other people want.

MORALITY IN POLICY ANALYSIS

Whatever the combination, speaking truth to power remains the ideal of analysts who hope they have truth, but realize they have not (and, in a democracy, should not have) power. No one can do analysis without becoming aware that moral considerations are integral to the enterprise. After all, analysis is about what ought to be done, about making things better, not worse. I have never been sympathetic to the view that facts and values, except as intellectual constructs, either are or ought to be kept separate in action.

In what, then, does the morality of the analyst consist? Are policy analysts "hired guns" paid to do the bidding of their clients, whatever that might be? Should they subvert their superiors for a higher cause? Discovering that a required course on moral dimensions of policy analysis in Berkeley (When do you resign? Who do you serve? How can moral implications be made more explicit in analysis?) did not satisfy a longing to be proved virtuous, I made our students a standing offer: when in doubt, the "Dean of Morality" would provide instant replies about which actions under what conditions were moral.[6] Some questions are easy to answer. Analysts should not abuse a client's trust by working sub rosa for others who are believed to be more deserving. Other questions are more difficult. If a study shows that a program supported by a worthy group with whom the analyst identifies lacks positive results, should that conclusion be made known? Yes, of course, though if the personal discomfort is excessive, the analyst may wish to move to other subjects. Suppose, however, the program as a whole appears desirable but contains flaws. Is the analyst duty-bound to reveal faults not only to clients, but, when challenged, to adversaries as well? Analysis, which is in part rhetoric, should be persuasive. Presenting a preferred policy in the most persuasive manner, by finding arguments that will appeal to others, is not only personally permissible but also socially desirable. One promise of policy analysis is that through repeated interactions, common understandings (though not necessarily, of course, common positions) will grow, so that action will be better informed.

Still greater difficulties arise. What the analyst does in one situation often is connected with opportunities to exercise influence in others. Should analysis be moderated or even withheld if action taken in this instance would damage future prospects? Clearly, careful balancing is rerequired. Here, however, the "Dean of Morality's" offer to decide the matter was rejected. "Who set you up as our Grand Inquisitor?" students asked. "After all, we have our own moral sensibilities and are able to take our own risks." And so you have and so you are.

Suppose you are working in the White House in order to be persuasive in recommending billions for inner-city urban areas. When within striking distance, should you oppose the president on Israel or condemn his proposals on civil service reform, rendering suspect your advice on urban aid? Analysts must not lie but they may be silent.

Still, there must be and there are, limits: *everything is not allowed.* Just as science cannot tolerate mob rule, in which claims are settled by force, or nihilism, in which every claim is as good (or bad) as every other just because it is made, so policy analysis, without being self-defeating, cannot be based on violence or fraud. The more violence, the less information, as coercion displaces cogitation and intimidation replaces interaction. Action that appears to be individual is actually mass manipulation. Unfortunately, the absence of force does not guarantee the presence of authentic expression. That depends on, among other things, self-awareness and social trust. Interaction cannot operate if social actors withhold their true preferences and cogitation cannot calculate on false data. Although these norms rejecting force and fraud may appear overly dramatic when baldly stated, they are, in fact, quietly included under accepted modes of craftsmanship.

Designing problems is an art but justifying solutions is a craft amenable to various conventions: some distinguish work of quality and others select forums for securing agreement on what counts as evidence. The detailed biblical directions for building the temple, specifying quality of material and workmanship, as well as the endlessly elaborated procedures for preparing whales in Melville's *Moby Dick,* are reminders that the morality of ordinary people like us (but not like Moses or Ahab) consists of maintaining the quality of everyday activity that is craftsmanship. High standards and healthy habits are protection against the demonic. To be sure, there can be no guarantee that truth will be discovered or, if it is, that it will make mankind free or even increase agreement rather than conflict. But maintaining acceptable standards for convincing others (including not lying to oneself) is surely superior to doing the opposite.

What about me? Will I make good my promise to tell the truth about analysis of policy? Maybe. It depends not only on what I have to say but also on what you are looking for. Suppose I summarize: Analysis is *descriptive* in that it is designed to explain how a difficulty has come about. Analysis is *prescriptive* in that it aims to give advice on what should be done. Analysis must be *selective*, therefore, in that it is oriented to particular people (in specific slots within locatable levels of an organization) who have the authority, money, and other resources required to do what is recommended. Analysis may be *objective* by getting people to agree on the consequences of a variety of alternatives. Insofar as it is relevant to future choices, however, analysis inevitably is *argumentative,* leaning toward this view and rejecting that other one. The ability to rationalize is not to be rejected once it is recognized that the capacity to convince is essential for social support. Analysis is *retrospective* because it involves establishing a view of the past (this is why we need change) that will justify a desired future.

But, I have said also that analysis is *inventive,* representing a creative juxtaposition between resources and objectives. Analysis is *prospective,* seeking its rewards in the future, which is always in doubt. Analysis must also be *subjective,* therefore, in that the choice of problems to be solved, as well as the alternatives considered, is not specified but must be worked out by particular people with individual interests.

Is analysis, then, a union of opposites — prospective and retrospective, objective and subjective, descriptive and prescriptive — or, different things under different circumstances? Both.

As philosophers of science say of discovery (origins of ideas and their formation into theories, which we call policies), analysis is indeed an art. But as we proceed to justification (why we should tentatively accept evidence), rules of craftsmanship become more important. Distinctions may be made between work that is better and worse on such grounds as inclusion of variables that can be used by decision-makers, sensitivity of design to difficulties of implementation, viability of assumptions, and anticipation of counterargument. How policy is created may be a private affair, but whether it is justified is part of a public proceeding.

By this time suspicion dawns: there can be no one definition of policy analysis. As old-time cooks used to say when asked how much spice a recipe required, "as much as it takes." Policy analysis is an applied subfield whose content cannot be determined by disciplinary boundaries but by whatever appears appropriate to the circumstances of the time and the nature of problem. When confronted by excessive expectations, my father would tell the story of how Yoshke answered an advertisement calling for a butler who had his own livery, could pilot an airplane, speak French, and set table for full service. When the major-domo asked about livery, Yoshke said he preferred underwear. Could he fly a plane? Actually, he even got sick in cars. Did he speak French? His English wasn't really that good. Could he set table? Maybe one knife and fork. By this time, the major-domo was getting angry: why had Yoshke come if he evidently lacked every qualification? "Well," Yoshke said, "I came to tell you, on me you shouldn't depend."

Do not ask from me what you should not want — a definitive definition of policy analysis good for all times, places, and circumstances. If you are looking for the secret of analysis, you will not find that here (or anywhere else, for that matter) but if you want to debate about different ways of thinking about public policy, I hope this book is a good place to begin.

THE ART OF POLICY ANALYSIS

Policy analysis is an art. Its subjects are public problems that must be solved at least tentatively to be understood. Piet Hein put this thought-twister,[7] "Art is the solving of problems that cannot be expressed until they are solved." Policy analysis must create problems that decision-makers are able to handle with the variables under their control and in the time available. Only by specifying a desired relationship between manipulable means and obtainable objectives can analysts make the essential distinction — between a puzzle that can be solved definitively, once all the pieces are put in place, and a problem for which there may not be a programmatic solution.

The technical base of policy analysis is weak. In part its limitations are those of social science: innumerable discrete propositions, of varying validity and uncertain applicability, occasionally touching but not necessarily related, like beads on a string. Its strengths lie in the ability to make a little knowledge go a long way by combining an understanding of the constraints of the situation with the ability to explore the environment constructively. Unlike social science, however, policy analysis must be prescriptive; arguments about correct policy, which deal with the future, cannot help but be willful and therefore political.

Analysis is imagination. Making believe the future has happened in the past, analysts try to examine events as if those actions already had occurred. They are strongly committed to "thought experiments," in which they imagine what might have been in order to improve what may come to pass. Theories are discarded instead of people. Naturally, this is risky. Often we do not know where we have been, let alone where we would like to go or how to get there. Retrodiction ("predicting the past") may be as much in dispute as prediction. Because what our past should have been, as well as what our future ought to be, is defined by differing values, one person's analytic meat may be poison to another. Following the practices of the analytic craft — norms for disciplining private imagination by making it more publicly assessable — can reduce but cannot eliminate disagreement over future consequences that no one has yet experienced.

Policies should be considered not as eternal truths but as hypotheses subject to modification and replacement by better ones until these in turn are discarded. Dogma is deleterious; skepticism is sound. Yet dogma is indispensable; without taking some things for granted some of the time, everything is in flux so that nothing comes amenable to examination. Drawing the balance is not easy: how much dogma versus how much skepticism?

The good organization is devoted to correcting errors, but is subject to exhaustion itself if it does not reject a high proportion of the allegations against its current practices. Anyone who knows contemporary education will acknowledge that. Error correction itself has to be traded off against error recognition, for the very visibility of error, which facilitates detection, is correlated with large size, which makes correction difficult. The widely acknowledged error in indexing social security against both wages and prices is easy to spot because its cost is huge, but difficult to end because so many millions benefit. Whether errors are recognized or eliminated depends on the interests of the people who participate in producing policy.

People make problems. How are they to be encouraged to do the right thing? How does one individual know what is right for others? What gives anyone the right to decide for others? How are preferences shaped and expressed? One way of shaping and expressing is to ask people, and another is to tell them. "Asking" means setting up institutions, such as voting for public office and bargaining over prices, to help people evolve preferences. "Telling" means deciding intellectually what is good for people and moving them in a predetermined sequence toward a preselected destination. Asking (which we will call social interaction or just plain politics) and telling (intellectual cogitation or just plain planning) both belong in policy analysis. When things go wrong, analysts, at least in a democracy, play politics. By altering the franchise or by imposing a cost constraint or by making monopoly less likely, analysts seek to adjust institutional interaction so as to secure better behavior. Planning is preferable when interaction is not feasible, because people can't get together, or when it is undesirable, because people might make morally impermissible choices. The highest form of analysis is using intellect to aid interaction between people.

Policy analysis, then, is about relationships between people. When we like the results of interaction between doctors and patients or teachers and students, we reinforce our approval of the institutional arrangements under which such persons come together. When we don't approve, we try to alter these relationships. Major changes take place when we shift the pattern of relationships (by paying doctors through government, or giving parents vouchers enabling them to choose public schools) so that outcomes change. Thinking about analysis as relations between people much like us — not as strange symbols or desiccated dollar signs — is not only more humane but also more accurate.

Policy analysis, to be brief, is an activity creating problems that can be solved. Every policy is fashioned of tension between resources and objectives, planning and politics, skepticism and dogma. Solving problems involves temporarily resolving these tensions.

But, if tensions do not have an end, they must have a beginning: what social forces do they reflect? Objectives may be infinite but resources are not; scarcity of resources is ubiquitous. Objectives, therefore, must be limited by resources; what one tries to do depends on what one has to do it with. But this does not always mean that resources are always good, so to speak, because they exist and objectives are bad, because they exceed what is available. On the contrary, objectives may demand too little (see Chapter 14, "A Tax by Any Other Name" and Chapter 15, "The Distribution of Urban Services") so that resources flow in the wrong direction.

How dogmatic and how skeptical one is about policies and the way they are produced — who gets what and why, as Lasswell said — is a measure of trust in social relations. What one likes may depend on how one does. A record of success in economic markets would naturally increase confidence in that form of encounter. Cogitation may appeal more to groups that gain less from interaction. The tensions about which we talk, then, are social as well as intellectual; they are about power in society as well as analysis of policy.

The list of the goals one is not attempting to reach is necessarily much larger than those one does try for. I make no pretense of writing a "how-to-do-it" book, other than by illustrating forms analysis can take. This book is comparative in that I compare a wide range of American domestic policies, but it is not exhaustive (by no means does it include all or most policies) or international (I do not discuss experiences abroad). My impression is that west European nations are no more successful than we are in most of domestic policy; the big difference is that America publicizes its failures and most of these other nations do not. Defense policy is not covered because the scope of this book is already too broad. My purpose is not to cover everything, a task best left to an encyclopedia, but to exemplify the main characteristics of the art and craft of analyzing policy. The book is organized so that readers who wish to consider the main lines of policy development can go straight through, skipping the last section, which pursues policies in depth, to get to the conclusion on craftsmanship.

Policy Analysis is about the realm of rationality and responsibility where resources are related to objectives. Rationality resides in connecting what you want with what you can do, and responsibility in being accountable for making that connection.

Policy Analysis is also about calculation and culture: What combination of social interaction and intellectual cogitation, planning and politics, leads us to figure out what we should want to do and how to do it? In the course or relating resources to objectives culture is created by shifting patterns of social relationships. Analysis teaches us not only how to get what we want, because that may be unobtainable or undesirable, but what we ought to want compared to what others are to give us in return for what we are prepared to give them. Calculation comes in deciding whether and which decisions will be made by bidding and bargaining or by central command.

Always there is a tension between dogma and skepticism, where analysis embodies skepticism but can't get along with dogma. When results do not live up to our expectations, or we think we can do better, which is most of the time, the question of error detection and error correction comes to the fore. Nothing is ultimately sacrosanct, of course, but at any given time a proper degree of doubt — how much will remain unchallenged if not unchallengeable — is essential but difficult to determine.

These, then, are the tasks and tensions of policy analysis: relating resources to objectives by balancing social interaction against intellectual cogitation so as to learn to draw the line between skepticism and dogma.

My life is spent reading, talking, and writing about public affairs. Yet I cannot keep up. And, though I have more time than most people, I cannot satisfy the endless demands for participation. Somehow we must be able to make sense out of public affairs without being consumed by them. How to help ourselves gain access to public life without becoming politicians is the challenge, for it means not only sporadic influence over policy but continuous participation as part of policy (as patients, postal patrons, donators to charities) as it is played out. Analysts are paid to spend full time on public affairs; citizens must relate time spent on their public activities to their private interests. I argue that citizens can act as analysts by becoming part of public policies through which they can determine what they are getting for what they give, by learning to perfect their preferences, and by exercising their autonomy so as to enhance reciprocity by taking others into account. Above all, policy analysis is about improvement, about improving citizen preferences for the policies they — the people — ought to prefer.

NOTES

1. *Implementation: How Great Expectations in Washington Are Dashed in Oakland; Or Why It's Amazing That Federal Programs Work at All*, by Jeffrey L. Pressman and Aaron B. Wildavsky (Berkeley and Los Angeles: University of California Press, 1973).
2. See Jeanne Nienaber, Aaron Wildavsky, *The Budgeting and Evaluation of Federal Recreation Programs, or Money Doesn't Grow on Trees* (New York: Basic Books, 1973).
3. See Aaron Wildavsky and Naomi Caiden, *Planning and Budgeting in Poor Countries* (New York: John Wiley, 1974).
4. See Michael D. Cohen, James G. March, and John P. Olsen, "A Garbage Can Model of Organizational Choice," *Administrative Science Quarterly*, 17:2, pp. 1–25.
5. For a fascinating discussion see Robert K. Merton, *Social Theory and Social Structure*, revised ed. (New York: Free Press, 1968), pp. 3–7.
6. For an excellent discussion, see Arnold Meltsner, *Policy Analysts in the Bureaucracy* (Berkeley and Los Angeles: University of California Press, 1976).
7. As quoted by R. K. Merton in *The Sociology of Science in Europe*, R. K. Merton and Jerry Gaston, eds. (Carbondale: Southern Illinois University Press, 1977), p. 3.

PART 1

RESOURCES VERSUS OBJECTIVES

The mainstreams of social science analysis and of the political consensus of the 1960's were the products of two converging currents of American history. The first of these currents, flowing from the Depression and the Second World War, was the conviction, unusual in American history, that the federal government was a beneficent and uniquely competent force for effecting social and economic change. The Depression carried the message that a market economy could be saved from economic catastrophe only by informed governmental management of the economy. The Second World War was a bloody titanic morality play in which the U.S. government successfully led the struggle to suppress totalitarian evil and following which the U.S. government aided war stricken countries around the world. The War was viewed as a triumph of governmental coordination and leadership.

The second current was the stream of civil rights activities that produced landmark legislation of the 1960's assuring legal equality to Blacks and other minorities. The issues of poverty and civil rights, of course, are logically and factually distinct. But they became joined because Blacks suffered more poverty and unemployment than did Whites for reasons that could be traced to legal and political discrimination. Whether one favored greater general equality or not, one could agree with Theodore Lowi's assertion that "the real task of our time was to attack injustice and to change social rules of conduct in order that poverty become and remain a random thing. . . ."

Together these currents led to the outpouring of social legislation that followed President Kennedy's assassination, and they shaped the research agenda and conclusions of the swelling cohorts of social scientists then emerging from graduate schools.

Moods changed in the late 1960's and early 1970's for three distinct reasons. The first was the collapse of that bubble of faith that government action is a force for good. Between the War in Vietnam and the revelations that led to the resignation of Vice President Agnew and President Nixon, the vague residual presumption that governmental actions could be guided to benign purposes by dedicated leaders was utterly obliterated.

The second cause of the changed mood was the *formal* success of the civil rights revolution that exposed a latent ambiguity in the goals of supporters of the War on Poverty and the Great Society. Many who had supported equal *rights* as a final objective had allied with others whose ultimate objective was equality of results. The coalition that united around the civil rights revolution had embraced both those who sought a fair process and those who wanted what they perceived as fair outcomes. When formal victory in the civil rights revolution removed it from the agenda of salient political issues, the coalition that had been organized around it dissolved.

A third reason for the change in the political mood in the late 1960's and early 1970's was the collapse of the intellectual consensus about the nature of and solution to the problems of poverty and unemployment, about how to improve education and training, about how to control inflation, and about many other objectives of social legislation.

How serviceable remain the faiths that motivated the reformers of the 1960's for the 1970's and beyond? The twin spectres of the Second World War and the Great Depression, both banished by governmental action, recede into the fog of past history, replaced in contemporary consciousness by another war without valid purpose or tangible success, by economic and social dilemmas still poorly understood, and by a recognition that modes of government action suitable to the past may be inadequate today. Fear of nuclear catastrophe, initially a source of shared responsibility, has turned to dull awareness. The moods of the post-war, post-depression years, the sense that humanity must act to improve the world and secure it from disaster while time remains, have ended. The almost mad sense of urgency will not be missed. But sober attempts rationally to solve increasingly complex problems may be advanced if we retain a bit of that sense of mutual obligation and community that flowed from economic catastrophe and the holocaust.

> From a speech by Henry Aaron,
> Assistant Secretary for Planning and Evaluation,
> Department of Health, Education and Welfare

The last words of this policy tale of our times return us to our task: how to retain a sense of mutual obligation in our political community amid the ruin of failed hopes without the deathly prod of war or the human waste of depression. The generation of the sixties has grown more wary about the fallibility of human design, but will it also become more wise? Pretending something that won't work, will, is of no use; we are too sophisticated for that and, besides, the institutionalization of these errors has already caught up with us. A self-conscious society has no choice except to think. Knowing what we know, that is, knowing more about what to avoid than what to do, we must nevertheless act. Looking life in the eye, knowing now that there are no permanent solutions, but only permanent problems, the question for us is how to make our failures more instructive and our dilemmas more expressive of our moral selves.

My aim is to alter the prevailing conception of policy analysis from problem solving to problem succession. The supposed sequence by which solutions are found for preexisting problems, as if they were fixed in quick-setting concrete, should give way to the notion that man-made solutions also create man-made problems. Policies don't succeed so much as they are succeeded. It is not resolution of policies but evolution that should interest us. How well, we should ask, have we detected and corrected our errors? More to the point, are we better able to learn from today's errors than we were from yesterday's? Do the problems we cannot solve today help us understand better what we ought to attempt to solve tomorrow? And will our future failures make better people of us than our past difficulties have?

The surveys and appraisals of American social policy that make up this section can be simply summarized: when citizens, acting through government, have tried to alter basic patterns of individual behavior involving large numbers of people, this effort has failed; but when citizens have sought to get government to reallocate resources, they have often succeeded. When the change lies within millions of people, their behavior remains the same, but when it is within government, basic changes do take place. Here is the evidence: although reading, crime, and health rates remain sticky, expenditures on social welfare have doubled and defense expenditures have remained the same, reversing their respective positions in 1960.

Why failure in "micro" social policy and success in "macro" movement of expenditures? Because we know how to do the latter and we don't know how to do the former. Because we find it easier to command government to change itself than to change ourselves. Why, for individual policies, has there been "The Strategic Retreat on Objectives in American Public Policy"? Because most people, including those in governmental agencies, seek to construct an intelligible universe within which they can lead lives they can justify to themselves. Building in failures from the beginning by seeking objectives that can't be met is not justifiable. Unless pious words are a substitute for good deeds, feasibility is part of morality. Reconsidering objectives, rethinking where we want to go, as well as how to get there, helps construct meaning, and revamp the values and beliefs we call culture.

But why, with all our experience at "standing on the shoulders of giants,"* even if they are only giant failures, do solutions become problems faster than we can cope with these new difficulties? When we speak of the welfare state or of growing government, one thing we mean is that

---

* Robert K. Merton, *On the Shoulders of Giants: A Shandean Postscript* (New York: Harcourt Brace Jovanovich, 1965).

there are many more large programs than there used to be, with many more unanticipated consequences, about which we are slow to learn, because these programs and those consequences influence each other faster than we have been able to catch up with them. We may be smart, but life is smarter.

In attempting to deal with social difficulties, public agencies propose programs that themselves act on the environment, thus becoming part of the problem with which they are supposed to cope. Of course, policies don't act, only people do. But once policies are no longer intentions but become actual programs, they implicate many people — those who operate them as well as those served by them. It is the people behind or, more accurately, within the policies who act, but that which they act upon, like any other idea embodied in action, has an independent existence. If it had not, programs (the specific embodiment in action of general policy ideas) would be mere shadows, puppets without will. Yet, we know no one will turn off social security or food stamps as easily as one cancels a performance, or turns up sick at work, or just decides to try a new idea. The solution for stabilizing policy — a new or bigger organization — is also part of the problem; namely, resistance to change.

There is tension between the organizational clients of policy analysis, who stress stability, and analysts, who champion change. Analysts may also welcome constraints because, by limiting feasible action, restrictions help make calculations manageable. If everything is possible, nothing or everything (which amounts to the same thing) need be done. Too many constraints, however, convert calculability into immobility. The bureaucratic response is to retain intelligibility by maintaining boundaries; if consequences of policies cannot be predicted, they can at least be contained by monopolizing the means of response within the boundaries circumscribing each substantive sector (health, highways, energy). Thus the force of the external world is blunted by restricting the variety of internal response. If Mr. Outside becomes Mr. Inside, we can also better understand bureaucratic responses that appear divorced from environmental stimuli.

If the organized sectors of society restrict responses to particular problems, how is it that the direction of total spending has been so responsive to popular preferences? One part of the answer is evident: they expand into the private sector. Because no sector gets smaller and most grow larger, why *should* they protest? The other part is so utterly obvious it has escaped attention: social-welfare expenditures have gone way up because, in effect, we the people want it that way. It is our communal conviction that has led us along this path. It is true, as everyone knows, that opposition to skyrocketing welfare and medical costs is widespread; it is just that whenever access to medicine or welfare has to be sacrificed to cost, it is always access that wins.

The moral meaning of public policy becomes clear in considering how there can be "Coordination without a Coordinator." What gives social-welfare policies as a whole, from medicare to aid for dependent children to unemployment compensation, their coherence and consistency is their adherence to moral norms, which affirm that need is more important than cost, that to include the deserving is more important than excluding the undeserving, to protect the elderly against inflation is more important than to protect workers against increased payment, and so on. When tax money is taken from some people and transferred to others, moral judgments are being made. Even when no moral declarations are made, we can see citizens' opinion influencing policy because now much more goes for welfare than for warfare.

Before we can turn to trends in public policy, however, we must first exorcize the ghost of rationality, which haunts the house of public policy. If all that matters is means, how hard you try, not what good you do, is all that counts. If all virtue is attached to ends, accomplishments are everything and aspirations nothing. Thinking of rationality as all effort or all ideal, as only resources or only objectives, is immoral as well as ineffective. It is immoral because people who depend on policies require results, not only remedies. It is hard to warm the home with promises. It is ineffective because this does not connect what we want with what we can get. My purpose in "Policy Analysis Is What Information Systems Are Not" is to rehabilitate rationality, not as either resources or objectives, but as the relationship between them.

POLICY ANALYSIS IS WHAT INFORMATION SYSTEMS ARE NOT

The task of analysis is to create problems, preferences tempered by possibilities, which are worth solving. A difficulty is not necessarily a problem; that depends on what I can do about it, including whether it is worth my while to try. My inability to go to Mars, a famous gap between aspirations and actuality, is not a problem but a longing to overcome my limitations. My inability to explain the influence of the tides on the rise and fall of the stock market is not a problem unless I have a hypothesis suggesting how I might influence factors by which the two events might be linked. Only by suggesting solutions, such as programs linking governmental resources with social objectives, can we understand what might be done. Policy analysis involves creating problems that are solvable by specific organizations in a particular arena of action. A problem in policy analysis, then, cannot exist apart from a proposed solution, and its solution is part of an organization, a structure of incentives without which there can be no will to act.

The perfect organization would have no problems. Mechanisms whose parts fit perfectly create no friction, make no noise, allow no error. Where there is no error there can be no analysis. Policy analysis serves organizations of people who want to correct their mistakes. These self-evaluating organizations[1] are the opposite of bureaucracy, which Michael Crozier defines as "an organization that cannot correct its behavior by learning from its errors."[2] How are organizations supposed to learn? By using the internal mechanisms specialized for the purpose, their own management-information systems (MIS).

MODERN MANAGEMENT INFORMATION SYSTEMS

Where traditional modes of decision-making were anti-analytical because they suffered arrested development at the stage of inputs (comparing effort instead of accomplishment), modern management information systems, by dwelling excessively on goals, have become fixated on objectives. Policy analysis, by contrast, compares programs. Only programs combine the compromises between resources and objectives that make for viable alternatives. Resources change objectives — a million dollars should make one think of things to do that would differ from the things a thousand would inspire — as much as the other way around. Each analytic iteration, as well as every practical application, should teach us as much about what we prefer as about how much we put in. We learn to choose by knowing what we cannot do as well as what we might wish to try. Ends and means are chosen simultaneously, and what life has joined, policy analysis must not rend asunder.

Yet information theory, as discussed in the literature, clearly refers to inputs and outputs of data, to data storage and data retrieval, but not necessarily to any external referent in the world of action. Information theory handles quantities (not quality) of data. For policy analysis, however, when analysis is part of organized action, information is any communication by which organizations detect and correct error. Thus management information systems are misnamed. They are really made up of dumb data, which assume the very intelligence that must be proved: that data, in fact, will be converted into information for public agencies to use in overcoming error. To no great surprise, this is the very same feat (turning data into information) that policy analysis is supposed to accomplish. By seeing what has gone wrong with MIS, perhaps we can discern by contrast what is supposed to go right with policy analysis.

I shall begin by discussing why major modern information systems — PERT, MBO, SI, PPBS — cannot convert data into information, and end by suggesting that policy analysis is an attempt to learn from these failures.* I will criticize information systems as untheoretical, nonorganizational and ahistorical. And what is policy analysis? The reverse.

---

* What exactly are management information systems? They are bodies of data reported regularly. Let us define data (a laundry list, a telephone directory) as any bit, information as data ordered to effect choice, and knowledge as information used to achieve desired consequences. Presumably these bits of data are tied together to form a "system." The usual meaning of "system" is any functional relationship among parts — a model or theory whose consequences, or their probability, are predictable from its constituent elements. Data become information by participating in a system or model or theory that organizations manipulate to produce knowledge. If knowledge about the complex interaction of policies in society were available (so that the conse-

The Longest Path

The system named PERT (Program Evaluation Review Technique) or, more specifically, the Critical Path Method (CPM), is supposed to help us manage a complex task by discovering what has to be the critical path, the longest, most difficult path, and planning everything else around it. Inherently, this seems plausible. Yet the few published studies suggest that outside of construction, where one activity usually follows another, PERT is rarely successful.[3] Why?

PERT depends on interrogating engineers. That is, you say, "Charlie, how long do you think this is going to take? You're the expert in the field." The question leads to problems: discount and motivation. The discount problem is, does Charlie know? How expert is his expertise? The motivation problem is that companies soon learn it is in their interest at times to estimate slower or faster. If they want the contract, they may say faster; if they want to get more money, they may say slower. Because employees are often rewarded for their ability to meet or exceed targets, they have a further interest in biasing their estimates toward the higher rather than the lower side. How can we be sure, then, whether these people really know, and whether they are motivated to tell the truth as they see it? A deeper puzzle: why is there only one critical path? After all, the larger the project, the more separate paths are needed, and the lower the absolute probability that any path will be the critical one.

Using a mathematical function to calculate the critical path lends PERT a spurious specificity, but Harvey Sapolsky's splendid book on the Polaris missile contains the true story.[4] Constuction of Polaris is an example of brilliant management, and one feature of this brilliance was to be known as an organization with such inspired management that external agencies would leave it alone. When asked if they would use PERT, Polaris's managers said they would not use a formula for anything so important. Rather they told somebody to develop a method that would "look scientific," so that innovative management could be cited as a rationale for escaping outside control.

Nonetheless PERT spread, not only in governments but to industrial firms all over the world. This rapid expansion raises an intriguing question: what are all those wise men thinking when they adopt it? One possibility is simply that PERT is fashionable and they go along, as so many do, with fads. A better answer, however, is that PERT serves functions not anticipated by its creators. Following Robert K. Merton,

quences of alternatives could be known in advance of experience) and organizations were willing and able to use it, the object of management information systems would be achieved as soon as their moniker (MIS) was applied. Where there was a system, by definition, there would be a way.

I impute latent functions — hidden purposes — when patterns of behavior persist though the manifest function or purpose is not achieved. After all, PERT was designed to figure out the probability distribution of paths to achieving a target; now it has been adapted to do just the reverse — to decide what the original target should be. The PERT system gives managers a brush with which to smooth a scientific patina over their activities. PERT also provides a vehicle for negotiation over scheduling and a plausible answer to another disturbing question: why are we here? The answer often is, because the flow chart shows that we are on the critical path.

From this experience we should learn that the function of information systems need not be the manifest conveyance of information to the sponsoring organization but rather the latent rationalization of the organization to a world that (it is hoped) will be less critical. The lesson of Management by Objectives (MBO), on the other hand, is that a technique which may begin as deception — look what wonderful objectives our organization has! — often winds up as self-deception, as if ranking objectives equals analyzing problems.

Management by Objectives

The idea behind Management by Objectives (MBO) is that goals should be specified and that management and workers should agree on the results by which workers are to be judged in accordance with these objectives. What could possibly be wrong with so appealing an idea? Managers should have objectives for their organizations, and workers should be held to account for achieving results. In a word, MBO is but a restatement of good management based on rational choice for effective decision-making. The trouble is that the attempt to formalize procedures for choosing objectives without considering an organization's dynamics leads to the opposite of the intended goal: bad management, irrational choice, and ineffective decision-making. It is not that sophisticated analysts do not realize the pitfalls but that, having dug the pits themselves by semantically separating objectives from resources, they are surprised when client organizations fall into them.

The main product of MBO, as experience in the United States federal government suggests, is literally a series of objectives. Aside from the unnecessary paperwork, such exercises are self-defeating because they become mechanisms for avoiding rather than making choices. Long lists of objectives are useless because it is rare that resources are adequate for carrying out more than the first three or four. If choosing objectives means having to abandon choice, choosing objectives is a bad idea.

The more numerous the objectives, the more likely it is that an organization's activity will somehow contribute to one of them and the less will be the need to give up one thing for another. Public agencies prefer many objectives rather than few because the consequences of their actions, whatever they may be, are more likely to fit into one of the goals. Everyone knows that objectives of many public agencies are multiple, conflicting, and vague — multiple and conflicting because different people want different things with varying intensities, and vague because often people will be unable to agree about exactly what they do agree on, especially if they are forced to agree beforehand. Reconciling conflicts is not made easier by telling bureaucrats that their strategic behavior, staking out their own objectives as a prelude to bargaining, has become an object of virtue, indeed, the essence of rationality itself.

In sum, a rational manager does not manage by objectives alone. To this the evident riposte is that MBO is just another way of smuggling analysis into government. Obviously, its proponents say, MBO must deal with allocation of resources, personnel systems, planning for the future, incentives for performance, adaptation to trends — that is, with practically everything. By the time Peter R. Drucker (a founding father of MBO) gets to the end of an article in which he effectively challenges every tenet of this movement, he winds up with the one conclusion on which everyone can agree about every information system: "However, its success depends upon the administrator: in applying MBO he or she must obtain the right results, both with respect to objectives and to management."[5] This, of course, is not a particular answer but a general restatement of all the questions. Listing objectives is the operational part of MBO, which is why it keeps happening, and the hortatory part tells managers to achieve "right results." Amen!

The other side of MBO is the assumed community of interests between a manager who wishes to exert control and a worker who wishes to be judged fairly. Supposedly, they will concur on criteria against which the worker's efforts are to be measured. Leaving aside the knotty problem of what these objectives are supposed to be, and how one can tell whether a particular kind of effort contributes to them, a substantial literature warns about unanticipated consequences of inappropriate criteria.[6] If there is only one criterion, chances are it will not encompass the multifaceted activities. Rewards based only on the quantity produced may lead to deterioration in quality, just as incentives based on minimizing costs of operation may lead to deferred maintenance. With many criteria it becomes difficult to establish the contribution of each worker or unit.

Instead of assuming a compatibility of interests, it is wiser to realize that it is in the nature of things for different individuals and units to have somewhat opposed desires; thus it is more productive to concentrate on devising mechanisms that will either make it worthwhile to cooperate or compensate them for expected losses. When agreement about objectives is emphasized, critical problems of organizational design — how to relate people and activities so that mistakes become evident and get corrected — are hidden under the surface sentimentality of human-relations jargon.

Social Indicators

Similarly, the lack of theory to predict where we are heading is submerged under slogans about social indicators (SI). Their purpose is to find measures, usually a numerical time series, showing the health or welfare of sectors in the population. Social indicators sometimes are supposed to have normative force in that they not only tell us where we are but suggest where we ought to go.

Social indicators are modeled on economic indicators. If one can estimate freight-car loadings or know how many corrugated boxes are sold, such trends might give an indirect measure of economic activity. But their usefulness depends on how the economist conceives the economic system, a conception more substantial than the sociologist's (nonexistent) view of the social system.[7]

Social theory is supposed to be broad, to show how one change in society affects another. If we do not care about interaction effects, however, dealing with only one indicator (separating "social" from "indicator") is surprisingly simple. Hence Wildavsky's Law: movement on any indicator can be maximized provided society is willing to ignore all other indicators. Here is a suitably simple-minded solution to the problem of dope: catch addicts, not pushers. The error (the government then would say) is to believe that pushers create addicts, whereas the truth is just the other way around; without addicts there wouldn't be pushers. The solution would be first to warn and second to shoot addicts. The pain of addiction would then exceed the pleasure. It would be easy to stop addiction, evidently, so long as we didn't care about life, liberty, and the pursuit of happiness.

Social indicators supposedly measure outputs of social processes. Yet, without being anchored in theory that is part of practice, social indicators can be neither "social" (i.e., partake of social relations) nor "indicators" (i.e., point to anything that is likely to occur). Social indicators are meaningful only when knowledge and power meet, which is only when they indicate right action. What is the matter, then, with seeing indicators as attention-getting devices that suggest inquiry leading to remedial action? Nothing and everything; nothing, in that by capturing public attention, critical numbers or trend lines have been known to serve as catalysts for action. Everything, in that because knowledge is lacking, time and money are likely to be wasted in action, likely to have unforeseen and unfortunate consequences, including preemption of better programs in the future. A fast train is worse than a slow one if it takes you in the wrong direction.

Program Budgeting

Planning Programming, Budgeting Systems (PPBS or program budgeting) require a structure in which all policies related to common objectives are compared for cost and effectiveness. Not just one theory for an area of policy is called for, but a series of related theories for all policies. If we can barely sense the relation between inputs and outputs in any one area of policy, how likely are we to know what these relationships are across the widest realm of policy? As one area of ignorance interacts with other areas, we get not an arithmetic but a geometric increase in ignorance.

Program budgeting has not succeeded anywhere in the world it was tried.[8] The reason for this failure can be deduced backward. What would it be like if it worked? Program budgeting is like the simultaneous equation of society in the sky. If every major program were connected to every other with full knowledge of their consequences, then all social problems would be solved simultaneously. Program budgeting fails because its cognitive requirements — relating causes to consequences in all important areas of policy — are beyond individual or collective human capacity.

But wouldn't program budgeting be desirable even if it is not feasible? Who can deny the desirability, not to say the rationality, of establishing priorities among objectives and allocating resources according to the amount that programs contribute to them? I do, for economic and organizational rationality are not the same. By sacrificing organizational incentives in the name of economic efficiency, program budgeting serves neither.

The good organization wants to discover and correct its own mistakes. The higher the cost of righting errors — not only in money but also in personnel, programs, and prerogatives — the slighter the chance anything will be done about them. Organizations should be designed, therefore, to make errors visible and correctable, that is, noticeable and reversible, which in turn means cheap and affordable.

Error recognition and error correction, alas, are not always compatible. Without recognition, to be sure, there is unlikely to be correction. The trouble is that something that facilitates recognition often inhibits correction. To be readily recognized, error should be conspicuous and clear. The larger the error, and the more it contrasts with its background, the easier it is to identify. Easy correction, however, depends on mistakes that are small in both size and cost and are necessarily close to what has gone on before. Small errors, therefore, are likely to lack sharp resolution, blending imperceptibly into their backgrounds. Because they are likely to be cheap and reversible, these errors would be correctable if only they were detectable. Alternatively, giant policies generate big mistakes which makes them simple to spot, but difficult to reverse, because the sunk cost of change — throwing good money after bad — soars. If only big mistakes can be recognized, we will be able to detect only those errors we cannot correct.

Program budgeting increases the cost of correcting error. The great complaint about bureaucracies is their rigidity. As things stand, the object of organizational affection is the bureau as serviced by the usual categories of expenditure from which people, money, and facilities flow. From the standpoint of bureau interests, programs are somewhat negotiable; some can be increased and others decreased while the agency stays on an even keel or, if necessary, adjusts to less happy times, without having its very existence called into question. Line-item budgeting, where each line covers a special activity, such as operation and maintenance, rather than a general program, is easier to change precisely because its categories (personnel, maintenance, supplies) do not relate directly to programs. Budgeting by programs makes it difficult to abandon objectives precisely because money flows to objectives without abandoning the organization that gets its money for them.

Notice I do not say that analysis should not take place at the level of programs and policies. On the contrary, there is every reason to encourage analyses from different directions and aspects of policy, provided only that no one is encased in concrete and considered final. It is better to use nonprogrammatic categories in formal budgets permitting a diversity of analytic perspectives through which money is funneled.

Error should be relatively easy to correct; but PPBS makes it hard. The "systems" in PPBS are characterized by their proponents as highly differentiated and tightly linked. The rationale for program budgeting lies in its connectedness — like programs are grouped together. Program structures are meant to replace the confused concatenations of line items with clearly differentiated, non-overlapping boundaries; only one set of programs to a structure.

This linkage means that a change in one element must send change reverberating throughout the system. Instead of alerting only neighboring units or central control units, which would make change feasible, all are, so to speak, wired together, so that choice is total or there is none. The more tightly linked the elements, and the more highly differentiated, the greater the probability of error (because tolerances are so small), and the smaller the likelihood that error will be reported (because with change, every element has to be recalibrated with every other one that was previously adjusted). Why idealize an information system such as PPBS that causes many more mistakes than it can correct? Being caught between revolution (change in everything) and resignation (change in nothing) has little to recommend it.

At one time I knew only that program budgeting data were not used; now, I believe I know why PPBS did not provide information relevant to the user at any level. At bureau level the question addressed had to do with whether programs should be abolished or replaced. This, to be sure, was a question bureaus not only did not want to answer positively but could not even respond to negatively because it was beyond their jurisdiction. To take programs from one bureau and place them in another is reserved for higher authorities — the department, the president, and Congress. Because the advice was for "them" and not for "us," it was either doctored to appear impressive or ignored because nothing could be done about it. Secretaries needed information on how they might allocate resources better within their departments. Instead they got rationalizations of bureau enterprises.[9]

In the past it was said that PPBS might have succeeded if it had produced better analysis. This, as structuralists say, is no accident. It is hard to do useful work for clients who are nonexistent or uninterested. PPBS produced bad analysis because it ignored organizational imperatives, as if analysis could be considered apart from the structure of incentives under which it is done.

Not a plain solution, PPBS is a fancy way of restating difficulties: if we could agree on what we wanted, if people would cooperate, if resources were available, if knowledge were adequate, if power were sufficient, if.... If PPBS is a question in the form of an answer, what is policy analysis? An answer in the form of a question.

Comparison

There is no denying the attractive aspects of information systems. Why accept a crazy quilt if we have a critical path that leads through the maze? Isn't it better to manage by objectives rather than by procedures for which managers can hardly be held accountable? Shouldn't budgeting be done by programmatic outputs instead of administrative inputs? Why should society suffer later if social indicators of future problems are available now? Who, indeed, would not want to be able to plan today for a better society tomorrow?

Although some have scrutinized the information systems we have been discussing, so far as I know they have never been compared critically as modes for solving problems. It is assumed always that their strengths lie in assisting rational choice (that is, helping clients to solve problems) and their weaknesses in coping with the irrational features that political self-interest unfortunately brings to policy-making (because clients measure solutions only by self-benefit). My argument will be different. These information systems are defective because they are bad advice on what good policy analysis is (and how to get it). Analysis is an attempt to get around the lack of theory rather than assume a theory's existence. Analysis works toward embedding itself in organizational incentives, holding that information is good only if organizations actually use it to do better.

THEORY

A promise underlies public policy: if the actions we recommend are undertaken, good (intended) consequences rather than bad (unintended) ones actually will come about. Causal connections are strict — if this, then that — so failure to match promise with performance is likely to be frequent, as is reluctance to acknowledge error.[10] Objectives are kept vague and multiple to expand the range within which observed behavior fits. Goal substitution takes place as the consequences actually caused by programs (say an increase in client's self-esteem) replace the objectives originally sought. Displacement of goals becomes the norm as an organization seeks to make the variables it can control — its own efforts and processes — the objectives against which it is measured. This is how organizations come to justify error instead of creating knowledge. On all sides theoretical requirements are abandoned, by considering inputs or outputs alone, until there seems to be no error (and hence no truth), and it is impossible to learn from experience.

Social indicators assume the prior existence of a model of society without which SI's are meaningless. Managing by objectives alone (MBO) is better seen as a misguided effort to violate an analytic theorem — treating objectives apart from resources — than as a mode of analysis. The trouble with experts is not only that they may not know what they ought to know, but that they may pretend to know things that are actually unknown. Routines and rote formulas, such as PERT, risk becoming the problem for which they were supposed to be the solution. Instead of discovering critical paths, they assume them, becoming the chief obstacle to undertaking a quest everyone now believes is over. Swallowing one's own entrails is not a recommended method of nourishment.

The question never is whether a theory is there (it always is), but whether it is only a veneer to mask error or an actual hypothesis whose testing uncovers error. Economists call this a production function, specifying the mix of instruments or inputs that is expected (within some range of probability) to lead to the desired output. Let us suppose the problem is to improve the reading ability of deprived children. It is not enough to think of this as a great idea. Without a production function (an idea of what result can be produced at what cost), school systems can spend three or four times as much as others without showing marked differences in the reading or mathematical achievement of their pupils; examples of this kind — inability to convert government action into desired changes in personal behavior — abound throughout public policy.

If our society lacks production functions (which is to say, theories connecting what government does to the changes we desire, that is, policy-relevant theory in most areas we wish to affect) how much more profound must be our ignorance about the consequences of alternative programs for whole areas of policy across spans of time. Program budgeting and multisectoral planning make huge demands on theory that cannot be met. Who is most misled, the proponents who sell these information systems or the politicians who buy them? The answer is debatable. But if these systems are the best in rational analysis, as many believe, and if this presumptuous rationality is doomed to failure, as it certainly is, then the sure loser is policy analysis, with its idea of applying intelligence to policy problems.

Does policy analysis have anything positive to say about relating available knowledge to today's problems? Though analysis has yet to be codified as a craft, its practitioners have developed devices to compensate for ignorance. In one, analysts test their faith that the variables omitted from consideration (always far more numerous than those which complexity permits to be included) are less important than the few they can include. Sensitivity studies may bolster their own intuition by showing that their recommendations are unaffected by large variations in excluded variables. A variety of redundant schemes may insure against uncertainty if the recommended solution turns out to be wrong.[11] Work may proceed in parallel until events reveal what prediction cannot. The dependence of recommendations on assumptions may lead to critical reexamination of these newly discovered basic premises. Where analysis does not consist of applying tested theory to clearly defined contexts, which is most of the time, its major aim is overcoming limited knowledge.

Furthermore, analysis welcomes constraints.[12] If everything is seen as possible, nothing can be done. To a point, constraints usefully limit the field of inquiry or range of alternatives. By focusing consideration on those instruments available to the organizational level that must act, and by dealing only with variables relevant to policy, analysts restrict themselves to things that can matter.[13] The art of analysis consists in finding problems — relating resources and objectives — worth solving at the level of action where they occur, within the time available, using instruments that interested organizations can control.

ORGANIZATION

The tension between analysis, which seeks out error and promotes change, and organization, which seeks stability and promotes its current activities, is inevitable. If analysis were natural there would be no need to impose it, and if it were powerful it would not so often be defeated. Analysis must win support from bureaucracies while pursuing antibureaucratic policies. That is why most analysis is rejected by the organizations for which it is intended.[14] Better information alone will not matter without worthwhile incentives for organizations to use it. Struggling with organizational incentives, therefore, is a perennial (perhaps the paramount) problem of policy analysis.

Evaluation, for example, is an organizational problem. Suppose one asks why the multitude of evaluations of governmental programs now carried on is so seldom used to improve them? An important part of the answer is that merely asking whether a program is accomplishing its objectives does not necessarily tell anyone what to do about achieving these objectives — no variables relevant to policy, no possibility of intelligent action.[15] Learning that a program is terrible might be relevant to a body with the authority and the desire to abolish it, but it is useless to a program manager who needs to know which of his present (or alternative) activities might be less terrible, in order for improvement to take place. If evaluation does not communicate desirable new alternatives to managers, moreover, they can use evaluation as their own message to the outside world: leave us alone (remember the Polaris managers and PERT) because we have been tried and tested and proven truly efficacious.

Ignoring organizational levels, and the proper approaches to each, is the original sin of modern information systems. Thus PERT is perverted because the organization that has to supply the data is not interested in (on the contrary, hostile to) attempts at accuracy. PPBS is pulverized because no organizational level can get information that it is willing to use and that is relevant to the resources at its disposal. MBO either obfuscates objectives, so that higher levels will be unable to understand them, or drowns the upper echelons in objectives, so that they cannot figure out which ones apply. After participating in a lengthy MBO exercise, as a result of which it was decided that the status quo was splendid, a business participant reported: "I suggest this is a conspiracy by the Board to prove the fruitlessness of deviation from established group practices."[16]

The most elaborate evaluation of an MBO operation, "The Case of the Social and Rehabilitation Service,"[17] shows that its chief effects are to increase paperwork and discussion of objectives, and to decrease time spent in programmatic activity. When asked what they would recommend as improvements beyond MBO, "Both regional and central administrators mention management accountability and responsibility . . . better teamwork . . . coordination . . . a need for clear mission goals and priorities . . . and the development of management information systems"; in other words, exactly what MBO was supposed to accomplish in the first place. Interviews with 159 top administrators reveal that MBO "is generally perceived by managers and supervisors as a system which reinforces such bureaucratic norms as centralized organizational control and decision-making, paperwork, efficiency emphasis and lack of participation."

Oftentimes MBO, like other information systems, is valued less for its formal apparatus than for the impetus it allegedly gives to policy analysis. If so, the first task of analysts introduced into an organization under the guise of MBO must be to abolish it as an impediment to achieving that rational behavior which must connect thought and action.

HISTORY

To say that contemporary information systems are ahistorical is to conclude that they increase the sources of error while decreasing the chances of correcting mistakes. If history is abolished, nothing is settled. Old quarrels become new conflicts. Both calculation and conflict increase exponentially, the former worsening detection and the latter impeding correction of errors. As the number of independent variables grows, because the past is assumed not to limit the future, ability to control the future declines. As mistrust grows with conflict, willingness to admit, and hence correct errors diminishes. Doing without history is a little like abolishing memory — momentarily convenient, perhaps — but ultimately embarrassing.

The ideal specimen of an ahistorical information system is zero-base budgeting. The past, as reflected in the budgetary base (common expectations as to amounts and types of funding), is explicitly rejected. There is no yesterday. Nothing is to be taken for granted. Everything at every period is subject to scrutiny. As a result, calculations become unmanageable. At last report, the state of Georgia — in which zero-base budgeting became most famous — was trying to budget by somehow surveying some 10,000 elements. Conflict might be catastrophic if state governments did not, in fact, end up doing business very much as it was done before.[18]

By comparison, traditional budgeting is extensively historical. Base is to budgetary systems as habits are to organisms. A budgetary base is the routinized retention of old solutions. Clinging to last year's agreements is enormously economical of such critical resources as time and good interpersonal relations, which would be greatly impaired if all or most past agreements were reexamined yearly. If there is a mechanism for holding on to adequate solutions and proceeding sequentially to solve remaining problems (which focus on increases and decreases to the base[2]) knowledge is more likely to result. Similarly, an agreement-producing system is more likely to work if past agreements can be retained selectively while the system works on unresolved issues.

Only poor countries come close to zero-base budgeting, not because they wish to do so but because their uncertain financial position continually causes them to go back on old commitments. Because past disputes are part of present conflicts, their budgets lack predictive value;

little stated in them is likely to occur.[19] Ahistorical practices, which are a dire consequence of extreme instability and from which all who experience them devoutly desire to escape, should not be considered normative.

Analysis aims to bring information to bear on current decisions that do have future consequences. Taking these consequences into account (acting now to do better later) is the soul of all analysis. Because prediction comes at a premium, however, analysis uses history — what has been tried in the past, how past patterns have led to present problems, where past obligations limit future commitments — as a source of both limits and possibilities. And what could be more historical than time series of social indicators? But, at any time, what did they indicate? If there were models of social systems into which these indicators fit, so that their relationships were known, one year's indicators could indeed be related to another's. But there weren't and aren't so they can't. Time alone is not history. Retrodiction, not prediction, is the first task of social indicators.

Policy analysis may be viewed as a reaction against major modern information systems. The pretension of theory is replaced by continual efforts to reformulate hypotheses through action. It is more important to create organizations that want to learn than to tell them what they ought to learn. Structure becomes strategy; an organization that expects to self-destruct when it has outlived its usefulness will use analysis because its self-interest demands self-evaluation of errors. Analysis uses the legacy of the past to make manageable the present, for creating a future is immensely more difficult when one must invent a past simultaneously.

Policy analysis means transforming the inevitable weaknesses in the formulation of public policy — theoretical aridity, organizational rigidity, historical passivity — into sources of strength. Policy analysis is not so much in being as in a state of becoming. Becoming what? What information systems are not, correctors not protectors of error, changers not maintainers of preferences.

How are preferences changed? When they are hammered on the anvil of incompatibility between objectives and resources. Changing our conception of what we ought to prefer under the discipline of our limitations as well as the spur of our aspirations is the highest form of learning. If attempting to learn from failure in social policy is the ideal, then we should have had plenty of practice.

NOTES

1. See Chapter 9, "The Self-Evaluating Organization."
2. Michael Crozier, *The Bureaucratic Phenomenon* (Chicago: University of Chicago Press, 1964), pp. 186–187. See also Martin Landau, "On the Concept of a Self-Correcting Organization," *Public Administration Review*, Vol. 33, No. 6 (November-December 1973), pp. 533–542.
3. C. R. Odom and E. Blystone, "A Case Study of CMP in a Manufacturing Situa-

tion," *Journal of Industrial Engineering*, Vol. 15 (November-December 1974), pp. 306–310; C. P. Gray and R. Reiman, "PERT Simulation," *Journal of Systems Management*, Vol. 20 (March 1969), pp. 18–23; K. MacCrimmon and C. Ryavec, "An Analytical Study of the PERT Assumptions," *Operations Research* (January-February 1964), pp. 16–37; and an excellent student paper by Jonathan Bendor, "The Seven-Fold Path to PERT."

4. Harvey M. Sapolsky, *The Polaris System Development: Bureaucratic and Programmatic Success in Government* (Cambridge, Mass.: Harvard University Press, 1972). For anticipatory interpretation, see Robert K. Merton, "Manifest and Latent Functions," *Social Theory and Social Structure* (New York: Free Press, 1969).

5. Peter F. Drucker, "What Results Should You Expect? A User's Guide to MBO," *Public Administration Review*, Vol. 36 (January-February 1976), pp. 1–45.

6. A brief introduction to this literature might include Joseph S. Berliner, *Factory and Manager in the U.S.S.R.* (Cambridge: Harvard University Press, 1957), pp. 318–329; Frank J. Jasinsky, "Use and Misuse of Efficiency Controls," *Harvard Business Review*, Vol. XXIV (July-August 1956), pp. 105–112; V. F. Ridgway, "Research Notes and Comments: Dysfunctional Consequences of Performance Measurements," *Administration Science Quarterly*, Vol. 1, No. 2 (September 1956), pp. 240–247; and works too numerous to mention by Chris Argyris.

7. See Eleanor Bernert Sheldon and Howard E. Freeman, "Notes on Social Indicators: Promises and Potential," *Policy Sciences*, Vol. I (Spring 1970), pp. 97–111.

8. For evidence see Aaron Wildavsky, *Budgeting: A Comparative Theory of Budgetary Processes* (Boston: Little Brown, 1975), passim.

9. Jeanne Nienaber, Aaron Wildavsky, *The Budgeting and Evaluation of Federal Recreation Programs, Or Money Doesn't Grow on Trees* (New York: Basic Books, 1973), pp. 116–142.

10. See Martin Landau, "On the Concept of a Self-Correcting Organization," *Public Administration Review*, Vol. 33, No. 6 (November-December 1973), pp. 533–542.

11. See Martin Landau, "Redundancy, Rationality, and the Problem of Duplication and Overlap," *Public Administration Review*, Vol. 29 (July-August 1969), pp. 346–358.

12. Giandomenico Majone, "The Role of Constraints in Policy Analysis." *Quality and Quantity*, new series, Vol. 8 (1974), pp. 65–76.

13. See James S. Coleman, *Policy Research in the Social Sciences* (Morristown, N.J.: General Learning Press, 1972).

14. David H. Stimson and Ruth H. Stimson, *Operations Research in Hospitals: Diagnosis and Prognosis* (Chicago: Hospital Research and Education Trust, 1972); they evaluate several hundred analyses of hospital administration and suggest that a good 90 per cent were ignored or opposed by the sponsoring agency.

15. For an informative study see Victor G. Nielsen, "Why Evaluation Does Not Improve Program Effectiveness," *Policy Studies Journal* (June 1975).

16. John Brandis, "Managing and Motivating by Objectives in Practice," *Management by Objectives*, Vol. 4, No. 1 (1974), p. 17.

17. Jong S. Jun, "Management by Objectives in a Governmental Agency: The Case of the Social and Rehabilitation Service," Social and Rehabilitation Service, Department of HEW (August 1973).

18. See Wildavsky, *The Politics of the Budgetary Process*, 3rd edition (Boston: Little, Brown, 1978).

19. For numerous examples see Naomi Caiden and Aaron Wildavsky, *Planning and Budgeting in Poor Countries* (New York: John Wiley, 1974).

CHAPTER 2

STRATEGIC RETREAT
ON OBJECTIVES:
LEARNING FROM FAILURE
IN AMERICAN PUBLIC POLICY

Mistakes are, after all, the foundations of truth. . . .

Knowledge rests not upon truth alone but on error also.

 Carl Jung

How does one group of preferences (say for governmental provision of medical care) succeed another (such as for fees for service by private doctors)? Do people observe what is happening and adjust their preferences accordingly? Preferences, then, would be determined by individual cogitation. Or do people relate to others, modifying their values and beliefs in these engagements? Preferences thus would be a product of social interaction. If preferences result from thinking, our interest should turn to the individual mind; if preferences are molded by interaction, then it is social relations that deserve our attention.

Where do preferences come from? An economist will tell you simply that they exist and therefore can be revealed.[1] For some sociologists and anthropologists, preferences are caused by culture, but culture itself has no cause, it just is.[2] Political scientists disagree about whether people really have chosen their preferences, so that these can be taken as genuine, or whether the so-called preferencs are manipulated — caused by capitalist culture — and may, therefore, be demystified as forming a false consciousness. Psychoanalysts, with exceptions, think of preferences as passed on to the child at an early age: the rest of life seemingly is spent in figuring out how to fulfill these preferences. Policy analysis would then consist of replacing irrational, ineffective behavior with efficient means to the same ends. This is not my conception of policy analysis. People like us are not purely passive; we try to learn from our experience. Learn what? Learn to know what we should prefer until we again change our preferences.

If culture may be conceived as values and beliefs that support a social structure, policy analysis is part of creating culture. Culture is created by the continuous confrontation between objectives and the re-

sources — knowledge, power, money, talent, trust, and others — necessary to achieve the objectives. Culture is creative if it makes use of the
effective intelligence, which we call policy analysis — simultaneously re-
combining resources and objectives, means and ends, instruments wielded
by government with public preferences so that they, together, form an
improvement.

Analysis has the task of creating problems (defined earlier as preferences tempered by possibilities) that are worth working out. Remember
that a difficulty is a problem only if something can be done about it. A
problem can be distinguished from a puzzle, moreover, only by hypothe-
sizing what might be done, by suggesting a solution. Other people, to be
sure, define problems as puzzles whose parts do not yet (or may never)
fit together. But analysts, who are supposed to be helpful, understand
problems only through tentative solutions that take on the character of
programs linking governmental resources with social objectives. Policy's
prescriptive questions do not have to imply answers but, for analysts,
problems do imply the real possibility of solution, for there would be no
policy analysis if there were no action to recommend.

Analysis, in which solutions tell us whether we have problems, involves learning what we collectively are constrained to prefer by finding
out what we cannot get. If there were no obstacles to realization of desires, no analysis would be necessary; everything could be had at once.
With no need to allocate statuses through a social structure, not only
analysis but also government and possibly society would be eliminated.

Analysis also helps us discover what we might prefer by suggesting
problems that call for new solutions. Expanding the range of the acceptable may push against constraints — available finance, social norms,
political power, time limits — hitherto considered inviolable. Constraints,
then, become part of the implicit objectives to which policies, whatever
else they are designed to accomplish, must conform.[3] Constraints are not
always accepted. Occasionally they are tested; either they give way, or we
must. By attempting to transcend past limits, we may learn about future
possibilities.

Usually analysis involves small adjustments to the status quo. Solutions are sought in existing problems.[4] Search is incremental, remedial,
and serial.[5] Feedback from error leads the governor to make repeated
small corrections (the incremental or cybernetic school) — both normal
and desirable under most but, of course, not all conditions. For present
purposes, however, the very virtues of incrementalism (limited aspirations, mini-moves) become scientific vices; inability to discern changes
because they are so many and so small, or to relate changes to learning
about preferences (because the effects are too tiny and too close to their
causes to be separated from each other). To see that analysis does contribute to changing culture by altering preferences we need big (costly)
policy and large (conspicuous) changes. A medical museum, after all, is
not there to display "normal" pathology; on the contrary, it stresses the

very abnormal — organs not slightly swollen, but enlarged several times over — so that disease can be detected unmistakeably.

Because we are living through it, we do not recognize the extraordinariness of our public experience with social programs. During the period starting in the mid-sixties, one social program after another (to make things manageable, I shall write mostly about education, crime, and health) failed as measured by ostensible objectives — and the failure was common knowledge. The remarkable thing was that the very professionals who ran these programs, their clients, and interested publics all acknowledged to themselves (and to others who were relevant) that these programs were unsuccessful. Moreover, this was going on in public, remarked on in the mass media as well as professional publications. The main difference between the United States and other Western nations is not that these other countries succeed but that — unlike us — they do not publicize failure. America is larger than life. Because Americans have hung their dilemmas out on public display, we have an opportunity to watch what happens not only when programs fail, but when everyone knows they are failing.

By concentrating on examples of failure to achieve objectives in major American public policies, I hope to show more clearly how government agencies in charge of making them work try to change not only means to ends, but the objectives themselves. We shall see how agencies negotiate between what they would have liked and what they can get, by finding either new objectives they can achieve for former clients or a new clientele that can use old objectives, or, as a last resort, by transferring responsibility to other levels of government. Policy analysis then should stand revealed as central to culture: how we reconstruct our values, beliefs, and social relations.

RETREAT ON OBJECTIVES

Constellations in the American public policy universe seem to be moving in remarkably similar directions, from concentrating on aggressive design (the war on X, the crusade against Y), through the current quagmire of implementation, and into the strategic retreat on objectives. The age of design is over; the era of implementation is passing; the time to modify objectives has come. A brief comparison of trends in public policy will show a headlong retreat from objectives; the paths taken while in flight have much to tell us about how preferences change.

Crime

In the recent past, prison reform aimed for rehabilitation as measured by reduced rates of recidivism. Rehabilitation, however, is rare. What goes on inside prisons apparently has little to do with what happens outside.

Old inmates don't just fade away; they keep going back into the same society that sent them away. Has anything changed in their environment or personalities that would lead a reasonable person to expect that a different prison routine — vocational training, group therapy, more leniency — would affect behavior outside the walls?

So far no approach has appreciably lowered the rate of recidivism. Prison administrators understandably are on the defensive; they spend too much and accomplish too little, if nonaccomplishment is measured by the propensity of released prisoners to go on committing crimes for which they are again caught and returned to prison. (A wag has it that a high recidivism rate is good because it shows that the right people are in prison.) In fact, all connected with the prison system are on the defensive: inmates who balk at forced therapy; guards caught between conflicting philosophies of strictness and leniency who find it hard to exercise control; and wardens and public officials who cannot point to results in reduced recidivism and end their terms feeling like failures.

I can project a different future. Though organizational behavior may not change, there will be radical transformations in the objectives by which it is judged. Soon enough, the effects that programs have been discovered to cause will become the objectives they have been designed to achieve.

If prison officials have their way, recidivism as a measuring rod will soon recede into the distance. Normative theory will replace empirical evidence. At worst, our punitive impulses will prevail and prisons will be expected to punish. Retribution will be its own reward. If nobler feelings dominate, prisons will be seen as reflections of American moral values. On one side, we say some citizens must be removed from society to protect its members; on the other, that they ought to be treated humanely because, while incarcerated, they are easy objects of oppression. Decent standards should be maintained, not for them alone, but for us as well, for prisons are a test case of our humanity. If one accepts as a leading objective maintenance of decent expenditures, then spending money almost guarantees that goal will be achieved.

Other elements of criminal justice also may produce desirable objectives. If crime rates by chance should go down, policemen, judges, and probation officers — without understanding what they might have done — will take the credit, even as they take the blame when crime rates rise for reasons also beyond their comprehension. The criminal justice system cannot change family structure, mobility patterns, distribution of income, social mores, age cohorts, or whatever it is that affects crime. Though it may be possible to mitigate the consequences of crime — shift its targets, make criminal justice more fair or more efficient — policemen, judges, or probation officers cannot decrease its incidence. If these people want support for what they can do, they must shift attention from crime itself and toward criminals and what happens to them.

Until recently it would have been considered counterproductive (though courageous) for the Director of the National Institute of Law Enforcement and Criminal Justice in the Law Enforcement Assistance Administration of the Department of Justice to tell anyone, much less Congress that, after seven years of research, he had discovered "knowledge about controlling our worst impulses has grown but little over the last few thousand years. . . . Crime control is not one of those fields of study where the word 'breakthrough' is applicable [if one wishes] to avoid the disenchantment that inevitably follows grandiose promises. . . ."[6] To be blunt, let me paraphrase: we have never understood crime, we do not understand it now, and there is little chance we will do so in the future, or maybe ever.

What, then, can be done? Though in truth no one knows how to increase efficiency, there are "fixes." The size of jury pools can be reduced and police patrols redirected. Improved information might facilitate more nearly equal sentences for similar offenses. Decisions about parole may be rendered less arbitrary. Inequities in charging and plea bargaining can be reduced. Individuals can make their homes harder to enter unlawfully and thus less attractive to burglars by installing better locks and alarm systems, and by burning identification numbers on valuables. Bus drivers are less open to attack if they carry no money and the fares are deposited in locked receptacles. Better insurance and more appropriate medical care can lighten the consequences of crime for its innocent victims. Court witnesses can be better treated and not forced to sacrifice so much time.

All this and more can be done, "If," as Director Caplan delicately observes, "these advances are not eclipsed by the quarterly release of crime statistics. . . ."[7] Emphasis may well shift from the causes of crimes to the consequences for victims, if only because we can do something about the latter but not about the former. We will hear less about safety and more about equality because we can learn more about comparable treatment of criminals than we can about how to limit their propensity to commit crimes.

Health

Similarly, it is much easier to equalize access to medicine than to improve health. The small truth is that a modest amount of medical care is essential for health. The large truth is that, at the all-important margin where additional costs must be justified, expenditures on medicine bring almost no improvement in health. Until new knowledge suggests efficacious medical intervention, then, health rates measured by morbidity or mortality are not likely to improve.[8]

By now we should have learned to ask not only what government can promise but what, in fact, it can do. Government, with programs such as medicaid for the poor and medicare for the elderly, can help equalize the number of times each person — rich or poor, black or white — visits the doctor each year. In this way equality of access to medicine has come to replace improvement in health as the operational objective of government medical programs. The shift to an attainable objective means that at long last progress can be reported.

Education

Educators also used to think they could report progress. The idea was that parents should be able to understand how well their children were doing in school by having access to figures that would tell them about achievement. The way to do this was to test students at regular periods and compare achievement levels with those of other children in the same school and with pupils in schools across the United States. Parents could then hold educators accountable for variations in students' achievement.

Unfortunately, the idea of making measurement public preceded the ability of educators to show students' accomplishment. No matter what schools have done — spend three or four times as much on each student as other schools, reduce class size, try different methods and structures of teaching — performance, especially of students who are poor or judged to be deprived, appears little affected. Whatever students bring with them to school seems more important than whatever they get at school. These findings are continually challenged but they keep reemerging. Perhaps our measures are bad or the underlying theories wrong, but for the time being no school district can feel sure that its teaching will lead to appreciable and demonstrable improvement in cognitive skills. No known technology or production function will turn teaching inputs into cognitive student outputs. No one should be surprised, therefore, when educators seek to substitute objectives they can achieve for those which appear unattainable.

Unobtainable Objectives

Why this headlong retreat, this separation of resources from objectives? Because the objectives originally chosen are beyond the ability of any democratic government to achieve at this time. The qualifying "democratic" is inserted to cover considerations on the consent of the governed. As a general rule, progress can be made on a social indicator providing people are not worried about or are unable to prevent deterioration on other indicators. Dope addiction will illustrate. Because addicts love the stuff and the dope traffic is so lucrative, the incentive for buyers and sellers to get together is far stronger than governmental ability to keep them apart. Government might fractionally limit the traffic by making it harder for the parties to find each other and complete their business, but it cannot impose penalties stringent enough to deter most of these tempting transactions.

But why, you ask, do governments set objectives they cannot achieve? For many reasons. For one thing, society's capacity for measuring results has outstripped its ability to cause consequences. We know that programs have failed but we have been unable to bring about the changes in behavior that would have labeled them successful. A while back I wondered out loud why, in retrospect, the social programs under the New Deal in the thirties seemed so much more successful than those of the sixties. "That" someone rapidly retorted, "is because they didn't have evaluation then." Indeed, evaluation itself embodies this gap between measurement and power because it is devoted to telling agencies whether they have achieved their programmatic objectives (not likely!) rather than telling them how to show results that might be judged superior.

For another, these objectives (improve health, reduce crime, increase cognitive capacity) seem terribly attractive and politically seductive. (President Ford promised to reduce crime, though his Justice Department knew better, and his Democratic Party challengers in 1976 pledged better health, though their advisors knew better.) Perhaps, with effort, new methods can overcome old problems: you can't tell until you try; or, failure can be blamed on conditions (group antagonisms, vested interests, bureaucratic bickering, personal selfishness, class conflict) other than defects in the instruments available for pursuing policy objectives.

All these rationalizations have in common the inability to appreciate or reluctance to admit that some of the social objectives of the sixties require drastic changes in deeply rooted aspects of human behavior. Even worse, this behavioral change must be in the client, not in the resources government has at its command. Let us turn, as before, to crime and health for evidence.

Some kinds of crime actually seem to be a way of life for many. We know that perpetrators of violent crimes for gain often decrease their rate of activity after their middle and late thirties, but we don't know why. White-collar criminals, on the other hand, apparently improve their skills with age and continue a life of crime well past retirement. While they are at it, criminals of all kinds hold onto their preferred life tenaciously. They must do so because they resist both blandishment and punishment. To go straight they would have to work regular hours, accept reduced pay, lead duller lives, postpone gratification, associate with regular people — in other words, give up not just isolated criminal acts but their way of life. Whatever the causes of large national variations in amounts and types of violent crimes, no government has been able to substantially reduce the rates. Criminals will no more abandon crime because it is bad for society than you and I will change unattractive but seductive habits merely because they are bad for us.

Delivering medicine (doctors, hospitals, drugs) is supposedly as simple — and quite as futile — as giving lectures to criminals. Except for the classic public-health measures of sanitation and inoculation, and a few major medical procedures, only people themselves can maintain and help improve their own health. In a word, Mother was right. You should eat a good breakfast every day; you shouldn't smoke and you shouldn't drink; you should sleep seven or eight hours a day and not four or fourteen; and you shouldn't worry because worry is bad for you. The rich person who does all these things is likely to be slightly healthier than the poor person who does them all, but the poor one who does all or most will be much healthier than the rich one who does half or less.

The system euphemistically called delivery of health services is a misnomer. The service delivered is access to medicine, which is far from health. Only when one focuses, clear-eyed and in literal detail, on the centrality and depth of the behavioral changes necessary to improve health does the immensity of the task become apparent. We are not talking about peripheral or infrequent aspects of human behavior but about some of the most basic and often experienced aspects of life: what one eats, how often and how much; how long, how regularly, and how peacefully one sleeps; whether one smokes or drinks and how much; even the whole question of personality. Health, then, until a technological breakthrough comes (the famous pill that's good for all that ails you and has to be taken only once), is a product of innumerable decisions made every day by millions of people. To oversee these decisions would call for a larger bureaucracy than anyone has yet conceived and methods of surveillance bigger than big brother. The seat-belt buzzer that screeches at us if we do not modify one small bit of behavior would be but a mild harbinger of the restraints necessary to change bad health habits. When the magnitude of the task is understood — that it means a revolution in human conduct — it is no wonder that health is not delivered.

Let us learn by looking at programs that have shown at least some success — Alcoholics Anonymous, Weight Watchers, and Synanon (for drug addicts). They share the enormous exertion and concentration of common social pressure, surrounding the sinner with recovered abusers who are on call day and night (all of which today would be widely regarded as impermissible for government to do). Government could not afford to do this task. Besides, the populations are preselected — made up of people who want to change and are willing to accept some sacrifice. Government must deal with whom it can get unless, as we shall see, it decides to change the kinds of people it will take.

THE SEARCH FOR ATTAINABLE OBJECTIVES

Were we to study transfer programs, such as food stamps or social security supplements, we would discover that government has been successful in delivering money and food. Why? Because it has what it needs to attain the objectives — the capacity to supply food and money to people who need *and* want them. When government writes checks or supplies food stamps, it has done its job. Difficulties arise, to be sure, in getting the correct amount to the right people, but government does not have to interest itself in what people do with the money or food.

In concentrating on social programs, by contrast, we have discovered that other objectives of major American social policies are not being achieved because "Human Beings Are Not Very Easy to Change after All."[9] We also have reconfirmed, according to well-known theory on the sociology of organizations, that agencies unable to achieve some objectives will replace them with others that can be reached.[10] The usual explanation — goals are displaced from external effects on people to internal organizational processes — though correct as far as it goes, is too narrow and needs to be expanded. The principle remains the same but it may be helpful to express it more broadly: because organizations wish to be regarded as successful, they try to replace objectives whose achievement depends on variables either unknown or outside their control with objectives that can be attained by manipulating the instruments that those groups do control. Organizations may either choose new objectives they can achieve with their clientele, or organizations may retain their old objectives and concentrate on substituting clientele with whom they can achieve these objectives. Alternatively, organizations can dismiss both objectives and clientele by passing on responsibility to some other agency. Sometimes this is called decentralization.

Let us suppose that an organization cannot come close to accomplishing its desired objectives. If it cannot control the behavior of people in society, what can this organization control? Its own efforts. If success in welfare or education policy is judged not by effects on recipients or students but by efforts of welfare agencies and schools — money spent, time devoted, compassion offered — there is a fighting chance of success. Compared to their control over employers in private sectors of society, to use another example, public agencies are in a better position to control the makeup of their own work force. A government employment agency is supposed to find lasting jobs for the hard-core unemployed at modest cost. By experience the agency discovers either that this clientele cannot hold jobs or the training required is so expensive it would be cheaper to pay them not to work. What can the agency do? The usual tactic is called creaming, finding jobs for the best of the worst, who are closest to being successful in the job market. Can anything be done, however, for the real hard-core unemployed? Yes; hire them in the employment agency itself, thus manipulating the variable closest to its own control.[11]

Suppose clientele prove perverse; "these people," as they are then called, do not want to do what's good for them and the agency does not know how to induce or impel them to change; agency achievement calls for cooperation from clients who either cannot or do not wish to change. But though people are hard to change, agencies may be able to create programs that (1) require no change in clientele, as in a prison, or (2) alter the clientele, as in denying work incentives (the famous WIN program – "Whip Inflation Now") to people unlikely to hold jobs and offering them only to people likely to work anyway.[12] Having trouble altering the behavior of present clientele? Find a new clientele that you can change or, better still, that needs no changing.

Now we know how any organization can succeed even though aspirations outrun achievements. Our Ordinary Organization (the organizational Everyman) can stress adherence to internal techniques, such as standardizing employee work loads and client pathways; it can equalize the amount of resources devoted to its clientele; and it can improve the caliber of, or metamorphose (literally, turn into different people) its clientele. Standardizing techniques results in the action Merton called displacement of objectives from external clientele to internal procedures.[13] Behavioral change among clients is replaced by manipulation of organizational processes. Equalizing output makes success depend on organizational effort rather than outcomes for people. Metamorphosing clientele leads to a shifting of objectives, that is, retaining the old goals but for new clients. So what? Now we can interpret the strategic retreat on objectives in American social policy as movement by Ordinary Organizations from clients for whom objectives were unattainable either to objectives that fit clients or clients that fit objectives.

Which of these modes are likely to be tried and in what order? That depends. Every lawyer knows circumstances alter cases. A rule that is safe (because it invokes the principle of least effort) for the Ordinary Organization to follow is this: when in doubt, standardize; if that fails, equalize; under real pressure, metamorphose; and, if nothing else works, decentralize.

Equalizing Organizational Outputs

Why do organizations representing the broadest span of public policies stress equality of outputs? The major reason, no doubt, is that equality is a value widely recognized in American society. But though equality has been popular for a long time, organizations, based on hierarchy, have not rushed to embrace it. Organizations now seek to equalize, with force and fervor I suggest, mainly because they can. If true organizational objectives are to deliver health, prevent crime, decrease recidivism in prisons, and improve cognitive performance in school, soon failure darkens the horizon. But, beginning with medicine, if organizations interpret their task as equalizing the financial capacity of different income groups to see doctors every year, it is an objective more likely to be achieved. Of course, visiting doctors is viewed as a means of improving health. In time, however, medical programs come to operate as if equalizing the number of visits, which can be sustained by subsidizing poor people, were the end, not the means, of medical care. This trend is more advanced in medicine but has become visible also in education: in many states equalizing the tax dollar behind every child has become the focal point of educational policy. Nor are goals in crime and prisons far behind. Prison reformers today are vitally engaged in equalizing the length of sentences for comparable crimes. Police activities are influenced not only by efforts to make minorities on the force equal to their proportion in the population but also (if I may bring in the wider criminal justice system) to bring equity in grand jury pools, waiting time for juries, length of time before trial, and even, by insurance schemes, the consequences to victims of burglaries. Equality is good not only because it is desirable — so too is improving health and reducing crime — but because it is achievable.

If equalizing organizational outputs were accepted as equivalent to accomplishing social objectives, success would be ensured. Consequently, the goal of improved results in education, health, and crime has been mocked by the release of rates, which fail to indicate the desired results. Rather than face failure, program professionals have turned to the search for a new clientele capable of (and interested in) achieving those original objectives.

Metamorphosing Clientele: The Five De's

"De old gray mare she ain't what she used to . . ." and neither is any clientele of major American public policies. If at first you don't succeed (in recalling an example of either improving the caliber of clientele or returning responsibility for them to the localities whence they came), try again, after calling to mind "the five de's" — deinstitutionalization, demedicalization, deeducation, decriminalization and (our old friend) decentralization.

The first of the five de's — reinvented in recent times, as far as I know — was deinstitutionalization of the mentally ill. The rationale, as usual, was part repulsion and part attraction: repulsion against scenes of gross neglect that appeared inseparable from (and all too susceptible to) shocking publicity about large mental institutions; attraction to the ideal of shared responsibility for the mentally ill by the human, personal, caring communities whence they came. There was reason to believe in this possibility, to be sure — the doctrine of deinstitutionalization does remain plausible. But there was no evidence it would work when, in little less than a decade, large mental institutions are beginning to exude patients from all their pores. The price for violating a perfectly obvious principle of policy analysis — no instrument is good for every purpose — is high, but how high no one can say, because the connecting of communities with their own obligations already has collapsed.

Now decriminalization is in dispute. Making possession of marijuana a misdemeanor either will release police to catch real criminals or drag soft-headed youths along the path to hard drugs. Prostitution is either crime without victims, if you're not one, or victims without crimes, if soliciting occurs in your neighborhood. For our purposes, however, it is clear that the trend is to reduce overload in the criminal justice system by redefining what is enforced or prosecuted as a crime. It is clear also that unclogging the courts cuts both ways: it can move in a civil libertarian direction, as in legalizing sexual relations between consenting adults, or appear as a restriction on access to federal courts in cases "in which public or private projects are delayed pending challenge . . . on environmental grounds, medical malpractice . . . and procedural rules used in civil cases."[14]

Deeducation and demedicalization are just beginning to be mentioned as harbingers of trends dimly discernible on the horizon of public policy. Deeducation is being tried out in California (and for all I know, elsewhere) in that students who wish to leave school may do so early upon passing a proficiency examination testing basic skills. Whether students who most want (or need) to leave can pass this exam remains to be seen. Whether the cure might not be worse than the disease — leaving public schools with the best and worst but nothing in between, much as active parole programs leave prisons holding hard-core criminals — will be interesting to observe.

Deschooling now is a matter of public policy because the state has made education (through high school at ages 16 to 18) compulsory. Until now, demedicalization has lacked institutional embodiment because presumably there is no legal way to force citizens to consult doctors. Demedicalization is the ultimate in decentralization because it demands that people take responsibility for following healthy habits, reducing the load on doctors, whose help can be reserved for times when people need, and can be helped, by medicine.

Decentralization may represent an effort to alleviate overburden at the center by delegating some decisions to the periphery. Decentralization even may be a method of devolving power upon (or even constituting) local authorities so that an additional capacity for decision-making can be encouraged. By the same token, decentralization can be a device to shift responsibility from central to local authorities so as to reduce political pressures on the national government. Has it not, indeed, been commonly held that the American federal system manages conflict by dispersing disagreement throughout many localities? The reluctant gain in responsibility by local levels may turn out to be the central government's welcome loss.

The question of which level of government will take responsibility (and hence blame) for failing to achieve objectives is, as always in the United States, changing with the times — the major difference between past and present being that state and nation used to fight to keep functions where now they fight to give them away. The Model Cities program — exemplifying devolution as an organizational response to unattainable objectives — was designed to give responsibility to local authorities for a host of objectives (urban redevelopment, housing, hard-core unemployment) that the federal government was tired of failing to achieve. The right to choose priorities among these objectives, including disagreements over them, was passed along to community-action agencies. If those agencies were no more successful than Washington in figuring out how to reconcile economic growth with social services, at least the federal government wasn't blamed. Everyone sees Model Cities as failing because it was so woefully underfunded. Look at revenue-sharing, and the proposed mini-bloc grants to consolidate a variety of social programs, which supply appropriations on the same premise: by moving money to states and localities, without tying funds to specific categories of expenditures, not only responsibility for success but blame for failure was deflected in their direction.

The National Health Planning and Resources Development Act of 1974 was to lead to establishment of 231 Health System Agencies (HSA) charged with providing better care at lower cost to more people. Because the federal government has been unable to reconcile these irreconcilables, now it will allow these decentralized Health System Agencies to fail in a decentralized way, that is, on nonfederal turf.

The "five de's" have their defects. Although being good is almost impossible, doing good is even harder. Schooling, bad as it is, may be better than the alternatives now available. People may prefer medicalization to mending their ways. (Health takes time, time is money, and because money can buy medicine, why not medicine instead of exercise?) In short, we should be prepared to discover that public policy ultimately will be left with the task of providing schooling and medicine for both the classes and the masses, whether it is good for them or not. What, then, would we like government to do to keep the retreat from objectives from becoming a rout?

RETREAT OR ROUT?

The strategic retreat from objectives in American social policy, as we have been discussing it, may be inevitable but the forms certainly are not predetermined. There are better and worse ways of retreating, which need to be discussed according to criteria meant to do them justice. Let us start, appropriately I believe, by trying to match the kind of perceived problem with the type of organizational retreat.

The common view that displacement (followed by replacement) of objectives is bad in itself must be rejected in favor of the position that it depends on circumstances. To recapitulate briefly, standardization displaces objectives from results in society to procedures in the organization. Equalization replaces objectives from those which come from clients (requiring behavioral change) to goals set for government (amenable to its own ministrations). To what kind of problems, then, might standardization or equalization be appropriate solutions?

Standardization of internal procedures is most appropriate when a crisis of confidence has to do with the main activities of governmental agencies. Do they hire the right people? Are they fair to employees and in letting contracts? If these are the questions — as they were during the era of Civil Service reform in the late nineteenth century — then standardization (when the way government does what it does may be more important than the action taken) can be a reasonable response.

Equalization of agency outputs fits best into recognized needs for achieving equality of opportunity; groups that feel left out may be assured that they are getting as much as everyone else. The National Labor Relations Board, established in the midst of the severe labor-management conflict of the thirties, succeeded in providing this assurance to trade unions, and eventually, to most managements as well. This approach has also been followed with mixed results, as observed earlier, in education, medicine, and criminal justice. For our purposes, it will prove most interesting to take the sector that has gone furthest in achieving equality of outputs, namely medicine, and examine the causes of dissatisfaction.

The number of times a year that rich and poor, black and white visit a doctor has just about been equalized nationally. Moreover, health rates for all groups in the population, except for upper-middle and upper-class white males, have improved over the last few decades. Why, then, has there been no acclaim that equalization of outputs has been achieved by the medical system — at least for the poor and elderly whose utilization has vastly increased? Many explanations are possible. Nationwide equalization in a large and diverse country may hide substantial local inequalities. In addition, to say that a person has visited a doctor does not necessarily mean that the quality of care has been equal. If high-priced private medicine in the whole society is seen as the epitome of excellence, then publicly provided medicine, the main vehicle of equalization, must ipso facto be judged inferior. And the shortage of physicians willing to practice in inner-city areas means that minorities may have to travel farther or use crowded hospital facilities, further diminishing apparent equality. In the end, evidence of inequality may be deduced from health rates: those of the poor are absolutely worse than those of the better off. That the difference may not be caused by differences in medical care is not generally entertained. Why? Because the poor and minorities want all the good things going including good health, and some believe government programs are the way to get it. In other, more familiar words, after demands changed from equality of opportunity to equality of results — equalizing outputs of government rather than access to these outputs by its people — accomplishments that would have been acceptable in the past are no longer acceptable today.

If displacing and replacing objectives won't work, goals can be abandoned by giving responsibility to another level of government, or shifted by being attached to another client. The justification for erasing objectives by yielding responsibility depends on which principles are best, under what conditions and at what government level, for handling what sort of problem for which sort of people. Such considerations come under the heading of federalism or (in a unitary state) decentralization. But there are few firm principles. Economies of scale, though often proclaimed, are rarely seen in practice.[15] My own preferred principle is the federal bias: a larger number of smaller units is, if we lack compelling contrary evidence, superior to a smaller number of larger units. The federal bias is attractive from the vantage point of error correction but is just beginning to get empirical support.[16] Besides, the curvilinear relationship — there must be a size below which it is unwise to go for various purposes — remains unspecified and unexplored.

Within a purely private medical system, complete decentralization by market mechanisms may work best by limiting use through prices. Under the mixed public and private system America has now, however, decentralization to Health System Agencies will be more apparent than real. From the standpoint of medical providers this decentralization will decrease the number of decision-makers by forming barriers to entry of new participants who might offer better ways to supply services. From the standpoint of offering a decentralized alternative to a nationalized health system, again HSA will fail because neither providers nor patients need confront the consequences of their actions so long as private policyholders and public taxpayers pay all costs. Only when all expenditures are incurred at the federal level will there be an incentive to limit use (and hence cost) of medical facilities.

Why Retreat?

Under some limited circumstances, one can see a point in cutting everyone's use of services, for improving "clientele," or even for cracking down on the worst off. Persuading people to depend less on the medical system and more on themselves would bring resources (health habits) into closer correspondence with objectives (better health). The nearly poor may be better candidates for education and employment than are the extremely or permanently poor. An obvious objection is that such a policy would violate Rawls's principle of justice: no action for the better off can be justified unless it helps the worse off.[17] Following Harsanyi's convincing critique,[18] however, one could argue against expanding resources to no (or little) good purpose when other clients could benefit greatly. If it were true that most violent crime is committed by people in their teens and twenties, it might make sense to crack down on that age group, even though older criminals who had committed more crimes might deserve more punishment.

Unless retribution is its own reward, however, it might be better if we asked less who is to blame (or even to praise) and looked harder at those whose interest and competence lie in producing results we would like. This is the spirit in which Calabresi and Gilmore approach the question of how damages for accidents should be assessed:

> Who can seriously assert that the most effective way of preventing behavior that we have collectively decided to prohibit is to charge the actor's insurance company for the damages that behavior *happens* to cause? . . .
>
> Assuming the goal is "optimal deterrence" — the minimization of the sum of accident costs and accident prevention costs — we are very likely to do better if (a) when we are certain that prevention is worthwhile, we coerce prevention, and (b) when we are uncertain, we attach incentives to decide *whether* prevention is worthwhile to that class which is best suited to decide the question.[19]

Instead of focusing on who has done harm it might profit us more to make a collective judgment on who could do most good.

In no way do I mean to suggest that retreating from objectives is necessarily good. On the contrary, it is easier to cite examples — denigrating cognitive skills in education, placing organizational procedure above the people it is supposed to serve — where retreat is ruinous. My main purpose is to suggest that retreating from objectives that cannot be achieved at all, or only at prohibitive political, social, or economic cost, is not always or necessarily bad. It can be good if the retreat leads to individual, group, or governmental decisions in which more desirable problems replace less desirable problems.

For analysis is done not only in the mind of the analyst but also in activities of social interaction, as public agencies move from one batch of programs to others until they find one that is temporarily supportable. In this way new preferences grow out of old tensions. Prisoners' preferences turn out to be widely shared, and victims of crime, as well as citizens on juries, receive overdue consideration. When rehabilitation of criminals receives a lower priority, the connection between what is good for the law-abiding and what is bad for law breakers comes to the fore. Vouchers can open new vistas in education as choice becomes more attractive than compulsion. And health habits receive overdue attention along with medical practices. None of these shifts in operations or perspectives would be likely to have occurred without a social scene in which public agencies had to face up to failure. Out of this desire to escape being branded as failures, out of the retreat on objectives in American social policy, new policy preferences are beginning to come in sight.

REDEFINING THE PROBLEM

You're not solving the problem, comes the inevitable response, you're just redefining it. That's right. The assumption behind this criticism is that problems force themselves upon us as though untouched by human hands. My view, for which I shall summon distinguished support, is that problems are man-made. There are always multiple conceptions. What, for instance, is *the* problem in health: too much or too little doctoring, the failure of individuals to follow healthy habits, or the failure of the medical system to deliver health services? Does *the* problem of education lie in the inability of some students to learn, or in the incapacity of teachers to teach? Or would it be better for student and teacher to be relieved of the pressure to serve outmoded instrumental values in order to concentrate on developing their innate capacity for self-expression? Actually, the objectives implied by answers to these questions, however one answers them, are all being pursued. The universal tendency for the grab bag of objectives to be multiple, conflicting, and vague should be evidence enough that problems are not uniquely determined. A pithy formulation is that of Charles Hersch:

> The conservative viewpoint sees the problem as residing in the individual and tries to change him; the reform viewpoint sees the problem as residing in the environment and tries to change it. A conservative viewpoint sees a troubled environment and blames it on individuals; a reform viewpoint sees troubled individuals and blames that on the environment.[20]

Even so, the conservative who would rather change people may despair of success and turn to altering the environment. The liberal reformer may discover the environment is elusive or resistant and end up seeking individual change instead. Indeed, conservative and liberal alike may proceed seriatim from one formulation to another until they find some configuration of ends and instruments that seems to cohere or until their attention shifts to another formulation of a different problem.

It could be argued that most problems are solved by redefinition — substituting a puzzle that can be solved for a problem that cannot. Sir Geoffrey Vickers writes that changing the appreciative framework within which problems are perceived may do more than any other act to affect future events.[21] If one can alter conceptions of what is problematical (not inevitable), as happened with mass unemployment, an entire series of actions may be affected. Community action on the poverty programs of the sixties had a quintessential characteristic: altering the view not only of the problem — personal deficit versus systemic failure — but also of the power to decide who should define it.[22]

I do not usually recommend the argument from authority, but here it may be useful to show that others in diverse fields — policy analysts, sociologists, philosophers of science — consider definition of problems as the critical and creative part of solution. Otherwise my insistence that objectives ought not to be conceived apart from resources may be considered as abandoning rather than abating problems. "Learning about objectives," Charles Hitch tells us, "is one of the chief objects of . . . analysis"[23] and E. S. Quade adds that the "honors go to people who . . . find out what the problem is."[24] In formulating problems, Albert Wohlstetter continues, "we are always in the process of choosing and modifying both means and ends."[25] According to Melvin Webber and Horst Rittle, "The information needed to *understand* the problem depends upon one's idea for *solving* it. . . . The problem can't be defined until the solution has been found."[26]

Although policy problems may be man-made, it is easy to imagine that they are not in natural science. Untrue J. R. Ravetz tells us:

> only when there is some specification of the new conclusion to be drawn, can we say that a problem exists.
>
>   . . . It is insufficient to characterize a scientific problem simply as "a question put to Nature," or "an hypothesis to be tested." Judging such questions on purely internal features, as their surprise, improbability, or organizing and unifying power, can lead to utterly unrealistic accounts of the evaluation of scientific problems. The question must contain, in addition to its implied answer, some plan (implicit or explicit) for the attainment of the answer. For the solution of genuine scientific problems is not merely having bright or even brilliant ideas; these are empty unless they are developed and enriched by the hard, complex and sophisticated craft work of scientific inquiry. Unless there is some idea of how the work will be done, there is no way of knowing whether the solution can even be achieved; and in general the form that the tentative solution takes will depend on the projected means of its accomplishment.[27]

Solving one set of problems, moreover, leads to creating others.

> For I am arguing that whatever a scientist does, it is best conceived as the investigation (including both the creation and the solution) of problems. We shall see that problems can vary in depth from the trivial to the profound, and that when genuine scientific knowledge comes to be, it is achieved through a complex social endeavour, where the materials embodied in the solution of one problem are tested and transformed through their use in the investigation of subsequent problems.[28]

Robert Merton says that a problem's importance depends on the knowledge produced that can help to formulate new and more interesting problems. He quotes a biologist to the effect that the "difficulty in most scientific work lies in framing the questions rather than in finding the answers," and comments:

> This scientific opinion is paradoxical in the sense that it runs against popular opinion. But the discord can be resolved by recognizing that, in science, the questions that matter are of a particular kind. They are questions so formulated that the answers to them will confirm, amplify, or variously revise some part of what is currently taken as knowledge in the field. In short, although every problem in a science involves a question, or series of questions, not every question qualifies as a scientific problem.[29]

What qualifies for us? A problem that will change the way we define the problem. For, in creating problems, beliefs and values are related to each other by testing environmental constraints. What we would like to do is tested against what we can do, clarifying our preferences.

If problems are man-made, so is culture. Mary Douglas argues against the position found in cultural theory that "the individual himself was very much downgraded. The human person was made into an automaton whose choices are controlled, whose thoughts and values are passively received from the ambient culture."[30] Her own position is that:

> Among all living beings, humans are the only ones who actively make their own environment, the only ones whose environment is a cultural construct. Culture is no passive object of negotiation; it is not a solid deep-storage system, nor a fixed set of logical pigeonholes for retrieving embedded memories. A living thing, with some pliability and some toughness of its own, there are limits to its negotiability.[31]

How might we discover these limits? If we take our preferences for granted, we need only keep asking how they might be achieved. Experience would be confined to means and not to ends. Long ago, Frank Knight insisted:

> We cannot accept want . . . satisfaction as a final criterion of value because we do not in fact regard our wants as final; instead of resting in the view that there is no disputing about tastes, we dispute about them more than anything else; our most difficult problem in valuation is the evaluation of our wants themselves and our most troublesome want is the desire for wants of the "right" kind.[32]

I could not agree more "that life is fundamentally an exploration in the field of values itself and not a mere matter of producing given values."[33] Creativity, then, consists in conceptualizing new problems. Though it is, Karl Popper writes,

> possible to formulate all universal laws . . . as prohibitions [constraints, we call them] . . . these are prohibitions intended only for the technicians and not for the scientist. They tell the former how to proceed if he does not want to squander his energies. But to the scientist they are a challenge to test and to falsify; they stimulate him to try to discover those states of affairs whose existence they prohibit, or deny.[34]

For the policy analyst, then, constraints are not mere obstacles but are opportunities asking (daring, pleading) to be shown how they can be overcome.

Always we must be prepared to learn that we are wrong. For, as Popper tells us, "*It is through the falsification of our suppositions that we actually get in touch with 'reality.'* It is the discovery and elimination of our errors [read, policy failures] which alone constitute that 'positive' experience which we gain from reality."[35] Reduction of error consists of formulating new hypotheses that we may think of as new policy problems. When we discard worse hypotheses in favor of better ones we refine our preferences, which is to say, we learn to formulate more interesting problems. Perhaps we should judge policies not by whether they promise final solutions — no interesting problem can be solved once and for all — but by the greater interest of the new problems to which they lead.

NOTES

1. Richard Easterlin says, "Economists have generally insisted that the determination of tastes is not their business." "Does Economic Growth Improve the Human Lot? Some Empirical Evidence," in *Nations and Households in Economic Growth: Essays in Honor of Moses Abramovitz,* Paul E. David and Melvin W. Reder, eds. (New York: Academic Press, 1974), p. 119.
2. See the introduction to Mary Douglas, *Implicit Meanings: Essays in Anthropology* (Boston: Routledge & Kegan Paul, 1975). Even when sociologists see social interaction as alleviating social norms, they are held back by lack of theory. Robert K. Merton wrote, "the economist, the political scientist, and the psychologist have increasingly come to recognize that what they have systematically taken as given, as data, may be sociologically problematical. But this receptivity to a sociological outlook is often dissipated by the paucity of adequately tested specific theories of, say, the determinants of human wants or of the social processes involved in the distribution and exercise of social power. Pressures deriving from the respective theoretic gaps of the several social sciences may serve, in time, to bring about an increasing formulation of specific and systematic sociological theories appropriate to the problems implied by these gaps. General orientations do not suffice. Presumably this is the context for the complaint voiced by an economist (J. R. Hicks): [The economist always seeks to refer his analysis for a problem] back to some 'datum,' that is to say, to something which is extra-economic. This something may be apparently very remote from the problem which was first taken up, for the chains of economic causation are often very long. But he always wants to hand over the problem in the end to some sociologist or other — if there is a sociologist waiting for him. Very often there isn't." From Robert K. Merton, *Social Theory and Social Structure* (New York: Free Press, 1958), p. 143.
3. See Herbert A. Simon, "On the Concept of Organizational Goal," *Administrative Science Quarterly,* Vol. 9, No. 1 (June 1964), pp. 1–22. See also the "Zone of Indifference" as developed by Chester I. Barnard in his *The Functions of the Executive* (Cambridge, Mass.: Harvard University Press, 1968).
4. See R. M. Cyert and J. G. March, *A Behavioral Theory of the Firm* (Englewood Cliffs, N.J.: Prentice-Hall, 1963).
5. See David Braybrooke and Charles Lindblom, *A Strategy of Decision: Policy Evaluation as a Social Process* (New York: Free Press, 1963).
6. See the statement by Gerald M. Caplan before the House Committee on Science and Technology, July 18, 1975.
7. From Caplan's statement.
8. See Aaron Wildavsky, "Doing Better and Feeling Worse: The Political Pathology of Health Policy," *Daedalus,* Vol. 106, No. 1 (Winter 1977), pp. 105–123.
9. Title of an essay by Amitai Etzioni in *Saturday Review,* June 3, 1972.
10. See Robert K. Merton, *Social Theory and Social Structure* (New York: Free Press, 1957).
11. See Mike Preston, "Manpower Politics in California" (Ph.D. dissertation, University of California, Berkeley, June 1974).

12. See Mildred Rein, "Work Through Requirements" (draft, May 11, 1976). See also her "Social Services as a Work Strategy," *Social Service Review* (December 1975), pp. 515–538.
13. See Merton, op. cit.
14. Lesley Oelsner, "Burger Urges New Ways to Resolve Court Disputes," *The New York Times,* April 8, 1976, at a meeting of the National Conference on the Causes of Popular Dissatisfaction with the Adiministration of Justice, after a speech with the same title delivered by Dean Roscoe Pound in 1906.
15. Jonathan P. Sher and Rachel B. Tompkins, "Economy, Efficiency and Equality: The Myths of Rural School and District Consolidation" (Washington, D.C.: National Institute of Education, July 1976).
16. See Aaron Wildavsky, "A Bias Toward Federalism," *Publius,* Vol. 6, No. 2 (July 1976), pp. 95–120.
17. John Rawls, *A Theory of Justice* (Cambridge, Mass.: Harvard University Press, 1971).
18. John C. Harsanyi, "Can the Maximin Principle Serve as a Basis for Morality? A Critique of John Rawls's Theory," *American Political Science Review,* Vol. 69, No. 2 (June 1975), pp. 594–606.
19. Guido Calabresi and Grant Gilmore, "Optimal Deterrence and Accidents: To Fleming James Jr.," *Yale Law Journal,* Vol. 34, No. 4 (March 1975), p. 671.
20. Charles Hersch, "Social History, Mental Health and Community Control," *American Psychologist,* Vol. 27, No. 8 (August 1972), p. 749.
21. See Sir Geoffrey Vickers, *The Art of Judgment: A Study of Policy Making* (New York: Basic Books, 1965).
22. See Judith May, "A Struggle for Authority: A Comparison of Four Social Change Programs in Oakland, California," (Ph.D. dissertation, University of California, Berkeley, December 1973).
23. Charles K. Hitch, "On the Choice of Objectives in Systems Studies" (Santa Monica: Rand Corporation, 1960), p. 19.
24. E. S. Quade, *Analysis for Military Decisions* (Chicago: Rand McNally, 1964).
25. Albert Wohlstetter, "Analysis and Design of Conflict Systems," in Quade, *Analysis for Military Decisions,* p. 122.
26. Horst W. J. Rittel and Melvin Webber, "Dilemmas in a General Theory of Planning," *Policy Sciences,* Vol. 4 (1973).
27. J. R. Ravetz, *Scientific Knowledge and Its Social Problems* (New York: Oxford University Press, 1971), p. 135.
28. Ibid., p. 135.
29. Robert K. Merton, "Notes on Problem-Finding in Sociology," *Sociology Today: Problems and Prospects,* Robert K. Merton, Leonard Broom, Leonard S. Cottrell, Jr., eds. (New York: Basic Books, 1959), p. v.
30. Mary Douglas, *"Cosmology: An Inquiry into Cultural Bias,"* The Frazier Lecture 1976 at Cambridge.
31. Ibid., p. 5.
32. Frank H. Knight, *The Ethics of Competition and Other Essays* (Chicago: University of Chicago Press, 1935), p. 42.
33. Ibid., p. 43.
34. Karl R. Popper, *Objective Knowledge: An Evolutionary Approach* (New York: Oxford University Press, 1972), pp. 360–361.
35. Ibid.

CHAPTER 3

POLICY AS
ITS OWN CAUSE

The foremost of all illusions is that anything can ever satisfy anybody. That illusion stands behind all that is unendurable in life and in front of all progress, and it is one of the most difficult things to overcome. . . .
   Only that which can destroy itself is truly alive.

   Carl Jung

We forget the solution that generally comes to pass and is also favorable: we do not succeed in changing things according to our desire, but gradually our desire changes. The situation that we hope to change because it was intolerable becomes unimportant. We have not managed to surmount the obstacle, as we were absolutely determined to do, but life has taken us round it, led us past it, and then if we turn round to gaze at the remote past, we can barely catch sight of it, so imperceptible has it become.

   Marcel Proust, Remembrance of Things Past: The Sweet Cheat Gone

Why do we feel that public policy problems never seem to be solved? As knowledge and skill grow in society, why do efforts to control public policies lag behind their ability to surprise us? Why don't organizations that promote public policies seem to learn from experience? If they do try, why do their actions lead to ever larger numbers of unanticipated consequences? One answer, I will argue, lies in the growing autonomy of the policy environment. Because policy is evermore its own cause, programs depend less on the external evironment than on events inside the sectors from which they come. The rich inner life of public agencies helps explain why there appears to be so much change for its own sake. If bureaucracies are the principal opponents of change, as is often alleged, however, how can they also be its chief sponsors? How, if major sectors of public policy can control their internal response to external events, does the world outside specifically affect organizational behavior in government? If external forces matter, why do organizational responses often appear to have so little relation to what actually goes on out there in society? Why, in a word, do supposed solutions turn into perplexing problems? Because the Law of Large Solutions in Public Policy — when the solution dwarfs the problem as a source of worry — is inexorable.

THE LAW OF LARGE SOLUTIONS IN PUBLIC POLICY

The way to solve large social problems is to keep them small, because as problems grow, solutions create their own effects, which gradually displace the original difficulty. I do not say that large problems have no solutions or that small solutions are always preferable but only that big problems usually generate solutions so large that they become the dominant cause of the consequences with which public policy must contend.

The larger the problem the less that can be done about it. Moreover, because so many people are implicated in large problems, counteraction demands support from those who think they gain from the status quo. The Law of Large Solutions implies that the greater the proportion of the population involved in a policy problem, and the greater the proportion of the policy space occupied by a supposed solution, the harder it is to find a solution that will not become its own worst problem.

Big enough solutions transform their own problems. It may not be possible to make an accurate cost-benefit study of a large project in a small country; if the project is large enough in relation to the economy, it will distort the relative prices on which the appraisal of its own economic desirability depends.[1] American experience with medical policy, a deceptively different matter, shows that medicaid for the poor and medicare for the elderly were supposed to increase access to the medical system for people whose rate of utilization we thought to be low. And just as they were supposed to, these programs increased use of medical resources. Consumption increased without corresponding growth in production, however, so that access to doctors became more difficult for most people and costs rose astronomically. The evils that worry us now spring directly from the good things we tried to do before; prime public interest has shifted from the poor and elderly to the cost of (and access to) the medical system for almost everyone else.

The business of economic regulation (the Interstate Commerce Commission, say, or the Civil Aeronautics Board) teems with examples of the solution (regulation of prices and conditions by government) becoming the problem — higher prices, barriers to entry, shortages. Fixing natural gas prices led to all three difficulties. The same is true as efforts to reduce court congestion lead to fewer convictions, or diverting criminals from jail produces a tougher prison population or increases the number and proportion of youthful offenders under governmental control. In the past when they came to sentence youths, judges had to choose between jail and home. Today a third choice is available — a juvenile home — increasing the probability that more youths will end up somewhere in the criminal justice system without the safeguards available to ordinary criminals. Wherever they go, which takes us to the next point, these youthful offenders are more likely to come into contact with a criminal subculture because, when we say that crime has become a major social problem, one of the things we mean is that there are many more criminals than there used to be.

A large problem implies subgroup support for those who produce its behavioral effects. Criminals must have friends; they can count on subgroup solace. Don't laugh; so can heavy drinkers, eaters, and smokers whose habits harm their health. Even low achievers in school, when there are enough of them, may band together to create or reinforce group norms holding cognitive skills in low repute. Should these deviants become dominant, they undoubtedly would pass laws penalizing people for intellectual progress.

The enervating effects of increasing the ratio between size of solution and size of problem become obvious when we look at tax assessment and collection. Where only a slight percentage of the people knowingly and blatantly try to cheat, efforts to improve the tax take (by more accurate assessment or careful collection) usually succeed. If 72 per cent or 92 per cent of the population don't want to pay, nothing works. Where would one find a jury pool that did not contain a majority of tax evaders? Where would there be enough judges and courts to try them? If one proposes amnesty to reduce the number of those subject to criminal sanction, amnesty will then become the norm and most people will refuse to pay. The government is caught between two unhappy alternatives. It must choose between ridicule, in accommodating to the prevailing practice of paying a small proportion of the assessment, or incapacity, in being overwhelmed by the deluge of cases that clog administrative machinery.[2] In addition to replacing the presenting problem, then, what is it that makes large solutions generate new problems?

Large Solutions and Policy Interdependence

The force of the Law of Large Solutions increases when there are so many big programs that the policy space — if we can think of public policies as divided into sectors — is densely rather than lightly packed. For as large programs proliferate, they begin to exert strong effects on each other, increasing reciprocal relations and mutual causation; policy A affects B, B has its effect on C, and C back on A and B. An immediate effect of new large programs amid this increased interdependence is that their consequences are more numerous, varied, and indirect, and thereby more difficult to predict.

The double indexing of social security against both wages and prices has the immediate effect of substantially increasing payments to the elderly, and the more lasting effect of threatening the financial stability of the social security trust fund. It also affects consumption patterns among the elderly (who can spend more) and among younger people (who can spend less) as social security payments increase to meet the expected shortfall. Indexing unexpectedly affects different industries and their employees. As social security payments increase, moreover, billions are taken out of savings, where they were a source of capital. The current controversy over an alleged shortage of capital thus becomes entwined with social security. The concurrent financial difficulties of cities and states are involved also, though no one, so far as I know, anticipated it, because they are coming to look on social security as a burden from which they might escape. Should many cities, or even private employers, decide it would be more economical to go it alone on pensions, the stability of the social security system would suffer, and there is more. Lower rates of population growth combined with higher rates of social security mean that current classes of workers, in effect, are paying for past participants who did not contribute enough to make future payments. Generational conflict is in the making. One could go on, but perhaps you will agree that these samples are enough to show how far-reaching and unexpected the consequences of policy moves may be in a sector.

To sum up, interdependence among polities increases faster than knowledge grows. For each additional program that interacts with every other, an exponential increase in consequence follows. These consequences, moreover, affect a broader range of different programs, which, in turn, affect others, so that the connection between original cause and later effect is attenuated. One program affects so many others that prediction becomes more important and its prospects more perilous, because effects spread to entire realms of policy.

Looking back at the original new program, now a cause of complication in many others, we see that the advantages of specializing in one area, with its attendant concentration of resources, are rapidly lost. Why? Because with so many large programs around, attention must focus on external consequences and resources must be diverted to other purposes now endangered. This preemption of attention happened to Daniel P. Moynihan's family assistance proposal, a form of negative income tax, when its intersection with food stamps, medical care for the poor, and other kinds of income transfers made it extraordinarily difficult to serve the original objectives of income maintenance combined with work incentives.[3] As a result, programs may be in peril long before they have had a chance to work. They may be aborted in mid-flight or compelled to land at another destination because, in a dense policy space, they keep colliding with bigger craft or menacing the safety of smaller ones.

Understanding the relative density of policy spaces enables us to add to incrementalism as an explanation for the favored position of old programs. The desirability of being early comes partly from the usual practice of awarding incremental increases. The older a program is, the more time it has had to accumulate add-ons; as its base grows larger, each increment is worth more. Early occupants of a policy space are fortunate also because newcomers will be forced to adjust to these existing programs. As the policy space gets crowded, no reduction of benefits (the usual "hold harmless" provision) is allowed for older programs; hence, benefits may actually increase for all ("upgrading," it is called) every time newcomers do better. New programs must be designed to get around old obstacles; preexisting programs therefore may be misshapen or contorted (if not aborted) unless the total policy space is increased so that all can breathe easier. This diaphragmatic activity, needless to say, puts pressure on the policy spaces that are threatened, including, of course, taxation. All expansionary forces may win (potential conflict in the public sector is mitigated by expansion at the expense of the private sector), but if they do not, the older and better established — say social security for the aged in America, and family allowances in France — which started at the bottom will be sure to come out on top.

This progression, by which late arrivals endanger early ones, may be what Hugh Heclo had in mind when, ruminating on the consequences of "a crowded policy environment," he observed that:

> Our difficulties have developed out of the successive logic of policy development itself; well before generally accepted aims in one policy area are achieved, serious difficulties are generated for the achievement of other, widely supported aims in proximate policy areas. . . . As policy effects accumulate and interact, the explosion of costs becomes less important than the implosion of spillovers. . . .[4]

It is not only that everything depends increasingly on everything else, but that ever larger proportions of the population are living off one another. Actually, it is not only the rich who subsidize the poor but also the poor, the rich, and one kind of rich subsidizes another kind: the flow increases but its sense of direction is lost. We follow Heclo again:

> The modern welfare state intermingles benefits, dispensations and transfers to such an extent that it is practically impossible to separate dependents and nondependents. Virtually all citizens are involved in paying and receiving or are in some other way tied into the family of social policies. The difference in degree of dependence is hardly self-evident between the single mother receiving public assistance, free medical care and welfare milk, and the rugged individualist dependent only on the tax law for subsidizing interest payments on his otherwise too-costly home, state-enforced credit regulations to multiply his purchasing power, tax indulgences for his lucrative retirement plan and expense account, and government agencies planning to make others bear the social costs of urban renewal, private transportation and fighting inflation. Considering only cash trasfer payments of the U.S. government, in 1970 approximately

40% of U.S. families benefited and 22% of families with over $25,000 annual income received some type of transfer grant via the government.[5]

Make a program big enough and it will generate its own support, as proven by accelerating increases in social security. Because social security payments lagged behind inflation, the Nixon administration proposed, and Congress passed, a bill indexing payments to inflation. This was done, however, without considering the proclivity of congressmen to gain constituents' credit by voting increases. There we have automatic increases by indexing on top of payment increases voted by Congress.

INTERNALIZING EXTERNAL EFFECTS

Often the task in policy analysis is not to convince people that a policy is bad, which they already know or suspect, but to find a substitute for their dependence on a relationship. Let us move the discussion closer to the cutting edge (analysis begins at home) by previewing our later discussion of the reliance of private universities on governmental support by the income tax write-off as a way of subsidizing charitable contributions. It is easy to show that the tax write-off gives rich people 70 to 2,000 times more power than poor people to direct government money to selected charities. It would be fairer for government to subsidize each dollar contributed equally, whether or not the giver pays taxes or is in a high tax bracket. As a rule, however, the poor give mainly to churches and the rich to universities. Reducing the subsidy to the rich, therefore, means universities would suffer a decline in income they cannot afford. To make progress, consequently, ways must be found to cushion the influence on private universities of a transition to more equitable arrangements.

But "buying out" beneficiaries can be expensive. The usual rule when changing welfare programs is that no person should suffer financial loss. This may mean that all classes of beneficiaries will have to be upgraded to the highest current level. Where different classes of beneficiaries and types of subsidies intersect, as often happens, securing equity in one class may lead to inequity in others. The subsequent readjustment looks much like a policy game of musical chairs, except that no one is allowed to lose. Small wonder, then, that those unaware of the convolutions and contortions introduced by the powerful internal relations among programs may view them as divorced from reality. They are not. It is just that the external world increasingly is filtered through the internal lenses of the agencies. If change appears divorced from cause, it is because the causes, being internal, are clearer to the organizations than to external observers.

"We need a theory of the environment," James March and Johan Olson write, "where the actions and events . . . sometimes have little to do with what the organization does."[6] Indeed, the internal adaptations being made by public agencies do not appear strongly related to the external environment. Decentralization — via revenue-sharing — comes along when state and local units have markedly increased their share of governmental expenditures. Deeducation at the secondary level is seen now that far fewer students enter schools, leaving much capacity unused. Youth unemployment is so high that it is doubtful those who leave early can get jobs. The proportion of youths in judicial custody increases as the criminal-justice system staggers under its heavy load. And proposals already implemented (Health System Agencies, for example) and receiving strong backing (such as vastly increased federal subsidies recommended in the 1976 Democratic Party platform) promise to further flood the medical system with financial inputs just when medical inflation is running two to three times the national average.

Now we can explain this seemingly deliberate defiance of environmental evidence: because the environment in each major policy sector is more internal than external, it reacts more to internal needs than to external events. That is, each sector creates the environment to which, in turn, it best responds. Can this be? Unless this report of policy development is wholly false, the ability of agencies to respond to the environments they create only sums up what I have written before. Why, after all, does policy become its own cause? It has to do with both the absolute growth of the public sector and the increasing density of the sectoral spaces within it. Large problems, I recapitulate, beget large solutions, which become their own problems, further enlarging the scope for action. (Such a sequence is equivalent to historical explanations in which past effects become future causes.) As more of the policy space is occupied, its organized occupants necessarily exert most of the force in their sectors. As each sector enlarges, the surplus resources available for innovation grow also. A $100 million agency may have difficulty spending 10 per cent or $10 million on research, but a $1 billion agency will have little trouble in getting a small percentage (say $30 to $60 million) for the same purpose. There are even more people whose task is (or whose continued existence requires) new departures. Division of labor and specialization have done their work. Because most interested experts as well as occupants of powerful positions are within the policy sectors, so also are most initiatives from which consequences flow. All that has happened within a policy space determines most of what will happen in that space.

Few would challenge James Q. Wilson's list of the most significant new social legislation of the sixties: amendments to social security, civil-rights acts, medicare, the Elementary and Secondary Education Act, the Safe Streets Act, various consumer and ecology laws, the Model Cities program, and the Economic Opportunity Act. Others may disagree, but I find that Wilson's conclusion about the power behind this legislation — "the great, almost overpowering, importance of the existing government and professional groups in shaping policy" — fits the facts:

> School administrators demanded ESEA [Elementary and Secondary Education Act]; social workers fought for the 1962 welfare amendments; HEW [Department of Health, Education and Welfare] bureaucrats and certain hospital administrators, together with the AFL-CIO [American Federation of Labor-Congress of Industrial Organizations], created Medicare; Justice Department lawyers drafted the Safe Streets Act; senatorial staffs and their allied activists, together with sympathetic "advocacy journalists," were the determinative influence behind the consumer and ecology laws; the representatives of the Labor Department, HEW, the Budget Bureau, and President Johnson were the architects of the poverty program, with each person struggling to see that his agency's interests were protected.
>
> In short, I am impressed by the extent to which policy making is dominated by the representatives of those bureaucracies and professions having a material stake in the management and funding of the intended policy and by those political staffs who see in a new program a chance for publicity, advancement, and a good reputation for their superiors.[7]

Unanticipated Consequences

For a moment, forget the relative weakness of external forces and ask why, if internal forces are so firmly in control, there are so many unanticipated consequences? Because large solutions become problems for neighboring sectors a lot faster than they can be predicted and controlled. If large programs increase the variety and number of consequences, many more are likely to be unanticipated than in the past.

The latest example of unanticipated consequences to come to my attention is the California high school proficiency certificate.[8] By passing an examination after tenth grade or age sixteen, students can get a certificate and need no longer continue in school. As usual, the rationales are many, from a desire to liberate students from compulsory attendance to letting troublemakers leave. An early study reveals numerous and unanticipated (though not always undesirable) consequences. White students do considerably better than blacks, raising the question of discrimination. Higher educational aspirations in the home are strongly related to passing the exam, removing the more — rather than the less — motivated from school. Though encouraging students to take the test may relieve behavioral problems, districts also lose students and state money, therefore teaching jobs and school income. A sizable student minority, in addition, uses the test to get school, with its mandatory course requirements, off their back. A program designed to reduce pressure in the schools in one direction may unhappily end up increasing it in another. And if the program is successful in encouraging many students to get out of school, pressure on the job market and juvenile justice may well increase, thereby transferring the difficulties to new sectors.

This transformation of solutions back into bigger problems is a way public agencies create conditions under which successor agencies become better able to survive. American medicine appears headed in such a direction. Its mixed private and public sectors pour ever larger amounts of money into the medical system, vastly increasing both individual costs and government spending. Costs are diffused over millions of insurance policyholders and citizen taxpayers, meaning that no one has enough incentive to limit use of medical facilities. Increases in expenditure are so huge that government risks seeing all other efforts swamped by tides of medical deficits. Eventually, government either will divest itself of the expense, by setting up universal medical insurance, or will take over all expenditures so that it can at least set a total. Both solutions — mandating insurance and a national health service — dwarf their predecessor programs and both will create huge problems of their own, from excessive costs in the private sector to immense bureaucracy in the public. Again old answers become their own new problems; why then, are large solutions still pursued?

The sectors deal with the external environment, not by anticipation but by absorption. They do not (because they cannot) predict what will happen out there that might affect them. Instead, the sectors try to internalize these external effects, so that whatever happens, they remain in charge. Size buffers adversity; the bigger they are the better they can absorb flaws. The wider their scope, the more objectives they legitimate, the more they can accommodate unforeseen events. The greater their autonomy, the fewer their rivals and the more likely it is that any new solution will have to come from the sector in their charge. Size and autonomy working together can make internal, controlled operations into solutions for external problems.

Unanticipated consequences, moreover, lead a life of their own. Not all unpredicted results are necessarily bad for everyone who experiences them. Some satisfy. Consider the Interstate Commerce Commission. Originally created as a response to discontent among small farmers and businessmen stemming from discrimination in favor of larger users, it began as a vehicle of equalization. But almost from the beginning the transportation industry saw that at the minor cost of subsidizing some politically popular activities, they could achieve the greater goal of government regulation of competition. Why worry about the outside world if government can smooth out the sector for business? Thus it happens that programs initiated for one purpose end up serving others.

Again we see that policy problems rarely appear to be solved because past solutions create future problems faster than present troubles can be left behind. When policy spaces were lightly filled, programs could be pursued on their own merits. They could be judged satisfactory until new external conditions made small adjustments inadequate. Today, however, policy spaces are dense; any major move sets off series of changes, many of which — because they are large and connected — inevitably transform any problem they were originally supposed to solve.

THE CORPORATE STATE?

Is the tendency toward containing conflict within broad functional sectors by combining public agencies and private interests part of a movement toward corporatism? Philippe Schmitter gives us the most sophisticated definition of the ideal type of corporatism:

> Corporatism can be defined as a system of interest representation in which the constituent units are organized into a limited number of singular, compulsory, noncompetitive, hierarchically ordered and functionally differentiated categories, recognized or licensed (if not created) by the state and granted a deliberate representational monopoly within their respective categories in exchange for observing certain controls on their selection of leaders and articulation of demands and supports.[9]

Comparing corporatism with Madisonian pluralism, as he does, helps distinguish crucial differences in the philosophy that has been and the one that is growing.

> Practitioners of corporatism and of pluralism would heartily agree with James Madison that "among the numerous advantages promised by a well-constructed union, none deserves to be more accurately developed than its tendency *to break and control* [my emphasis—PCS] the violence of faction." They would also agree that "giving to every citizen the same opinions, the same passions and the same interests . . . is as impracticable as [suppressing them altogether — PCS] would be unwise." Where the two practitioners would begin to diverge is with Madison's further assertion that "it is in vain to say that enlightened statesmen will be able to adjust these clashing interests and render them all subservient to the public good." Corporatists, basing their faith either on the superior wisdom of an authoritarian leader or the enlightened foresight of technocratic planners, believe that such a public unity can be found and kept. Their "scheme of representation," to use Madison's felicitous phrase, instead of extending the "number of citizens" and the "sphere of interests" would compress them into a fixed set of verticalized categories each representing the interdependent functions of an organic whole.[10]

Here, to close students of American politics, is a real conundrum: How can interest groups grow into sectors when prevailing American ideology as well as existing institutions militate against it? Federal structure, reinforced by the separation of powers, makes centralization and coordination of interest groups difficult to achieve, and the suspicion of "special interests" leads to restrictions on their efforts. This is why there are even anti-interests, like Common Cause, that specialize in weakening other interest groups, though anti-interests are also handicapped by the need to appease state units. "Peak" associations — one interest, one group — have been slow to start in the United States. With institutions and ideology unfavorably disposed, who will organize these or, more interestingly, how will they be organized? By government around programs. If interest groups relate to programs through government, they need not belong to the same organization or even take a similar position on all issues so long as they keep conflict within the same sector. This would be a singularly American solution — channelizing conflict without destroying diversity.

Schmitter's scheme, combining pluralism with corporatism, may be extended by following Harold Wilensky's effort to understand why there has or has not been a severe "tax-welfare backlash" in various western countries. Comparing the conditions for dampening protests against rising social expenditures, Wilensky finds an important insight in the relationship between well-organized interest groups and governments sufficiently centralized to be able to take into account the advice of such groups in relating finance to social policy. In this way distinctions between public and private are blurred as peak associations of interest groups, such as the National Association of Manufacturers, and agencies with power to bargain in the same areas are able to commit themselves to the necessary agreements and bring their constituents along. They are able to achieve an "effective social contract" because, as Wilensky puts it,

> Social policy is in some measure absorbed into general economic policy. One reason for the relative effectiveness of this type of consensus is that the big issues are economic growth, prices, wages, taxes, unemployment, and the balance of payments; welfare, housing, health and social security are absorbed into these broad discussions. This tends toward an important result in a time of slow growth and rising aspirations: labor, interested in wages and social security, is forced to take account of inflation, productivity, and the need for investment; employers, interested in profit, productivity, and investment are forced to take account of social policy. . . .[11]

A trend toward sectoralization of policy is evident; whether this trend will result in the "new corporatism" or stop someplace short no one knows. Uneven rates of development not only among nations but within them make predictions poor. For the present, to show how policy becomes its own cause, it is apparent that the welfare state is becoming a solution to its own problems. By expanding public and quasi-public sectors in size and scope, the welfare state generates interdependencies that are increasingly difficult to resolve without sectoralizing government by linking it to strong centralized interest groups who can speak for members. The more governmental taxes and transfers become part of arrangements in other sectors, the higher the level at which agreements have to be struck and the more inclusive must be the units that do the bargaining.

As the public sector enlarges, it takes an ever higher proportion of national income; and expansion in one area increasingly becomes part of negotiation in another. Labor relations include bargaining with government over the tax take and social benefits, because these have become part and parcel of real wages. British Minister for Education Shirley Williams believes that in "a marginally balanced economy" — in which actions in one place are immediately felt in many others — no program stands alone.[12] The same is true for the policy sectors: how do they cope with interdependency without giving up autonomy?

GOVERNMENT AS A FEDERATION OF SECTORS

If the question (I adapt Lenin) is, who will change whom, the answer is that each sector seeks stability at the expense of the others; "it" will remain stable so that "they" can be changed.[13] The best-organized sectors will try to change the least organized. During the sixties the social sectors expanded as society sought to make them solve social problems. When they did not (after the strength of the social sectors had increased), they attempted to throw back problems that proved intractable onto the least well organized governmental units — state and local governments. States and localities now are increasing lobbying efforts to decrease their burdens by getting the federal government to do such things as assume the whole cost of welfare. The one certain outcome of any accommodation they reach is that it will lead to a welfare sector that is larger, more centralized, and better able to defend itself.

Multisectoral Treaties

With every sector generating consequences for all others with increasing frequency, each is tempted to move into the other's domains; but these moves are rebuffed. If departments "made waves," each would seek to limit the discretion of the others until none could act without all; then the requirement of all acting together would mean that none could act. Whenever departments share the same rules, these are extremely slow to change, for either all must be altered or none. Overload would lead to stalemate.

There is always the chance that one or the other sector will lose out or that both will be subsumed under a larger entity ready to take advantage of their weakness. Though agencies have been intervening in private behavior for a long time, they have little knowledge and less hope of ordering each other around. To do so would require appeals to central authorities with unpredictable outcomes, except for the likelihood that all operating departments will lose in favor of the center.

Why risk a capricious and possibly malevolent environment when things can be negotiated in advance? Soon it becomes clear that treaties demarcating lines of influence are far less dangerous than all-out warfare. The abstract argument is in the language of systems; if elements (like departments) are related, so that a change in one mandates a corresponding chain of changes in others, the interaction costs would be prohibitive and the uncertainty boundless. If it were possible, however, to decouple linkages between departments and substitute a division of labor involving their respective spheres of responsibility, a minimum of interaction and a maximum of predictability could thus be maintained.

These treaties internalize externalities by creating even larger departments so that a subject formerly outside of several is now internal to the one. As the sectors grow so too does the need for central intervention. But the center's capacity diminishes, for as each sector becomes both larger and more unified, it also becomes like the departments of Defense or Health, Education and Welfare — more opaque and less penetrable from outside.

Behind the arguments of economies of scale, behind the rationale of consolidation to avoid overlap and duplication of a pluralistic administration, lies an apolitical politics: government as a federation of departments.[14] Decentralization becomes a form of national sectoralism. This — increasing size so as to facilitate the division of labor necessary for liaison with sectional specialists (including trade unions) — is what we see in the vast amalgamations of local governments in England, Norway, and Sweden (the last of which has reduced the units from 2,500 to 300 in a few years). Nor should anyone be surprised to discover that the most extensive development since World War II in American elementary and secondary education has been consolidation of rural schools.[15]

National sectoralism is what we mean throughout the Western world when we speak of the understanding — part informal, part binding regulations — between finance ministries and departments, in which finance gets greater control over totals in return for allowing the departments greater discretion in allocating internal resources.[16] Finance, in other words, has become specialized to macroeconomic management and taxation, viewing the level (rather than the kind) of spending as instrumental to its major purpose. In the chief executive, reorganized into just another grand department, public policy-making is more centralized at the department level and less so at the governmental level. Hence the contemporary riddle of government: as it becomes more centralized, the center disappears.

Why, summarizing our previous questions, does policy-making become more segmented just as the relationships among policies grow stronger? Why sectoral segmentation rather than any other approach to managing complexity? Let us proceed by elimination.

Why Sectoral Segmentation?

Because, reversing a familiar theme, social interaction is too clever and intellectual cogitation is too dumb. Interaction opens up the possibility of unanticipated failure and cognition of planned disaster. Complete fragmentation in the form of total decentralization is too threatening. It would place bureaus in competition so that more than one could bid to take over new work or replace others whose legislative mandates have expired. Departments would resemble holding companies — supporting diversity rather than similarity among bureaus — so that they could shift resources away from those which fail. Nothing and no one would be sacrosanct. This service would not be civil. Centralization of all sectors is equally threatening. There is no telling what a central authority would do, because it would have too much power and too little brain to deal with all the interconnections; it brings to mind the long since vanished dinosaur with its huge body and tiny brain. Instead, governmental agencies have adapted to greater interdependence by combining the two approaches: sectors want greater autonomy, thus disaggregating policy by subject matter, and, within that, they seek centralization to encompass adverse effects within their own ever-larger jurisdictions. Autonomy and centralization are traded off in the form of sectoral supremacy.

Individuals choose between alternatives made available by the structure of their societies.[17] If professionals want to influence policy or just exercise their skills, sectors are the place for action. To pull out of the sectors would mean losing the chance to participate in policymaking. For whether they wish to advance their careers as professionals or to identify with the clienteles who are supposed to be served (usually both), their interest lies in expanding the sectors right to the point of threats to their autonomy.

That the professionals who operate them support federation among sectors at the center is not strange; it invokes the ordinary experience of people in policy sectors as they try to come to grips with everyday difficulties. The simple appears simple only, however, when placed among complex considerations that connect individual interests with institutional incentives. Gudmund Hernes tells us, "social change is mediated through individual actors. Hence theories of structural change must show how macrovariables effect individual motives and choices, and how these choices in turn change the macrovariables."[18] Of course, as Hernes cautions, change or constancy may be motivated "even when actual outcomes deviate from the intended."[19] Indeed, even when individual actors believe their deeds are efficacious, they may be wrong or they may be thinking self-interest, not social service.

This dissociation of perception and outcome may take place for one of two reasons; organizational equilibrium is equated with social harmony, or organizational growth is mistakenly understood to show desired social behavior. In both instances behavior may be reinforced because it is wrongly assumed to be adaptive. According to Campbell:

> A process of habit meshing takes place within any organization, in that each person's habits are a part of the environment of others. Encounters which are punishing tend to extinguish [the habit]. . . . Rewarding encounters increase the strength of behavioral tendencies on the part of both parties. Thus any social organization tends to move in the direction of internal compatibility, *independently of increased adaptiveness* [italics added].[20]

Wieck, who first drew my attention to habit meshing, goes on to explain how selection may be adverse:

> Whenever the different members of a group contribute portions of a finished product, and the group is given feedback about performance only in terms of the group product (e.g., it is acceptable, it is unacceptable), individual members have no way of knowing how adequate their *individual* contributions were. If the outcome is judged acceptable, this could mean that individual members will repeat their actions even if they were actually irrelevant or detrimental to the outcome. Thus we would have yet another instance in which certain behavior was selected (reinforced due to the success of the group) without any relation to adaptation.[21]

Habit meshing, when combined with adverse selection, helps explain how individuals and units in an organization can believe they are doing well, for others as well as for themselves, when their clienteles or other people outside their purview see it quite differently.

But don't the professionals know how unsatisfactory their sectors are? Yes, they do and no, they don't. The specialization made possible by size divorces most professionals from direct contact with clients. By equating more effort with better results, by identifying with their clients, professionals find it easy to believe more is better. As big solutions make for larger new problems, more effort (which creates a bigger sector) simultaneously enhances professional prospects and acts to meet the present problem. This effort in turn leads to other problems that, with the best of will, further enlarge the sectors.

Back at the sectors, as we saw in "Strategic Retreat on Objectives," realization dawns that clients are with them for a long time, while unsatisfactory evidence of progress on their behalf is being reported. Sectoral professionals begin to doubt the quality of the programmatic life —for processes are how we live — within which clients are trapped, albeit for their own good. Lack of results could ultimately end in collapse of the organizations that fail to produce. Because no one would let that happen, whatever changes public agencies produce in themselves must be their measure of progress. At times it is not clear whether the purpose of the organizational changes is survival or solution. It is entirely clear, however, that any intellectual rationale for this position must be oriented toward inputs and instruments within the sectors and not toward people who cannot be controlled.

Here, where bureaucracy and policy meet, lies the preference of public agencies for instrumental rather than substantive rationality.[22] By identifying rationality with instruments rather than results, their procedures become their purpose. They can control their procedures but not yet their results, making this a wise choice. The rationality of instruments is a self-protecting hypothesis: here is a form that cannot be disproved because beauty lies in the eyes of the bureaucratic beholder. But what a form! Systems are highly differentiated and mutually exclusive; each sector has a single objective and for each objective just one organization. The one best organizational form is large (including all policy in a sector), and hierarchical (headed by one executive). Single executives, single organizations. Instrumental rationality rejects dualism — federalism, and separation of powers — because crisscrossing jurisdictions sow confusion and create multiple rather than single lines of access to power. When this Noah's Ark called American Government (with two of everything), and this Tower of Babel called federalism[23] and separation of power (with no one knowing who is in charge) are destroyed in favor of a monotheistic administrative structure, the sectors of social policy will be safe, for then they will control the responses to their own revolutions. Whatever happens, there are rewards: if the sectors produce, they can build on success, and if they fail, they alone will control the means to counter the manifestations of their mistakes.

It is one thing for sectors to control their own actions, quite another for them to control the actions of others, on which they must depend. Sectors cannot expect to avoid adversity, but they can avoid competition by monopolizing the means of response in their own spheres. The response may be better or worse: the main concern is that it be theirs.

The sectionalization of policy-making explains why public agencies are increasingly isolated; autonomy of policy does not mean absence of interdependence but the sectors' success in escaping from it by controlling the means of response. Agencies do not appear to learn because the experiences their critics have in mind are outside their consciousness, not inside their sectors.

THE WORLD OUTSIDE

Small people and giant bureaucracies alike occupy a world they never made and are subject to forces outside society itself, located in the international economy and polity. The increased price of oil (fourteen times since 1970) has profoundly affected cost of living, value of labor,

comparative advantage of different forms of energy and hence transportation, housing, and political power — none of which is controllable
by those ostensibly in charge of social policy. The same is true for other
commodities. Would food stamps be feasible in America if food were in
such short supply that the price to nonrecipients soared? Nor do inflation
and unemployment respect national boundaries. If competitive deflation
(in which each nation tries to gain foreign exchange by decreasing the
international price for its goods) results in de facto devaluation of the
designated currencies, for example, import and export sectors of the
economy will be treated differently — upsetting labor-management
agreements, accepted levels of taxation, employment policy, kind and
extent of welfare services, and much else. In addition, the unpredictability
of the outside world makes our intellectual devices (other things being
equal, under current conditions, for the time being) rather lame. Contingency is alive and well in public policy.

The size of the economy limits what can be done. Constraints on
resources are real. Total government expenditure must bear some relation
to tax effort. Yet if spending rises because of unemployment or falls as a
result of inflation or changes its pattern due to more selective efforts to
combat stagflation, the effects on sectors of social policy may be profound.
Welfare agencies can no more control the employment consequences of
reducing the money supply than can the proverbial goatherder in the
hills of Bavaria.

Yet the ability of the sectors to affect other governmental policies
is considerably greater than their capacity to control social rates — individual decisions that may add up to social problems. Birth rates, marriage
and divorce rates, crime, drug addiction, and alcoholism rates are, so to
speak, properties of people conceived of as populations. Unless governments have far greater force than the ones we are talking about, these
properties stand as societal resultants rather than as end products of
national decisions. Still, it would be hard to overemphasize the powerful
effects of these rates on schools, demand for housing, size of police forces,
and too much more to mention.

Just as the international, economic, and social realms constrain the
sectors of social policy, so too the sectors constrain each other. Much
more for one, taken as a whole, has to mean much less for the others.
According to the Law of Large Solutions, the stronger the recognized
need, the larger the programmatic response, the greater the effects in
other sectors, the less the ability to anticipate them. Efforts of the sectors
to absorb their own effects by growing larger, by unifying their forces,
and by demarcating their boundaries paradoxically make their actions
more important (because more massive) and their consequences for
others less predictable (because more numerous, diverse, and lasting).
Even attempts to shift responsibility, in a society increasingly organized
by sectors, must shift consequences from one to the others. Former

mental patients and former school children — if society is not prepared to accept them — are going to end up in welfare or criminal justice or some other sector.

Policy cannot be its only cause. The outside world does intrude. The question is not whether policy is connected to society, but how? If the sectors cannot anticipate or direct social change, at least they can mediate the responses government makes to what is going on out there. And the two phenomena are connected: inability to control social change generates the modes of organizational response. The main mode of adaptation used by public agencies is their own internal structure, the one variable over which they have most complete control.

CHANGE FOR ITS OWN SAKE

What do government agencies do when they cannot control the behavior they are expected to change? Change themselves to show that they can. The time-honored tactic is called "change for its own sake," or "if you can't change what you should, change what you can."

Organizations may change in order to influence people in the manner intended by some specific public policy. If this doesn't work the difficulties may be traceable to defects in the organization's structure or inadequacies of its personnel or inefficiencies in its procedures. Unable to achieve desired external effects, organizations may exert influence in the one place where their powers are most nearly adequate to their preferences — their own internal affairs. Agencies may be reorganized because they are a lot easier to change than social structure. It reminds one of the old joke about looking for a missing button, not where it was lost but in the kitchen because the light is better there. Nor need this be done cynically; it is only natural to take up the instrument closest at hand, namely, one's very own organization.

For instance, no one can accuse local educators of inertia; they are always in motion, tinkering with the organization of their schools. Teachers teach alone, in twos, and in teams. They are supervised by specialists in subject matter, by specialists in presentation, by specialists in age groups, and by generalists whose virtue is that they are not specialists. Students are arranged by ability, by age, and by interest to secure homogeneity, and they are regrouped by ages, interests, or disabilities to secure homogeneity. School districts are centralized and decentralized; principals are given and denied hierarchical authority; teachers are assigned in almost every conceivable combination, as are the curricula and methods they use. No one can accuse schools of being unresponsive. In a manner of speaking everyone gets what they want. But innovation may turn into obfuscation when the assertion of multiple objectives — the whole child, the emotional child, the social child, even the educated child – creates a moving target, blurring the achievement of any one. Changing objectives and changing organizations becomes the object of change. And the more things change. . . .

The medical system also has generated a cornucopia of organizational change. Doctors are reviewed by local medical societies, by hospital review boards, by PSRO's (Professional Service Review Organizations), and more, much more. Hospitals are paid by so many formulas, and costs are monitored through so many different arrangements – retrospectively, prospectively, before, during, and after patients are sick – that it would be tedious to list them all. Yet, against this flux, cries of crisis, rise in prices, and complaints about access to medical care are the most constant element.

The attempt of governmental employment agencies to become perfect employers – that is, to hire in their own agencies minorities whom they could not get private employers to accept – is a nice illustration of using the instrument closest to hand. They meet their objectives in the only possible place, their own agency. One hardly need go further to document the observation that inability to attain objectives usually is accompanied by organizational upheaval.

What can be learned if the same organizations that make errors are also those that are supposed to correct them? Our common perception – the more they appear to change, the more they remain the same – is correct, but only half the story. Two phenomena occur: as the policy sectors grow and the spaces they occupy become more crowded, detection of errors becomes more difficult and correction of them less likely. Detection is harder because varied and numerous effects get farther from their causes. Correction is less likely because as policy increasingly becomes its own cause, sectoral size increases the capacity for self-protection.

By this time it appears we have come full circle: policy initiation is vested in the same sectors that contain change. How is it possible for public agencies to be the main force behind, as well as the main engine opposed, to change?

SECTORS OF POLICY AS PROHIBITERS AND PROPONENTS OF CHANGE

It is common in current criticisms to blame governmental bureaucracies for resisting change. Bureaucracies resist adaptation to new conditions, it is alleged, because public agencies, with their huge stake in the status quo, stymie any such efforts by activating agency clienteles, who can lobby in Congress, drag their feet, distort implementation, and otherwise throw up roadblocks to progress. No observer of bureaucratic behavior can doubt the truth of these assertions as far as they go. But they do not go nearly far enough. For as we have seen, public agencies are also the chief motivators of change in public policy — both the pace and extent of which have increased markedly in the last ten to fifteen years. Why, then, if public agencies are so powerful in resisting change, has there been so much of it? Our hope for explanation lies in the simultaneity of these trends.

As policy becomes more and more its own cause, public agencies are ever more involved in making adjustments to past programs, creating new ones to overcome difficulties, and responding to forces originating in other sectors or in society. In their own interest, public agencies change, even if only to maintain their current status, and to keep their most talented people. A large part of this action is negative: unwanted changes must be fought off; they must stabilize themselves if only to change others. Because the best defense is offense, as folk wisdom has it, they seek to preempt the field of action. Their guiding rule, it is clear from Chapter 2, is to sponsor changes that strengthen their sectors by making the variables they can manipulate (internal procedures, the organization's structure, the form of their outputs) into the measures of their success (due process, unity of command, equalization of expenditures by classes of clientele).

Still it seems strange that so many initiatives can be carried through in a decentralized, pluralistic political system famous for its "veto groups" and for its devotion to consent as opposed to efficiency. According to Clark and Wilson,[24] organizations (or, for our purposes, governments) characterized by large numbers of independent and heterogenous units are likely to bring forth many initiatives very few of which will be adopted or become live innovations. Contrariwise, systems composed of a small number of unified entities are hypothesized to produce far fewer initiatives but a much higher proportion of actual adopted innovations. Nothing is said, however, about the presumably powerful effect that the rate and number of initiatives can have on the number of real adoptions. The larger the number and the faster the rate of increase of new proposals, I suggest, the greater the influence of very low propensities to turn initiatives into innovations.

Imagine, as an illustration for this proposition, that the United States government generates 10,000 initiatives a year and accepts one percent, while a unitary West European democracy, Europa, which spawns only 1,000 initiatives, enacts 10 percent of them into law. Both America and Europa, then, would end up with 100 initiatives, though the United States goes through many more motions to come out with the same absolute number. At the initiation stage, Americans have to work ten times harder than Europeans.

Suppose, however, for any number of reasons, that the rate of initiation in America goes up to 100,000 while the acceptance rate remains the same. Then America would have 1,000 new programs though its rate of acceptance had not changed. To show the potential significance of exponential increases in initiation consider what would happen if, with the same number of initiatives, the rate of acceptance doubled in Europa and was halved in America. The resulting acceptances would number 200 in Europa (1,000 times 20 percent) and 500 in America (100,000 times one-half of one percent). Hence the consideration that now Europa has 40 times as great an acceptance rate (20 percent over one-half of one percent) could be overwhelmed by America's enormous increase in initiation from 10,000 to 100,000. And this is all I wish to show: it is possible for policy spaces to become denser at the same time as many, if not most, initiatives are doomed to failure.

What might account for the ever-increasing rate of new initiatives? Another way of putting the question is to ask why congressmen now find it (1) possible, and (2) desirable to introduce constantly increasing quantities of legislation? Why, also, are there so many more administrative regulations?

I have been arguing that policies feed on each other; the more there are, the more there have to be in order to cope with new circumstances, effects on other policies, and unexpected consequences. New legislative amendments and new administrative regulations become a growth industry as each makes work for the others. Sectoral symbiosis reigns supreme. The policy sectors to which I have been alluding include not only the bureaucracies (federal, state, county, and city) that enlarge with the proliferation of programs as well as the interest groups and collective "peak" associations that lobby for whole industries, but also the burgeoning congressional staffs on legislative committees, appropriations committees, and the new House and Senate budget committees as well as the Congressional Budget Office. Bureaucracies generate corrections to old programs and ideas for new ones; lobbyists add their own. Congressional staffs make modifications as well as feed in ideas from policy communities outside, ensuring a steady stream of initiatives.

Paradoxically, these trends have created countervailing forces — paradoxically, because the only way to stop changes you don't like is to initiate new regulations or legislation. If, for some people, change can hardly come fast enough, and if for others it is already much too fast, all may push to speed up or slow down. The one thing all have in common is the only thing we all observe and seek to explain — change. How strange, then, that we should think of policy not as a temporary resting place but as a permanent cure.

PROBLEMS AND SOLUTIONS

My purpose has not been to say that nothing works or that government is more trouble than it is worth. In this chapter I do not analyze the effectiveness of programs. If I did, I would not consider individual programs alone or in their infancy, but ask whether, as a whole, the nation is better or worse for what has happened in this last quarter century. (I would say, "better, but. . . .") No, my purpose is to reveal how policy becomes its own cause and the conditions under which internal causes may be overwhelmed or modified by external ones. The moral I wish to draw is not what is wrong but rather how to think right about public policy as a beginning, not an end.

Why do we think of public policies in the language of death? Our words (hence our thought) imply that problems have solutions, as if they could be solved once and for all, but our experience suggests that, like the poor, they are always with us. It is our expectation of closure, of decent burial, rather than of regeneration and rebirth (albeit with an occasional mutation), that is misleading.

Policy problems are man-made in that we choose among infinite possibilities to attack one sort of difficulty rather than another. Problems are defined by hypothetical solutions; the problem's formulation and the proposed solution are part of the same hypothesis in which thought and action are fused. Problems, then, are difficulties or dilemmas about which we think we might do something so as to create a new problem that is more worthy of trying to solve. Problems are not so much solved as superseded.

If we thought of solutions as inverse Chinese boxes, whose successors are found each folded outside the other, the idea of a final resolution could hardly occur. Instead, we would ask more interesting questions, such as whether we would prefer one set of problems to another. I would, for instance, still prefer today's medical inflation to yesterday's systematic exclusion of the poor from medical services or even to improved access conditioned only on noblesse oblige. We might also find more helpful answers (such as setting up structures like school vouchers) for converting errors we know we will make into corrections that will enable us to learn about the next generation of problems.

These difficulties, I wish to make clear, do not involve rejection of all social policy, nor even of the whole panoply called the welfare state. On the contrary, I will next suggest, in some ways, an affirmation, quite possibly an expansion of past trends in size and scope of the public sector. No, these preferences have less to do with how much we try to do and more with what we try to do. The strategic retreat is not from conscience but from failure. Negative knowledge of what doesn't work is being put to use. The question is whether it will lead to resignation or, as I would prefer, redesign of public policies. Our efforts have been substantial; it is our results that need correction.

To understand where future policies are likely to lead us, we need to know about past policies. For, as policy becomes its own cause, the future problems in which we are increasingly interested are a response to our past solutions.

NOTES

1. A. R. Prest and R. Turvey, "Cost-Benefit Analysis: A Survey," *Economic Journal*, Vol. 75 (December 1975), pp. 683–775.
2. Alex Radian, "Politics in Administration of the Taxing Process in Poor Countries," (Ph.D. dissertation, University of California, Berkeley, June 1977).
3. Daniel P. Moynihan, *The Politics of a Guaranteed Income: The Nixon Administration and the Family Assistance Plan* (New York: Random House, 1973).
4. Hugh Heclo, "Frontiers of Social Policy in Europe and America," *Policy Sciences*, Vol. 6 (December 1975), pp. 404–405, 407, 411–413.
5. Ibid., pp. 413–414.
6. James March and Johan Olson, "The Uncertainty of the Past: Organizational Learning under Ambiguity," *European Journal of Political Research,* Vol. 3 (1975), p. 153.
7. James Q. Wilson, in "Social Science: The Public Disenchantment, A Symposium," *The American Scholar* (Summer 1976), p. 358. The last clause, "those political staffs" requires greater elucidation than is possible here. Someone should study the rise of congressmen who view advocacy of ever-larger numbers of new programs as good in itself. (For conclusive evidence of their existence, see the illuminating paper by Jack L. Walker, "Setting the Agenda in the U.S. Senate: A Theory of Problem Selection," delivered at the Annual Meeting of the American Political Science Association, Chicago, September 2–5, 1976). The consequences of the vast increase in congressional staff for advocacy will undoubtedly be profound. What part will they play in the policy sectors?
8. Ellen Polgar, "The California High School Proficiency Exam," (mimeographed, Graduate School of Public Policy, University of California Berkeley, June 1976).
9. Philippe C. Schmitter, "Still the Century of Corporatism?" in F. B. Pike and T. Stritch, eds., *The New Corporatism: Social Political Structures in the Iberian World* (Notre Dame, Ind. and London: University of Notre Dame Press, 1974), pp. 93–94.
10. Ibid., pp. 96–97.
11. Harold L. Wilensky, *The "New Corporatism," Centralization, and the Welfare State* (London and Beverly Hills: Sage Publications, 1976), p. 23.
12. Shirley Williams, Secretary of State for Prices and Consumer Protection, *The Times* (July 6, 1976), p. 18.
13. See Aaron Wildavsky, "The Self-Evaluating Organization," *Public Administration Review*, Vol. 32 (September-October 1972), pp. 509–520.
14. See Hugh Heclo and Aaron Wildavsky, *The Private Government of Public Money: Community and Policy Inside British Political Administration* (London: Macmillan; Berkeley, Los Angeles: University of California Press, 1974).
15. See Jonathan P. Sher and Rachel B. Tompkins, "Economy, Efficiency and Equality: The Myths of Rural School and District Consolidation" (Washington, D.C.: National Institute of Education, July 1976).
16. See Aaron Wildavsky, *Budgeting: A Comparative Theory of Budgetary Processes* (Boston: Little, Brown, 1975).
17. See Arthur Stinchcombe, "Merton's Theory of Social Structure," in Lewis A. Coser, ed., *The Idea of Social Structure* (New York: Harcourt Brace Jovanovich, 1975).
18. Gudmund Hernes, "Structural Change in Social Processes," *American Journal of Sociology* Vol. 82, No. 3 (November 1976), p. 2.
19. Ibid., p. 36.
20. Quoted in Karl E. Weick, *The Social Psychology of Organizing* (Reading, Mass.: Addison-Wesley, 1969), p. 58.

21. Ibid., p. 63.
22. See Karl Mannheim, *Ideology and Utopia,* translated by Lewis Wirth and Edward Shils (New York: Harcourt Brace and World, 1959).
23. Martin Landau, "Federalism, Redundancy and System Reliability: The Federal Polity" in *Publius,* Vol. 3, No. 2 (1973), p. 188.
24. Peter B. Clark and James Q. Wilson, "Incentive Systems: A Theory of Organizations, *Administrative Science Quarterly* Vol. 6 (September, 1961), pp. 129–166.

CHAPTER 4

COORDINATION
WITHOUT A COORDINATOR

Should the United States government spend for war or for peace? Crudely expressed, that was a major dividing line in the debates over public policy in the late fifties through the sixties and seventies. The course followed by enlightened liberal opinion was clear: much more for welfare programs designed to help deserving groups, such as the poor, the aged, and minorities; much less for military preparedness or, worse still, for actually fighting wars. Less clear but still pronounced was a preference for a strategy specifying income over service for transferring money rather than goods, so that people could exercise more choice. No specific decision declared that government would do these things and no announcement came that this reallocation of resources would be governmental policy from a chosen day onward. We have no Domestic Welfare Day like an Independence Day. That these trends were not summed up and announced as deliberate governmental policy one day may account for their continued lack of recognition. People are still waiting for this revolution in public policy to come when it has already been. That we may not like it as much as we thought (viz. "Strategic Retreat on Objectives") doesn't mean it didn't happen.

National defense expenditures accounted for 41 percent of the 1965 federal budget while social welfare expenditures accounted for less than 19 percent. Critics of public policy in the mid-sixties attacked the priorities implicit in our heavy defense expenditures. Hence President Johnson declared the War on Poverty. As it became apparent that trying to do good was not quite the same as doing good, the Vietnam War began to siphon away resources. The optimism of the early sixties disappeared, leaving both liberals and conservatives disillusioned, the one because too much had been attempted by government, the other because it had not accomplished more. Then came the "stagflation" (unemployment and inflation) of the early seventies, the energy crisis, Watergate. . . . While we were occupied by this confusing cacophony of experiences, the priorities implicit in the federal budget changed. By 1976, a scant decade later, an almost complete reversal had occurred: national defense accounted for less than 25 percent of the budget as social welfare expenditures expanded to more than 38 percent. Although defense expenditures have shrunk slightly in real dollars, expenditures on welfare have more than doubled. If this doubling in a decade is a revolution, then we have surely had one.

THE REVOLUTION WE ARE WAITING FOR IS ALREADY HERE

The cause of this revolution may be charted among the major programs increasing expenditures on social welfare. Social insurance is the federal government's largest category of welfare. Therefore, we have chosen to study the growth of social insurance programs: OASDI ("social security"), medicare for the elderly, and unemployment insurance (UI). The second largest category of welfare programs is public assistance — direct cash payments to individuals financed by general revenues. From this category we include AFDC (Aid to Families with Dependent Children), medicaid for the poor, and Supplemental Security Income (SSI). A third category, in which goods are given instead of cash, is in-kind transfer programs; within this category we look at the growth of housing assistance and food stamps. I choose these programs because of their size, growth rate, and political salience. I have omitted several programs, such as federal employment retirement benefits and nutrition programs, which are large but not aimed at helping the poor or other needy segments of the population.

Table 4.1 summarizes, in three ways, the growth of these programs over the years between 1965 and 1975. How much these programs have grown can be absorbed quickly from column 3, which shows the percentage of increase for each program's share of federal budget outlays. The smallest growth was in OASDI, which increased "only" 30 percent; medicare increased 10,400 percent. The rest of the programs range between these extremes. Tables 4.2, 4.3, and 4.4 detail the record of federal expenditures on these programs and reveal their rapid and substantial expansion.

TABLE 4.1

SOCIAL-WELFARE EXPENDITURES; GROWTH OF SELECTED SOCIAL PROGRAMS, IN CURRENT DOLLARS, REAL DOLLARS, AND AS A PERCENTAGE OF FEDERAL BUDGET OUTLAYS, 1965–1975

Program	(1) Current dollars (factor of increase)	(2) Real dollars adjusted for price increase (factor of increase)	Percentage of increase, share of federal budget outlay
AFDC	5	2.7	60
SSI	4	2.2	30
UI	4	2.4	120
OASDI	3.6	2.1	30
Housing assistance	25	14.8	800
Food stamps	143	84	4,600
Medicare	230	139	10,400
Medicaid	253	146	9,000

KEY

AFDC:	Aid to Families with Dependent Children.
SSI:	Supplemental Security Income.
UI:	Unemployment Insurance.
OASDI:	Old-Age, Survivors, and Disability Insurance.

SOURCES. AFDC, SSI, UI, and OASDI figures from *Statistical Abstract of the U.S.,* issues 1965–77, U.S. Department of Commerce, and *The Social Security Bulletin,* vol. 41, no. 5, May 1978, Social Security Administration, U.S. Department of Health, Education and Welfare. Housing, medicare, medicaid, and food stamps figures from federal budgets prepared by the Executive Office of Management and the Budget from 1965 to 1975.

TABLE 4.2

SOCIAL-WELFARE EXPENDITURES, INCREASE IN CURRENT DOLLARS, 1965–1975
(IN MILLIONS OF DOLLARS)

Year	AFDC	SSI	UI	OASDI	Hous- ing	Medi- care	Medi- caid	Food stamps
1965	1,809	2,697	2,283	18,311	81		27	32.5
1966	1,924	2,564	1,852	20,048	391	64	77	64.8
1967	2,280	2,561	2,181	21,407	478	3,400	1,200	105.5
1968	2,851	2,491	2,151	24,396	948	5,300	1,800	173.1
1969	3,565	2,771	2,262	26,751	871	6,598	2,285	228.8
1970	4,857	2,939	4,131	31,863	1,280	7,149	2,607	549.7
1971	5,653	3,108	5,422	37,171	1,243	7,875	3,362	1,523.7
1972	7,020	3,392	5,198	41,595	1,595	8,819	4,601	1,797.3
1973	7,292	3,418	4,415	51,459	1,420	9,479	4,997	2,131.4
1974	7,991	5,246	6,646	58,521	1,819	11,343	5,833	2,718.3
1975	8,639	5,878	12,560	66,923	2,052	14,787	6,840	4,409.9
Total Increase 1965–1975	6,830	3,181	10,277	48,612	1,971	14,787	6,813	4,377.4

TABLE 4.3

SOCIAL-WELFARE EXPENDITURES, INCREASE IN REAL DOLLARS, 1965–1975
(IN MILLIONS OF DOLLARS)

Year	AFDC[a]	SSI[a]	UI[a]	OASDI[a]	Housing[b]	Medicare[c]	Medicaid[c]	Food stamps[d]
1965	1,914	2,854	2,416	19,377	85		30	34
1966	1,979	2,638	1,905	20,626	402	69	82	65
1967	2,280	2,561	2,181	21,407	478	3,400	1,200	106
1968	2,736	2,391	2,064	23,931	910	4,995	1,697	167
1969	3,247	2,524	2,060	24,363	786	5,818	2,015	210
1970	4,176	2,527	3,552	27,397	1,077	5,928	2,162	478
1971	4,660	2,662	4,470	30,464	1,000	6,133	2,618	1,286
1972	5,603	2,707	4,148	33,196	1,235	6,656	3,472	1,455
1973	5,410	2,568	3,317	38,662	1,052	7,053	3,629	1,507
1974	5,410	3,552	4,500	39,622	1,208	7,540	3,876	1,681
1975	5,359	3,646	7,792	41,516	1,230	8,767	4,057	2,514
Total Increase 1965–1975	3,445	792	5,376	22,139	1,145	8,698	4,027	2,480

[a] Deflated by consumer price index for all products, 1967 = 100.
[b] Deflated by consumer price index for all housing, 1967 = 100.
[c] Deflated by consumer price index for medical care, 1967 = 100.
[d] Deflated by consumer price index for food, 1967 = 100.

TABLE 4.4

SOCIAL-WELFARE EXPENDITURES, INCREASE AS A PERCENTAGE OF THE FEDERAL
BUDGET, 1965–1975

Year	AFDC	SSI	UI	OASDI	Housing	Medicare	Medicaid	Food stamps
1965	1.5	2.3	1.9	15.5	0.0		0.0	0.0
1966	1.4	1.9	1.4	14.9	.2	0.0	0.0	0.0
1967	1.4	1.6	1.4	13.5	.3	2.1	.7	0.0
1968	1.5	1.4	1.2	13.9	.5	3.0	1.0	0.0
1969	1.9	1.5	1.2	14.5	.5	3.6	1.3	.1
1970	2.9	1.3	2.1	16.2	.7	3.6	1.3	.3
1971	2.7	1.5	2.6	17.6	.6	3.7	1.6	.7
1972	3.0	1.5	2.2	17.9	.7	3.8	2.0	.8
1973	3.0	1.4	2.1	20.8	.6	3.8	2.0	.9
1974	3.0	1.9	3.9	23.7	.7	4.2	2.2	1.0
1975	2.6	1.8	3.9	20.5	.6	4.5	2.1	1.4
Total Increase 1965–1975	24.9	18.9	23.9	178.0	5.4	32.3	14.2	5.2

RULES CONTAINING THE CONSENSUS

Our explanation of the sharp relative and absolute increases in expenditures on welfare is that they have followed changing values. Doing more for welfare and less for war is what decision-makers wanted to do. Yet these changes were not planned, in the sense that decision-makers decided they would do this or agreed on how to do it or necessarily were aware that they were actually doing it. I wish to explain how, without apparent coordination, there came about a uniform pattern of rapidly increasing expenditures on welfare. Our first explanation is moral consensus: when decision-makers were in doubt as to how they should implement values in which they believed, they adopted several implicit rules for resolving uncertainty that invariably led them to choose more costly alternatives. Having decided to try harder, policy-makers instituted new kinds of program characteristics that permitted old welfare programs to expand more rapidly than intended. Benefit increases, for instance, were set up to occur automatically rather than at the discretion of Congress. Sometimes program costs were increased unthinkingly because policy-makers were distracted by more pressing questions. This phenomenon we shall call "the policy eclipse," because the programs were, in effect, hidden from view by other concerns. We find consistency because, when program characteristics were changed or their nature was eclipsed, the result was always the same — higher expenditures. We are retrospectively rationalizing disparate events by finding (inventing) common elements as if decision-makers had these interests. In the end, we will consider alternative hypotheses for higher expenditures — increased population, pressure groups, inflation, and so on.

Can there be coordination without a coordinator? Yes, when interaction over policy takes place within a moral consensus specifying the rules for resolving conflicts. And I shall now specify the rules containing that consensus. Suppose a rule for making decisions in welfare policy is that no one should receive benefits who is not entitled to them. Another is that all who are entitled should receive them. Regulations meant to screen out all the undeserving will inevitably eliminate some who should be covered, and regulations designed to include all the deserving will undoubtedly catch up some who should be left out. If the injustice of excluding the deserving is considered worse than including the undeserving, coverage can be broadened (overlapping categories of recipients) without worrying about those who should not qualify but do. So long as the right fish are caught, so to speak, the rest of the catch doesn't matter. Even if such a rule is not explicitly formulated, it may be implicit in the actions of decision-makers: no law will be passed that values exclusion over inclusion of beneficiaries. Thus, whether or not the rule is specifically stated, one may speak of these laws and regulations on social welfare "as if" they operated in conformity with such rules.

What, then, would be a test of the actual operation of these rules for resolving uncertainty? Of necessity, our test is historical: do past policies conform to the rules we propose? Because we formulated these rules by thinking about the past, however, it would be better to test them on new data. Prediction is better than retrodiction. Against the view that President Carter's 1977 proposals on welfare reform would be compatible with his previously pronounced ideas, we shall place our hypothesis that because these proposals come from the political process, they will instead conform to the rules we set down. Because the future is slow in coming but eventually arrives, readers will have a better opportunity than we do now to test our hypothesis against future developments in public policy.

RULES FOR RESOLVING UNCERTAINTY ABOUT VALUES

Analysis and explanation are intertwined tasks. The more that can be explained, the larger the target for a strategy for intervention based on analysis. In a completely random world statistical descriptions are possible but causal explanations are not. Analysis is not possible in a world governed by randomness. But, in a world governed by partially known causal chains, where motives are sometimes effective and where intentions are occasionally realized, instrumental knowledge is possible. Explanation and hence analysis make sense.

Values and Analysis

Analyzing the history of legislation on social welfare, we ascribe values to the historical settings as the causal origins. Historical values are like intentions, motives, and objectives. We say that as legislators increasingly valued "consumer sovereignty," they designed welfare programs to follow market techniques, supplementing income, or reimbursing for expenses rather than providing services directly. In another example, we say that because decision-makers valued equality, they were led to reduce the inequality of benefit levels between blacks and whites. These values are read into history for their explanatory power. There are risks in interpreting history in this way.

At one extreme, analysts may mistake *effect* for *intention*. Our desire to explain may lead us to read values as causes into the images of effects. In our example, the fact that welfare programs use existing markets leads us to read "consumer sovereignty" as the intention. These imputations, however well suited for explanation, may be factually wrong. The value of consumer sovereignty may not really have been operating. Unfortunately, there is no certain method to identify values held by decision-makers.

Students must settle for incomplete explanatory schemes. Luck, chance, and randomness must be given their due. Causal networks are tenuous, ruptured by unanticipated results, interaction effects, mixed motives, and conflicting values. At the other extreme, too much tenuousness can be bad, for as the unexplained portions grow, explanation and therefore analysis suffers.

We choose a middle ground. Intentions are sometimes realized, but room is ample for unintended consequences. Values sometimes exist prior to behavior, but often ascribed values are post facto rationalizations of current behavior. Values, like goals, are mixed; intentions are not always aligned. The direction of causality is not necessarily clear. Do we design programs with clear scales of values in mind or do we design programs and then modify our values once we see what we have? Once programs are devised, they become part of the experience that may modify our behavior.

Values for Designing Means

Programs, in the abstract, are the means for achieving broad end-state goals, such as equality of opportunity, protection from loss of income, and improved health care. Programs incorporate more instrumental interests as well. We can list a number of these instrumental values, that is, values for achieving broad end-state goals. Programs should be flexible rather than rigid, efficient rather than wasteful, fairly administered rather than arbitrary, inexpensive rather than costly, helpful without being paternalistic, and centralized in cost but decentralized in administration.

Broad End-State Goals

There was a time when the prevailing belief was that individuals were responsible for their own problems and government was responsible for the rest. Individuals suffer the consequences of their own making; the government must remedy natural disasters, situations beyond the control of individuals (depressions), and congenital handicaps (blindness). Over the last fifty years, our notions of the boundaries of individual fault have shifted, placing more responsibility on government. So long as poverty was caused by individual traits, such as laziness, public assistance could be discretionary. But when poverty was seen as caused by the government in a recession, then remedy by a governmental program was seen as a right or entitlement. Thus persons "earned" their social security payments by lifelong contributions to a trust fund. After much litigation in the sixties, welfare benefits were deemed to be "rights" (though the contrast was fought over procedural fairness, not justice of the outcomes). The more characteristics for which the individual is blameless, the heavier the demands upon government to respond. Equality of opportunity applied at first between blacks and whites, then between males and females, later between physically disabled people and the nonhandicapped, and still later between heterosexuals and homosexuals.

Moving from a world view of personal to societal fault suggests that values are embedded in policies. There is, we think, a consistency in what the government has tried to do about welfare.

Sources of Uncertainty

Rules for designing means and ends are directional but not magnitudinal. They tell us to do something but not how much of it to do; to reduce inequality, but not by how much; to use private markets more, but not how much more. Thus, morality is associated with intensity of effort. If reducing inequality is moral, then reducing it even more must be "more moral." Moral considerations therefore leave us uncertain about the precise design for a public policy. Attempts to operationalize several precepts in one program, moreover, often demonstrate that they conflict. You can reduce interstate inequalities or you can increase flexibility, but you may not be able to accomplish both. There is doubt then about which precept to follow as well as how extensively it should be implemented. If, as usual, we want to include several values, what is the optimal mix among them?

We believe that the development of welfare policies in the last fifteen years shows implicit rules for resolving uncertainties over values. In this sense, our welfare policies have developed a moral consistency that we will attempt to delineate with these rules.

It is better to give to the undeserving than to withhold from the deserving
It seems almost tautological to point out that one of the goals of most welfare programs is giving aid where it is needed. Yet this general goal does not tell policy-makers exactly who should be eligible for welfare. Nor does it tell the policy-maker, after the goal has been converted into a specific income level, how to achieve the standard. A standard that covers only a narrowly defined class of beneficiaries risks the possibility of missing someone who deserves to be covered. The greater this risk, the greater the chance the goal will be missed. The program's moral gravity is correlated with the degree to which it is designed to cover every possible beneficiary. Therefore, the rule for dealing with uncertainty is to *broaden coverage* and to *overlap coverage* among welfare programs so that no deserving persons slip through, even if this broadness also means that the undeserving will sneak in.

The tendency to continually broaden coverage is clear in the history of OASDI (social security). The percentage of the work force covered rose steadily from 64.5 percent in 1950 to 90.0 percent in 1974. Similarly, the percentage of the work force covered by unemployment insurance rose from 60.0 percent in 1950 to 79.8 percent in 1974. Eligibility for food stamps was increased in 1970 and 1973 by amendments extending the program to all areas of the country. Just prior to 1970, about 55 percent of the poverty population lived in counties offering food stamps; by the end of 1974, nearly 100 percent of the poor had food stamp programs. The history of housing-assistance programs reveals a tendency to extend eligibility by creating new programs as well as expanding old ones. New programs were created to subsidize rent (Section 236) and low-income home ownership (Section 235). Section 8 of the HUD Act of 1974 expanded eligibility for low-income rent subsidies.

Uncertainty over eligibility for welfare led policy-makers not only to broaden but also to overlap the coverage of several programs. One of the main ideas behind creation of SSI was that social security and the other welfare programs provided inadequate benefits for some beneficiaries and therefore should be supplemented. The overlapping coverage of many welfare programs has resulted in the "notch effect," as some observers call it: if you're eligible for AFDC, then you can also get food stamps and medicaid, and you're probably also eligible for housing assistance. If, in addition, you are old or disabled, you can get SSI and social security benefits. Thus, government reduces the risk that deserving people will not receive some kind of welfare.

Give too much rather than too little   Another goal of welfare policy is that the poor should be given enough to survive. But this goal is not easily put into operation in some times and places. How much is enough? Uncertainty has led policy-makers to adopt an implicit rule for setting benefits: when in doubt, raise the benefits. The policy's moral character is presumably enhanced by higher benefits, lowering the risk that someone will be shortchanged. The rule also increases the likelihood of paying some people more, however, so that the rule may be read: when in doubt, overpayments are preferable to underpayments.

The average monthly social-security benefit for a retired worker and his wife in 1975 dollars increased from $124 in 1960 to $390.30 in 1978; for a disabled worker from $89 to $226. As a percentage of weekly wages, unemployment benefits rose from 32.9 percent in 1960 to 80.2 percent in 1977. The maximum duration for unemployment benefits was extended from 26 weeks to 39 (1970), then to 52 (1973), and 65 weeks (1974). The average monthly payment to an AFDC family increased from $108 in 1960 to $240.86 in 1977 (in current dollars), or from $122 in 1960 to $144 in 1975 (in constant dollars). The average monthly payment under Aid to the Permanently and Totally Disabled (prior to 1974) and SSI (after 1974) increased from $44 in 1950 to $265.53 in 1978 (in current dollars), or from $61 in 1950 to $87 in 1975 (in constant dollars). If raising benefits enhances the morality of a welfare program, then we have reached new moral pinnacles almost every year since 1960.

The need justifies the cost   The goals of raising welfare benefits and broadening coverage conflict with a more general governmental goal — saving the taxpayers' money. How have policy-makers resolved this potential conflict? The history of the welfare system reveals that the implicit rule for resolving this conflict is to subordinate cost to the goals of broadening coverage and raising benefits.

Several pieces of evidence suggest the existence of the "need justifies cost" rule. First, despite the ebb and flow of public furor over rising welfare costs, there was little congressional debate over the costs of welfare proposals. Cost considerations were completely overridden in debate over expanding the services component of AFDC between 1962 and 1967. Similarly, Presidents Kennedy, Johnson, and Nixon all proposed (and Congress enacted) expansions of the food stamp program despite projections of increasing costs. Although it was understood that Nixon's "permanent extended benefits" unemployment proposal would significantly increase costs and federal involvement, Congress overwhelmingly passed the provisions.

The importance and pervasiveness of the "need justifies cost" rule is particularly evident in the legislation giving open-ended budget authorization (benefits must be given to all who qualify regardless of cost) to parts of several programs: food stamps, medicare, medicaid, and the services component of AFDC. Congress saw such an overwhelming need for these programs that it was willing to relinquish control over their cost.

A number of explanations are possible for the failure of cost criteria to receive greater consideration. One is the expectation that revenues will grow, and that therefore, costs can always grow. In a sense, supply of revenue creates its own demand for expenditure. A different (but not conflicting) explanation is that the optimistic, "can-do" spirit of President Kennedy's New Frontier, the belief that any problem can be solved with enough money and brains, led to a nearly complete disregard for cost.[1] To us, however, the best explanation is the belief that some people's need matters more than some people's money.

We have attempted to explicate some of the moral meaning behind the increase in welfare expenditures. We can now examine patterns of program characteristics resulting in part from these rules.

PROGRAM CHARACTERISTICS AS DETERMINANTS OF COST

Once a program is in being it has a life of its own: as conditions in the outside world change, they interact with the preexisting features of the program to create new consequences. A program's characteristics transmit not only decision-makers' values but also convert external factors, such as shifts of population, into program outlays. These characteristics are themselves a cause of expenditures. Most important, program characteristics are controllable, and are therefore appropriate subjects for the policy analyst's inquiry. The patterns of change in program characteristics that we describe are partly responsible for the increases in welfare spending.

Use of Commercial Markets

Shift social-welfare programs from direct governmental provision of services to existing (commercial) markets Many governmental programs for income transfer had their beginnings as services directly provided to the poor. The earliest federal food-assistance programs were distributions of surplus commodities. Produce purchased by the government from private farmers to support prices was redistributed to low-income persons: little choice of food was available to ultimate consumers; they took what they were given. Commodity distribution took place alongside of existing commercial outlets for food; whatever was procured through the distribution programs therefore suffered reduced commercial demand. Food stamps changed this effect at least; under the program recipients increased their buying power for food in commercial markets.

The first federal programs to house the poor were initiated during the late thirties. Built and administered by local public-housing authorities, and supported by federal funds and mortgage insurance, public-housing projects offered government-provided housing to eligibles too poor to afford standard commercial-market offerings. Public housing was to solve the problem of regular markets' inability to meet the needs of poor tenants. Later, during the sixties, rent supplements and mortgage-interest subsidies provided low-income families with the ability to enter private-housing markets. When critics claimed that these subsidies discouraged private initiative, the programs' proponents replied that the subsidies were less socialistic than public housing.

Before medicaid began, the medical needs of the poor (when they were met at all) were served mainly by city, state, and county-run welfare hospitals, Thus, for those unable to afford private hospital care, the local governmental unit would directly supply medical services. As early as 1950, the Social Security Act was amended to allow payments directly to providers of medical services for welfare recipients. But these "vendor-payment" programs were small because financial participation was limited by ceilings on cost. Nevertheless, this amendment signalled a trend away from governmental provision of medical services to the indirect payment for services provided by others. When the medicare-medicaid legislation was passed in 1965, the separation of government from the industry had already become quite clear:

> Nothing in this title shall be construed to authorize any Federal officer or employee to exercise any supervision or control over the practice of medicine or the manner in which medical services are provided. . . . (Section 1801)

After medicaid became law, many county-hospital patients became eligible for care in private hospitals. Since in some states (California, for one) counties pay a share of the medicaid budget, many have attempted to reduce their own costs by closing county hospitals, wiping out the last vestige of directly provided governmental care. (Recent attempts to close U.S. Public Health Services hospitals, though mostly ineffective, have followed a similar trend.)

Social services also fit this model of consumer choice. In 1962, a committee of welfare professionals recommended to President Kennedy that the orientation of public assistance be changed from monetary relief to rehabilitation. Whereas, prior to that time, social services were provided by the state or local welfare agency alone, the Public Welfare Service Amendments of 1962 authorized federal reimbursement for services provided by the welfare agency or by another state agency. In 1967, the purchase provisions of the amendments were extended to allow reimbursement for services purchased not only from other state agencies, but from private sources as well.

The extension of all these programs from direct governmental provision of services to commercial markets was a necessary condition for growth of expenditures. As long as distribution of food was limited to surplus goods, an inherent cap on the amount of aid was in place. But when the food stamp program was enacted, the cap came off. With commercial markets open to recipients of government subsidies, significantly larger numbers could and did become involved in the system. Although average monthly participation in the commodity-distribution program never exceeded 7 million (1962), with a maximum yearly cost of $321 million (1971), the food stamp program currently services in excess of 18 million people at a cost approaching $6 billion.

When assistance with medical care became indirectly provided by federal reimbursement to private health-care facilities, the growth of the program became completely dependent upon how comprehensive the individual states decided their programs should be. When state welfare agencies were allowed to purchase social services from other agencies and outside providers, incentives to increase such use were great. With new and nearly unlimited sources of services available to the state agency, the use and subsequent cost of the programs mushroomed.

The early systems were two-tiered. The regular market provision of services was paralleled by food, housing, medical assistance, and social services intended solely for the poor. The present systems allow low-income families, subsidized by governmental transfers of in-kind benefits, to use the commercial markets. Not limited by how fast government could get its bureaucratic machinery in motion to provide services, benefits could expand much faster. Because most of these programs had open-ended budget authorizations, their growth was potentially infinite.

Automatic Scale

Social-welfare benefits should increase automatically as conditions change. Many benefit increases and expansions require no specific congressional action but are triggered by prearranged circumstances Benefit levels of social-welfare programs at one time were changed by specific congressional acts mandating an increase. The history of the social security program illustrates that such increases came often: 1950, 1952, 1954, 1958, 1965, 1967, and 1971. In 1972, another increase was coupled with an automatic cost-of-living escalator. Whereas previous increases irregularly offset inflation, their cumulative effect greatly exceeded the rise in cost of living. With extreme inflationary trends, the "indexing" of benefits was expected to regularly offset the effects of inflation (against price changes to keep purchasing power constant).

"Indexing" is not peculiar to social security. In 1970, when food costs were rising at an annual rate of 3 percent, an amendment to the Food Stamp Act indexed benefit levels to the consumer price index (CPI) for food. Between 1972 and 1974, when food costs were rising more than 14 percent a year, further amendments stipulated that the indexing was to occur semiannually. Such action was not intended to provide greater benefits to recipients but only to automatically assure them of constant purchasing power. The index makes changes nondiscretionary. And, unlike the indexing of social security, food stamp benefits can be adjusted upward or downward with the CPI (though no decreases have yet occurred). Legislators may see such automatic increases as either favorable or unfavorable. Some may miss the almost yearly opportunity to show their constituents how much they have contributed to the nation's welfare. Others may be happy to continue constant benefits without being seen as wasteful spenders.

The automatic effects of indexing Supplemental Security Income (SSI) payments are more complicated but serve the same purposes. Many SSI recipients receive state supplements to the federal-income guaranteed level, and many (70 percent) receive social security benefits. Because dual recipients must pay a 100 percent marginal tax rate on regular increases in social security benefits (above the first $20), any cost-of-living increases granted for social security beneficiaries could decrease SSI payments by the same amount, leaving recipients relatively worse off in inflationary times. A "pass-through" provision for benefit increases specifies that no individual component of the overlapping programs can reduce its benefit payment because another part is raising theirs.

Expansion in the medicare and medicaid programs occurs automatically because third-party reimbursement is used. Inflation in the cost of medical care is directly passed through as increased charges to the payer (the federal government) or the taxpayers.

Another type of expansion in a nondiscretionary program is the automatic triggering of lengthened benefits when the rate of unemployment rises above a specified threshold. Prearranged "on" and "off" indicators of state and national unemployment rates determine how extended benefits will be provided in a way that is expected to adjust quickly in a "crisis," without requiring legislative discretion. (The proposed Humphrey-Hawkins Full Employment bill included a variation of this triggering mechanism.)

The values behind these nondiscretionary changes are a desire for flexibility in the program, which allows quick adaptation to economic trends, and an interest in keeping recipients at a predetermined standard of income regardless of such trends.

The difficulty with flexibility lies in its interactions. Indexing in response to inflation breeds its own inflation. As the price index for food increases, and the benefits increase correspondingly, more money is pumped into the market for food, raising prices further. Then, as prices rise, the indexing mechanism is again triggered. The increased demand for medical care caused by the introduction of medicare and medicaid, along with a reimbursement scheme having no incentive to keep prices low, has contributed to the very high rate of inflation in the medical-care field. Thus, the effect of the flexibility and responsiveness built into the automatic mechanisms of indexing, makes the cost of individual programs increase at accelerated rates.

Federal Responsibility

If the state and local governments won't (can't) pay for increases in cost of welfare, the federal government should   Policy-makers can agree easily enough on the general goal of trying harder to alleviate the welfare problem by spending more money, but agreement on the instrumental question of who will pay for increased costs is harder to come by. In recent years, however, the federal government has facilitated agreement on the question by assuming the cost of most new welfare programs as well as a larger share of the cost of the old ones. In effect the "feds" have become the "payer" (as well as employer) of last resort.

As welfare has grown, so too has the volume of complaints from local and state governments that they cannot afford increased costs of welfare. A sort of moral hazard was created: the federal government's willingness to finance welfare reform was an incentive to ask for, even to demand, increasingly expensive reforms. Let us consider several examples of this pattern of developing welfare policy.

The Supplemental Security Income (SSI) program of 1972 replaced more than 1,000 assistance programs for the aged, blind, and disabled, which had been jointly funded by federal, state, and local governments. In their place, basic monthly cash payments financed from general revenues of the Treasury pay recipients the difference between an individual's "countable income" and a federal guaranteed income level. Prior to SSI enactment, states had administered the Aid to the Blind, Aid to the Permanently and Totally Disabled, and Old Age Assistance programs on a federal-state matching formula. The new legislation was expected to reduce interstate variations in benefits and lessen the financial burden on states. Grandfather clauses were inserted to ensure state supplementation of federal payments up to the previous state-supplied level. But the federalization of the program exempted states from future increases in program payments; in any year, states could be charged up to their share of assistance only for the aged, blind, and disabled paid during calendar year 1972. Extra costs for increased case loads (resulting from more liberal eligibility standards) were paid by the federal government.

The Unemployment Insurance program (UI) is administered by the states according to minimum federal standards. It is supposed to be a self-sustaining insurance plan with all benefits paid out to be covered in full by the payroll tax. Originally, the only federal expenditures for UI were in grants to the states for administration of the program. Generally, the law left to the states determination of the qualification period, waiting period, duration of benefits, amount of benefits, and coverage beyond that required by federal law. The federal share of UI costs has increased mainly when federal policy-makers have chosen to manipulate the length rather than the level of benefits. In 1970, this type of extension was financed by an increase in the payroll tax rate. Extended benefits (beyond the standard twenty-six-week period) were financed half by federal funds and half by state funds. In 1971, another increase in the payroll-tax rate was used to cover emergency benefits, financed again under the 50 percent matching of funds.

Until 1970, most of the state unemployment trust funds were solvent; the Treasury Department recently loaned the Labor Department $10 billion to shore up dwindling state UI trust funds. In addition to taking over a greater share of benefit payments under extended and emergency benefit programs, the federal government is subsidizing the state UI funds. Although the recession of the mid-seventies has been a prime reason for a federally expanded role in UI, it is unclear whether an end to the recession would reverse this expansion.

The Aid to Families with Dependent Children (AFDC) program is administered by the states with the federal government reimbursing them for a percentage of their costs. Program costs have risen dramatically because the federal government has increased its own share so often. In 1935, states could be reimbursed one-third of the first $18 per month for the first child and the first $12 for the second child. By 1969, states were being reimbursed for five-sixths of the first $18 per recipient, and 50 to 65 percent of the payments up to $32 times the number of recipients. More important, HEW started reimbursing states for costs of services provided: at 50 percent of cost in 1956, 75 percent in 1962, and up to 90 percent for some services in 1975. In addition, federal reimbursement for services to former and potential AFDC recipients were permitted as of 1965. In the same year, states were allowed to use medicaid reimbursement formulas when they were more attractive to the state. Most states chose this schedule, which allowed for 50 to 83 percent of costs (depending on state per capita income), and which specified no maximum amounts.

Counterexamples to this rule are difficult to find. In some areas, individual congressmen attempt to reverse the regime of increasing federal support, but they usually fail. Throughout the legislative history of the food stamp program, efforts were made to have the states assume partial payment for the program beyond their share of administrative costs. In 1970, the House Agriculture Committee reported a food-stamp bill proposing that participating states help defray an increasing share of the bonus value of food coupons. The measure was eventually rejected in conference committee on the grounds that many states would drop the food stamp program completely rather than participate in its ever-increasing costs.

MISUNDERSTANDINGS THAT ALWAYS COST MORE

We do not claim that our hypotheses explain all the variation in welfare expenditures. Some of the increase in expenditures is attributable to random or isolated phenomena: accidents, misunderstandings, and unintended consequences. Few of these phenomena display much rhyme or reason. One of them, however, occurred quite consistently: the policy eclipse.

The Policy Eclipse

Social-welfare programs that evolved following larger policy initiatives have come to have significant lives of their own, often with unanticipated cost consequences   It is not unusual for Congress to consider several major bills simultaneously. In the last half-century it has greatly extended government activity in many areas. As the scale of government has grown, Congress has been compelled to address a larger number of increasingly complex issues and to make policy decisions regardless of whether it has had time to fully consider the issues. Seemingly innocuous changes in social-welfare programs, adopted without close legislative scrutiny, have later proved costly. Consider these examples:

The 1965 legislative debates over a suitable health program for the nation focused on medicare, because its social-insurance features were "radical" in contrast to medicaid's "conventional" liberalization of the Kerr-Mills program. Medicare, with its compulsory payroll tax, would automatically affect larger numbers of people, whereas the influence of medicaid was thought to be marginal. If history was any indication, the medicaid program would be small because states had spent conservatively on its forerunner. The medicaid program itself stole the limelight from an amendment to the Social Security Act allowing states to use their medicaid formula in figuring reimbursement for AFDC expenses. In the heated discussion over the health programs, a friendly amendment was proposed that would make planning for public-assistance payments administratively easier by combining the two reimbursement formulas. Floor managers for medicaid claimed that the amendment would tie up loose ends in the health program and suggested passage. Congress did not take time, because of the medicaid discussions, to scrutinize the estimate that the cost of the amendment would be only $5 million.

In 1967 the Office of Management and Budget (OMB) proposed to extend the purchase provisions of the AFDC amendments to allow reimbursement for services purchased not only from other state agencies but from private sources as well. The OMB proposal was included in the administration's draft of the 1967 social security amendments. Congress, however, focused mainly on the Work Incentive Program, the extension of benefits to unemployed fathers, medicaid amendments, and the welfare freeze. No one spoke for or against the purchase provision, and it passed without notice.

Although President Nixon's welfare-reform initiative in the early seventies included programs for both adults (aid to the aged, blind, and disabled) and dependent children, legislative debate was concentrated on AFDC. The supplemental security program for adults moved through the legislative works in the shadow of Nixon's Family Assistance Plan ("guaranteed income"). Congress focused its debate on FAP because it was a complex and radical program aimed at a politically volatile problem. Pressed for time and sensing that no compromise was possible, the House and Senate conferees deleted all provisions relating to FAP. The smaller and less-controversial SSI came away intact from the legislative procedures.

What have been the fiscal consequences of these program changes that were eclipsed by the more controversial programs of the times?

Costs increased beyond expectation and intention. The fiscal ramifications of an open-ended, federal match from general revenues became known as populous states like New York and California adopted "overly liberal" medicaid programs. The sleeping giant was roused. The Kuchel amendment that allowed states to use their medicaid formula for AFDC reimbursement was also costly. Instead of the estimated $5 million, the federal cost of this change rose to $240 million in 1968 (88 percent of this amount occurring in New York and California) and $1.1 billion in 1972. The AFDC expenses for purchase of services increased fivefold between 1967 and 1972 from $280 million to $1.6 billion. The growth was concentrated in the few states that learned to exploit the service amendments, notably California, New York, and Illinois. The SSI has been plagued by a case error rate of nearly 25 percent. Erroneous payments for the first two years of operations may have reached $800 million. Where the number of recipients of SSI's predecessor programs had been falling before SSI was passed, the number increased substantially with implementation of SSI in 1974.

We have examined several of the moral rules that rationalize increase in welfare spending and some of the patterns in the development of welfare-program characteristics that permitted costs to increase rapidly. We have found that "accidental" decisions always led to cost increases. In some cases, therefore, policy-makers' intentions to spend more on welfare were directly realized; in others, their intentions were realized accidentally on purpose. As always, however, alternative hypotheses will explain the same pattern of events.

ALTERNATIVE HYPOTHESES

We believe that examining the individual policy decisions that contributed to the revolution in budgetary priorities reveals patterns of development. We have attempted to define the logic of this development. We contend not that our explanation is complete but that it is correct as far as it goes. So far, we have neglected some of the more conventional explanations for the turnaround in budgetary priorities. These alternative explanations may conflict with or complement our own.

The Civil Rights Movement Caused the Welfare Explosion

Numerous writers have claimed that the growth of federal welfare spending was a response to organized political pressure from civil rights groups. Nick Kotz, a *Washington Post* journalist, writes: "there was real political pressure for change that came from a rapidly evolving civil rights movement that already was engaged in the struggle against poverty as well as against segregation and discrimination."[2]

Piven and Cloward wrote in *Regulating the Poor:* "we think that the Great Society programs were promulgated by federal leaders in order to deal with the political problems created by a new and unstable electoral constituency, namely blacks — and to deal with this constituency not simply by responding to its expressed interests, but by shaping and directing its political future."[3]

One cannot deny that the civil rights movement influenced the general tone of this nation's politics in the early and mid-sixties. But to argue generally that the welfare explosion was a response to the civil rights movement courts the post hoc fallacy. One must ask very specifically how the civil rights movement affected the development of the programs in question.

Medicare and medicaid   Although varied interest groups were important in the debate over medicare, civil rights groups had a very minor part. Medicaid, a program that would disproportionately benefit blacks, was almost ignored by all interest groups.

AFDC   The costly Kuchel amendment (1965), which permitted states to be reimbursed for money payments according to their medicaid formulas rather than their AFDC formulas, was ignored by civil rights proponents. The public-service amendments of 1962, which greatly expanded the services component of AFDC, were generally neglected by civil rights groups. The services component was further expanded in 1967 with little discussion.

In the late sixties, the National Welfare Rights Organization (NWRO), which might be very loosely called a "civil rights" organization, successfully sued local welfare agencies for improperly withholding AFDC benefits. The NWRO also encouraged eligible families to apply for AFDC benefits. The NWRO was not successful in lobbying for increased benefits or increased coverage. Overall, NWRO probably increased AFDC expenditures through existing benefit structures.

Social Security   OASDI benefit increases were supported by organized labor but received little attention from civil rights groups. Because social security benefits do not accrue disproportionately to blacks (unlike AFDC), there was no reason to view the program racially.

The SSI   NWRO spent most of its political resources lobbying for a $6,500 minimum income following the Nixon welfare proposals in 1969. SSI was generally ignored by interest groups and constituents.

Unemployment Insurance   Although blacks benefit disproportionately from UI, the program is not viewed as a welfare program whose primary purpose is to aid the poor or minorities. Rather, UI is thought primarily to benefit the middle class. Therefore, civil rights groups have generally ignored UI legislation.

Food Stamps   In 1969, NWRO strongly supported the Nixon proposals to expand the program to nationwide coverage. Prior to 1969, civil rights groups had generally ignored food stamp legislation, perhaps because it was considered an agricultural rather than a welfare program.

Housing   Inadequate housing is the most visible problem of inner-city blacks. Civil rights groups, including the Urban League and the NAACP, have provided much of the political impetus behind housing legislation. In 1961 the NAACP's support of Kennedy's housing proposals was couched as advocating an open-housing clause for all federally funded housing programs. In 1967 the Urban Coalition strongly urged the Senate to approve the full administration budget request on rent supplements.

Many observers have suggested that the rioting of inner-city blacks in the late sixties was a strong political impetus for housing legislation. Indeed, passage of the Housing Act of 1968 during the burning of downtown Washington after Martin Luther King's assassination suggests that the timing of the legislation was not entirely coincidental. Urban unrest, however, is one thing, and specific activities of civil rights organizations are another.

At best, the civil rights movement may have had a modest expansionary effect on food stamps, AFDC, and housing assistance; the movement had little or no effect on social security, SSI, Unemployment Insurance, medicare, and medicaid.

Inflation, Demographic Shifts, and Unemployment Caused the Increased Spending on Welfare

The decade from 1965 to 1975 was one of economic instability. The post–tax-cut boom of the mid-sixties gave way first to the stagflation of 1970, then to the worst recession since the thirties. Inflation, however, was the most consistent fact of economic life during this period. Prices increased every year, with a total from 1965 to 1975 of more than 70 percent.

Inflation has exerted a strong upward pressure on most social welfare expenditures. As prices rise, wages do too. With social security benefits based partly on earnings, higher wages result in higher benefits. Moreover, social security benefits are also indexed to increase with prices (hence, double-indexing). The indexing provisions of the food stamp program and SSI translate price increases directly into increased benefits. Since the medicare, medicaid, and AFDC programs directly reimburse third parties for goods and services, inflation in the price of those goods and services increases expenditures on programs. Although the effect of inflation on expenditures varies considerably from one program to another, we "guesstimate" that inflation caused between 35 and 45 percent of the increase in expenditures on welfare from 1965 to 1975.[4]

The rising unemployment of the early seventies explains a large proportion of the increased expenditure of the unemployment insurance program. The provisions for extended and emergency benefits of UI, with their automatic triggering, made program expenditures particularly sensitive to fluctuations in the rate of unemployment. Rising unemployment explains a relatively small proportion of the increased expenditure in the food stamp program; nevertheless, some people who were long unemployed apparently found they could save a little money by getting food stamps. The more stringent qualifications of the other categorical and social-insurance programs prevented unemployment from substantially affecting those program expenditures. We think that the overall effect of rising unemployment on the increase in social welfare expenditures was about 10 percent.

The continuing rise in proportion of the population over sixty-five is significantly affecting the programs that benefit the aged. As the over-65 segment of the population increases, so too must social security, SSI, and medicare expenditures. Another demographic trend, the growing number of families headed by females, has caused AFDC expenditures to increase somewhat. We estimate that these demographic trends caused about 20 percent of the increased expenditures on social welfare.

Altogether, demographic trends, inflation, and higher unemployment explain about 70 percent of the increase in social welfare expenditures. The remaining 30 percent of "unexplained variance" is therefore explicable only by the changes in policy that exemplify our hypotheses. Whether we have correctly interpreted the patterns in these policy changes is another matter.

Some of the changes in characteristics of program, such as automatic modifications in scale, have *permitted* inflation and higher unemployment to have more influence than they would have otherwise. Without the indexing of social security and the other programs, for instance, inflation would have had a considerably smaller effect on welfare expenditures. Therefore, it is probably more accurate to say that the changes in policy of the last decade explain *at least* 30 percent of the increase in welfare outlays.

It is evident that task forces engage in the kind of thinking about welfare that we have described. They invariably recommended spending more rather than less and urged adoption of expensive modifications of program characteristics. But the experts were only one of several powerful participants, including Congress, the executive, and interest groups, that thought about welfare policy in this way. Neither the president nor the Congress always accepted the advice of the experts. Nixon and his cabinet, for instance, significantly modified the proposals put forth by the

1969 welfare task force, and Congress eventually rejected most of the proposals. In sum, the argument about the influence of professionals is not inconsistent with our own hypotheses. It is, however, pitched at a different level: *who* caused events rather than *how* they happened. If we had to make a judgment on influence, it would be in favor of bureaucrats, the people paid to work full time on these programs.[5]

Evidently, coherence of values, at least among active participants, can provide coordination. But why was this vast redistribution of income, from these with more to those with less, allowed to occur? To say that this was the inevitable price of social peace — that poorer people were bought off by richer ones — merely rephrases the question: how were people with money and therefore political resources, persuaded to part with it? A possibility is that they didn't look at it that way. Each issue came up separately, at different times. Asked, in effect, whether they were in favor of helping the elderly with medical care or providing food for the hungry, they could well answer positively. Had they been asked whether government should spend so many hundreds of billions for welfare or that they should pay so much personally, they might have responded differently.

Actually, many of the most important choices are not made by direct decision — we don't "decide" the distribution of income or the size of families — but are resultants of other forces. Changing the frame of reference so that resultants do become decisions is an extremely important way of changing public policy.

How explicit to make public choices is a great question of public policy. Would we, for example, want to decide individual incomes or racial relations by direct decision? Usually, outcomes in these areas are products of social interaction modified at the edges by intellectual guidance. When we ask ourselves how much interaction versus how much cogitation is needed in policy analysis, we are raising issues that have vast influence on patterns of public policy.

NOTES

1. We are not suggesting that costs were always intentionally ignored; Congress sometimes received inaccurate projections of cost or did not have time to consider a proposal adequately.
2. From *A Decade of Federal Antipoverty Programs*, reply by Nick Kotz to "The Social and Political Context of the War on Poverty," by Lawrence Friedman, p. 49.
3. See Frances F. Piven and Richard A. Cloward, *Regulating the Poor: The Functions of Public Relief* (New York: Pantheon Books, 1971), pp. 248–249.
4. For a more precise treatment, see Martin Holmer, "The Sensitivity of Transfer Payments to Changes in Economic Conditions and Public Policy," Brookings Institution, unpublished.
5. See statement by James Q. Wilson on p. 69.

PART 2

SOCIAL INTERACTION VERSUS INTELLECTUAL COGITATION

The model of the intellectually guided society, Model 1 [or intellectual cogitation], specified that some people in the society are wise and informed enough to ameliorate its problems and guide social change with a high degree of success. . . . According to Model 2 [or social interaction], however, "every one well knows himself to be fallible," as John Stuart Mill argued in *On Liberty*.

Since some people *know* how to organize society, the test of an institution or policy is that it is correct. . . . Since, in Model 2, people are not competent to know what is correct, they fall back on their own volitions, however imperfectly understood, as a test. . . .

Since it is knowledge rather than volition that guides society in Model 1, the intellectual elite is simultaneously a political elite. . . . In Model 2, there exists no such elite.

In Model 1 is postulated an underlying harmony of men's needs that can be known to the guiding elite. . . . In Model 2, by contrast, it is assumed that harmony of needs is not only undiscoverable but nonexistent. . . .

Suppose a small society of three people wants to decide which restaurant to go to for dinner. In the style of Model 1, it would study the question on the assumption that there exists one correct solution discoverable by diagnosis. In the style of Model 2, it would look for a process of interaction to make analysis unnecessary. It might take a vote. Or agree on some rule such as choosing the first restaurant they encounter as the three set out to walk. Or negotiate a decision, letting each of the three bring persuasion or other influence to bear on the others.

Now suppose a large society wants to decide how to allocate its resources. In the style of Model 1, an elite would study the question in an attempt to find correct decisions. Economic planning of the communist variety is the obvious example. In the style of Model 2, it would establish an interaction process that would make the diagnostic study unnecessary — the market system is the obvious example. . . .

Charles E. Lindblom, *Politics and Markets*
(New York: Basic Books,
1977), pp. 249–250, 254–255.

If an idea about social life is any good, it should resonate with reality by appearing in daily life. Once we know what to look for, we should be able to interrogate experience to test the appropriateness of our conceptions. This sort of probe is especially important when the terms of discourse do not directly correspond to observable phenomena, like political parties or the Super Bowl, but are supposed to represent convenient categories of thought like social structure or national culture or even public policy imposed by analysts on a recalcitrant world. Although "social interaction" and "intellectual cogitation" may be more felicitous expressions than some neologisms we know (such as psephology for the study of political parties), they are not exactly in common use. What evidence is there that these refer to something out there that is more than an item of curiosity like the pet name of the family dog? By my lights, the phenomena to which these words refer appear any time you read (or just pick up) a newspaper.

On Friday, January 21, 1978, the day I wrote these lines at the airport in Denver, Colorado, a fellow passenger offered me his copy of the *Rocky Mountain News*, made up of some 143 pages, of which 38 contained domestic news, apart from sports and stock market quotations. That this will qualify as a random sample, I doubt, but it should nevertheless be interesting to see whether and to what extent appropriate illustrations appear. Lacking a better rationale, suppose I start at the beginning.

The third page (the first is about the war between Somalia and Ethiopia and the second has advertising) contains a report of President Carter's press conference in which he says that his energy policy is fair, meaning he has the intellectually correct solution, though Congress keeps insisting he must interact with it to bargain over an agreed policy. If Congress fails to act, Carter says, invoking the inexorable logic of a system beyond our control, "we may have conservation forced on us by unexpected increases in oil prices in the future." Apparently, the logic of health is not so deterministic, for Carter spoke out in favor of leaving smoking to social interaction, saying it was not up to his administration "to tell an individual American whether he can smoke or not." There is evidently no automatic mechanism to decide which behavior shall be proscribed and which permitted.

Similar state and local issues surface on page 5, where officials wrestle with the problem of whether or how to comply with federal clean-air standards. Evidently, state officials want to see how far they can rely on social interaction, for they are holding hearings "to find out how many changes the public is willing to make in its driving habits." The trouble is that even if all drivers joined car pools or rode in buses and trains, air pollution would be cut back by only a quarter of the amount needed to meet federal standards. Elsewhere, it is proposed that the state buy ranchlands as open space, for fear these lands will be swallowed up in normal commercial activity.

On the next page is discussed efforts by the Occupational Safety and Health Administration (OSHA) to seek evidence of the causes of headaches at a plant so that it could require more stringent preventive efforts. Everyone is uptight. An OSHA hygienist refused comment "for fear of giving the firm 'legal grounds to do some screaming.'" A company official said he was "very, very gun shy" about talking to the *News*. If you can read alphabet soup, you will discover that "OSHA, taking advantage of its parallel jurisdiction with COSH (Colorado Occupational Safety and Health), got into the act because the COSH suit dragged on, and because a NIOSH (National Institute for Occupational Safety and Health) regional industrial hygienist . . . was stopped by [company] officials when he attempted to visit the plant last Nov. 19." Neither leaving safety up to the interaction of workers and management nor mandating measures by bureaucratic cogitation seems to be working. The whole matter may become moot because workers are leaving in large numbers to take better-paying jobs elsewhere. (The article on the same page entitled "Sociologist Pleads Guilty to Misusing U.S. Funds" is omitted here because fortunately it is irrelevant.)

On page 16 we learn that "The Civil Aeronautics Board has set Aug. 15 for hearing of a consolidated route case that could thoroughly reshuffle air service between Denver and Aspen, Vail, Steamboat Springs and Gunnison." Rocky Mountain Airways wants to place in service a short-take-off-and-landing (STOL) plane but is facing opposition from Aspen Airways. Because other businesses do not need the government's permission to introduce new products, one wonders why airlines should be in that position, or why, in an ostensibly capitalist country, one enterprise is trying to use government to block competition by another.

This weariness with competition (understandable as fear of failure) comes through nicely on the other side of the page in a story of farmers' efforts to get government to support farm prices at 100 percent of parity, "loosely defined as a government guarantee that farm prices will be high enough to cover costs." Companies controlled by the farmers reported their relief in knowing that farmers weren't trying to get (perish the thought) "government subsidies, guaranteed profits or a guaranteed income," distinctions without much of a difference. The farmers argued that without this action they will be forced to sell their family farms to giant corporations who, they allege, farm only as a tax dodge. Executives in corporate food chains, on the other hand, welcomed parity as a stabilizing force in food prices. Food stores "told the farmers they were tired of trying to second-guess the market in pricing of food items and would welcome a stabilization of prices." It seems the one certainty is that the presence of stabilization signifies prices higher than they would be without stabilization.

Lest I be accused of dealing with dead issues, though they do have a way of coming back to life, page 26 reveals that an agency whose demise was one of the most celebrated successes of Colorado's Sunset Law (requiring agencies to expire periodically unless deliberately continued) may be about to be resurrected. Responding to suggestions that the State Morticians Board be reestablished, Governor Lamm asked only, if it revives the board, that the legislature take a "real look at consumer problems" in the funeral industry. In the past, such boards have acted to restrain price competition; that is, government intervention in favor of setting standards somehow seems to lead to higher prices.

The same story suggests that the governor is in a quandary over proposals to introduce metropolitan government to the Denver area. Would it be desirable to have five separate counties and numerous local jurisdictions or just one regional government? Will bargaining among governments lead to better or worse decisions than choice by one?

A story on page thirty two concerns a 10 cent cigarette tax designed to impose a penalty on smoking as well as to bring in revenue. Experts observed that many states were losing money as high taxes led to substantial illegal sales. A cartoon contained the caption: "Warning: fools in government want you to quite smoking while they subsidize tobacco" (page 62), a reference to federal price supports.

The last word goes to columnist Nicholas von Hoffman, who (page 61) argues against maintaining the monopoly of first-class mail by the post office department. The McNally cartoon claims this caption: "Come on Grandma! [who is reading 'Federal Fairy Tales'] Not that dumb one again about the post office making a profit!" What would happen if there were private post offices?

At first blush it may appear that we are back to the continuing question about which activities should be carried on in the public or private sectors. If farmers and food stores are not exactly asking government to set food prices, they are asking for a floor below which they cannot descend. And someone is suggesting that postal service be opened up to private companies. But to be accurate, most of the examples do not involve direct governmental operation of an industry or facility. Instead they are about regulating the health or safety conditions under which industry may operate. Even if we were to frame the question in terms of which interests in society would be harmed or helped by government or private operation, however, decision-makers would still have to decide how much cogitation or interaction was desirable. There could be far more interaction among competing government bureaus than within a private monopoly. A private postal monopoly might not differ much from what we have now, whereas setting up, say, a half-dozen government corporations to compete for customers might be drastically different. And if government decided that family farms should be subsidized, this need not be done by limiting price competition for food; it could also be done by direct payments to farm families. Similarly, there is a wide range of options for regulation. Pollution could be taxed, penalties could be applied to accidents, funeral parlors could be compelled to advertise their rates, all of which preserve competition without replacing interaction by cogitation.

But how can one distinguish between the two modes of choice when plainly cogitation is surrounded by interaction and interaction contains cogitation? Rule by one individual must be rare. No doubt even elites who rule with absolute power negotiate internally over the correct decision to impose on others, and bargainers think about their next interaction.

It is easy enough to speak of correcting errors either through cogitation or interaction by bringing resources and objectives closer together. It is not so simple to specify how this is to be done. Policy analysis proceeds by recommending changes in the structure of social interaction or by advising larger doses of direct control by bureaucratic orders under the guidance of intellectual cogitation. How much of each under different conditions is the question?

CHAPTER 5

BETWEEN PLANNING AND POLITICS: INTELLECT VS. INTERACTION AS ANALYSIS

Professors and policy analysts share one thing at least: they prefer explanations depending on latent rather than manifest functions — theories that are not obvious because they can account for action more profound than the specific behavior to be explained. After all, if things are just as they seem on the surface, who needs theorists? These academic scribblers have differed critically, however, in their evaluation, of the mysterious mechanisms that guide society.

Beginning with the two Adams — Ferguson and Smith — the "invisible hand" of self-interest was found to guide buyers and sellers to serve each other, and hence society at large, without anyone necessarily intending this serendipitous outcome. The results before us (increase in national income, bread and butter on the table, each without conscious central coordination) and the theory (each actor trying to make a better deal) are on different levels. A closer look shows that this (in)famous theory is based on the superiority of social interaction over intellectual cogitation. The interactions in economic markets, where alterations in outcomes go on all the time, lead to better results than central direction by one mind that decides everything once and for all. Observe that it is not conscious intent but actual outcomes, even (perhaps especially) when unintended, which provide the criteria of success.

Let me recapitulate: motives may be base; outcomes can be unintended; intelligence is interactive. If self-interest is the motive, where (after all, Adam Smith was a professor of moral philosophy) does virtue come in? Through exchange! Morality does not depend on what motivates individual actions but on the results of social interaction. How are collective objectives set? They aren't; collective objectives are by-products of individual interactions. No one sets out to make the nation richer or to achieve a decent distribution of income. If these come about, they are not the results of public objectives but rather the collective consequences of private acts. Individuals make decisions; their social exchanges make outcomes.[1] How is intelligence brought to bear on human activity? By many minds interacting. How is coordination of these multitudes accomplished? Pretty much as crowds are coordinated when crossing streets; by each individual adjusting to the others. Coordination does not require a coordinator; coordination takes place so long as there is mutual benefit in the individual transaction.

Just as constitutions are written to guard against previous predators, so, too, theories react to the past as well as point to the future. Adam Smith saw himself as a radical critic of the mercantilist doctrine that justified a vast variety of state interventions in economic life.[2] As the doctrines of his school became the prevailing wisdom, they were in turn challenged by succeeding generations who found Smith's ideas self-centered, reactive, and fatalistic. His "hidden hand" had four unappealing aspects: (1) its motivation — selfishness over altruism; (2) its passivity — resultants instead of decisions; (3) its irrationality — interaction rather than intellect; and (4) its unpredictability — the future had become fate.

The secret was out. That hidden hand was a mailed fist. Capitalism was a legalized form of robbery, an institutionalized exploitation. Law, government, philosophy, all were rationalizations of capitalist class interests who owned the means of production. What else could one expect of a corrupt class that made a virtue out of evil by elevating self-interest to a moral principle?

Who, then, should be the repository of communal interests? If virtue resided in everyman alone, anarchy was the result. People were good but contaminated by a selfish state. They needed liberation not only from capitalism but from all forms of state power. Where the people collectively exercised their power through the state — for it was the people as a whole who represented virtue — the regime was called democratic socialism. When the masses did not recognize their own interests — failed, on their own, as Lenin said, to develop a revolutionary consciousness but instead retained the false consciousness of bourgeois reformism inculcated by the capitalist class — virtue resided in a revolutionary fragment. This vanguard of the proletariat, able to cleanse its consciousness of illusion, became the Communist Party.

Under socialism men would control their own destiny; fatalism would be replaced by conscious collective coordination. The name for this enterprise was scientific socialism. It was socialist in that, as the fraternal community of the dispossessed, it spoke in the name of all. It was scientific in professing a historical, developmental theory of society, which explained where it had come from and predicted where it would go (or where socialists would take it). Scientific socialism fused modern consciousness and medieval community. In the name of all, a collective consciousness, acting as one mind, would make rationality serve fraternity. And, best of all, the end would be known at the beginning because of planning.

Of special importance to students of policy analysis, however, is a difference among socialist traditions. As the participants themselves were wont to say, social democrats were likely to sacrifice socialism to democracy but their communist rivals would give up democracy for socialism. Social democracy therefore legitimized social interaction as a mode of decision-making in politics. Once political forces are allowed free rein, including party competition, there cannot be one correct solution apart from the consent of the political actors. Politics becomes part of planning. The parties must establish and maintain rules (or conventions) for the give-and-take, bargaining, and negotiation by which political decisions must be made. It is essential also that they accept these decisions, apart from whether they wholly approve of the outcome, because they cannot expect to prevail on every occasion. Decisions no longer can be correct but can only be acceptable in that the criteria for truth are established by agreement through social interaction.

Between capitalism and socialism, then, between choice through social interaction and intellectual cogitation, where does policy analysis come in? Policy analysis is an effort to combine elements from the two traditions — infusing social interaction with intellectual direction and vice versa. I shall approach this attempt at synthesis by trying to clarify these opposing tendencies in the form of ideal models of pure intellect (called planning), and pure interaction (called politics).

If interaction does not demand common objectives, can our actions make sense if they are not goal-directed? They can. Do objectives have any place in policy analysis? They do. Efforts to modify intellect by interaction raise doubts about whether policy can be rational. I argue that it can. But can it also be moral? Applying social interaction in analysis of policy leads one to wonder whether one must morally accept whatever comes forth from this pulling and hauling. No. Must a collective conscience, then, guide all interaction? That depends on how we interpret the conversion of individual preferences into collective choices.

Consider the implications of Jung's wise words: "If a man is capable of leading a responsible life himself, then he is also conscious of his duties to the community." The intuitive meaning is clear enough: people who meet their immediate obligations to family and friends are those also more likely to recognize their implication in wider matters to which they ought to contribute. Obligation is learned most readily at home. At the communal level, however, this argument presupposes a compatibility between the individual and the collective that is open to challenge. Suppose what is good for General Motors (or for you and me) is not necessarily good for the country, and that such a clash of interests rends the fabric of society. Do citizens, then, have any right to base actions (that is, to do analysis) on selfish motives? It is argued that selfishness can serve society; in the clash of interests, citizens must give up part of what they have to get part of what they want; this exchange moderates their demands and, willy-nilly, serves others. If their motives were altruistic, the critical response goes, the general interest would have been paramount, and vulgar trades would be less necessary. To trade in values is to lose virtue. From this viewpoint, analysis would seem to be immoral, either because good motives would make it unnecessary to trade or because better motives would forbid it. We had better discuss this further, for if individual interests and collective exchanges are ruled out, policy analysis will be prohibited.

EXCHANGE

Analysis is based on exchange: what individuals or groups will give up for what they can get. If we can get what we want without ceding anything, then we are either in a condition of perfect freedom — no obstacles to the realization of desires — or of absolute constraint — no movement can take place, because (all desires being absolute) nothing can be given up. Either there is no need to think because all desires are compatible, or there is no point in thinking because it can lead to no action. Neither thought leading to action, nor action influencing thought, makes sense.

The fundamental objection to exchange is that its motivation is seen as immoral. By reducing mankind to mere individual wants, citizens become sybarites: self-centered, indulgent, materialistic bundles of appetites — mouths without morals. Empathy gives way to selfishness. The citizen in a democracy, who should be an active contributor, becomes instead an apathetic ingestor driven by purely personal desires. Economic man, who recognizes no goals transcending himself, makes decisions that affect others thinking only of his own private profit. Democratic choice becomes perverted into the sum of individual choices based on materialist motivations. If exchange is dirty, policy analysis is culturally contaminated.

It is not always clear whether the objection is to exchange or to the motivation behind it. If the motivation were collective rather than individual, if its objective were moral and not material, would it then be all right to give up one thing for another? If justice for all could not be achieved, could more justice for some (as in preferential hiring of minorities) be traded off, in the vulgar jargon of the profession, for less to others? If the object of a political community were to inculcate virtue in its citizens by establishing and enforcing norms of proper conduct, could one consider that some means of obtaining virtue might be sacrificed in order to obtain others?

A nice example of this objection to exchange is the requirement that proposed federal government programs contain environmental impact statements showing absence of significantly adverse consequences before action can take place. Protecting the environment becomes a constraint around which other interests must work; that is, it becomes part of the objectives that must be satisfied in all other policies. We can describe the environment with the phrase fashionable in the sixties; it is a nonnegotiable demand. A reasonably rich society undoubtedly has room to accommodate the environmental consideration. Suppose, however, more than one objective becomes a nonnegotiable (nonexchangeable) constraint? There is now a requirement for inflationary impact statements, and few would argue that reducing inflation is unimportant. Recent proposals also call for impact statements on health, safety, education, and employment. Now the plot thickens. Where nothing is allowed to vary, everything remains constant. If all or most basic values are untouchable, change becomes impossible. The environment must remain sacrosanct, yet energy must be saved; how, then, can auto exhaust devices (which use more gas) be justified? If energy must be conserved and nuclear proliferation halted, how can one justify abandoning breeder reactors — which increase energy but also the opportunity to make nuclear explosives? Evidently, exchanges for good causes are being made. Once one escapes this *reductio ad absurdum* by saying that only comparatively few values must remain nonnegotiable, we are back again to exchange.

MOTIVATION

Perhaps it is not exchange itself but the bad motives that lie behind it that are found objectionable. Mandeville's dictum — private vices, public virtues — may be rejected if we hold that public virtue reduces private vices. By acting for community and common interest, it is thought, public life may be elevated.

Motives, however, are (almost) always mixed. The question of which motive should prevail, therefore, is often crucial to public policy. Suppose some doctors make excessive income from medicaid for the poor. Should programs be designed to prevent their abuses, programs that make life difficult for doctors who behave honorably? Obviously, profiteering cannot be allowed. Or can it, *if* our objective is not only to deter the few but help the many? The moral of the story may take more palatable form if we consider people who are called "welfare cheats" because they deceive the government in order to receive payments. Should governmental programs be designed to catch cheaters, if this means also (as it does) denying or delaying welfare for the honest majority who need it? Just as citizens have varying motives, governmental programs that are meant to serve them also exhibit multiple motivation.

To suggest that anyone believes justice can be achieved and virtue inculcated by fiat (down with self-interest and up with community!) would be absurd. Everyone knows that governments that choose public over private interests often achieve neither and may even end up elevating a favored few in the name of the many. Clearly there is an empirical question about which sort of motivation leads to the best ends. The reverse — how can justice and virtue be achieved if they are not explicitly recognized as the proper wellspring of human motivation? — is more nearly arguable.

This argument has two components that are of the utmost importance for analyzing policy. One is that motives must be acceptable, and the other that justice must be knowable. Another way of putting it is that results, however good, do not count if they lack justification according to motives acknowledged to be good. If it is intentions rather than consequences of our actions that matter, evaluation of public policy would be about internal states. We would ask if intentions were good rather than looking to external effects and asking if accomplishments have been realized.

Evaluation of intentions would require knowledge of how to achieve justice (or other ultimate goals) because it would then be appropriate that good motives be distinguished from bad motives just as good results are differentiated from bad results. If intent were equivalent to accomplishment, good motives always would be the harbinger of good deeds.

President Jimmy Carter's presentation of his energy program illustrates the contemporary importance of good motives and conscious intent. Conscious emphasis on good motives is evident from his reiteration of the theme that the burden of conservation and cost would be shared fairly under his programs. After the Organization of Petroleum Exporting Countries (OPEC) raised the price of oil many times over, the federal government, to prevent precipitous price increases in the United States, controlled the price of old oil at less than half its price abroad. Now one way to encourage conservation is to let the domestic price of crude oil rise to the price it would bring if sold abroad. If oil were valued within the United States at the international price, motorists, homeowners, industrialists, indeed, all consumers of oil would take steps to reduce consumption, or switch to alternatives if that made sense. But the solution has two fatal flaws. For one thing, oil companies would profit by selling their old oil at new prices, widely considered unfair; for another, unseen hands — namely, market prices — would be determining what America would do.

On the surface, President Carter's oil policy appeared anomalous: old domestic crude remained price controlled while — on top of this subsidy to bring the price down — a substantial tax on oil was recommended, a tax that would, in effect, bring the domestic price up to the international price. What's the difference between letting the market set the price and setting a similar price by taxes? Nothing and everything: nothing in that the economic consequences are equivalent; everything in that when the government sets the price it is acting with conscious intent rather than appearing to give way to impersonal forces. Instead of letting the oil companies make money and taxing it away afterward, the government gets its share first. The important thing for us to understand from this example is the two ways in which decisions are made: interaction among people or intellectual determination of what would be just and effective.

Here is the distinction we have been seeking between intellectual and interactive modes of analysis — between analysis as an intellectual construct and analysis as a product of social interaction of which thought is but a part. If analysis is a social phenomenon, based on interaction among interests, then analysis must stem from a variety of motivations, not all of which are necessarily good. Nor, without knowledge of means and ends — what is good for man and how to achieve it — would it be either desirable or possible to completely control man's motives and aspirations or make them equivalent. But contingency is a condition of life. Only if analysis were solely a product of the mind and that mind knew the difference between good and evil and could therefore integrate motives and aspirations, could policy be judged by intention rather than execution.

PLANNING AND POLITICS

Let us call analysis as an intellectual construct "pure planning" and analysis as social interaction "pure politics" or hereafter, in short, planning and politics. Here planning is defined as current action to secure future consequences; the more future consequences planners control, the better they have planned.[3] Planning, therefore, requires causal knowledge — theories of society to predict the paths of the complex sequences of desired actions and power to sustain this effort. Once conflict is admitted over whose preferences are to prevail (there being ineradicable differences between the needs, wants, desires, and hence preferences of people), comprehensive national economic and social planning fails either from intellectual presumption or political persuasion. Planners do not have adequate knowledge or power. The more planning fails to secure intended results, the more it tries to become relevant by accommodating itself to social forces. Consequently, by shortening time horizons (annual plans), by reducing the need for prediction (adaptive planning), and by limiting coercion (indicative plans, which merely point the way), planning becomes indistinguishable from whatever means of decision it was meant to supplant.

Planning

Suppose, however, to sharpen the contrast, we say planning does have perfect knowledge and power in a context without conflict and thus deserves its new nametag, "pure planning." With compatible (indeed, mutually supportive) desires and preferences, there could be right or wrong solutions to all problems. Reason would reign supreme. Decisions would be made as if a single mind were supporting a single set of preferences. Nor would there be need for error correction because, with knowledge, there would be no error. Dissent would either be unnecessary, in the absence of conflict, or uncalled for, because the Grand Planners would know what is right; acting in the common interest, their motives are above suspicion. Hence, also, there would be no need to hedge them about with restrictions on term of office or extent of authority. Centralization and comprehensiveness would be valued because they are possible and desirable. Attributes that might lead to further differentiation, such as race, religion, class, ethnicity, sex, and language, would be discouraged; after all, why worry about diverse viewpoints or alternative hypotheses when there is only one right way and that is discoverable by reason? Ends do justify means. If ends are in harmony, and means are always appropriate to them, what else would justify means if not ends? To get an answer to that question, we must leave planning and turn to politics.

Politics

Politics is about preferences. The point about preferences is that they are not ultimately knowable, either by those who profess them or by those who propose to act for those who prefer them. Because there is no one source of ultimate wisdom, no one knows people's preferences better than they, themselves, do. And, hoping to learn, people reserve the right to change preferences frequently to suit their experience. Ends or objectives, therefore, are held to be provisional — to be modified by experience or to accommodate others.

> Political choice is never purely a matter of being for this program or against that policy. It is always partly a matter of being willing to compromise and adjust desires to various conflicting factions. Therefore, as soon as any group's wishes are revealed everyone else's wishes may, and indeed normally do, shift. . . . Priorities, that is, depend upon estimates of preference distributions. They may change whenever any particular set of preferences becomes known, and they never exist as entities separate and apart from their strategic possibility of enactment. Political options must always be understood to include some commitment to the decision-making process itself and to the value of agreement.[4]

The criterion of choice in planning is obvious — the one policy known to be right — but what is the correct criterion for politics? That there is no correct criterion. Does this mean that whatever is done is right? Hardly. It does mean that short of agreement no one is authoritatively able to say another alternative is better.

What takes the place of the correct criterion? An incorrect one? Not quite. Correction of error. All politicians and political institutions are considered, Martin Landau said, risky actors.[5] Power in American politics, for example, is limited in time and tenure, so that no one can impose a truth without opposition. Power is divided through the separation of powers, subdivided through federalism, and checks and balances are multiplied at every level. Conflict is desired (both to use the self-interest of one group or institution to counter the others and to refine preferences under pressure) and feared (because it may undermine the understanding that decisions will be considered acceptable, providing they get through corrective procedures giving everyone a chance to be heard, allowing parties to alternate in office, specifying due process, and so on).

The political equivalent of original sin is that men and the institutions they create are fallible if not fallacious and error-prone if not erroneous. They must be hedged with restraints, especially when they are sure they are right. It is hard to say whether criticism is valued more for its constructive aspects — making improvements — than for its destructive ones — exposing error. In practice, however, if there must be a choice, destructive criticism is preferable; procedures must be pursued in the realization that no one knows ultimate ends. All the more reason, then, to protect criticism politically. A decentralization of authority, the very untidiness of politics that contrasts with the neatness of planning, allows for alternatives rejected at one time and place to be available at others, should they have been passed over by mistake.

Politics does not consider preferences to be finally formed, as in planning, but to be undergoing continual reformulation. Personal preferences are not infallible, coming *ex cathedra*, as it were, from *homo politicus*, but they must be presentable, regarded as coming from a person who is entitled to them.

Political preferences are personal. They belong to a person (group or organization) until that person changes them. If the charge of "false consciousness" (propaganda, advertising, and indoctrination that make people mistake their true interests) merely meant that people did not realize they should have other preferences, it might be seen as just another effort at suasion. Surely, if we knew better, we might feel differently. But if false consciousness means that there are others with "true consciousness," who know what is better for us than we do, then we have been stripped of our political persona. Politics declines and planning takes over.

Comparison

Both politics and planning, at least in their modern manifestations, claim as their territory the general welfare of citizens. One shows this through interaction, the other through cogitation. The choice would seem to lie in whether one expects better or worse outcomes from intellectual or from interactive modes of decision-making.

Wait a minute! Haven't I turned the usual understanding upside

TABLE 5.1
ALTERNATIVE STYLES OF POLICY ANALYSIS

	Social interaction	Intellectual cogitation
Institutions	Markets and politics	Planning
Calculations	Partial	Comprehensive
Calculators	Many minds interacting	Single-minded decision
Decision-making	Exchange and bargaining	Comprehending and deciding
Error	Correction	Avoidance
Criteria	Agreement	Right
Administration	Reactions	Orders

down? Isn't it governmental planning that is commonly considered to be social, and economic markets and pluralistic politics that are said to be individualistic? Yes, of course, but no, not necessarily. An important distinction is to be made between the *locus of decision* and the *mode of calculation*. As larger proportions of the national product are redistributed through the government, or as government owns and operates more of industry, no doubt government is an increasingly important locus of decision. Because individual citizens are not directly deciding for themselves, but through government, such decisions commonly are called collective. The locus or site or arena of decision is collective. My interest, however, is policy analysis — recognition, reformulation, and resolution of problems. Looked at as modes of calculation, markets and politics are social because they are based on interaction among many minds. Planning, by contrast, is pursued as if there were but one collective mind whose intellectual operations posed and solved problems. As suggested in Table 5.1, politics and markets share the same analytic style: decisions are made through social mechanisms — exchange and bargaining by many minds — aimed at correcting error and securing agreement (rather than avoidance of error and a single proper choice) and administered by reacting to the other participants rather than by sending down orders and expecting obedience. As for the style of policy analysis, appearances are deceiving: politics appears to be individual but is in fact social, whereas planning seems to be social but actually is single-minded.

If we accept this socially interactive view of markets and politics, what is one to make of common criticism that these institutions prejudice decision-making? Markets accept the prevailing distribution of income when some say public policy should be designed to make it more egalitarian. Politics, others say, leads those who have less to use government as a lever for redistributing income to themselves, in effect expropriating property that doesn't belong to them. Monopolies let manipulators of markets administer prices for their own benefit, and political parties mobilize masses to monopolize government, denying minorities the medium to express their own message. Where there is agreement that these conditions (and their subsequent consequences) break the rules for decent decision-making, they are regarded as imperfections in the respective arenas and institutions. Rules for regulating interaction (such as conditions for allowing monopoly or of specifying who may vote) are subject to change, both through evaluation and intervention, so as to improve interaction. Social interaction may be preferred to intellectual cogitation as a style of analysis without the need to accept only current modes. Indeed, the stress on correcting error suggests that alteration in interaction is desirable.

Of course, I do not pretend that planning or politics exist in pure essence; they are ideal types, designed to display differences when they are pushed to extremes. What happens, however, if they are merged? If the reader will allow me my preference for two-thirds politics and one-third planning, this hybrid of social interaction and intellectual cogitation may be called policy analysis.

ANALYSIS

If analysis were purely intellectual, analysts would be everything, or if analysis were purely interactive, analysts would be nothing. Are we faced, then, with a choice between mind without matter or force without foresight? No. Our task is to develop a hybrid, called policy analysis, which uses intellect to help guide rather than replace social interaction. This peculiar amalgam called policy analysis may be better understood if we ask why either pure planning or pure politics alone are unsatisfactory as modes of making collective choices.

The effects of interaction may not be visible to participants. They may have to be identified mainly through intellectual constructs, for direct observation has severe limits. When many agencies are operating numerous programs in any area of policy, which they are most of the time nowadays, it may be hard to connect acts with consequences. Efforts of agencies to act and observe what happens may be unsuccessful without theories to tell them how things are connected. Agencies can hope, of course, that if other agencies are adversely affected by these consequences, they will act to correct them. This sort of defensive action, which Lindblom calls mutual partisan adjustment, is a major rationale in favor of social interaction as a mode of decision-making. Unfortunate consequences for other actors need not be predicted if those who already have suffered can take effective corrective action. Instead of having to figure out what various groups want, or will accept — as if it all had to be done in and by a single mind — policy preferences are registered directly through interaction on actual programs. Aside from whether, without analysis, anyone knows what is happening and what might be done about it, turning consequences over to others raises fundamental questions about the basis for social interaction.

A political system in which all interests are fairly represented would work differently from one in which important ones are left out or occupy a weak position. The outcomes of political processes cannot be considered apart from their design, which is an intellectual construct as well as a social fact. Outcomes may be altered not only by seeking them directly but also indirectly by redesigning interaction (who participates under what rules).

Action outside the rules (monopoly, for instance) may not be socially desirable. The classical conditions of the marketplace — competition, information, internalization of costs — must be satisfied for prices to represent optimal choices. If not, governmental intervention may be justified to restore competition, to provide as public information that which is not in the interest of any firm to supply privately, and to arrange compensation when the behavior of one party imposes burdens on another that, like pollution, cannot be alleviated through the marketplace. All these market imperfections depend upon theoretical schemes for recognition and for correction.

Dependence upon social interaction is inappropriate, moreover, when the acknowledged objective is that nothing should happen. The purpose of analysis of nuclear warfare is precisely to ensure that the main hypothesis need never be tested.[6] The trouble with experience is that one needs so much of it. The attraction of analysis is that one need not live through everything.

At first glance, the purely intellectual mode seems ideally suited to policy analysis, which seeks to bring intelligence to bear on policy. But this identity is achieved at the cost of triviality. Instead of innumerable minds, each with somewhat different perspectives, there is really only one. Instead of conflict there is consensus. Instead of problem solving, in short, there is suppression of problems. Everyone either gets what he wants, or has to want what he gets. Thought is made supreme at the expense of having anything worth thinking about.

When planning is infused with politics, however, social forces guide intelligence. The danger, of course, is that interest will overwhelm intellect. By being tied to power, intellect becomes the handmaiden of power, the excuse for inexcusable behavior. Autonomy is exalted above reciprocity. The alternative, however, is worse: when intellect alone is powerful, there can be neither autonomy, because the Great Planner is always right, nor reciprocity, because the good of all has been determined by intellect, not by interaction. My conclusion is that policy analysis makes more sense as an aid to (rather than substitute for) the politics of social interaction.

The way things stand, however, the world does not appear to be suffering from a surfeit of intelligence. Usually things work the other way around: social forces use analysis to advance as well as to understand their own interests. The task of policy analysis, therefore, is the weighty and ancient one of speaking truth to power.

For policy analysis to modify pure politics (if social interaction automatically produced social welfare there would be no need for intelligence), it must expect to lose more often than it wins. And this is as it should be. Who said analysts possess wisdom? False prophets abound now as before. Who said analysts exemplify virtue? They have interests of their own, and they are also part of social life that is suspect. And who expects social forces to give way without much travail? There is a place for the voice of experience, which says "show me!" to self-deluded theorists.

Yet there is something to be said for invoking intelligence. Aside from the small victories and larger number of defeats, analysis, not in one instance but in many, not at one time but over decades, performs a critical function. Citizens must be able to decide what is in their interest, to interpret their own experience in some way they can explain to themselves. This requires thought. When that thought leads them to reinterpret their experience so as to shift their notion of what is problematic, policy analysis, accepted as a body of thought about public policy, may be more influential than is apparent from isolated acts.

Practitioners of policy analysis seek to have it neither absorbed into social interaction nor substituted for it. Analysis supplements social interaction by using the theoretical mode to formulate and test hypotheses that can help bring precision to the judgment of decision-makers. Analysis uses social interaction both to understand what is happening and to suggest how it might be altered. Studies of political feasibility, for instance, may help with the allocation of analytic time: which programs are most worth pursuing because change is possible. The purpose of studying feasibility, however, is not to equate the feasible with the desirable but may also be to make the desirable do-able. Merely to say that something should be done — without saying anything about how — is an abdication of responsibility.[7] But it is one thing to notice organizational resistance to change, still another to use this understanding to help bring out necessary changes. The purpose of analysis is improvement — how to get from a worse to a better place — not to curse the fates.

If analysis is to aid judgment, it must simplify calculations. The world in the analyst's models must abstract from the overwhelming complexity of experience. Otherwise, experience itself would be a better guide. Analysis makes use of social forces to simplify calculations about preferences. The alternative would be to invent preferences and imagine interaction. To do so would be morally wrong — the people already involved are the best experts on how they feel — and intellectually obtuse — that is, to reinvent the wheel.

A difficulty with health policy — how we should seek to restrain exploding medical costs — illustrates the question of calculation because there is now no alternative to governmental regulation. One approach is to apply controls to each doctor, patient, and hospital for each service and capital cost. This form of direct regulation, covering hundreds of millions of transactions, would involve almost every person in the United States. Implementation would become intolerable. Obviously, if anyone is to understand what they are doing, the social relationships among doctors, patients and hospitals (rather than their individual transactions) have to be regulated. One alternative is to set much higher deductibles for private insurance and governmental subsidies, forcing cost consciousness on consumers. But this alternative is politically unfeasible today because most people are not willing to pay much more in direct costs for a service they believe is their due. In the long run, one might hope to persuade people to take greater responsibility for their own health. Right now, however, private solutions are not possible, nor will Americans accept a wholly governmental system by abolishing private medicine. If these interpretations are reasonable, government must move in with regulations that create incentives for the actors to consider cost as part of their everyday transactions. Hospitals might be given fixed budgets,[8] depending on the number and kinds of patients, and left to decide what mix of services should be offered. Regulating social interaction appears to be a better way of doing analysis than is minute control of mass behavior.

Here I am again appearing to accept miserable motives by founding analysis on manipulating self-interest rather than on expanding altruism. Surely, a critic would say, giving rein to brute empiricism — nudging interactions this way or that — is no substitute for a more rational and humane health policy. Have I, then, by emphasizing interaction, subordinated intellect? Is there a larger role for rationality than I have been prepared to admit? That depends on what rationality is about — intelligence, interaction, or both.

RATIONALITY

In the world of action we know that politics and planning — social interaction and intellectual design — coexist. Problems are discovered, solved, and reformulated both by interchange among organized actors and by their efforts to guide events along paths they anticipate in their minds. Not only our thoughts but our institutions may be conceived of as attempts to increase the probability of some desired outcomes and decreases the probability of others. Once we abandon pure planning, which occurs only in the mind, or pure politics, in which action carries its own (and only) interpretation, intention commingles with interaction. What are we to make of the rationality, of the conscious design, in policy analysis?

1. Rationality is real.
2. Rationality is relative.
3. Rationality is retrospective as well as prospective.
4. Rationality is a property of politics as well as of planning.

I shall begin by arguing that politics follow the same form as planning; any differences do not reflect commonly considered components of rational choice. The substantial difference is that the norms of planning: efficiency, comprehensiveness, and others have no content, and the norms of politics: agreement, bargaining, and so on, do. Because of their inherent ambiguity, I shall argue further, objectives absent in the present are retrospectively rationalized into the past. We then act as if we once knew what we were doing and, therefore, can be trusted to know what to do next. Nor is retrospective rationalization (we act, review the effects of what we have done, and then decide what our objectives really were) necessarily a bad thing because it enables us to (re)create a past as we make a future. If rationality can be retrospective as well as prospective, then it follows that planning and politics, as they are practiced, do not differ with respect to reason.

POLITICS AND PLANNING ARE EQUALLY (IR)RATIONAL[9]

Once human ignorance and recalcitrance are reintroduced into planning and unlimited knowledge and power are taken away, so that planning has to cope with politics, planners must revise what they do in order to take account of events they can neither predict nor control. When planning is placed amid continual adjustment to a changing world, it becomes hard to distinguish from any other method of decision. By making planning reasonable we render it inseparable from the techniques of decision it was designed to supplant. One plans the way one governs; one does the best possible at the time hoping that future information will make for improvement as circumstances change. Some call this adaptive planning; others call it muddling through. Under the criteria of adaptation, almost any way of making decisions in a social context can be considered to be planning.[10] One cannot, for instance, discuss democracy for long without using the words goal, alternative, appraisal, objective, which are at the heart of almost any contemporary definition of planning.

May electoral democracy then be considered a mode of planning? The United States does not seek to achieve goals stated in a national plan. Yet that does not mean the country has no goals for its decision-makers to aim at. There are institutions — the Federal Reserve Board, Council of Economic Advisers, Office of Management and Budget, congressional committees, among many — whose task is to find goals and policies that embody these goals. Specific pieces of legislation are dedicated to full employment, ending or mitigating the effects of pollution, building highways, expanding recreational opportunities, improving agricultural productivity, on and on. When goals conflict, new decisions must be made on how much of each to try to achieve. Moreover, these goals are related to ultimate objectives. The Preamble to the Constitution states national goals, and the body presents an institutional plan for achieving them. The government of the United States seeks to achieve domestic prosperity and to protect its interest overseas; while these broad objectives remain constant the intermediate goals change in response to forces in society.

West Churchman (in *The Systems Approach*)[11] postulates that planning has to do with muti-stage decision-making and "hence it must study (1) a decisionmaker who (2) chooses among alternative courses of action in order to reach (3) certain first-stage goals, which lead to (4) other-stage objectives." It is easy to parallel this model for electoral democracy as the operation of (1) the electorate which (2) chooses from a group of candidates in order to reach (3) certain first-stage goals, which lead to (4) the implicit goals of the society at large. Table 5.2 illustrates more thoroughly the parallels between models of the planning system and the electoral system. Please notice the close correspondence not only between the broad outlines of the two systems, but also between the components that comprise the system.

Similar comparisons could be made between the system of planning and that of legislation and administration. Consider a recent description of how public policy is made: "Generically, one can identify at least six different steps in the process of making government policy — publicizing a problem, initiating a search for a solution, evaluating alternative solutions, choosing a solution or a combination of solutions, implementing the measures decided upon, and finally, evaluating the consequences of a measure."[12] At this level of description there appears to be no significant difference between the United States (and almost any other government, for that matter) and societies that engage in planning.

In reality, planning is not defended for what it accomplishes but for what it symbolizes — rationality. Planning is conceived to be the way in which intelligence is applied to social problems. The efforts of planners are presumably better than other people's because they result in policy proposals that are systematic, efficient, coordinated, and consistent. Words like these convey the superiority of planning, and the virtue of planning is that it embodies universal criteria of rational choice.

THE IMPERATIVES

Key words appear over and over: planning is good because it is *systematic* rather than random, *efficient* rather than wasteful, *coordinated* rather than helter-skelter, *consistent* rather than contradictory, and above all, *rational* rather than unreasonable. For deeper understanding of why

TABLE 5.2[13]

The planning system (PS)	*The electoral democratic system*
Program 1: Legitimacy	Program 1: Legitimacy
Relationship between the planning system (PS) and the decision-makers.	Relationship between the constitution, etc. and the electorate.
(a) Justification (why the PS should exist and its role).	(a) Justification (why democracy should exist and its role).
(b) Staffing the PS and establishing responsibility and authority.	(b) Designing the institutions of democracy and establishing responsibility and authority.
(c) The communication subsystem	(c) The communication subsystem
(1) Persuasion (selling the PS)	(1) Persuasion (e.g., the Federalist, etc.)
(2) Mutual education.	(2) Public schools and media.
(3) Politics identifying and changing the power structure of the organization.	(3) Politics (constitutional amendments, judiciary).
(d) Implementation (installing the plan).	(d) Implementation (setting up the institutions and operating them).
Program 2: Analysis	Program 2: Analysis
Measurement (identification, classification, prediction, etc.)	Measurement (identification, classification, prediction, etc.)
(a) Identifying the decision-makers, and customers of the larger system.	(a) Identifying interest groups, setting the franchise, etc.
(b) Discovering and inventing the alternatives.	(b) Selecting candidates for office.
(c) Identifying the first-stage goals.	(c) Identifying and lobbying for first-stage goals and policies.
(d) Identifying the ultimate objectives.	(d) Identifying the ultimate aims of society (e.g., Goal for Americans, Bill of Rights, etc.)
(e) Measuring the effectiveness of each alternative for each first stage goal.	(e) Assessing the candidate and his policy platform.
(f) Measuring the effectiveness of each first-stage goal for the ultimate objectives.	(f) Assessing the effectiveness of policies for ultimate objectives (e.g., the Vietnam war as protecting democracy).
(g) Estimating the optimal alternative.	(g) Voting for the candidates of one's choice.
Program 3: Testing (*verifying the plan*)	Program 3: Testing (*does the democracy work?*)
(a) Simulation and parallel testing.	(a) Comparison with other nations, self-appraisal by the citizenry.
(b) Controlling the plan once implemented.	(b) Checks and balances, news media, public debate, the opposition.

Table adapted from student paper by Owen McShane

planning is preferred, consider these norms as instructions to decision-makers, observing what they do.

System

What does it mean to say that decisions should be made in a systematic manner? A word like "careful" will not do because planners cannot be presumed to be more careful than other people. Perhaps "orderly" is better; it implies a checklist of items to be taken into account, but anyone can make a list. "Systematic" as a designation implies further that one knows the right variables in the correct order to put into the list, and can specify their relationships. The essential meaning of systematic, therefore, is having qualities of a system — that is, a series of variables whose interactions are known and whose outputs can be predicted from knowledge of their inputs. System is another word for theory or model, a device explaining and predicting events in the real world in a way that permits manipulation.[14] To say that one is being systematic, consequently, implies that one has causal knowledge, whether one does or does not.

Efficiency

Modern man has a deeply rooted belief that objectives should be attained at the lowest cost. Who can quarrel with that? But technical efficiency should never be considered in a vacuum. It does not tell you where to go, but only that you should arrive there (or go part of the way) with the least effort. The great questions are: efficiency for whom and for what? Some goals (destroying other nations in nuclear war, decreasing the living standards of the poverty-stricken in order to benefit the wealthy) one does not wish achieved at all, let alone efficiently. Efficiency, therefore, raises once more the prior question of objectives.

Stress on efficiency assumes agreed-upon objectives. Knowledge of the general welfare, to which the plan is supposed to contribute, turns out to be one of its major assumptions. Without this knowledge, planners would have no legitimacy to tell others what part they should play in this grand scheme.

Coordination

Coordination is one of the golden words of our time. Offhand, I can think of no way in which the word is used that implies disapproval. Policies should be coordinated; they should not run every which way. No one wants his child described as uncoordinated. Many of the world's ills are attributed to lack of coordination in government.

But what does it mean? Policies should be mutually supportive rather than contradictory. People should not work at cross-purposes.

Participants in any activity should contribute to a common purpose at the appropriate time and in the right amount to achieve coordination. A should facilitate B in order to achieve C. From this intuitive sense of coordination four important (and possibly contradictory) meanings can be derived.

If there is a common objective, then efficiency requires that it be achieved with the smallest input of resources. When these resources are supplied by a number of actors (hence the need for coordination), they must all contribute their proper share at the correct time. If their actions turn out to be efficient, it means they contributed just what they should have, no more, no less.

Coordination then equals efficiency, which is highly prized because achieving it means avoiding bad things: duplication, overlapping, and redundancy. These are bad because they result in unnecessary effort, expending resources that might be used more effectively for other purposes. But now we complicate matters by introducing another criterion that is (for good reason) much less talked about when planning is discussed. I refer to reliability, the probability that a function will be performed. Heretofore we have assumed that reliability was subsumed in the definition of efficiency. It has been discussed as if the policy in mind had to work only once. Yet we all know that major problems of designing policies can depend on the need to have them go on working at a set level of reliability. For this reason, as Martin Landau brilliantly demonstrates, redundancy is built into most human enterprises.[15] We ensure against failure by having adequate reserves and by creating several mechanisms to perform a task in the event one should fail. Telling us simply to avoid duplication, therefore, gives us no useful instruction. We need to know how much and what kind of redundancy to build into our programs. To coordinate one must be able to get others to do things they do not want to do. Participants in a common enterprise may act in a contradictory fashion because of ignorance. But when shown how they fit into the scheme of things, they can generally be expected to behave properly. If we moderate the assumption that a common purpose is involved, however, and admit the possibility (indeed the likelihood) of conflict over goals, then coordination becomes another word for coercion. Because actors A and B disagree with goal C, they can be coordinated only by being told what to do, and then doing it. Coordination then becomes a form of coercion.

When bureaucrats tell one another to coordinate a policy, they mean that it should be cleared with other official participants who have some stake in the matter. This is a way of sharing the blame if things go wrong (each initial on the documents being another hostage against retribution). Because they cannot be coerced, their consent must be obtained. Bargaining has to take place to reconcile the differences; thus the policy may be modified, even at the cost of compromising its original purpose. In this sense coordination is another word for consent.

Coordination means achieving efficiency and reliability, consent and coercion. Telling other people to achieve coordination, therefore, does not tell them whether to coerce or bargain or stipulate what mixture of efficiency and reliability to attempt. An apt illustration is "consistency."

Consistency

Do not run in all directions at once. Consistency may be conceived of as vertical (over a series of periods extending into the future) or horizontal (at a moment in time). Vertical consistency requires that the same policy be pursued for a time, horizontal consistency that it mesh with others at the same time. The former requires continuity of a powerful regime able to enforce its preferences; the latter, tremendous knowledge of how policies affect one another. These are demanding prerequisites. One requires rigidity to ensure continuity, the other, flexibility to achieve accommodation with other policies. Be firm, be pliant, are hard directions to follow simultaneously.

The divergent directions implied suggest that the virtue of consistency should not be taken for granted. It may well be desirable to pursue one task with energy and devotion but it may also prove valuable to hedge one's bets. Consistency secures a higher payoff for success but also imposes a steeper penalty for failure. If several divergent policies are being pusued in the same area they may interfere with each other but the chance may be greater that one will succeed. Like other admonitions, this one, "Be consistent" has its opposing proverb "Don't put all your eggs in one basket."

Consistency is not wholly compatible with adaptation. Although it may be desirable to pursue a steady course, it is also prudent to adapt to changing circumstances. There is the model of the unchanging objective pursued along numerous detours and tactical retreats but never abandoned and ultimately achieved. There is also the model of learning in which experience leads men to alter their objectives as well as the means of attaining them. They may come to believe the cost is too high or they may learn they prefer a different outcome. Apparent inconsistency may turn out to be a change in objectives. If both means and ends, policies and objectives, are changing simultaneously, consistency may turn out to be a will o' the wisp that eludes one's grasp.[16]

The resulting inconsistency may not matter so much, however, as long as alternative courses of action are thoroughly examined at each point of decision from this follows the usual advice to consider alternatives. Which ones? How many? Answers here depend on the inventiveness of planners, the acknowledged constraints, and the resources (in time, talent, and money) that can be spent on each. Though it used to be popular to say that all alternatives should be compared systematically, it has become evident that this method will not work. Knowledge is lacking and the cost is too high. The more diverse the society, by religion, race, class, region, the broader the span of alternatives likely to be considered and the more difficult it will be to secure agreement about their desirability. The number of alternatives considered should be infinite if the dimensions of the problem (such as time, money, skill, and size) are continuous.

Let us suppose that only a small number of alternatives will be considered. Which among the many should receive attention? Unfortunately no rules are written to tell us when to intervene in which possible decisions and how much time to devote to each.

We have gone a long way from the simple advice to consider alternatives. Now we know that this command does not tell anyone which decisions should interest him, how many alternatives he should consider, how much time and attention to devote to them, or whether he knows enough to make the whole enterprise worthwhile. To say that alternatives should be considered is to suggest that something better must exist without being able to isolate it.

Rationality

If rationality means achieving one's goals in the optimal way, it refers here to technical efficiency, the principle of least effort. Paul Diesing argues,[17] however, that one can conceive of several levels of rationality for different aspects of society: the rationality of legal norms and of social structures; political rationality, which affects the maintenance of structures for decision; and economic rationality, devoted to increasing national wealth.

Strict economic rationality means getting the most national income out of an investment. The end is to increase real gross national product (GNP), no matter who receives it; the means is an investment expenditure, no matter who pays for it. To be economically rational is to increase growth to its maximum. What is good for the political system, however, may not be good for the economy and vice versa. The political effects of raising national income may differ according to who gets the increase or whether this increase strengthens or weakens governmental institutions. An analysis of public policy that does not consider incompatibilities among the different realms of rationality is bound to be partial and misleading.

Rationality is used also in the broader sense of reason. The rational man has goals that he tries to achieve by being systematic, efficient, consistent, and so on. Because rationality in the sense of reason has no independent meaning, it can have only such validity as imparted by the criteria that tell us what reasonable action is about. The injunction to plan (Think!) is empty. The key terms associated with it are proverbs or platitudes. Pursue goals! Consider alternatives! Obtain knowledge!

Exercise power! Obtain consent! Or be flexible but do not alter your course. These imperatives have a noncontroversial ring to them, in part because they contain no operational guidance.

"RETROSPECTION"

By "rational," it should now be clear, we mean something like intended, designed, or purposeful. Something happens because it is supposed to. Rational behavior is action appropriately calculated to achieve a desired state of affairs. Yet we have seen that this definition is so broad it readily fits the disjunctive and disorderly world of politics. So-called norms of rationality, moreover, are devoid of content in that they do not tell anyone what to choose. No doubt the difficulty lies in confusing the wrongly reasonable — specifying alternatives, comparing them, and so on — with the really rational — securing intended results, with all that is implied of knowledge and power. Instead of analysis connecting instruments of policy to its objectives, we are offered criteria of what would constitute rationality on the supposition that actions embodying them will prove efficacious. Instead of devices for correcting errors, we get norms alleged to be errorless. In a way, this self-protective behavior is not surprising: why risk failure — which lies in comparing intentions with results — when one cannot ever fail if the success of a norm lies in its form?

Herbert Simon has made a valiant effort to save rationality.[18] By introducing "bounded rationality," Simon argues that people are intendedly rational, their behavior is goal-directed but, because their ability to calculate is limited and the world is complex, they do less well than they would like. Human rationality being bounded, people who would like to maximize end up "satisficing," that is, being satisfied with a solution sufficient to get them past the present decision. With this, I have no quarrel. Rationality is treated as a relationship between means and ends, which, because of human limitations, is necessarily circumscribed. There is, in a word, a little rationality, though not a whole lot.

Intention and Inference

For present purposes, however, I would like to open up the question of intention: what do rational actors intend to do? Move toward their goals. But in what direction? How can we be goal-directed if we don't know what our goal is until we get there?

We are able to choose as we go along, so that we have the opportunity to choose objectives not only before we act but afterward, too.

Actions are undertaken; along the way they intersect others, which together cause consequences — some of which may be attributed to what has just been done, others which belong to external causes, still others which are unexplained. This multiplicity and ambiguity may be used selectively to make the objectives we attribute to the past serve our aims for the future.

Any action can be related to a number of possible objectives. When the number of hospital beds is curtailed it may be related to reducing costs, decreasing unnecessary surgery, increasing income for doctors and hospitals, increasing control over the mix of surgical procedures, or improving the quality of care. The meaning of an act does not necessarily inhere in it like a sign naming a railway station; it must be inferred. This inference can take place only after the act — and numerous others related to it — are safely in the past. At that time there is no single self-evident "there there" for goal direction. It is possible always to invoke a number of possible goals as connected to the action. No one need be surprised, therefore, at retrospective rationalization, which is done to increase the coherence of past actions. We make sense of our past by considering future needs. The multiple potential in each act gives us opportunities, not only before we act but also after, when we know more about how to present ourselves and our objectives.

Karl Weick, whose theorizing has helped me make sense of organizational objectives, holds:

> Rationality seems better understood as a postdecision rather than a predecision occurrence. Rationality makes sense of what has been, not what will be. It is a process of justification in which past deeds are made to appear sensible to the actor himself and to those other persons to whom he feels accountable. It is difficult for a person to be rational if he does not know precisely what it is that he must be rational about. He can create rationality only when he has available some set of actions which can be viewed in several ways. It is possible for actors to make elaborate, detailed statements of their plans. However, the error comes if we assume that these plans then control their behavior. If we watch closely, it will become clear that the behavior is under the control of more determinants than just the vocally stated plan. And at the conclusion of actions, it will never be true that the plan as first stated will have been exactly accomplished. But something will have been accomplished, and it is this something, and the making sense of this something, that constitute rationality.[19]

All is not lost. Once we recognize that rationality has much in common with "rationalization," it may yet be saved. Rationality is like a rocker that goes both forward and back; it tries by intention and is saved by rationalization. One acts first and makes sense of it later. We rewrite history from present motives. By attributing new motivational meaning to what we have done, we try to learn what we ought to be doing. We get three strikes before we're out, the first by acting in the present, the second by interpreting the past into the present, and the third by imagining the future as if it had occurred already so that we can correct and control it before it happens. Is this, one wonders, an example of creativity or of hypocrisy?

Retrospective Rationalization

The word "rationalize" or "rationalization" has at least two distinct meanings. One, according to Webster, is "to make conformable to principles satisfactory to reason." Here the question is whether reason resides in form or in function, in procedures or in consequences. The other meaning is deceitful: "To attribute (one's actions) to rational and creditable motives without adequate analysis of the true motives." Obviously, if I meant deceit, I should have said so. A word is needed that expresses our ability to make what we have done conform to reason as we understand it after we have acted. "Rationalization" has that meaning.

The word "rationalization" is often modified by "mere" as if it were only a poor excuse disconnected from real motivations. To rationalize, however, carries also the connotation of relating apparently disparate elements of behavior so as to make sense of them after, as well as before, we act. In this way, retrospective rationalization (hereinafter called "retrospection") is essential in policy analysis.

Retrospection is a method of incorporating the past into the present that we wish to become our future. For as the times change so also do the values we wish to turn into future objectives. Why, it is these very objectives, retrospection tells us, that we have been pursuing all along — dormant, asleep but still alive, immanent in our acts, ready for resurrection. Retrospection links what we now think we should do with what we ought to have done. Rationalization allows us to reformulate our problems without rejecting our past. If we want to act as analysts in prospect, we must also be able to make sense of our public lives in retrospect.

When social scientists speak of goal-directed behavior they mean that they try to understand and predict behavior as if it were geared to securing this or that objective. This is the origin of maximization models. Thus one speaks of maximizing sales or profits or budgets or survival or whatever. A successful prediction or explanation, however success is defined, does not mean that the true motive was discerned but only that the behavior produced in the model was similar to that observed in the world. Without a good fit between the model and observed behavior, that model must be reformulated (retrofitted, engineers say) to do better. Other objectives must now be introduced to produce a better fit. What is this but a retrospection of results?

Two stories, one far away in Nepal and the other near in the United States will show the potential of retrospection. Years ago in Nepal, I observed that bureaucrats in the field were reluctant to spend governmental funds allotted to them. Underspending authorized amounts was a major difficulty. Because studies of budgeting follow the desire of agencies to spend (often they are called spending agencies), I thought the difficulty could not lie with bad bureaucrats who, engaged in repetitive activities, must know what they are about, but with simple social scientists who assumed the wrong motivation. Investigation revealed that in the old regime of the Rana Prime Ministers, budgetary authorizations required numerous rules for proper accounting, which, if not punctiliously met, resulted in a fine of seven times the amount in question. Caution in spending was plainly advisable. Often, in the ordinary course of events, it is difficult to determine what is or is not correct accounting. Suppose a tractor was called from its home station to a farm and broke down there. Who was responsible for the repair, the station or the farm? Only if officials had connections, with the protection this implies, would they risk taking responsibility for the expenditure. Hence the tractor would remain unrepaired for months or years until higher authorities removed the risk by assigning accounting responsibility for repair.[20]

Was spending a bureaucratic objective or wasn't it? Yes, it was — but not the only one. Spending was an objective until it ran afoul of risk. It became possible to reformulate the problem from irrationality among field bureaucrats to inappropriate incentives applied by the government. It turned out further that the king and his advisors did not want to solve the problem as formulated, because their spending was tied to an even stronger objective — preventing unauthorized expenditure. How did they resolve this duality? In the usual way: they pressed alternatively on each front (one year spending and the next, accounting) without ever resolving the tension. Was their behavior rational? It depends on which motive you are willing to assign them at what time. Whenever the powers that be want to change, they will be able to choose what their objectives were as well as what they will be.

President Carter said the nation had a physical shortage of oil and that, therefore, the American people must support policies requiring sacrifice. Informed opinion was not agreed about the truth of such a shortage nor will we decide that here. Let us, instead, ask about the consequences of deciding after the fact that there had or had not been a shortage. If there was no oil shortage, there was little rationale for asking people to conserve or to pay higher taxes. If there is no shortage, why are prices so high? Either American oil companies are profiteering, which calls for attacks on them, or the foreign oil cartel, OPEC, is price gouging, which calls for an attack on it. Both approaches are unsatisfactory for a president who wishes to show that he is peaceful abroad and a protector of private enterprise at home. If, however, it could be argued that the world would run out of petroleum, the preferences of ecologists (who want less use for the environment's sake) and of business (which wants less use for cost's sake) could be reconciled under a motif of national unity. By making the one essential to the other, President Carter was trying retrospectively to rationalize the conflict between conservation and consumption. Amid massive change "Retrospection" is a bridge between experiences and future policies to maintain meaning within a recognizable universe.

REPRISE

Policy analysis, as I conceive it, is about change in patterns of social interaction. How does change happen? By joining planning to politics, social interaction gives analysis a historical outlook made up of the past pattern of agreements, including agreements to disagree until next time. From the organized actors, the constituent elements of this interaction, analysis gets its abiding interest in incentives to alter their behavior. And planning helps analysis bring intelligence to interaction, by rationalizing movement to a different pattern that may lead to improved future outcomes.

The trouble with social interaction is that you don't know how it will turn out in advance. People can't be trusted to be predictable. Lord knows what they'll do next, as the saying goes, for we surely don't. Accepting the consequences of social interaction is not only hard on the nerves but may be disquieting to a sense of justice. Who ever said that the way things turn out when we bid and bargain is how they ought to be? Not I. If the decks are stacked, the dealer always wins. Enter intellect to guide behavior and motivate morality. Intellect, however, can also be imperious; it can make things turn out right by rigging the rules. By limiting aspirations to internal consistency, intellect can always plead itself innocent of contamination with consequences. So long as reason is about right rules rather than right results, it remains internally consistent and externally vacuous. How can principles of rationality be reasonable if they are not operational?

If rationality is about results, however, how are results to be judged? By relating outcomes to objectives. Yet objectives are as much produced by social interaction as by intellectual postulation. There may be disagreements about what the original objectives were. In any event, we know objectives are likely to be multiple, conflicting, and vague. A way is needed to try out objectives posthumously, so to speak, after the act or, at least, as we go along. Rationality, therefore, is as much (or more) retrospective as it is prospective. Retrospection is a species of policy midwifery through which objectives are revamped to fit new conceptions of what is problematic and hence worthy of attempted solution. Retrospection is how we change without saying so.

Of what, then, does rationality consist? If reason is reduced to intention — the launching of glorious objectives and breathtaking procedures — then the reasonable becomes irrational, productive of cruel (and possibly unusual) consequences. Rationality is a reflexive relationship between acts and consequences, either one being used to justify the other. Sometimes we seek and subsequently achieve objectives postulated in advance; at other times we learn to change objectives as we act; occasionally we examine consequences and decide these were the results we should have wanted to achieve. Thus, if rationality can be retrospective as well as prospective, it can also be interactive as well as intellectual.

Where does one find social interaction and intellectual cogitation? Everywhere and nowhere: everywhere in that they are important components of choice in designing policies; nowhere in that they do not come labeled as such like the products of a sausage machine. With or without brand labels, they are independent of us. Because these categories do not force themselves upon us, however, we see them only where we choose. Therefore, it is important to view cogitation and interaction as general phenomena, operating at different levels, which can be made manifest when convenient. Our interest extends to the institutions through which policies are made and the doctrines (ideologies, if you prefer) on which they are based as well as the policies themselves. That is why I will illustrate here the tension between interaction and cogitation within institutions (the "Bias Toward Federalism" is, in fact, a rule for resolving this tension), among doctrines (opportunity costs are calculated interactively and merit wants by cogitation), and among policies as the environmentalist drama is played out in "Ritual and Rationality, Economy and Environment."

NOTES

1. Adam Smith, *The Wealth of Nations*, Andrew Skinner, ed. (Harmondsworth, Middlesex, Eng.: Pelican Books, 1970); Adam Ferguson, *An Essay on the History of Civil Society, 1767,* Duncan Forbes, ed. (Edinburgh: Edinburgh University Press, 1966).
2. Aaron Wildavsky, with Frank Levy and Arnold Meltsner, *Urban Outcomes* (Berkeley and Los Angeles: University of California Press, 1974).
3. Aaron Wildavsky, "If Planning Is Everything, Maybe It's Nothing," *Policy Sciences,* Vol. 4, No. 2 (June 1973), pp. 127–153.
4. Elaine Mates, "Paradox Lost — Majority Rule Regained," *Ethics,* Vol. 84, No. 1 (October 1973), p. 49.
5. Martin Landau, "Federalism, Redundancy and System Reliability," from *The Federal Polity* in *Publius,* Vol. 3, No. 2 (1973), pp. 173–196.
6. Aaron Wildavsky, "Practical Consequences of the Theoretical Study of Defense Policy," *Public Administration Review,* Vol. 25, No. 1 (March 1965), pp. 90–103.
7. Giandomenico Majone, "On the Notion of Political Feasibility," *European Journal of Political Research,* Amsterdam: Elsevier Scientific, Vol. 3 (1975); Arnold J. Meltsner, "Political Feasibility and Policy Analysis," *Public Administration Review,* Vol. 32, No. 6 (November/December 1972), pp. 859–867.

8. Stuart H. Altman and Sanford L. Weiner, "Constraining the Medical Care System: Regulation as a Second Best Strategy," Working Paper #73 (Berkeley: Graduate School of Public Policy, University of California, 1977).

9. Aaron Wildavsky, "If Planning Is Everything, Maybe It's Nothing," *Policy Sciences*, Vol. 4, No. 2 (June 1973), pp. 127–153.

10. Imre Lakatos, "History of Science and Its Rational Reconstructions," from *Boston Studies in the Philosophy of Science* VIII, 1970; Roger C. Buck and Robert S. Cohen, eds. (Dordrecht, Holland: D. Reidel, 1970), pp. 91–136; Paul Feyerabend, *Against Method* (Atlantic Highlands, N.J.: Humanities Press, 1975); Giandomenico Majone, "Policies as Theories," paper presented at the joint European Consortium for Political Research Workshops, Louvain, 1976.

11. C. West Churchman, *The Systems Approach* (New York: Delacorte Press, 1969), p. 150.

12. Richard Rose, "The Variability of Party Government: A Theoretical and Empirical Critique," *Political Studies*, Vol. 17, No. 4 (December 1969), p. 415.

13. Aaron Wildavsky, "If Planning Is Everything, Maybe It's Nothing," *Policy Sciences*, Vol. 4, No. 2 (June 1972), pp. 127–153.

14. See David Berlinski, "Systems Analysis," *Urban Affairs Quarterly*, Vol. 7, No. 1 (September 1970), pp. 104–126.

15. Martin Laudau, "Redundancy, Rationality and the Problem of Duplication and Overlap," *Public Administration Review*, Vol. 29, No. 4 (July/August 1969), pp. 346–358.

16. It is, by the way, often difficult to know when actions are inconsistent. Leaving aside obtaining accurate information, there are serious conceptual problems. Policies often are stated in general terms that leave ample scope for varying interpretations of their intent. Ambiguity sometimes performs a valuable political function by enabling people (who might otherwise disagree if everything was made clear) to get together. There cannot then be a firm criterion against which to judge consistency. There is also the question of conflicting perspectives among actors and observers. The observers may note an apparent commitment to a certain level and type of investment and see it vitiated by diversion of funds to wage increases. To the observer this means inconsistency. The actor, however, may feel consistent in pursuing his goal of political support. Given any two policies that lead to conflicts among two values one can always find a third value by which they are reconciled. Investment seemed to bring support when it was announced, and so, subsequently, does spending for other purposes when its turn comes. The actors' values may be rephrased as "the highest possible investment so long as it does not seriously affect immediate political support." In view of the pressures to meet the needs of different people variously situated in society, most decisions undoubtedly are made on such contingent basis. This is what it means to adapt to changing circumstance. As the goals of actors shift with time, consistency becomes a moving target, difficult to hit at best, impossible to locate at worst.

17. Paul Diesing, *Reason in Society: Five Types of Decisions and Their Social Conditions* (Urbana: University of Illinois Press, 1962).

18. Herbert Simon, "Cognitive Limits on Rationality." See also the demonstration that "satisficing" is compatible with prevailing doctrines of decision-making under uncertainty in M. A. H. Dempster and Aaron Wildavsky, "Yes, Virginia, There Is No Magic Size for an Increment," in *The Political Economy of Spending: A Predictive Theory in the United States Federal Budgetary Process* (in progress).

19. Karl E. Weick, *The Social Psychology of Organizing* (Reading, Mass.: Addison-Wesley, 1969), p. 38.

20. Aaron Wildavsky, "Why Planning Fails in Nepal," *Administrative Science Quarterly*, Vol. 17, No. 4 (December 1972), pp. 508–528.

CHAPTER 6

A BIAS TOWARD
FEDERALISM

To govern this nation do we want an operative federal structure? If so, where do we want the balance between national and state power to be drawn and on which issues? Under a national regime, states and localities carry out national instructions; the problem is how to improve their obedience. In a federal regime, states and localities are disobedient. The operational meaning of federalism is found in the degree to which the constituent units disagree about what should be done, who should do it, and how it should be done. In a word, federalism is about conflict. It is also about cooperation, that is, the terms and conditions under which conflict is limited. A federal regime, therefore, cannot be coordinated from the center any more than it can be controlled or coerced. Coordination, as we have seen, does not necessarily imply a coordinator. Under an operative federalism, coordination occurs by interaction among many governments, not by intellectual cogitation by a single one. Federalism means mutuality, not hirearchy, multiple rather than single causation, a sharing instead of a monopoly of power. One can determine if the federal beast is alive only by whether it kicks — and then whom it kicks and who kicks it back. The rationality, responsiveness, and responsibility of a regime, its overall decency and effectiveness, should not depend on its appearance (it may appear untidy) but on results. Self-government need not come from one center, but from interaction among many, which leaves room for plenty of participation.

If there is a federal principle, it cannot be limited to relations between national and state governments. If it is good for power to be divided and shared, that principle must prevail also in relationships among states, and their cities, counties, and special districts. Let us call this principle — that under most conditions a larger number of smaller units will deliver services better than a smaller number of larger units — the federal bias. It is alterable bias (circumstances do alter cases). It is, however, a bias in that, with no evidence to the contrary, it is assumed that interaction among a larger number of smaller units produces better service to citizens than cogitation by a smaller number of larger ones.

The promotion of economic development is a "classic" function of government, long acceptable in many quarters and antedating contemporary conventional wisdom about the planning and organization of government for serving the public. In the past generation, the federal government has experimented with several ways to promote economic growth, particularly in the country's less-developed areas.

Most relevant research on economic development falls within two opposing traditions in the study of planning and federalism. On one side, long-range comprehensive planning is ranged against short-term, piecemeal adjustment; on the other side, concentration of power is posed against its dispersal. One uses a metaphor of bureaucratic planning — hierarchy, coordination, consistency — and the other makes use of political interaction — competition, conflict, bargaining, markets. To make an interactive analogy good in the political arena calls for many participants to bargain for increased mutual advantage. The cogitational image necessitates as few bureaucratic units with as little conflict as possible. Although political interaction is designed to clear any number of antagonistic interests, bureaucratic planning depends on a few agencies operating among agreed objectives. The normative prescriptions of the two models can be summarized: Because units should cooperate, when they conflict they ought to be coerced. When units ought to differ, they can resolve their differences only by consent. To simplify exposition, I shall refer to one as the cooperative-coercive and to the other as the conflict-consent model. The characteristics of these are summarized in Table 6.1.

THE COOPERATIVE-COERCIVE MODEL

A good statement of the cooperative-coercive model comes from William I. Goodman, whose major contention is, "Modern administrative requirements for area development cannot be met by the old order, in which each plane of government either fights its battles in a sovereign and isolated way or is frustrated in attempting to carry out a program in conjunction with other units. Cities and states have for too long engaged in a profitless conflict which neither side can expect to win . . . because of the rigid system in which they are caught up."[1] The assumptions are clear: the old order of innumerable sovereign units of government engaged in profitless conflict is counterproductive and must go. How? By coordination.

Goodman's discussion of that elusive term is sharp and to the point:

TABLE 6.1
TWO MODELS OF ECONOMIC DEVELOPMENT

Element	Cooperative-coercive	Conflict-consent
Time span	long-range	short-term
Planning span	comprehensive	piecemeal
Power	concentrated	dispersed
Decision	cogitation	interaction
Rank or degree	hierarchy	equality
Operational values	coordination, con- sistency	competition, conflict bargaining, markets
Number of participants	few	many
Intensity of goal variation in environment	low, agencies with agreed objective	high, many antagonistic interests
Normative	Norm: Cooperation .·. coercion permitted to eliminate conflict	Norm: Conflict .·. differences resolved by consent

"Coordination ... requires a hierarchy of units wherein the coordinator exercises supremacy and, at least, tacit coercion against units lower in the hierarchy. The power to coordinate places a club over the head of those who are to be coordinated. The dilemma therefore is this: coordination is likely to founder when exercised by the planning agency against operating departments, if planning itself is set up as an operating department."[2] If coordination is a synonym for coercion, how will planners acquire the necessary power to impose their will? By comprehensive planning.

One might be accused of creating a straw man of comprehensiveness in planning if Carlisle P. Runge and W. L. Church had not written: "Our review has led us to conclude that there is an unfortunate lack of coordination of efforts [on] all [planes] of government and that the programs involved would be more effective if governmental procedures required a higher degree of interagency and intergovernmental cooperation."[3] Further coordination, Runge and Church believe, will not be fully achieved unless a local planning unit "has some minimal capacity to enforce its recommended priorities within the guidelines of comprehensive plans."[4] What role would there be, then, for states or for the federal government? How, then, will conflicts be resolved among levels of government? Will federal and state agencies provide funds to areas that thwart their own plans?

"One can only hope," Runge and Church say, "that ... elected representatives would be willing to forego their traditional direct influences over federal programs in their home states in recognition of the breadth and complexity of administering shared federalism."[5] Here we have it all: faith, that interests and objectives are similar; hope, for a voluntary renunciation of power; charity, toward other levels of government, without expecting a return in the form of change in policy. If there is too little consent, according to this model, there must be more coercion.

In an important modern work on federalism, James L. Sundquist and David W. Davis state that efforts to make the federal system work better by providing "planners, coordinators, expediters, facilitators, communicators" have given us "a more complicated federal system — one with five, six, or even seven levels of government where three or four sufficed before."[6] How, they ask, should the federal system be organized to accommodate the new neighborhood structures and multi-county organizations? They believe "A coordinated approach to intergovernmental relations requires the introduction of a new force [on] the regional [plane] — a supradepartmental official with responsibility and authority to speak for the federal government as a whole in matters of intergovernmental relations. In the absence of such a spokesman, there will not be a satisfactory channel of central communication between the federal government as a whole and state and local governments."[7] These coordinators would not control substantive programs, but would be in charge of managing, overseeing, and coordinating, which may or may not be the same thing.

What role are the states supposed to have in this picture? Sundquist and Davis suggest "a differential approach to federal-state relations,"[8] by which they mean taking into account the considerable variation in the competence of state governments. To make such an approach possible, federal-state relations have to be converted from a *legal* concept, in which the states collectively negotiate in the legislative and administrative process for rights and powers that all possess, to an *administrative* concept, in which the federal government exercises judgment as to how much reliance can be placed on each state and reaches "an individual understanding with that state governing federal-state administrative relationships."[9] American states thereby would be reduced to European prefectures.

The authors feel that there is a place for coercive action by state governments, which should compel local jurisdictions to comply with comprehensive Model Cities plans. "If the model cities coordination process is to succeed," the authors assert, "state agencies will have to be directed by their governors and their legislatures to enter without reservation into that process and to conform their programs to the model cities plans, and it will require state leadership — and perhaps coercion at times — to bring counties, school districts, and other independent governmental bodies into that process also."[10] The role of the states, apparently, is to enforce federal programs on recalcitrant localities.

And the localities? It is all for them. "The central premise," the authors state, "is that the effectiveness of the execution of federal programs depends crucially upon the competence of community institutions to plan, initiate, and coordinate. The federal contribution of money and ideas and leadership to community programs is indispensable, but it is still only a contribution. . . . No amount of review by, and coordination among, federal agencies is a satisfactory substitute for what must be done properly in the first place within the community itself."[11] Communities, apparently, must be forced to be free.

"Somewhere in the Executive Office must be centered a concern for the structure of federalism — a responsibility for guiding the evolution of the whole system of federal-state-local relations, viewed for the first time as a single system."[12] Only from the standpoint of intellectual cogitation would the inherent dualism of federalism turn into a single system. The authors' unitary bias is clear: "federal agencies cannot be bound absolutely by whatever the local planning process comes up with. They must guard not only against waste and extravagance but against proposals that may distribute the benefits of federal programs unfairly or in other ways inconsistent with the national purpose."[13] The feds, in their view, must be a bulwark against proposals by one community which might adversely affect others, or which might cost more than the federal government felt it it could afford.

> Yet [they continue], it is one thing for federal officials to draw the line against a local proposal on grounds of illegality, waste, inequity, discrimination, spillover effects, or unavailability of funds and quite another for them to substitute their judgment for that of local communities on matters that do not involve these considerations. Our field interview notes are filled with assertions by local officials that federal decisions are being made on matters that should be wholly within the competence of the communities.[14]

Naturally, no federal agency would ever substitute its judgment for that of a locality; it just happens that all these other reasons (illegality, waste, and others) are good ones for turning down or altering what the localities wish to do.

After this, it is some surprise to read that: "Yet the principle of decentralization is sound." Local decisions "are *potentially* better than those made [on] the national [plane], because only [on] the community [plane] can the community be seen as a whole, only there can all the community programs be interrelated, only there can the systems of comprehensive planning and program coordination be established and operated, and only there can widespread citizen participation be organized and the contributions of the citizens blended with those of the professionals in the decision-making process."[15] Only there, apparently, does perfect liberty consist of the right to agree with the Grand Federal Coordinator.

On the national plane, according to Robert Warren, despite lip service to the contrary, "elected Federal decision-makers have, on numerous occasions, clearly rejected a policy of granting subnational entities the power needed to control the range of socio-economic phenomena necessary for economic development programs or for effectively coordinating the activities of Federal agencies within a specified territorial area. An agency can be charged with the responsibility for coordination of planning or development without being delegated the requisite authority or resources to perform these functions. Consequently, officials of regional bodies tend to be in the position of claiming to achieve goals for which they are statutorily responsible but for which they have no formal power to accomplish."[16] Why is there so large a gap between objectives and resources, rhetoric and responsibility?

One answer appears in a splendid study by Robert Warren and Geoffrey Wandesford-Smith. The Federal Field Committee (FFC) was created in October 1964 to develop "coordinated plans for Federal programs which contribute to economic and resources development in Alaska."[17] But the FFC failed. Why?

The difficulty was that Congress wanted coercion in the abstract but conflict in the concrete. It wanted to give new powers to an areawide body so long as it didn't have to take old ones away from the functional federal departments. The FFC resulted in contradiction but, more significant, embodied these opposing impulses — let rival camps contend. The substantive theory of Congress was based on the cooperative-coercive model, but its procedural theory depended on conflict and consent.

THE CONFLICT-CONSENT MODEL

A division of power normally would not be thought of as good in itself but as a means to desired ends — peace, prosperity, domestic tranquility. Sharing powers geographically has been defended as aiding national defense,[18] diffusing by dividing domestic conflict,[19] and facilitating innovation (the states as laboratories).[20] The test of federal theory is federal action — superior delivery of services.

Evidently two measures are required, one of excellence in delivery of services (the dependent variable) and the other of governmental structure (the independent variable). A seemingly insuperable obstacle comes from inability to get agreement on the definition of federal structure. What kind of division or sharing of powers, on paper or in practice, to what degree, in regard to which objects, must a government have to qualify as federal in structure. No answer will be forthcoming here.[21] Instead, keeping delivery of services firmly in mind as the end in view, I shall concentrate on two structural attributes — size and number — without which no claim of federal superiority in delivery could be made.

If it were true that the fewer the units and the larger each was, the more effective the delivery of services, it would be hard to conceive of an effective argument for a federal structure. The more unitary the state, the more effective it would be. Field offices might be feasible but state and local governments would be gratuitous. Within loose limits, the pro-federal argument must be that the more numerous the units, and the smaller they are, the more effectively they will deliver services. To argue the reverse — bigger and fewer is better — is to reject federalism.

According to Sperlich's law (all interesting relationships are curvilinear) there must be sizes so small or so large as to render the units ineffective. The federal argument must be that beyond minimum size — a few thousand or tens of thousands of people — all useful division of labor and specialization can be achieved. Naturally, there are trade-offs between size and number. From the federal viewpoint, numbers take the curse off size: the more units involved, the larger each unit can be without decreasing effective delivery of services. The value of size, then, depends on number; the smaller the number of units, the more large size contributes to ineffective delivery of services.

The division and sharing of powers among one federal and various state governments is only one (and not necessarily the best) test of the federal principle's efficacy. It is difficult to arrange tests of federal principles; states are usually just a handful, rarely exceeding the fifty of the United States of America. Fortunately, there are hundreds of counties, thousands of cities and even more special-purpose districts (water, sewer, school, fire, irrigation, and others), whose operations involve variations in both number and size in the delivery of services. These endlessly proliferating units live by conflict and cooperation. Districts conflict because each is out to make the best deal for itself. Districts cooperate so long as arrangements suit each other better than any available alternative. How, then, if there is no central command, is economic development to be achieved?

Coordination, although frequently proposed, is not a real answer. But the suggestion of coordination does pose a great question, not only of economics but also of politics: who will coordinate whom toward what ends? By this time it should be apparent, as Robert Warren states, "that organizational and political theory are as central to area development as economic theory."[22] More than 800 counties are designated Economic Development Administration redevelopment areas, 75 multicounty districts, 5 multistate regional planning commissions with three to six states in each, and some additional structures in Alaska and the Delaware River Basin. "However," he observes, "the numerous subnational experiments in multijurisdictional organizations . . . have been designed in the absence of systematically developed generalizations or a set of testable propositions about the interrelationship of organizational structure to behavior and performance."[23] Few efforts have been made to relate experience on one level to that of another or to relate these general problems to organization theory.

Warren's thesis is that there are alternative ways of organizing agencies for area development and that these have political consequences. Extending the size, for instance, biases the result. Moving beyond one county to many makes a difference in who will exercise power over what. This is not merely a matter of efficiency, or of increasing the size of planning staffs, but of who will rule.

> By increasing the scale of the organization it is far more likely that the result will be an [economic development] committee composed of the representatives of a number of independent county-based politico-economic systems rather than a "community. . . ."[24] A high percentage of the counties in the districts are rural and it is assumed that actors with the high levels of economic resources wlil dominate decisions in both the public and private sectors. . . .[25] Organizations upon which the poor and minorities might rely for support within a city or even a county area, such as the union, church, the NAACP . . . are unlikely to be able to amplify whatever local influence they have to the district scale.[26]

Not everyone, then, can expect to gain from district or regional government.

It would be foolish to alter decision-making institutions without having a defensible notion of more desirable arrangements. Eugene Smolensky and others set out to determine how many problems in metropolitan areas are caused by defects in governmental structures.[27] In doing so, they hoped to learn whether action should be undertaken within current structures, or should be "designed to compensate for the awkward federal structure of the government." They chose to proceed theoretically by setting down general conditions for the design of a spatially dimensioned federal system. In that way, public servants could tell whether the boundaries of the policy are congruent with those of the problem.

> It may be fairly said that the present areal jurisdiction of our multi-level governmental units have been established by tradition and modified by expedience, rather than by the guidelines issuing from any widely recognized theory of governmental boundaries. In consequence, governments and their citizenry come together under circumstances in which the legally defined spatial boundaries are increasingly out of alignment with the boundaries of the substantive public issues on which they interact.[28]

This, at least, is the understanding supporting the conventional wisdom of reform.

> If the optimal production level for a public good is to be achieved (the guiding theorem goes), the spatial extent of the political domain in which the output decision is to be made must embrace all those upon whom taxes or other non-user costs are to be levied, as well as all those who will benefit from that output. Thus, one (remedial) solution to inefficiency in the provision of public goods caused by geographical spillovers is to create a new [plane] of government which, in effect, forces congruency

between the boundaries of a political unit and the boundaries of a spatial area affected by that political unit.[29]

A competitive solution, the authors observe, could not guarantee that districts would fill their uniform plain completely because it would take time for districts to reshuffle themselves when the gaps appeared.

> But in the meantime, there would be investment in the wrong places, which would have to be written off before the shifts could take place. In order to avoid this misplaced investment, a solution that considered the whole plain in the first step would be needed. That is, a planner would be needed to carve up the plain into equal-sized adjoining districts of the optimal size for the provision of the good. Then the households in each district would provide themselves with a facility of the optimal size, in a location consistent with a pattern in the plain, and no investment would be wasted. Thus the price of efficiency in our uniform plain is a greater concentration of power.[30]

The hierarchic bias is evident. Achieving efficiency within the boundaries of the plan demands that the planner (the federal government) decide who will perform what functions in which geographic locations. Whatever else besides the assumed efficiency of a hierarchic system recommends persuading local units to abolish themselves, the result will not look like the federal system we have come to know if not to revere.

"There seem to be more ideologies channeling the attention of multi-county agencies to state and federal levels," Pierre Clavel observes, "than there are ideologies directing their attention locally."[31] The co-operation-coercion model, assuming congruence of interests within a framework of comprehensive planning, allows only one correct answer, not many.

SIZE VS. NUMBER OR INTERACTION VS. COGITATION REVISITED

The most deeply ingrained assumption in all the literature on the relationship between governmental structure and policy outcomes is that rural and urban problems can be traced to the large number of overlapping jurisdictions, governments, and special authorities in America. In my opinion, the most critical issue in organization theory for area development is conflict-consent versus cooperative-coercive models of organization. Are externalities to be taken into account by internalizing them in ever-larger organizations so as to coerce cooperation? Or will those adversely affected give consent through a crazy-quilt pattern of interaction as a multitude of conflicting interests bargain out their differences? Which of these alternatives generates more information on preferences, imposes fewer costs, inculcates more dynamism, and leads to more integrative solutions?

Warren and Wandesford-Smith state this issue: "The assumption that the efficiency and responsiveness of government in an urban area decreases as the number of jurisdictions increases is open to serious question in relation to metropolitan areas." On the contrary, they argue that a large number of special districts "has frequently played a major role in the establishment of the infrastructure necessary for economic development. They provide tax and debt capacities, some degree of functional professionalization, and officials whose record for reelection or career advancement depends upon the production of public goods and services."[32] A growing literature is aimed at attempting to create a political economy of governmental jurisdictions in which competition (compared to bureaucratic alternatives) improves services.[33]

A normative theory of federalism should deal with the size and number of organizational units, and the areas within which they ought to operate so as to enhance the quality of public services. If it were in fact true that better education, or police, or welfare services are provided through larger units, states would be better than counties, which would overwhelm cities; all would lose out entirely to the central government. In fact (although the details are beyond the scope of this volume), there do not appear to be any economies of scale whatsoever for most services. "In summary," according to Niskanen and Levy, "the evidence developed by all the major studies in the last twenty years — by numerous scholars using different techniques and different data sources — is consistent and, in total, overwhelming: There do not appear to be any significant economies of scale in the provision of local government services (other than water and sewage services) above the level of the smaller cities."[34]

On the contrary, bits of positive evidence now show that the quality of service (below a minimum) declines with increasing size. Using a variety of measures of student performance in California, for example, Niskanen and Levy find that "school district size has a consistent *negative* relation to student performance."[35] And Elinor Ostrom has shown that smaller police departments either perform better, or do no worse, than larger ones on a variety of measures connected with crime.[36]

Now the type of the governmental service to be performed is clearly important. Defense and foreign policy are not readily made at the state level and constitutional provisions prohibit it. Besides, six good defense policies, all going in different directions, may be worse than one. But wait a minute. We are talking about the federal principle on size and number and not about division of authority. The need for an ultimate arbiter in defense policy, for instance, does not automatically dispose of the argument over several armed services departments possibly being better than one. Unification of the armed forces after World War II was proposed with the usual aim of securing extra efficiency by increasing economies of scale, and by central control to avoid overlap and duplication. When a public organization such as the Department of Defense (DOD) is several times larger than the largest corporation, the argument of efficiency has to grow from self-delusion. Who can understand what actually goes on in so overwhelming an organization?

Achieving efficiency (which is always problematical) ought not to have been the main issue — at least not to me. The question is always "efficiency for what?" Achieving creativity in concepts of defense and maintaining civilian control over the armed forces should have been the main intention. Here diversity was far better than uniformity, pluralism preferable to unity.

Suppose, instead of the three old services, a new hexagonal armed forces was formed — the old army, navy, air force, and marines, together with a new agency for procurement and one for producing weapon systems. The question of control by civilian outsiders would have been more readily answered because the quarrel among the six services would have revealed the most interesting secrets. Creativity, I think, would have been better served because of the incentive for each service to compete with the others to show that it could do whatever was worth doing in a better way. The separation between procurement and production, moreover, would have reduced collusion between armed forces and industry because designer and producer would have been different. At the same time, competition would have increased, both for creating the best design and for producing the best weapon according to that design. Coercing the services under the guise of a cooperative DOD may satisfy the appearance of neatness. The actuality of control and creativity that could have come from the consent supplied by conflict would have served our country better.

Advocates of federalism should start with the supposition that smaller is better. At least, they should consider that as a leading hypothesis. Under some conditions, the hypothesis may be invalid. But reliance on the structure of social interaction — more units interacting with greater frequency — should always be the leading hypothesis (a bias, I called it earlier) of people who profess to prefer federalism.

For present purposes, the important thing is recognizing that arguments over the structure of institutions are often disagreements about degrees of social interaction and intellectual cogitation. Cogitation implies coercion while interaction requires consent. The same is true, we shall see, over doctrinal disputes. Who cares about such arcane subjects as opportunity costs? Only those who understand that it provides the main underpinning for the economic theory that guides the economy and justifies public intervention.

NOTES

1. William I. Goodman, "Organizing for State and Multi-State Development Planning," mimeograph, 1968, p. 55.
2. Ibid.
3. Carlisle P. Runge and W. L. Church, "New Directions in Regionalism: A Case Study of Intergovernmental Relations in Northwestern Wisconsin," *Wisconsin Law Review*, Vol. 1 (1971), pp. 453–454.
4. Ibid., p. 509.
5. Ibid., p. 517.
6. James L. Sundquist, with the collaboration of David W. Davis, *Making Federalism Work: A Study of Program Coordination at the Community Level* (Washington, D.C.: Brookings Institution, 1969), p. 242.
7. Ibid., p. 273.
8. Ibid., p. 272.
9. Ibid., p. 271.
10. Ibid., p. 268.
11. Ibid., pp. 243–244.
12. Ibid., pp. 244–246.
13. Ibid., pp. 248–249.
14. Ibid., p. 249.
15. Ibid., p. 250.
16. Robert Warren, "Alternative Governmental Structures for Area Development," mimeograph, p. 6.
17. Robert Warren and Geoffrey Wandesford-Smith, "Federal-State Development Planning: The Federal Field Committee for Development Planning in Alaska," mimeograph, p. 17.
18. William Riker, *Federalism: Origin, Operation, Significance* (Boston: Little, Brown, 1964).
19. Aaron Wildavsky, ed., *American Federalism in Perspective* (Boston: Little, Brown, 1967).
20. William Anderson, "Federalism and Intergovernmental Relations, A Budget of Suggestions for Research" (Prepared for the Committee on Public Administration and the Committee on Government of the Social Science Research Council, Chicago, 1964); also, Anderson's *The Nation and the States, Rivals or Partners?* (Minneapolis: University of Minnesota Press, 1957).
21. See S. Rufus Davis, *The Federal Principle: A Journey Through Time in Search of a Meaning* (Berkeley: University of California Press, 1976), a superb survey of futile efforts from ancient to modern times.
22. Robert Warren, op. cit. p. 23.
23. Ibid., p. 3.
24. Ibid., p. 14.
25. Ibid., p. 16.
26. Ibid., p. 18.
27. Eugene Smolensky, Richard Burton, and Nicolaus Tideman, "An Operational Approach to an Efficient Federal System, Part 1, On the Specification of Horizontal Relationships," mimeograph.
28. Ibid., p. 4.
29. Ibid., pp. 5, 8.
30. Ibid., pp. 24–25.
31. Pierre Clavel, "The Politics of Planning: The Case of Non-Metropolitan Regions," mimeograph.

32. Robert Warren and Geoffrey Wandesford-Smith, op. cit.
33. These issues are splendidly posed in Elinor Ostrom's "Metropolitan Reform: Propositions Derived From Two Traditions" (mimeograph, 1971, done under support of NSF Grant #GS-27383). See also Vincent Ostrom and Elinor Ostrom, "Public Choice: A Different Approach to the Study of Public Administration," *Public Administration Review*, Vol. 31, No. 2 (March-April 1971), pp. 203–216. Vincent Ostrom, Charles M. Tiebout, and Robert Warren, "The Organization of Government in Metropolitan Areas: A Theoretical Inquiry," *American Political Science Review*, Vol. 55 (December 1961), pp. 831–842: Robert Warren, "Government in Metropolitan Regions: A Reappraisal of Fractionated Political Organization" (Davis: Institute of Governmental Affairs, University of California, 1966); Robert Bish, *The Public Economy of Metropolitan Areas* (Chicago: Markham Press, 1971); Jerome Rothenberg, "Strategic Interaction and Resource Allocation in Metropolitan Intergovernmental Relations," *American Economic Review*, Vol. 59 (May 1969), pp. 494–503; Bryan Ellickson, "Jurisdiction Fragmentation and Residential Choice," *American Economic Review*, Vol. 61 (May 1971), pp. 334–339; Wallace E. Oates, "The Effects of Property Taxes and Local Spending on Property Values: An Empirical Study of Tax Capitalization and the Tiebout Hypothesis," *Journal of Political Economy*, Vol. 77 (December 1969), pp. 957–971; and the literature cited in the papers by Elinor Ostrom and by Vincent Ostrom and Elinor Ostrom, op. cit.
34. William Niskanen and Mickey Levy, "Cities and Schools: A Case for Community Government in California," Working Paper No. 14 (Berkeley: Graduate School of Public Policy, University of California, 1974), p. 22.
35. Ibid., p. iv.
36. Elinor Ostrom and Gordon P. Whitaker, "Community Control and Governmental Responsiveness: The Case of Police in Black Communities, in *Improving the Quality of Urban Management*, David Roger and Willis Hawley, eds., Vol. 8, *Urban Affairs Annual Review* (Beverly Hills, Calif.: Sage Publications, 1974), pp. 303–334; Elinor Ostrom and Roger B. Parks, "Suburban Police Departments: Too Many or Too Small?" in *Urbanization of the Suburbs*, Louis H. Masotti and Jeffrey K. Hadden, eds., Vol. 7, Urban Affairs Annual Review (Beverly Hills, Calif.: Sage Publications, 1970), pp. 367–402, Elinor Ostrom, William H. Baugh, Richard Guarasci, Roger B. Parks, and Gordon P. Whitaker, "Community Organization and the Provision of Policy Services," in *Administrative and Policy Studies Series* (Beverly Hills, Calif.: Sage Publications, 1973).

CHAPTER 7

OPPORTUNITY COSTS
AND MERIT WANTS

The notion that the cost of any action can only be measured by the value of the opportunities foregone by taking the action is at the same time trivial and profound.

Walter Nicholson, in
Microeconomic Theory

If opportunity costs are about cabbages, merit wants are about philosopher kings. These rival doctrines may speak in the language of economics but the guiding hand behind them is that of politics. The great questions are there: Who should rule? How should they rule? Who will govern the governors? How might subjective preferences be converted into collective rationality? In short, the question of whether decisions should be made by social interaction, with many minds contributing, or by intellectual cogitation, with an elite acting, in effect, as a single intelligence, will reappear here in different doctrinal form. The better to get to know them, we shall approach opportunity costs analytically, by decomposition, and historically, by evolution, for from these seemingly simple garden-variety notions of cost and merit, we shall peel off layers of ideology. If our economic onion causes more than a few tears, we can say only that it's better to be sad theoretically than actually sorry for absentmindedly eliminating economics from public policy.

What happens when cogitation replaces interaction? By itself, economics, which is exemplified by opportunity costs, is composed of doctrine and folklore whose rationale is limited but real. Merit wants takes away both the reality and the rationale of economics without replacing it with an intelligible politics. This is the moral of our tale: better a flawed economics than a bogus politics.

TWO DOCTRINES

Can a doctrine be so embedded in discipline, so integral to its essence, that practitioners rarely recognize it explicitly? So it would seem for the doctrine of opportunity cost, defined as the notion that the cost of an action can be measured only by the value of the best alternative that must be foregone to undertake such action. Perhaps analysis of this term has been neglected precisely because opportunity costs are ubiquitous. Possibly analysis of opportunity costs has been avoided because the doctrine comes close to that core of values that a body of theory is designed to protect, the nonrational (unexamined) heart of its rational periphery. Maybe, in exposing the deep-seated presumption in favor of interaction versus cogitation, opportunity costs are vulnerable to attack by the opposing doctrine of merit wants.

Although costs of opportunity appear as crucial to economics as that of party competition is to proper functioning of a democracy, a review of recent economic literature reveals very little exclusively on the subject (with the exception of a book by James Buchanan). Practitioners may respond that understanding of opportunity cost has become internalized, assumed present in all economic analysis, and unnecessary to discuss among the initiated. Yet, in doing so, the discipline risks treating the doctrine of opportunity costs as profound (good for everything) or, when we return to merit wants, trivial (good for nothing), limiting its potential contribution to policy analysis in broader areas of political economy.

Reviewing the history of opportunity-cost doctrine, we seek to reemphasize its centrality to economics, for without it we believe almost anybody else — moral philosophers, politicians, citizens, even astrologers (who would have the virtue of appearing, as well as being, ridiculous) — would be worth more to consult than economists. If merit resides in will, it is the willful who ought to prevail.

COST VERSUS MERIT, OR INTERACTION AND COGITATION IN A NEW GUISE

In considering opportunity costs, the difficulty arises, for good reason, of distinguishing among merit, utility, price, and cost. When a person is asked how much a thing is worth, it makes a difference whether he argues an individual or social view (its worth to him alone or to all others), a subjective or objective view (the value he places, or what others will give him), or a unique versus a comparative view (intrinsic or alternative worth).

Consider the isolated individual. His notion of worth may result from feelings of intrinsic merit attached to some object. He may even go so far as to rank objects by their importance to him (he generally likes having birds around more than turtles). Yet there are obviously practical considerations: the individual may come to embrace usefulness (utility, to the economist) as more reflective of worth, and this perspective may result in rankings sharply divergent from the previous ones. If, for example, his food supply were to run out, he might be forced to forage for meat, and he'd rather try to hunt turtles than birds, which are harder to catch and tougher to eat, especially if he'd rather not pull off the feathers.

Opportunity Costs

Make way for market man. Surrounded by social relations, our formerly isolated individual finds a market where objects similar to his are traded. The exchange rate (or price, in everyday parlance) displaces his previous notions of worth: learning that one bird brings ten turtles is cause for reevaluation. The valuation of goods by others in society has become a part of his own calculus. As his evaluations become more social, then, they become more comparative, and hence at least somewhat more objective (in the sense of widely agreed upon).

Valuing goods by their intrinsic merit is purely personal; when subjectivity is supreme, whatever value the individual applies is right. Exchange value can be wrong only in a trivial sense, as when it is said, "the price is wrong," meaning something like an incorrect tag has been put on the garment. Socially speaking, "the price is right" because that is whatever other people are willing to give up in exchange when they interact in markets.

Prices are palpable, but systems are slippery. Prices are made (and seen) by people, but opportunity costs are made up by economists. Just as physicists once believed in ether (and some now commend quarks) though these entities cannot be seen, but only deduced from the traces they leave on other substances, so too economists have created a relationship whose only evidence lies in the indirect effects it has on the economy. Its name is opportunity cost.

To economists, the worth of a commodity is equal to the value placed on the best alternative good necessarily foregone in its production (its cost, they call it). If the economic system works well, goods will be given their highest use no matter who does the valuing. Resources will be bid away from inferior uses. Success means increasing the total national product, and failure lies in decreasing it. It is, hypothetically, a tidy world in which signals are loud, clear, and unambiguous.

Decision-makers, without some notion of error, are unable to learn from their action. When intellectuals impose a systemic notion, like "best alternative use" (defined by increasing national income, operated by redeploying resources toward higher returns), error becomes meaningful and failure possible. Failure, as Linus in *Peanuts* might say, is when resources run away. Opportunity-cost doctrine allows economics its chief contribution to public policy: estimating the value of a good or service by alternative use of resources.

Just as there is no free lunch, no doctrine (or discipline for that matter) is invulnerable under all conditions. Opportunity costs are tinged with subjectivity, cannot entirely overcome historicity, and depend upon comparability in their domain of applicability. They say something about the never-never land of what might have been, namely, alternative valuations either of what is or what might be. Yet history rules out more than one alternative at one time, place, and circumstance. The objectivity of opportunity costs, therefore, depends on the somewhat subjective capacity to estimate intellectually the consequences of alternatives that have not, and, in the nature of things, cannot historically have been tried. What is done, moreover, as with the establishment of governmental monopolies, may not be possible to undo, influencing all future choices by eliminating alternatives that might otherwise have proven viable. Now, no historical interpretation of how things came to be as they are can avoid a tacit supposition about how they would have been in other circumstances. The logic of experiment is assumed — unavoidably assumed — even when nothing is expressly said about the counter-to-historical-fact alternatives. We accept the use of thought-experiments (mental or imaginary exercises) but we also accept the weaknesses of their use.

The more markets there are, the broader their scope and the wider the experience included in their transactions, the greater their capacity to overcome the limitations inherent in opportunity-cost analysis. The fewer alternatives have to be made up, the more their costs can be estimated (because they have been experienced), the more educated guesswork about relative worth becomes. Should it be decided that medicine or education ought to lie outside the applicability of markets, comparison may still be made to private suppliers in other countries or to various cost elements in one's own. The fewer markets there are, however, the less comparability among prices, the greater their subjectivity until, in the end, administration replaces economics. If opportunity costs are rejected, not only in a few areas, but in most or all, if it is wrong to think of alternatives foregone, there is no place for economics. What is worse, without alternatives there is no place for policy analysis.

Merit Wants

Yet, in one field after another — environment, safety, health — thinking of opportunity costs has been rejected as vicious, disgusting, and just plain immoral. What sort of person would put a price tag on human life, or fail to use medical resources because the prognosis was poor, while the cost was high, or think that a million dollars for each accident prevented was too much? But there are, after all, alternatives that should be foregone and prices that should never be paid. It's not always clear whether evil inheres in monetarizing these considerations or just in thinking of alternatives. Whatever the rationale, economists have not unexpectedly been caught up in the desire to affirm morality by denying its cost. The trouble with social interaction is that it can lead to almost anything. From a time during which the normal values underlying economic action were neglected, these have now been raised to become the cornerstone of a new economics featuring *mirabile dictu* wants that are made meritorious.

We doubt that an ersatz economics will lead to pure politics. The only guarantee that intellectual cogitation will be judged moral is if cogitators do the judging. After studying the history of opportunity costs as the crux (some would say cross) of economic analysis, we review the economic manifestation of imposed solutions, merit wants, noticing how we stray from the main idea of alternatives foregone. In discussions of merit wants, some economists go beyond the traditional public-policy impasse of competing claims, allowing their not-so-invisible hands to offer scratchless solutions to thorny questions. After all, if some wants are meritorious and others are not, the problem of choice is solved without recourse to the old-fashioned notion that what you want has something to do with what you have to give up to get it.

COST IN ECONOMICS

The *International Encyclopedia of the Social Sciences* defines economics as "the study of the allocation of scarce resources among unlimited and competing uses."[1] This interest in scarcity has lent economics its characterization as "the dismal science," and is reflected in definitions found in introductory textbooks. Paul Samuelson writes:

> Economics is the study of how men and society *choose*, with or without the use of money, to employ *scarce* productive resources which could have alternative uses, to produce various commodities over time and distribute them for consumption, now and in the future, among various people and groups in society.[2]

And Walter Nicholson stresses the normative position inherent in economics: "Because resources are scarce, we must be judicious in allocating them among alternative ('competing') uses."[3]

Thus, economics is most broadly involved with use of the resources available to society — resources that potentially have alternative uses in satisfying wide-ranging demands. Efficient production in any sector of society requires combining resources in such a way as to minimize the cost of the output. A specified output should be produced with the least input. A broader view of efficiency is called Pareto Optimality: efficiency is achieved when no move can make one better off without simultaneously making another worse off. But if, as Samuelson says, economic decisions are sometimes made without money, what exactly is "cost"?

The concept of cost lies at the core of economics. Armen Alchian wrote:

> For some purposes the cost of an input is adequately represented by its market price. For others, one must turn to the more fundamental concept of *opportunity cost,* or alternative cost, which states that the cost of employing a unit of a factor of production in any activity is the output lost by the failure to employ that unit in its best alternative use.[4]

As every action has a reaction, any decision involving the use of resources has a cost — the ability to use those resources in another capacity. The pure economist hopes, from his perspective on efficiency, that the value of the action undertaken is greater than that of the forsaken alternative, that, with the objective of economic growth, no matter how it is distributed, the contribution to the economy outweighs its opportunity cost.

Alchian offers as an example the cost to the economy of changing the use to which a tract is put on the outskirts of a city from farming to residences, remarking that the cost of such a change is represented by the land's value as farmland, which in turn depends on its contribution to overall farm output. But "if there were several residential or industrial development plans in each of which the value of the land was higher than in farming, the cost of using it in any one plan would be its highest value in any of the others."[5] The doctrine of opportunity cost demands enumeration and evaluation of cost as the *best* available alternative necessarily foregone, the best being the most productive. Frank Knight turns the whole proposition around, perfectly emphasizing the crucial role of opportunity cost in economics: "Where there is no alternative to a given experience, no choice, there is no economic problem, and cost has no meaning."[6]

This notion of cost is different from that of "expense," "outlay," or "cost of acquisition" as they are normally understood.[7] These terms refer to putting out a specific amount of money. In effect, the opportunity-cost doctrine emphasizes the cost *to society* of using resources — the *social cost.* Alchian suggests, "If resources are used in less than their most valuable ways, their cost will not be covered, and the difference will be an economic loss";[8] Schumpeter speaks of opportunity cost as "an explanation of the fundamental social meaning of costs";[9] and Alchian and Allen say that the "cost of an *action* is the associated *reduction in total wealth.*"[10] All reaffirm the observation that the cost perspective of the economist is societal rather than personal. The loss of business from an old restaurant to a new one, for example, does not involve any economic cost, because no formerly available alternatives are forsaken by society; wealth has merely been transferred. There is a loss of opportunity for the individual, but not to the society as a whole. Opportunity costs, then, are measured, when possible, by contribution to net social product, and as such are considered objective.[11] But, we may ask, to set the stage for later discussion, can something be objective for society (which is, after all, a reification as if it were a person or thing), but not for any of the individuals in it, who may be affected differentially, and feel differently about what happens to national income?

Removed from its societal context, the notion of opportunity cost is intuitively easy to grasp, perhaps having been first presented in the form of the warning, "You can't have your cake and eat it, too." If we choose to see a movie, the cost to us is not just the three-dollar price of admission, but the value of three dollars in some alternative use, plus the time spent at the theater — a leisurely lunch, perhaps. The depth of actual analysis by an individual varies from situation to situation, but in choosing to do any one thing, whether we realize it or not, we are rejecting alternative activities, at least at the same time, usually making at least implicit decisions on how we personally value things by actually giving up some for others. To those interested in economic rationality — the growth rather than the distribution of economic values — the effect on society's productive output as a whole is what counts.

HISTORY

Although the expression "opportunity cost" itself is relatively recent, having first appeared in 1894,[12] the fundamental idea has been evident in and essential to the writings of economic thinkers from Adam Smith on.[13] The question of worth has been the chief interest of economic theory from the start, and Smith was the first of many to hold it to be a function of the cost of production, moving away from more philosophic discussions of merit. In so doing, Smith implicitly embraced the idea of opportunity cost in 1776: "If among a nation of hunters ... it usually costs twice the labor to kill a beaver which it costs to kill a deer, one beaver should naturally exchange for or be worth two deer."[14] A hunter could allocate his time to killing deer, which would cost him the opportunity to kill beaver.

This worth as a function of cost-of-production approach, with its implicit opportunity-cost basis, was further accepted by Ricardo (1814) in dealing with questions of rent and capital stock (valued as a product of previous labor),[15] and even Marx, whose theories relied on a cost-of-labor view of valuation.[16] Although this cost-of-production approach never could handle problems of fixed supply (because its users did not consider that demand would make a difference), or the famous water-diamond paradox (the differing value of the two obviously not being a function of cost of production), it held forth in economic thinking until roughly 1870.

Here enter Jevons, Menger, and Walras, among others, and the *"marginalist* revolution" (1850–1880) begins. The value or utility of a commodity was what anyone was willing to pay for the last unit, hence the marginal theory of value. In consumer preferences, value is set by demand at the margin. Because diamonds were scarce, a few extra diamonds were very valuable, whereas a little more water, with its relative abundance, had little worth. The notion of worth shifted radically from the initial idea of intrinsic value, to cost of production, to a market-determined phenomenon, emphasizing value-in-exchange. What is a commodity worth? Not its essentiality or its cost of production, but what others will give you for it.

Because it emphasized the importance of demand as well as supply in economic analysis, marginalism necessitated a clarification and broadening of the concept of cost, and the Austrian school took up the task.[17] Joseph Schumpeter records that by relating the substitutability of factors of production to marginal utilities,

> the Austrian school arrived at what has been called the alternative-use or opportunity theory of cost — the philosophy of the cost phenomenon that may be expressed by the adage: What a thing really costs us is the sacrifice of the utility of those other things which we could have had from the resource that went into the one we did produce.[18]

As Blaug reemphasized, the Austrian alternative-cost theory "made both demand and supply dependent upon utility by tracing all costs back to utilities foregone."[19] Cost of production depended on value foregone just as demand for one thing meant that another could not simultaneously be acquired with the same resources. If the factors or resources that went into production could be viewed as alternatives, so too could demand for goods and services.

Although the idea of cost as benefits foregone was inherent in Adam Smith's model, it was the explicit analysis of the Austrian school that led to the theory that Roll characterizes as one "of great elegance which seemed to make the whole marginal-utility analysis . . . comprehensive and self-consistent."[20] Schumpeter goes so far as to suggest "the great contribution to the period to 1914 was indeed the theory of opportunity cost. . . ."[21]

Previously focused on either supply or demand, economic theory progressed with Marshall's synthesis in which demand and supply simultaneously determine price, leading to a more dynamic formulation of market exchange.[22] Two variables interacted instead of one being posited. Although Marshall's analysis never clearly contradicted the principle of opportunity cost, because he was primarily interested in explaining price formation, American economist Frank Knight sensed ambiguities in the neoclassical treatment and sought to reaffirm the standard Austrian position.[23] In doing so, he emphasized that the notion of opportunity cost is the only objective one, measured in units of alternate or displaced product, and further that it is not to be confused with "pain" or other undesirable attributes of production experienced by individuals. As the bulk of theoretical economics moved on to other matters, this basic understanding of cost remained intact. From Smith's capitalist interests through Marx's theories of socialism and the Austrians' socialist drift, the idea of opportunity cost had claimed for itself a validity independent of political distinctions.

TEXTS IN THE PRIVATE SECTOR

How do modern texts treat opportunity cost? Outside of cost-benefit analysis, which will be discussed below, the treatment of opportunity cost in the private sector texts is (at first) surprisingly small.[24] In Paul Samuelson's introduction to *Economics,* perhaps the most widely used text, he first discusses opportunity cost on page 443, in a chapter (23) amazingly entitled "Implicit- and Opportunity-Cost Elements: A Digression"![25] His brief discussion is fairly representative of textbooks, correctly conveying the notion that cost of doing one thing is really sacrifice of doing some other thing. Most of these definitions are presented as part of the discussion of the theory of the firm, which is an attempt to explain and predict production and pricing decisions, and therefore to distinguish cost as opportunity cost from "expenses" or the accountant's notion of cost as outlays. Texts then customarily proceed to (or, as in Samuelson's, are preceded by) analysis of such issues as fixed versus variable costs, short-run versus long-run costs, sunk and marginal costs, and others, most often using exactly what the accountant would name "expenses" or "outlays" to represent cost (in resources acquired or price paid). Buchanan has also mentioned this trend in texts: "Opportunity cost tends to be defined acceptably, but the logic of the concept is not normally allowed to enter into and inform the subsequent analytical applications."[26] An exception in some of the works is the discussion of theories of rent and capital, where the alternate use doctrine (owners must consider use of capital or rent elsewhere as part of their costs) is more fully considered.

How is it, then, that economists feel comfortable in presenting material in this less-than-complete way? Two hypotheses appear plausible. One is that the idea of cost as opportunity cost in the private sector is never challenged (it has not drastically changed over the past century) and the economist may feel that one definition of the doctrine will suffice throughout the entire presentation. The second reason, however, may be the more fundamental: just as markets are supposed to do the work of allocating scarce resources for society, so they appear to substitute for thought by economists. As Alchian and Allen write: "Cost of a specified output is defined as the *highest* valued of the alternative forsaken opportunities. The measure of that cost is the market-exchange value of the forsaken output."[27] Thus the market is assumed to do the work for the economist and for us: prices of resources used in production are assumed or argued to adequately reflect their opportunity cost. This explanation is worthy of further discussion, for if markets did not reflect opportunity costs, the inner sanctum of economics might turn out to be empty, or, even worse, contradictory. That is why we must delve deeper, first into what is meant by "cost" and second into what economists might have in mind by "opportunity."

FOUR CONCEPTS OF WORTH

Four notions are commonly confused when people speak of worth: *merit*, as intrinsic value; *usefulness*, as value-in-use, or utility; *exchange rate*, as price or value-in-exchange; and *best alternative*, as opportunity cost. Any of these four may be reflected in an answer to the question, "what's that worth?" Because most economics texts deal with these notions at different parts of their presentations, an explicit and direct comparison here appears useful. Without delving deeply into the exact theoretical history of each concept, what distinctions can we make among them?

Merit (Value)

The idea of merit or intrinsic value is probably the oldest notion of value, and yet is currently the most ignored by economists. It involves a totally individual and subjective evaluation. Based on a notion of worth that is exclusive of a good's usefulness by itself or in exchange, personal valuations of similar objects may vary widely. One's feeling about a family portrait or other heirloom is an easy example, like the classic bronzed pair of baby shoes.

Utility (Usefulness)

For the economist utility has come to mean "the quality of an object which causes it to be viewed as necessary or desirable."[28] The utility of any event, activity, purchase, and so on is determined by an individual weighing its good and bad consequences, its desirable and undesirable characteristics. This, then, too is a subjective notion of value, taking an individual perspective, not the social view of exchange, of what others are willing to give. The difference we seek to stress between this social understanding of utility and our previous discussion of merit is that in utility the situation is somewhat more comparative — the likelihood of individual estimations of worth falling within a specific range is higher, because they are based on more than individual sentiment.

Trying to determine why individuals value things is like trying to explain why some people like vanilla and others eat only chocolate ice cream. Because of this seemingly irreducible element of personal preference (apparently a throwback to intrinsic worth), economists, Nicholson writes, early "turned their attention to value-in-exchange, leaving value-in-use for philosophers."[29] No doubt this desertion of the philosophical field of battle — as if preferences revealed in action answered anyone's questions about where preferences came from or how they were changed — has been detrimental to economics. One windmill to a customer, however, and ours is now worth its relationshp to price.

Price (Exchange Rate)

Exchange rate implies social interaction, involving explicit comparisons between alternatives, presenting itself as somewhat objective (objective in the sense of measurement — widely agreed-upon estimations falling within a range). Price reflects the collectivization of subjective evaluations of any good. It results from exchange, or, as George Stigler says, "The price of a product is simply the terms on which it can be acquired."[30] Of course, nothing so profound as price can be that simple.

Prices are related to marginal utility — the value to the consumer of an additional unit of some commodity. In distinguishing between price (marginal utility) versus total utility (value-in-use), the concept of scarcity is most important. A loaf of bread has a low price because bread is abundant, whereas jade is expensive because it is relatively scarce. Obviously this price says little about the *total* utility of the two items; if one had to choose between a life of no bread or no jade, a continued supply of the staple would surely win out.

Cost as Best Alternative

If economic man exists, he will act on the notion of best alternative or opportunity cost: "the cost of employing a unit of a factor of production in any activity is the output lost by the failure to employ that unit in its best alternative use."

I reemphasize that opportunity cost, as understood here, embodies a notion very different from that of utility or value. Turning to the decision on whether to install a swimming pool, Alchian and Allen say:

[It] yields the pleasure of swimming and keeping cool, but it also involves the undesirable consequences of neighbors' children splashing up the yard. The desirable and undesirable are taken into account in assigning a *personal valuation*, but not the *costs*, of having a pool.[31]

Opportunity costs are not defined as the undesirable or painful consequences of some act, because the latter do not affect alternative opportunities (the highest-valued forsaken option remains the same). Such consequences may reduce the value of the pool, but they do not raise its opportunity costs. "This distinction between (1) undesirable attributes inherent in some event and (2) the highest-valued forsaken option necessary to realize that event is fundamental, for only the latter is cost as the term is used in economics."[32]

Yet, this notion of the highest-valued or best alternative forsaken is troublesome, as we said, because it is impalpable. Limited by one past and multiple futures, can individual decision-makers determine their opportunity costs anything but subjectively? Let us see what opportunity costs would look like if they were merely a matter of opinion.

Elements of Opportunity Cost.   Because estimation of alternatives lies in the future, which will never be realized for a particular person, James Buchanan, for one, argues that individual opportunity costs are purely subjective, reflecting only that person's evaluation of satisfaction he will forego by any action. To see how well his approach holds up, we deem it desirable to disaggregate opportunity cost into its constituent elements: *alternatives, competition, standards* of evaluation, possibility of *failure*, determination of *best, repetition,* and *prediction.* First we approach these seven elements of opportunity cost from the perspective of the individual decision-maker, taking a subjective (individually determined) versus an objective (widely agreed-upon) view. Consider, for illustration, the decision faced by X as to which among a number of items to purchase with an inheritance.

The first and most essential element in determining opportunity cost is recognition of *alternatives,* the notion of substitutability of one action for another. If there are no alternatives, there is no choice to be made, and hence no opportunity cost to action. The individual must first identify the alternatives available to him. Because the number of alternatives may be infinite, and the pain of acquiring information on their existence therefore high, the individual is likely to select some small number for immediate consideration: building a swimming pool, buying a car, or taking a trip around the world. The second element of opportunity cost consists of *competition* among alternatives, instead of, say, selecting the first to come into the decision-maker's mind. To be able to judge such a competition, we need to consider the third element of opportunity cost, the presence of a *standard,* or standards, of evaluation, which allow for a meaningful comparison on some scale, say, how long an individual will enjoy the chosen alternative.

The existence of standards by which to judge competing alternatives leads to a fourth element of opportunity cost, the possibility of *failure*. If some of the alternatives under consideration measure up poorly against others, they may be rejected; for this inheritor, the voyage is rejected as too brief.

The existence of standards also allows the fifth element of opportunity cost to appear, a *best* alternative, that which most strongly meets the standard applied. This individual may finally select the pool as the longest-lasting investment. In determining both worst and best, the evaluation here is totally subjective, and the individual may have difficulty stating operationally how this evaluation was made (some would consider memories of a trip as most lasting). The sixth element of opportunity-cost analysis, *repetition*, applies to the possibility that an individual's evaluation and decision takes place not once or twice but continuously, with outcomes often changing. Finally, the difficulty of evaluation is emphasized by the seventh element of opportunity cost, *prediction*. The alternatives forsaken, because they have been rejected (or just ignored) may not materialize. Their evaluation as well as that of the chosen option is based on the individual's experience with pools, cars, and trips, involving a prediction about how lasting each would be. In the end, only the consequences of the act actually chosen are experienced.

Applying these elements of opportunity costs is plainly a subjective exercise of little use to anyone but the decision-maker himself. Different people might apply different standards to the same alternatives, such as ability to share the item with others. Further, the individual is liable to ignore other available alternatives, perhaps purchase of a cottage in the mountains. Is the doctrine of opportunity cost doomed to such limited relevance?

OPPORTUNITY COST AND MARKETS

Economics texts, we said, though ignoring intrinsic merit altogether, plainly and freely substitute price for the notion of costs. Utility, too, it seems, gets replaced by exchange, as evidenced by one text's dictum: "For our purposes, the *value* of a good to a person *is* the exchange rate. . . ." The substitution is not new; Von Wieser wrote in 1914:

> In daily intercourse economic exchange value has completely overshadowed both personal exchange-value and utility-value. It is this to which men refer when they speak of value pure and simple. When one asks what certain goods are worth, he expects and is given the figure for their market value.[33]

The mechanism that provides the magic for this substitution of cost for value and value for price in economic analysis is, of course, the market. And a market is a mechanism by which offers to purchase or sell different quantities of a good at various terms are known. Is the market's magic real or sleight of hand?

Market Price as an Indicator of Opportunity Cost

Most economists use price, the market's reflection of exchange, in their general discussions of economic analysis for several reasons. The first was offered as early as 1888 by Von Wieser: "Exchange value is . . . without doubt the most important form of value, inasmuch as it governs the largest sphere — that of industrial economy generally."[34] Von Wieser wrote elsewhere that as societies became increasingly productive, the number of exchanges made drastically increased, with the consequent manifestation of value in exchange as true economic value.[35] Certainly it was obvious that the market represented the largest sphere of economic activity, and its valuation was therefore difficult to ignore.

Another reason for using the market price of goods or factors of production is its ease of calculation. Witness Von Wieser's analysis of markets:

> It is easy to understand that this value, uniformly the same for all persons interested, should obscure in common parlance all personal valuations. There is a social accord in regard to this value and its numerical expression which is clear and unequivocal. Compared with it, all other expressions of value are matters of sentiment, having standards which are personally experienced but are not readily susceptible to accurate interpretation.[36]

In a world of mixed motives and haphazard action, clarity and accord are two values readily embraced. But to say that there is no better mechanism is not to say that we can accept price as the private sector's reflection of value. There is a more appropriate question: is the market's substitution of price for cost correct, or at least appropriate?

Why should we accept price as indicative of opportunity cost? The underlying reasoning, according to Alchian:

> If some productive resources are used in ways that yield less than their highest achievable alternative, or "opportunity" values, these uses will not cover cost. The incentive to increase one's wealth induces shifts of resources to their higher-valued use until their cost is at least matched by the value of their currently yielded product.[37]

Why, a whole theology is there — a theory of human motivation (the incentive to increase wealth) and a vision of the promised land (the highest achievable alternative). All that is missing is divine guidance, which is supplied by Blaug in the name of the eternal equilibrium.

The costs of producing a commodity reflect nothing but the competing offers of other producers for the services of the factors to produce it; they represent the payments needed to attract the factors from their next most remunerative employment. In equilibrium, the marginal productivity of resources in all uses and the alternative opportunities foregone from producing an increment of any commodity will be equalized.[38]

In other words, if the standard conditions for competition are operational, the market tends to equilibrate price and cost; if the price of a good falls below cost, the factors of its production will be shifted (bid away) to a more productive use, and if price rises above costs, profits provide capital for subsequent use of these resources. Market price, in equilibrium, untouched, as it were, by human hands, seems to adequately represent opportunity cost, the best (read "most productive") alternative use.

The Market and the Elements of Opportunity Cost

Applying the seven elements of opportunity-cost analysis to the market offers a more mundane explanation. The existence of a market implies the presence of *alternatives;* if there were no alternatives, there could be no exchange, and if there is no possibility for exchange, there is no need for a market. A large number of individuals are able to derive multiple and often ingenious (alternative) uses of resources. And because a wide range of (alternative) resources may be able to satisfy any production idea, the number of options available in a market is extremely large, and constantly changing. Resources, however, are limited, introducing the second element of opportunity costs, *competition,* into the market setting. The offers for resources, representing alternative uses, must compete with each other, which means that property rights must not be monopolized.

Although we assume individuals in the market make their offers considering the value to them of having an extra unit of the resource desired, the market as a system holds firmly to one *standard* in judging alternatives: the highest bid or offer is the one to be accepted. *Failure* is thus experienced by those alternatives whose bids fall below the highest, the latter, of course, representing the fifth element of opportunity cost, or *best* alternative. Yet this analysis seems to leave us once again with a subjective *prediction* — made by competing individuals as to the use and subsequent value of the resources in question — which is not very different from our previous example. The only wider or more social aspect of opportunity-cost calculation seen so far is that more alternatives may become known in a market setting than by individual deliberation.

To analyze the market in this way, however, is to ignore the fact that markets are supposed to work their will in time. Whereas evaluation of alternatives and decisions by an individual customarily occurs within a limited time, evaluation in the market is *repetitive* as participants adjust and readjust their bids in response to the offers of others. Although the standard never changes, the best offer clearly may. Consider the individual who made the best offer for a resource. If he has overestimated the value of that resource to him, and consequently the good he produces with the acquired resources cannot bring in the amount of money necessary to continue in operation (to engage in further exchange; to trade money for labor or to compete successfully with others trading for a type of labor), he has failed. The market's notion of best may then be corrected downward by new educated bids, which reflect the fact that the previous level was too high to enable successful transformation of the resource into the profit necessary to continue in exchange. Individuals, then, receive signals from market activity.

A market's acceptance of an alternative as best is supposed to depend upon that alternative representing in the long run the most productive use of the resource in question. The higher one's bid for a resource, the more productive its use must be, in order to cover the cost. *Best, then, takes on a systemic meaning; it results from many interactions evaluated over a period of time, interactions that tend to make individual calculations conform to the experientially derived highest worth of a resource.* Viewed in this systemic fashion, resources are in equilibrium when bid away to their highest (most productive) use. As such, the amount successfully offered for a resource, or its price, tends to coincide in the long run with its opportunity cost, or best alternative use. *It is thus the system that is rational, not necessarily the individuals in it.*

Returning to the seventh element of opportunity cost, we find that *prediction* resulting from market observation takes on a broader significance. The ranking of alternatives has resulted from a large number of trials; it is objective in that it tends to be widely agreed upon by those exchanging in a market. Agreement is based on the fact that the market price is the price; the individual may not accept it as the price he anticipated, or an ideal price, but it is the terms on which a resource can be acquired. With this agreement, it becomes possible for the economist to predict the product displaced by any production decision — to predict the reduction in output elsewhere that comes about as a result of using resources in any particular way. The next highest price offered for the resource required is, of course, the measure of the best alternative foregone. Thus, although the concept of cost is not necessarily tied to a market, measurement efforts usually are, as we seek to make use of data on whose interpretation agreement is broader.

Market Price and Other Concepts of Worth

The argument for market price effectively reflecting value, either as utility or intrinsic merit, is similar. In the market, if the price of a good falls below its value to some people, those who value it will, presumably, offer more for it, which will eventually raise the price to this higher figure. If the price is greater than the value of the good to others, consumption will (in theory) fall off until the price returns to a level more in line with consumers' valuation. Von Wieser, once again, offers a philosophical argument as to why price equals value. He presents the case of someone who values an item more than its market price, and thus retains it for personal use. Here, it appears, is an irrefutable counterexample: if goods have intrinsic (only the insensitive would say sentimental) value, equilibrium will not operate, the market will fail to clear so as to maximize national income, and economics is undermined. Have no fear; Von Wieser is equal to the task. One need only imagine a situation (tragic, but true to life) of financial disaster in which conditions compel our formerly sentimental man to revert to his underlying real self as economic man. Price, or value as price in exchange, is like death and taxes: hard to avoid in the long run.[39]

Although overall value-in-use does conform to market price, individuals do not have to enter the market to sell goods, and, therefore, do often implicitly value things at more than their market price. Only when there is agreement to trade would anyone who valued something at less than its market price and still retained possession be irrational.

In the economy, to be sure, an economic loss ensues when values are not maintained. The market price can thus be viewed as an aid to calculation for the individual, in that it provides him with a clear alternative to his valued use of a good, an alternative he is certainly free to reject if it fails to meet his personal valuation. How free, of course, depends on his overall resource position, a personal consideration of little interest to theorists of economic markets, until, as we shall see, they enter the social realm.

Opportunity Cost as the Best Indicator of Worth

Thus worth as forsaken alternatives is a crucial concept. Like price, it involves an interactive mode of analysis, it is competitive (and thus allows for the possibility of failure), and therefore it is broader and richer in evaluation than concepts of merit or utility, which are more subjective and hence self-protective. Opportunity cost is also broader than price, for although we can speak of alternatives forsaken without reference to price (I think I'll go swim instead of taking a nap), we can't really think of prices without referring to alternatives (prices being derived from alternative offers in the market).

As the individual starts to use market signals as part of his subjective evaluation (he may know that he wants a recording until he finds out that it is quite expensive), we begin to get at the concept of alternatives in a more objective or social sense, reflecting more widely agreed-upon estimations. And, continuing in this direction, we arrive at the primary value of economics as a social subject exclusive of any decision-maker. Economics studies and estimates the best alternative use of resources that is foregone by any production decision. Though there are difficulties in calculation, the principle is unbending. Even Buchanan accepts this view, commenting that "cost is objective in any theory that involves genuine prediction."[40]

In general, evaluation of any activity is best accomplished by multiple, external, independent, and repetitive analysis, and the determination of the opportunity cost of resources by market interaction meets these criteria, as (multiple) individuals (independently) react, repetitively, to the (external) prices that result from market exchange. With this contribution, attempts by economists to preserve the range of market activity are understandable — the more alternatives the market allows individuals to collectively value, the more information results.

COST IN THE PUBLIC SECTOR

In view of its seemingly successful approach, it is tempting to embrace market price as a model for determining opportunity cost in any activity. Yet, the market is able to ignore effects (pollution, for example) that its offers do not capture. One need only recognize that it owes success to the simplicity of its goal — efficiency — to realize that transplanting the market mode of evaluation to other areas of decision-making may be unfortunate.

Recognizing this difference between private and public costs may lead to challenging the correspondence of price to opportunity cost, so that, Edwin Mansfield says,

> The social costs of producing a given commodity do not always equal the private costs, which are defined as costs to the individual producer. For example, a steel plant may discharge waste products into a river located near the plant. To the plant, the cost of disposing of the wastes is simply the amount paid to pump the wastes to the river. However, if the river becomes polluted, and if its recreational uses are destroyed and the water becomes unfit for drinking, additional costs are incurred by other people. Differences of this sort between private and social cost occur frequently.[41]

These social costs are frequently called externalities (having effects on individuals external to the consumer), and are not usually sold in the market, resulting in their possible neglect. Evidently, if we are to accept the results, these social costs must be reintegrated into market considerations.

The market's difficulty in recognizing values as derived from considerations other than those based on efficiency is similarly limiting. In the private sector, as Frank Knight observes, "Price 'tends' to coincide with value, but the notion of value also involves a norm to which price would conform under some ideal conditions."[42] The conditions necessary for perfect operation of the market are rarely present; lack of information, subsidies, and trade restrictions, among other influences, result in prices that are not perfect reflections of value.[43]

Arguing that the market is better at allocation than valuation, is a view that implicitly equates price with opportunity cost, but not with worth.[44] Phillip Klein emphasizes that preferences may be distorted by corporate concentration of power. Goods may move to their most productive use, but the decisions on production are seen as derived from consumer preferences, manipulated by advertising. If preferences are manipulated, or if markets are not ideal, two things are to be done: one is to reform markets so that they do a better job of forming preferences, and the other is to manipulate markets in a better way; the doctrine of social wants seeks improvement whereas merit wants, as we shall see, tries manipulation.

More alarming is the market's failure to embrace at all issues other than efficiency — such as distribution of income, which raises the broader question of whether we can claim market results to be objective for society if they are not for the individuals in it. Economic rationality does not always know best; it may be efficient to execute all criminals instead of jailing them, but the moral consequences of such a policy far outweigh the strictly economic calculus. Though it is never wrong to be rational, it can be dangerous to follow one rationality when another is the more appropriate.

In attempting to transplant the principle of opportunity cost to the public sector we encounter further resistance. In the private sector, as we have noticed, the cost of a good is usually conceived of (and almost always measured as) the price paid for it in market exchange. But government-produced goods (public goods) are not traded on the market; provision is determined by politics. A decision is made that we need some good or service the market is failing to supply, or supplying in less than an optimal quantity, and the government invokes the power to transfer resources necessary to produce it. Thus there is no market allocating mechanism to assist us in arriving at an efficient level of production, nor to bestow an objective (collective) value on the goods. And although we frequently can price what we put into public goods, this price is obviously not the same as the value of the benefits bestowed; inputs are not necessarily outcomes. The salary paid to a teacher is not necessarily an indication of ability to teach reading, and certainly is no indication of improvement in the educational ability of students.

Obviously the concept of public expenditures requires a broader understanding of cost than economists have come to embrace in private-sector analysis. Social values, such as liberty and equality, are often deemed more important than any specific dollar expenditure. And, where they conflict, more of one may mean less of another. How might economists using opportunity costs contribute to policy analysis in this complex social framework?

The existence and recognition of alternatives makes a contribution to the evaluation of any decison, public or private. Allowing for alternatives permits competition, failure, and hence learning and regeneration.

For public-sector analysis, then, the opportunity-cost doctrine offers two clear principles. First, if a private market price exists, even if it is for only a portion of the resources required to produce the public good, it has to be recognized as at least a minimum cost to be outweighed by some other value. Thus the cost of a police-community relations program may be greater than the salaries of the officers (crime and private property loss may go up on beats abandoned by the newly assigned officers), but we must initially recognize and accept that we are valuing the better community relations at least more than, say, the one million dollars in salary reallocated. With the difficulty not only of measuring, but even of identifying alternatives, we should make whatever limited use we can of market information, that widely agreed-upon measure of alternative cost, price. Second, whether or not relevant prices exist, the logic of cost as alternative dictates we recognize that, subject to budget constraints as we are, the cost of any government program is other programs foregone by use of resources. The cost of adding teachers in a vocational school may be the number of new textbooks that could alternatively have been purchased, or it may be two jobs in the private sector for the school's graduates, jobs produced by leaving tax resources in the private economy. The cost of a syphilis-eradication program may be a gonorrhea-eradication program, or it may be a new public tennis court. This approach obviously involves complex problems of conceptualization and calculation, because the market is not likely to offer an alternative, but that is all the more reason for the analyst to be worried about alternative uses of resources (trade-offs of economic growth for income redistribution, for example) involved in policy. With Mancur Olson, we agree that here microeconomic theory becomes, "more nearly a theory of rational behavior than a theory of material goods."[45]

ECONOMICS IN THE PUBLIC SECTOR:
PUBLIC GOODS AND MERIT WANTS

Economists have approached public policy issues in many ways, often moving from a predictive position (such and such will happen if you do such and such) to a normative one (government *should* do this). A discussion of two such proposals, that government should provide social wants (or public goods) and merit wants is in Richard Musgrave's classic public finance text, in a chapter entitled "A Multiple Theory of the Public Household"; other economists have reflected the views held by Musgrave.

We now turn to these two "economic" considerations in an attempt to de-cipher just how much economics there is behind them — that is, we ask how closely to the market and the principle of cost as alternatives fore-gone do these concepts adhere.

Social Wants (Public Goods)

Discussing the allocative role of government, Richard Musgrave defines "social wants" as

> those wants satisfied by services that must be consumed in equal amounts by all. People who do not pay for the services can not be excluded from the benefits, that result, and since they cannot be excluded they will not engage in voluntary payments. Hence the market can not satisfy such wants. Budgetary provision is needed if they are to be satisfied at all.[46]

Nonrival goods (my enjoyment of the service does not reduce yours) and nonexclusive goods (it is difficult to prevent others from enjoying all or part of the service provided) present pure social want. As Musgrave points out, though, the distinction between private and social wants is usually not of an absolute sort; it is essentially one involving the degree to which costs or benefits of some activity affect those other than the direct "consumers." Smith's education helps him get a job, and, because he is able to find work, I do not have to help subsidize him by an income-transfer program. Part of the benefit of his education accrues to me in the form of tax savings.

When satisfaction of a want creates large "spillover" benefits for other members of society, it tends to be underproduced by those who value only their own gain. Because all share a want, whether they pay or not, they lack incentive to pay the full cost. Members of society who benefit from such spillovers may not express their true preference for the service in question, fearing that they will be forced to pay more for it. Mancur Olson names this the "free-rider problem," in which the weak often exploit the strong: knowing that others must support an activity, they can get away with not paying their share. Unions seek closed shops in part to make such free riders pay. Inefficiencies occur because benefits cannot be related to costs. The difficulty is not that individuals are exploited by so-ciety or that they are not able to calculate their interests correctly but, knowing their interest all too well, they share public goods without pay-ing for their private benefits. Economists suggest that in such a situation the government must step in if an optimal amount of the public good — what individuals would want if they had to pay — is to be provided.

Opportunity cost is alive and well in this discussion as Musgrave ex-plicitly states his feeling for alternatives: "The central issue in the theory of public expenditures, and, indeed, in the theory of public finance, is how to determine the proper level and pattern of public services. Putting it differently, the question is how available resources should be divided be-tween the satisfaction of 'private' and 'social' wants."[47] He desires to correct inefficiencies, the potential loss if public goods remain solely in the private domain.

The analysis itself relies on opportunity costs. The normative theory of public goods begins with consumer preferences as obtained and expressed in market interactions, accepting the alternative chosen by members of society. There is competition and hence failure of alternatives to gain acceptance. The standard for evaluation is initially whether or not members of society are willing to pay for any amount of the good, qualified by a prediction as to the likely underevaluation of the good by individuals. Such a prediction results from estimating the amount of benefits that spill over because some pay for this good and partly from observation of rational behavior in the market: avoid paying when you can.

Based as it is on the idea of alternatives as reflected in market operations, the concept of social wants for public goods is arguably economic. Markets are imperfect, not immoral. Consumers are entitled to their preferences. Although they do not usually claim to give precise information on the amount of a good the government should produce, economists can argue that corrective policy is required to secure an allocation of resources that is (hypothetically, at least) in line with consumer preferences. Real markets are giving way to imaginary ones but, in conception, they are still markets. The next temptation is to substitute intellectual imagination for market interaction.

Merit Wants

Social wants, which would reflect real preferences if a market were available, give way to merit wants, which are good, according to Musgrave, precisely because peoples' preferences are not preferable.

> A different type of intervention occurs when public policy aims at an allocation of resources which deviate from that reflected by consumer sovereignty. In other words, wants are satisfied that could be serviced through the market but are not, since consumers choose to spend their money on other things. The reason for budgetary action in this case is *not* to be found in the technical difficulties that arise because certain services are consumed by all. Separate amounts of individual consumption are possible. The reason, then, for budgetary action is to correct individual choice. Wants satisfied under these conditions constitute a second type of public wants, and will be referred to as *merit wants*.[48]

In short, merit wants "become public wants if considered so meritorious that their satisfaction is provided for through the public budget, over and above what is provided through the market and paid for by private buyers."[49] Instead of following consumer preferences, merit wants seeks to shape them. As examples of government services aimed at merit wants, Musgrave offers publicly provided school luncheons, subsidized low-cost housing, and free education, and as an example of discouraging an undesirable ("demerit") want, penalty taxation of liquor.

So defined, five elements of merit wants may be distinguished: *preference distortion,* consequent *under- or overproduction* of the merit good, *knowledge of a correct or better preference* that represents *altruistic consumption* for others and hence justifies *preference interference.* Let's examine each in a little more detail.

Preference distortion   In the first major review of the merit goods idea in the economic literature, John Head stressed that in Musgrave's treatment "preference maps of individuals are no longer taken as given, but are themselves subject to critical scrutiny."[50] Merit wants analysis thus turns its back on consumer preferences in markets, the argument being that these preferences in some instances are distorted by incomplete or inaccurate information (consumers don't know their own minds), or worse, irrationality (people don't know what's good for them).[51] Musgrave suggests that "In the modern economy, the consumer is subject to advertising, screaming at him through the media of mass communication and designed to sway his choice rather than to give complete information."[52] Because all that follows depends on distortion of preferences, its existence is the essential element of merit wants.

We observe that when specific merit wants are discussed, they often involve redistribution of income. The distortion of preference may not be by the direct consumers of the good, but by those, namely, taxpayers, providing it. Poor people may want to buy housing, but lack the resources, which could come from government subsidies. When it is said that preferences are distorted, the statement may sometimes be taken to mean that poor people want things they can't have but would get if they had more money.

Under- or Overproduction of Merit Goods   Because the preferences of consumers are distorted, the market is unable to provide the merit good; it doesn't receive the signals it would need to respond correctly. The good may be underprovided (a merit good) or overprovided (a demerit good). Discussion is on either the level at which the good is provided, or, in some cases, on whether it should be provided at all.

Knowledge of a Correct or Better Preference   Someone must know what a correct preference is so that distortion in others can be recognized. Who that might be and how they might legitimate their claims raises the most intriguing questions about merit wants.

Altruistic Consumption   That an individual or a group of individuals would want to interfere in the preference patterns of others requires that they have something to gain by doing it and that they believe in the interest of these others. Pulsipher argues that merit goods have externalities, like social goods, but that they are "psychic."[53] This is an example of what economists call "interdependence of utilities," meaning that the individual who interferes with the preferences of others derives satisfaction from their consumption of the merit goods. This psychic consumption must be altruistic, for otherwise it would not differ from suppression by oppression. Interference is justified on the grounds that some people know what is best and also want to do what is best for others. Again cogitation is elevated over interaction.

Preference Interference "The implementation of such wants," Elisha Pazner writes, "involves to some extent imposing on individuals choices that they would not otherwise make."[54] Such imposition is intended to raise or lower the consumption of a good. There must be, therefore, some kind of institutional ability to provide or constrain consumption.

How close, then, is merit wants to opportunity costs? About as far as you can get.

How does merit wants deal with *resource scarcity?* It doesn't. If goods are intrinsically meritorious, they ought to be provided by government. How are *alternatives* to be generated? By people who know better than we do. By what *standards* would goods be judged meritorious? Automatic acceptance of markets gives way to uncritical acceptance of government. How *failure* in government is recognized and corrected receives no discussion. Failure must be what we do now, because it has not led to provision of goods and services that are meritorious. When someone tells you that a thing is good for you, you want to know why. Yet no general principles are offered for judging which preferences are distorted and which are meritorious. In a word, if we are told to leave it all to politics, why do we need economics?

What, then, is a successful application of merit wants? One situation Musgrave suggests — "interference in the preference patterns of families may be directed at protecting the interest of minors" — presents the problem: without standards, how does one know what is "in the interest of minors?" Baumol's complaint (echoing Mill) must be considered: "I want badly to be protected from those who are convinced that they know better than I what is really good for me, and I want others to receive similar protection."[55]

People might choose correctly if they knew what was good for them, so that it is difficult, without experience, to say what they would have done had they known better. Were people compelled to experience situations contrary to their preferences, they might learn to like it. Something of the sort is suggested in the Musgraves' text when they say that "Given incomplete consumer information, temporarily imposed consumption choice may be desirable as part of a learning process, so as to permit more intelligent free choice thereafter."[56]

The *predictive* part of opportunity costs, built on preferences, gives way to a different sort of calculation: what would people really like, even if they don't know it yet? This compulsory learning led Cuyler to consider and reject *"ex post"* evaluation by a merit-good coerced individual, who would be compelled to make complex calculations about past occurrences and feelings, which because of time and distance are not likely to be accurate.[57] It remains true, of course, that past policies shape future preferences; new experiences do matter. But who is to decide what sort of experience we now think we wouldn't like would be good for us? Would people prefer to expand their horizons by, as it were, being forced to be free?

Two ways come to mind of correcting the distorted preference by injecting a clearer conception of alternatives into merit wants. Charles McLure mentions one: if imperfect information is the problem, why not provide more information in place of a merit good?[58] Educating the consumer might prove less costly than having government provide the good, and further would result in consideration of a wider range of alternatives and a subsequent refinement of ideas about the good in question. If lack of resources is part of the problem (as with low-income housing), a subsidy could be given along with the relevant information.

The idea of alternatives can be injected into consideration of merit wants in another way. If the interdependence of utilities is important in providing merit goods (if my imposition of preferences on you makes me feel good), then the cost of not providing them is an unhappy element in society. Merit becomes a payment to buy off discontent. When redistributive aspects are involved in provision of a merit good, it could be argued that the alternative is a less stable society. Back again to politics, to man acting as a collective as opposed to an individual being. In sum, because the concept of merit wants ignores cost, rejects consumer preferences, and has no standards of applicability, it is appropriate to ask who is to determine the provision of merit wants, for we have no other questions left.

Merit Wants: Who Decides?

How do we allocate the right to coerce? Musgrave is on both sides of this issue. When discussing *social* wants, his reliance on the political system is always clearly relayed: "A political process must be substituted for the market mechanism, and individuals must be made to adhere to the group decision."[59] "Budgetary provision for social goods does mean that the supply of such goods and the assignment of their cost must be determined through the tax-expenditure process of government."[60] "It is thus left to the 'art' of politics to establish a workable system of preference determination and tax assessment."[61]

But in discussing derivation of merit wants, Musgrave does not explicitly refer to governmental processes, and seems to indicate that the "choosers" may come from a group overlapping (but not necessarily coterminous with) government, so long as they are leaders in an otherwise democratic society. Musgrave writes, "while consumer sovereignty is the general rule, situations may arise, within the context of a democratic community, where an informed group is justified in imposing its decision upon others."[62] Searching for an acceptable political principle, Musgrave associates determination of *social* goods with 'majority rule,' adding, "in the case of merit wants, however, the very purpose may be one of interference by some, presumably the majority, into the want pattern of others." If this sounds like a Supreme Court justice trying not to extend a right too far, the Musgrave and Musgrave text confirms the elusiveness of the arbiter: "even a democracy such as ours has aspects of an autocratic society, where it is considered proper that the elite (however defined) should impose its preferences."[63]

If Musgrave isn't exactly sure who will make the merit-goods decisions, others, extrapolating from his work, have ideas. Head spends a great deal of time analyzing reasons why political elites (party leaders, and others) would rarely arrive at the right decisions (too busy winning elections, for instance),[64] Cuyler sarcastically suggests an elite "possessing some distinguishing characteristic (such as great intelligence, sensibility, compassion, party membership, race) ought to impose its preferences,"[65] and Pazner finds that for analysis it is best to postulate "a perfectly informed elite on the shoulders of which rests the responsibility of social policy."[66] Two thousand years of political theory are thus abridged without going beyond (or indeed, doing as well as) Plato, who was far more aware of the possibilities of elites ruling in their own interest.

Although presented on the subject of social-discount rates and not merit wants, Turvey's reasoning suggests the dangers:

> My personal feeling is that the value judgments [of economists on discounts rates] are, by and large, better than those by non-economists. My assertion about value judgments is not as arrogant as it sounds. For one thing, it applies only to the sort of value judgments involved in public investment decisions, and even here it does not apply to all of them. . . . The point is simply that the people who are experienced at systematic thinking about a problem are usually those who make the best judgment about it. Thus whatever their theory of aesthetics, most people are prepared in practice to accept the judgment of an art critic about the merits of a painting.[67]

Looking at a modern museum, the consequences of this abandonment of choice to experts are clear enough. But Turvey, at least, is trying to find a place, if not for economics, at least for economists.

Aside from the observed fact that politicians rarely allow economists to decide for them, why should anyone think that judgments about the cost of money, the interest rate that asks how we value the future compared to the present, should be turned over to professors who do not represent the people? There must be a better way to delimit the domain of applicability so that economics, à la Musgrave, is not turned into politics or, à la Turvey, becomes a substitute for it.

Conclusions for Policy Analysis

We have argued that economic contributions to policy analysis can best be judged by the degree to which they adhere to opportunity costs. Economics provides information on at least one aspect of the alternatives involved in removing resources from the private sphere — their price. Economics can make adjustments to some prices, and derive others by proxy to allow a better representation of the costs of some government activities, although the further such analysis gets from price, the direct result of market activity, the less accurate it becomes. (As Steiner says, expressing a caution that should be a universal with economists toiling in the public sector, "I would rather measure only what I have confidence in measuring with some accuracy and leave 'incommensurables' to be decided upon by explicit choice." Where no prices exist, or where those derived receive little agreement, economics has little to offer to policy analysis beyond the principle of cost as alternatives foregone, a principle urging decision-makers to recognize that the cost of maximizing any one value (such as redistribution) may be minimizing others (stability). Prices may be merely economic; alternatives are the essence of rationality. Without alternatives, recognition of error would be irrelevant, for there would be no means of correction. Rejecting consumer preferences, analysis of merit wants loses the very foundation of its science — sequential modification of error — and its emphasis on externalities of consumption and interdependence of utilities reflects merely a jargonized description of politics. Yet, as politics, the proposition that some wants are more meritorious than others has neither theoretical foundation nor operational implications.

How do we agree on what is meritorious? It is better to ask people what is right for them, better to rely on social interaction in markets to set up institutions for that expression, better, we feel, to rely on political bargaining than on planning, as if through intellectual cogitation we could imagine what people should want and how to give it to them. Giving thorny questions technical auras does not solve them, as we shall see in studying the differences over social structure that shape environmental policy, it merely postpones the prick of the thorns.

NOTES

1. Armen Alchain, "Cost," *International Encyclopedia of the Social Sciences* Vol. 4 (1958), p. 472.
2. Paul Samuelson, *Economics* (New York: McGraw-Hill, 1976), p. 5.
3. Walter Nicholson, *Microeconomic Theory* (Hinsdale, Illinois: Dryden Press, 1972), p. 5.
4. Armen Alchian, op. cit., p. 477.

5. Ibid.
6. Frank Knight, "Notes on Utility and Cost," mimeograph, University of Chicago, 1935, p. 18, cited in James Buchanan, *Cost and Choice*, Chicago: Markham, 1969.
7. The distinction will be further developed below.
8. *International Encyclopedia*, Vol. 3, p. 406.
9. Joseph Schumpeter, *History of Economic Analysis* (New York: Oxford University Press, 1964), p. 917.
10. Armen Alchian and William Allen, *Exchange and Production Theory in Use* (New York: Wadsworth, 1977), p. 228.
11. For a discussion of an alternative view, that all costs are subjective, see Buchanan, op. cit.
12. David I. Green, "Pain Cost and Opportunity Cost," *Quarterly Journal of Economics*, Vol. 8 (January 1894), pp. 218–229.
13. Most of this survey is drawn from Nicholson, op. cit., Schumpeter, op. cit., and Mark Blaug, *Economic Theory in Retrospect* (Homewood, Ill: Richard D. Irwin, 1962).
14. Adam Smith, *The Wealth of Nations*, Andrew Skinner, ed. (Harmondsworth, Middlesex Eng.: Pelican, 1970), p. 47.
15. David Ricardo, *Principles of Political Economy and Taxation* (New York: Dutton, Everyman Press, 1933), chapter 1, section 1.
16. Karl Marx, *Capital* (Newark: International, 1967), Vol. 1, chapter 1.
17. See for example, Frederich Von Wieser, *Natural Value*, William Smart and Christian A. Mallock, eds., reprint of 1893 ed. (New York: Kelly Press), Book V, chapters 1 and 2, especially pp. 171–176.
18. Schumpeter, op. cit., p. 917.
19. Blaug, op. cit., p. 492. He suggests reading Wicksteed's *Common Sense of Political Economy* (London: G. Routledge, 1933, 1910), pp. 391 ff.
20. Eric Roll, *History of Economic Thought* (Chicago: Richard D. Irwin, 1974), p. 404.
21. Schumpeter, op. cit., p. 1044.
22. Alfred Marshall, *Principes d' Economique Politique*, 2 vols. (Gordon 1971).
23. See especially Frank Knight, "A Suggestion for Simplifying the Statement of the General Theory of Price," *Journal of Political Economy*, Vol. 36 (June 1928), 353–370.
24. For a list of the texts reviewed, see Bibliography. Indeed it is difficult to find any general articles on opportunity cost, theory, or history, written after Knight. A review of the American Economic Association Index from 1887 to the present and the Social Science Index from 1947 on turned up very little. James Buchanan has a fairly full treatment in his *Cost and Choice*, but it is written from a somewhat specialized perspective.
25. Samuelson, op. cit., p. 443.
26. Buchanan, op. cit., p. ix.
27. Alchian and Allen, op. cit., p. 234.
28. *Encyclopedia Britannica*, p. 344.
29. Nicholson, op. cit., p. 7.
30. George J. Stigler, *The Theory of Price*, 3rd ed. (New York: Macmillan, 1966), p. 22.
31. Alchian and Allen, op. cit., p. 22.
32. *International Encyclopedia*, Vol. 3, p. 404.
33. Friedrich Von Wieser, *Social Economics*, 1914, p. 234.
34. Von Wieser, *Natural Value*, 1893, p. 53. ftn.
35. Von Wieser, *Social Economics*, op. cit., A. F. Hinricks, trans., reprint of 1927 ed. (New York: Kelly Press, 1967).

36. Ibid., p. 234.
37. *International Encyclopedia*, Vol. 3, p. 405.
38. Blaug, op. cit., p. 492.
39. Von Wieser, *Social Economics*, p. 232.
40. Buchanan, op. cit., p. ix.
41. Edwin Mansfield, *Microeconomics: Theory and Applications* (New York: Norton, 1975) 1970, pp. 157–158.
42. Frank Knight, *The Ethics of Competition* (Chicago: University of Chicago Press, 1935), p. 245.
43. See, for example, Roland McKeon's piece on "The Use of Shadow Prices" in Samuel Chase, Jr., ed. *Problems in Public Expenditure Analysis,* Washington, D.C., Brookings Institution National Committee on Government Finance, Studies in Government Finance, 1968.
44. Phillip A. Klein, "Economics: Allocation or Valuation," *Journal of Economic Issues,* Vol. 8, No. 4 (December 1974).
45. Mancur Olson, Jr., "Economics, Sociology, and the Best of All Possible Worlds," *Public Interest* (Summer 1968), pp. 96–118.
46. Richard Musgrave, *The Theory of Public Finance* (New York: McGraw-Hill, 1969), p. 8.
47. Musgrave, "Public Expenditures," in *International Encyclopedia of the Social Sciences* (1968), Vol. 13, p. 156.
48. Ibid., p. 9.
49. Ibid., p. 13.
50. John G. Head, "On Merit Goods," *Finanzarchiv,* Vol. 25, No. 1 (1966), p. 2.
51. Ibid., p. 4.
52. Musgrave, *The Theory of Public Finance,* op. cit., p. 14.
53. Allan G. Pulsipher, "The Properties and Relevancy of Merit Goods," *Finanzarchiv,* Vol. 30, No. 2 (1971), p. 276.
54. Elisha Pazner, "Merit Wants and the Theory of Taxation," *Public Finance,* Vol. 27, No. 4 (1972), p. 461.
55. Peggy and Richard Musgrave, *Public Finance in Theory and Practice* (New York: McGraw-Hill, 1973), p. 81.
56. Ibid.
57. A. Culyer, "Merit Goods and the Welfare Economics of Coercion," *Public Finance,* Vol. 26, No. 4 (1971), p. 565.
58. Charles E. McLure, Jr., "Merit Wants: A Normatively Empty Box," *Finanzarchiv,* Vol. 27, No. 3 (1968), p. 481.
59. Musgrave, *The Theory of Public Finance,* op. cit., pp. 10–11.
60. Musgrave, "Public Expenditures," op. cit., p. 159.
61. Ibid.
62. Musgrave, *The Theory of Public Finance,* op. cit., p. 14.
63. Musgrave and Musgrave, op. cit., p. 81.
64. Head, op. cit., pp. 23, 27.
65. Culyer, op. cit., pp. 546–547.
66. Pazner, op. cit., p. 462.
67. Ralph Turvey, "Present Values Versus Internal Rate of Return — An Essay in the Theory of the Third Best," *Economic Journal* (March 1963), pp. 93–98. Notice that Musgrave does admit later that the satisfaction of merit remains "a precarious task," and that authoritarian determination is not permissible. Musgrave, *The Theory of Public Finance,* op. cit.

CHAPTER 8

ECONOMY AND ENVIRONMENT
RATIONALITY AND RITUAL

The Delaware River Basin Commission mounted a massive attack on pollution in their estuary,[1] "hailed by many as representing one of the few triumphs of American environmental policy."[2] The effort was (and is) the largest aimed to clean up our rivers. The work involves five states, hundreds of millions of dollars, and extensive attempts at the most modern technical analyses of costs and benefits. In its economic rationale and political procedures this large-scale attack on water pollution is typical of environmental policy-making. It is also a failure. Of course, the river will be cleaned up somewhat, except that, for the most part, the Delaware will remain unswimmable, unboatable, unsightly, and only slightly more fishable, smellable, and potable. That is not much gain for approximately three quarters of a billion dollars, not much, that is, if you value results. But if the cleaning is what you value, if your aim is the ritual of purification, then the whole thing is a rip-roaring success.

This outlandish behavior, which is intentionally rational but functionally absurd, is inadequately explained by economic profit, political gain, technical imperatives, organizational abuses, or legal hubris. Although each of these explanations has merit in its own sphere, they are like an unfinished skyscraper whose spaces are illuminated at night but whose superstructure, the grid that gives groups of spaces their meaning, is blacked out.

THE DELAWARE RIVER BASIN PROJECT'S FAILURE

A helpful rule to follow in analysis is that no instrument of policy or measure of results is good for everything. If one decides to build roads for the lowest cost per square mile consistent with safety, flat desert areas will win out and there the roads will be built, which may not be exactly where they would be most useful. The environmental equivalent is to relate dissolved oxygen (DO) to the biochemical oxygen demand of a river. This DO, like any other overly simple measure, does have an advantage. Immediately one can see that the river between Philadelphia and Wilmington suffers the most severe lack of oxygen. Would raising the DO from 1 part per million (ppm) to 2 or 4 ppm, the most that could be done without vastly increasing expenditure, enable urban dwellers to swim in the river or view its beauties? Yes, said the Delaware River Basin Commission (DRBC), judging by cost-benefit studies done by the technical staff that produced the Delaware Estuary Comprehensive Study (DECS). No, say the authors of a book on the subject: color would probably change from muddy brown to impenetrable green; swimming, unless municipalities were prohibited from pouring in sewage after heavy rainstorms, would be positively harmful. Besides, the shoreline is occupied by heavy industry and chemical plants. Even if it were not potentially fatal to do so, would you want to swim there?

"Instead of taking a consumer's perspective," Bruce Ackerman and his coauthors write, "the DECS suffered from a characteristic form of planner's myopia."[3] Instead of considering whether consumers had other and better locations for swimming, boating, or fishing, the staff confined themselves to the estuary for which they were responsible. The fact that people might prefer to go to the Poconos, or the Jersey or Delaware shore, was ignored in favor of considering recreation opportunities within the highly industrialized Delaware estuary.

Time was troublesome also. The DECS study was based on a steady-state model, but the river refused to conform: at intervals sewers let go with massive discharges, and the level altered radically under different conditions at times. If it rained, a promised DO level of 4 ppm might drastically decrease. The authors complain that the staff should have told (but did not tell) decision-makers about these limitations.

By playing down variability in the river and by narrowing the range of recreation facilities available to residents of the estuary area, the study considerably overestimated recreational benefits. By arbitrarily deciding that each fisherman needed ten feet of shoreline to be attracted to the area, and by failing to mention that less than a third of fishing capacity, even before cleanup, was being utilized, DECS predicted that full advantage would be taken of new opportunities, as if some natural law demanded that fishermen align themselves at the approved interval at all times.

The cost of reducing pollutants poured into the river and of clearing the wastes already there began to rise so fast that eventually estimates were suppressed in the interest of furthering the project. Even Ackerman's $750 million estimate, however — two to three times the original sum — would not have deterred those who believe that no price can be too high for preserving life forms. If one accepts the desirability of maintaining a broad spectrum of nonhuman life, the DRBC program still is insufficient. For one thing, the river would not support diverse forms of fish or animal life even after being cleaned. For another, the main life form in question, the Atlantic shad, had many other more favorable habitats, but still ran in portions of the estuary, and in any event would not have expanded its numbers there by much more than 10 per cent. When the project is completed, these will be among the most expensive fish in the world.

The main contention of *the Uncertain Search for Environmental Quality,* which I have been reviewing here, is that investing enormous sums in an effort to improve the Delaware's DO profile was wrong because:

1. It did nothing to control the discharge of poisons that may threaten the health of those who depend on the water for drinking.

2. It did little to improve the recreational opportunities open to residents of the region.

3. It did little to improve the environment of nonhuman forms of life, especially considering the probable results of spending a similar sum on preserving and developing areas as yet relatively untouched by urban industrialism.

4. It did little to minimize the long-term ecological risk to mankind's continued existence compared to probable results of spending like sums on other pollutants and in other river basins.[4]

In other words, even if the tactical moves suggested by the cost-benefit analyses were right, still the strategy would have been wrong; instead of spending large amounts to improve a bad area marginally, it would have been better to spend the same sum in an area capable of being restored or maintained for high-priority use.

The Root of the Problem

The punishment must fit the crime; the reward must be related to desired behavior. Bringing in outside parties, who must act like *dei ex machina,* is a sign that relationships among the participants are not structured to offer sufficient incentives. If the DRBC had a study prepared that was only half good, it might be because DRBC was only half interested, which in turn just might be because the states paid less than half the cost. If all costs of the study had been borne by the authorities who benefited, DRBC might have been more cautious about estimating benefits at twice as high and costs at half as much. In the same way as the organizational separation of procurement from production in the Department of Defense might do more to end abuses than would endless castigation, so too, payment of full costs by state and local governments — who could then hire anyone, including federal bureaus, to do a job — might encourage better studies and more efficient execution of projects.

In recent times, we can pursue the same point in another area of policy: state and local governments have discovered that their pension plans are woefully underfunded. A major explanation is that because fringe benefits are not part of wages, the real future cost of employing people is easily understated. As governments are faced with finding the money, they suggest new procedures designed to force future settlements out into the open by requiring adequate provision for funding "up front." This is wise and long overdue but is hardly self-enforcing. Imagine, instead, that governments contracted out for sanitation or highway or other services. Though this approach is subject to other abuses, such as corruption in letting contracts, by its very nature — the contracts include all expenditures, leaving pensions, health insurance, and other matters to the suppliers — this arrangement shows the true cost year by year. There is a difference between ordering people to do good and making good behavior part of the institutional arrangements for their interaction.

To test the notion that faulty technical studies prejudiced the result, we need look no further than the politics that resulted in the DRBC decision to choose an expensive proposal. Would that decision have been substantially different if the analyses had been better? Not likely.

The DECS Proposes

Table 8-1 shows the estimated cost and estimated range of benefits of five proposals made by DECS. No doubt it is standard practice to frame the "real" alternatives with evidently unsuitable alternatives I (in which costs are so high they exceed benefits) and V (in which costs are so low they do not produce benefits) arranged for quick disposal.

One might think that the choice among second, third, and fourth alternatives would be fairly obvious. Compared to alternative IV, alternative II is expected to cost $165 million more while estimated benefits increase only $20 to $40 million, depending on whether the figures are too high or too low. The third alternative raises estimated costs $45 million over IV but benefits rise only from $10 to $30 million. One would have

TABLE 8.1
Cost-Benefit Analysis of DECS Pollution Plans[5]

Objective set	Cost	High estimate-low estimate of benefits
I	$490 million	$355–155 million
II	$275 million	$320–135 million
III	$155 million	$310–125 million
IV	$110 million	$280–115 million
V	$ 30 million	- - -

expected the DRBC to judge unanimously alternative IV (the winner on points) to be the title contender. Instead, the winning alternative was number II, whose highest estimate of benefits barely exceeded costs. (At the midpoint, costs would exceed benefits by almost $50 million.) Why?

Not only is the political story instructive, it has a charm of its own. I believe what happened may be explained as a form of coordination by ideology. "More environmental than thou" appears to have been the decision rule used not only by top officials but by lower echelons as well. All actors knew that action in favor of the environment was good but they did not necessarily know how good. They resolved their uncertainty by going one step further than their predecessors. Think of this as a poker game whose pot is not provided by the players: everyone gains by upping the ante. If analysis suggests plan IV, the underlings say III, and the over-lords decide on II. The importance of the staff analysis lies in the fact that, had number I not been ruled out because costs vastly exceeded benefits, the political bidding might well have arrived at that pristine number.[6]

About the only thing the technocrats could have done to reverse the result was to load the deck against environmental action. Here the DECS may have a just complaint. Its technocratic analysis may well have been too good (rather than not good enough) for the uses to which it reasonably could have been put. Had it suggested there was no point in cleaning the Delaware Estuary, the DECS staff might well have been fired, accused of failing to do the job. As it was, the staff may have felt that it stuck its neck out by recommending a less expensive program than would come from the political process.

Trying to develop political consensus for whatever alternative was preferred, the DECS staff formed a Water Use Advisory Committee (WUAC) composed of four subcommittees — two representing the polluting municipalities, and two representing conservationist and so-called public-interest groups. Conservationists predictably came out for alternative I, which promised the most benefits regardless of cost. The public-interest people came out for alternative III, which was equidistant between the contending sides. The two classes of polluters, however, made the interesting choices. Municipal officials, whose cities would have had to pay by raising sewer rates, thought large expenditures futile. These officials opted for the least costly alternative (IV) short of doing nothing. Industrial polluters refused to perform their role: they believed their answer should be "no," but they said "yes." On cost-benefit grounds the industrial polluters preferred to do nothing; but, to appear "responsible," they, like the municipalities, had to choose something, which meant alternative IV. Leaders in this industrial group, however, desiring a better public image for industry on the pollution issue, asked for negotiating flexibility up to alternative III. That is how, for industry, V became III. The next step, explored below, is how III became II for the DRBC.

The DRBC Decides

When the DECS got the four subcommittee chairmen together, the DECS project director strongly recommended alternative III because he believed that "unquantifiable" benefits justified going beyond a strict economic calculus. By this time, congressmen and conservation groups were urging number II. As for the DRBC, its executive director came out for number II because ordinary cost-benefit calculations in no way reflected the real benefits of cleaning up the estuary. For DRBC's director, as for others in the environmental movement, "a clean stream, similar to a beautiful park, reflects the conscience of a community and is an attribute far beyond monetary benefits that may be assigned."[7] To take this position, it should now be clear, is not really to reject quantifying aesthetic benefits;[8] the DRBC position is that aesthetic benefits count for more than any conceivable financial cost. Here, in truth, is a decisive quantitative calculus.

Of the various state agencies interested in pollution, only one, Delaware, considered the DECS cost-benefit analysis and recommended number III, one beyond the place to which the numbers pointed. Elsewhere no attention was paid to analysis because the other states had already committed themselves to widespread adoption of standard facilities for treating wastes and welcomed the additional federal subsidies. Besides, the other states wanted, as the commercial has it, "an extra margin of safety." Knowing that plans for abatement of pollution frequently fell short of their targets, those states preferred doing more — alternative II — in order to get as much as promised in the less-expensive plans.

If one side demonstrates its noble nature by recommending a more expensive alternative than it would otherwise prefer, and if the other believes it must bid higher to secure the next level of achievement, the results are predictable: the chosen plan will be twice removed (from IV to II) as well as twice as expensive ($275 to $110 million) as the best alternative. This is known as the hidden hand of altruism. Once the industrial polluters settled for alternative III, the municipalities couldn't be less "responsible" and so went along. Once the polluters turned the other cheek, it remained only for politicians to walk that extra mile to alternative II.

The Secretary of the Interior, according to the Water Quality Control Act of 1965, had to approve the objectives of the DRBC before the goals could become legally effective. The secretary was not only one of DRBC's five voting members but also its Pooh-Bah — final judge — and, if it came to that, its Koko — Lord High Executioner. But there was nothing to fear, for all winds were blowing in the same direction. It was easy for Secretary Stewart Udall to move from alternative III, recommended by DECS, to alternative II. Udall could show his bona fide credentials as an environmentalist only by proposing to do more. A Democrat, Udall felt he could not allow liberal Republicans to take over the issue. If the Department of Interior ruled that a rich area like the Delaware Valley could not support a large effort, it could hardly expect poorer ones to act with vigor. The Democratic administration could not expect to lead an antipollution campaign without followers.

Similar considerations prevailed with Governor Rockefeller of New York. As Ackerman sees it, "While Rockefeller would incur no political costs by voting for high standards, he would obtain political benefits on both the state and national levels."[9] So long as there was a national Democratic administration, he wanted the initiative (upping the ante) taken by Republicans at the state level.

Pennsylvania was critical. Although Philadelphia and its environs would pay a substantial share of the cost, most state benefits would be reaped downstream in Delaware. Nevertheless, Governor Shafer, who wanted state initiative in this area, went for alternative II. The fact that Shafer accepted the view of his state advisors — that doing more was required to achieve a lesser objective — suggests analysis would not have mattered. What is more, Udall, Rockefeller, and Governor Hughes of New Jersey had previously agreed that even if Pennsylvania wanted the modest program of alternative III, they would insist on the more ambitious objective. Only Governor Terry of Delaware cited the DECS analyses in support of doing less. The DRBC voted 4 to 1 for doing more. Ackerman and company conclude:

> Our interviews with the leading politicians on the DRBC and their close political assistants provide an outstanding example of decision by cliché. To all of the leading decision makers, it was "obvious" that "pollution" was a "bad thing" and that the Delaware was a badly polluted stream. It followed from this simplistic perception that the thing to do was to "clean up the river as much as possible. . . ."[10]

The cliché to which they refer is noneconomic thinking — cleanliness is priceless; more of a good thing is necessarily better than less; money is no measure of morality.

Economists and Environmentalists

The exasperation with which devotees of economic thinking regard the behavior of environmentalists and their political allies would be fully justified if everyone agreed the goals could be expressed according to economic rationality. Then the means to this end would indeed be perverse — spending much to gain little; satisfying fewer people in fewer ways rather than more people in more ways; focusing on the condition of the water instead of on the uses to which people would put it. But it is precisely this mode of thinking in terms of opportunity costs to which environmentalists object.

Some things, after all, must be sacred. Environmentalists are trying to move the boundaries by which men distinguish between the profane — money, the economic calculus — and the sacred — man's relation to nature. God is not dead, only immanent in nature. We are not dealing with the usual organizational phenomenon — substitution of process for purpose. The process of cleansing is the purpose.

If purification is what you are after, more is better than less and you would expect to pay more for each increment. Confusion enters because the transactions occur between two worlds, so that homage must still be paid to the old economic costs and benefits whereas choices are predicated on quite different environmental values.

How else can one explain the extraordinary language of the Federal Water Pollution Control Act of 1972: "It is the national goal that the discharge of pollutants into the navigable waters be eliminated by 1985"?[11] This task might require all of America's national income or all its wealth.[12] Could Congress have been serious? Perhaps the politicians were escaping from the problem by pretending to solve it. Perhaps the legislators thought that by trying to get it all, the country stood a better chance of getting half. But then again, as is customary in many countries, progressive legislation may be a substitute for program implementation. Perhaps Congress meant it wanted to come clean and adopt a new morality but did not yet know what that was to be.

Are we dealing with a cognitive lack — politicians would be economically rational if they understood how — or with a phenomenological change — an alteration in the way the world of nature is conceived in relation to mankind? Is it that environmentalists cannot or will not speak the language of economic rationality?

ALTERNATIVES FOR CONTROLLING WATER POLLUTION

Under the "legal-orders" model, a governmental agency issues orders telling polluters what they must do to comply with the law, or face legal sanctions. This approach seems straightforward — if behavior is odious, compel the offender to cease his nuisance — but its implementation is complex. There are too many polluters to treat as individuals, and the differences among polluters are too great for convenient grouping. Equity is elusive because the criterion of equal effort among polluters conflicts with minimizing cost to the public. Naturally, polluters do not remain inert, but push back politically to place themselves in a less expensive zone. The results of DRBC regulatory efforts were neither fair nor efficient.

Alternative modes of regulation include market models, such as effluent charges, with polluters paying for their discharge, and exchanges of property rights. Though Ackerman et al. like the idea of effluent charges better than legal orders, they find it wanting in numerous respects. For one thing, the notion of effluent charges creates difficulties in charging the correct amounts and applying them to specific classes of polluters. The polluters do have an incentive to consider the costs of pollution, but it is difficult to determine whether the charge will be fair in assessing burdens among polluters.[13]

The strong preference of the authors, a preference I share if pollution is a difficulty rather than a taboo, is to auction off rights to pollute within an allowable limit. This is a real market solution. By creating a market in pollution, citizens would soon discover how much pollution was worth to all — polluters themselves and the government bodies that wished to buy back rights. Efficiency is ensured because, insofar as information permits, the price of the right to pollute will equal the capitalized marginal cost of treating an extra pound of pollution. Equity is approximated among polluters regardless of size or location or political pull, because each polluter's bid must reflect its own interests.

Can anyone imagine a president surviving a proposal to vest property rights in pollution? He would be accused of paying people to pollute when he should be prohibiting it. Economists understand they are being thwarted but cannot understand why. Environmentalists find it particularly offensive to allow a polluter to continue to emit waste simply by paying a fee. It is not clear how this fact alone distinguishes an effluent charge from any method of control that does not contemplate immediate cessation of pollution. Why is polluting in return for money worse than polluting for nothing under the legal-orders model?[14] Why, indeed, might anyone think this way?

Money repels environmentalists who find it a repulsive symbol. To environmentalists money has become a stigma, the invocation of the dollar sign, an emblem of the fall from grace. Money has become associated with man's lower functions, the odor of corruption following its appearance. Properly used, cash might nurture nature, making man at one with the land. But money has become a source of idolatry; mankind worships its own feces.

Environmentalists wish to change humanity's moral relationship to nature. Without law, there can be no sin, without sin no crime, without crime no punishment, and without punishment no repentance. For environmentalists the symbolic level is the real one. Ackerman et al. find this approach "inexplicable," because they think that environmentalists confuse the appearance of legal orders with the result of reducing pollution equitably and inexpensively. Actually, it is this assumption — it is wrong to pollute — that environmentalists value.

It is hard to avoid the implication that Ackerman, like many others thinking in an economic framework, regard extreme environmentalists as irrational. I am trying to find some way to call environmentalists rational. Only if environmentalists think they are talking in ordinary language to workaday people with prosaic interests in allocating limited resources would environmentalists be irrational, for then environmentalists would deliberately be choosing the most expensive way of doing the least good. Everyone knows what people are called who prefer pain to pleasure. That is why I wonder whether environmentalists are operating on a different level of rationality. There must be some other level of discourse into which an explanation can be made to fit.

THE RISKY ENVIRONMENT

Who deals with decidedly different schemes of values? Anthropologists, among others. The problem is that if environmentalists want a better policy, they are going about it in a peculiar way. Their arguments remind me more of Mary Douglas's *Purity and Danger* than they do of any specific discussion of the environment. Therefore I turn for enlightment to her seminal work.[15]

"Nature" as a Verbal Weapon

Anthropology, Professor Douglas argues, may be regarded as a kind of phenomenology, the study of how people in various societies arrive at their beliefs. Once there is a consensus on a moral order, it determines, within wide limits, how a community experiences physical conditions. This perception is then enforced by methods of social control. "Among verbal weapons of control," Mary Douglas continues, "time is one of the four final arbiters. Time, money, God and nature, usually in that order, are universal trump cards plunked down to win an argument."[16] There is no time or insufficient money, God is against it, and it is contrary to the laws of nature. In many tribal societies, dominant males enforce chastity among wives by finding a sanction in nature that applies only to women: they will miscarry if adulterous. The Cheyenne outlaw a man who murders one of his own tribe by contending that the buffalo, upon whom they depend for food, will not react to the murder of men in other tribes but will be offended by the smell of fratricide.

Charges of pollution are levied against those who seem to threaten the moral values that sustain a society. That which is to be considered risky in the environment is determined by a normative scheme of how social relations ought to be structured. The right to define pollution, in this sense, is power; those who can make the charge stick succeed in imposing or maintaining a social hierarchy they regard as favorable.

Economists say there is not enough money to do it all or to do it all at once. Therefore, we must choose among doing everything in one place, nothing in another, or something between the two elsewhere. Environmentalists say there is no time. We must act now, for it will be too late tomorrow. Both economist and environmentalist brandish nature as a threat: spending too much on nonproductive endeavors will cause the economic system to run down until it no longer supports society; failure to clean up the environment will cause the polluted world to produce cancer, deformation of babies, a new ice age, destruction of the ionosphere until the sun burns us to a crisp, and other evils too numerous to mention.

The Idea of System

Douglas observes "the deepest emotional investment of all is the assumption that a rule-obeying universe exists. . . . Hence the most odious pollutions are those which threaten to attack a system at its intellectual base."[17] She repeats the tale of an Eskimo girl who was banished to die for insisting on eating caribou meat in winter instead of summer, because this broke the fundamental moral distinction between things fit for the two seasons. The girl was condemned for a pollution that ignored a distinction without which the society would imperil itself by running out of meat.

Are these strange-sounding stories really so remote from our own experience? The radio pours forth proposals for segregating smokers from nonsmokers — the pure from the defiled — in restaurants. People mutter about tampering with the atmosphere that produces unusual weather patterns. Implicit theories about the interpenetration of biological and natural systems appear in the news. The papers report reluctance in Alaska, California, and the eastern seaboard to have the ocean bottoms penetrated by money-mad oil companies who would profit by pumping their vital fluids to other parts of the country (or, worse still, abroad). Oil inside the ecological system is sweet; oil outside is foul.

The idea of system, Douglas suggests, is not only exhilarating but frightening. System can take hold with a death grip. System is a seamless web: know one part, know it all; eliminate one element and the entire economy or ecology collapses, or so it seems.

The media convey the contention that by eating grain-fed beef, Americans deprive starving people of the staff of life. Economically speaking, the allegation is absurd. Wheat is not a depletable resource. The grain would go elsewhere if recipients could pay the cost of raising, transporting, and distributing it. A handout is not a right. Americans pay for what they produce. Americans return what they take from the land. Surely the real polluters are those who take but do not give. If, instead of a world of nation-states, there were a universal world ecosystem — both physical and animal — then overconsumption by one element might well take place at the expense of others.

The price of oil at the Persian Gulf increased over eleven times between 1970 and 1978, and four to five times from 1973 — when it was raised as an instrument of coercion during the October war in the Middle East. These increases destroyed the possibility of economic development in most poor countries for at least a decade and perhaps likely longer, generated an unprecedented flow of arms to the area, increased dispersion of nuclear materials from which bombs may be made, and otherwise reduced standards of living, while increasing inflation in the United States. Meanwhile, these price increases have benefited mostly reactionary feudal regimes, military dictatorships, or royal absolutisms.

Yet, these developments have been greeted, if not entirely with approbation, at least with evident satisfaction by environmentalists who welcome restraint in exploiting the earth's resources. Environmentalists know this much about economics: a rise in price means a decrease in use; less fertilizer also means fewer cars and less pollution. Relating man to nature requires sacrifices. So, too, I noticed when rummaging among the British Cabinet papers of the early thirties, did kindly ministers harden their hearts in order to lower payments to widows and orphans. In the fearful grip of a deflationary economics, those ministers believed society could recover its health only if expenditures were cut. No primitive people sacrificing youth to appease a vengeful god were more in the grip of system. Now it is the environmentalists' turn.

"System" as Compulsion

"If the study of pollution ideas teaches us anything," Professor Douglas asserts, "it is that, taken too much at face value, fears about rules of nature tend to mask social rules."[18] Disagreements about population policy among rich and poor nations, for instance, Douglas attributes to "a social problem about the distribution of prestige and power. . . ."[19] If that principle applied to the differences between those who (for want of better names) we have called environmentalists and economists — the two great systems-makers of our time — what would be their differences over status and power? Status distinctions are well known: rich versus poor countries — the developed who can afford to slow down and the developing who cannot; and, among the wealthy, the upper-middle versus the lower economic classes — those who wish to preserve the pastoral pleasures of the rich, versus those who wish to become rich before sacrificing growth to preservation. Power differences are appearing: the new contestants are the professional upper-middle class, who value power more than money and whose care for control is represented well by Common Cause and other "public interest" lobbies; versus an alliance of corporate management, labor unions, and minorities, whose immediate interests and mutual accommodation are best served by sharing the monetary rewards of economic growth. Common Cause, after all, wants to "clean up" political life. Its favorite disinfectants are the aptly named "sunshine laws" that require open meetings of political bodies, disclosure of campaign contributions, and limitations on lobbying. These weapons are aimed at every intermediary organization — political party, labor union, trade association — that attempts to mediate between government and society. These intermediaries are polluted by contamination with money. So long as conflict must be carried on by time and talk, surplus resources among the professional classes, instead of money or numbers, which corporations and unions can use best, the outcome is ensured. The movement of citizen lobbies into environmental issues in a big way — a pox on politicians who condone pollution — may confidently be expected.

If everything is allowed, nothing is sacrosanct; there can be no culture, only nothingness. Professor Douglas wants to make sure we realize that there can be no knowing without principles that tell us what is polluted and what is safe:

> In essence, pollution ideas . . . protect a system of ideas from challenge. . . . If this guideline and base is grossly disturbed, knowledge is at risk.
> . . . Pollution is the black side of Plato's good lie on which society must rest: it is the other half of the necessary confidence-trick. We should be able to see that we can never ask for a future society in which we can only believe in real, scientifically proved pollution dangers. We *must* talk threateningly . . . if we hope to get anything done. . . .
> Our worst problem is the lack of moral consensus which gives credibility to warnings of danger. This partly explains why we fail so often to give proper heed to ecologists. At the same time, for lack of a discriminating principle, we easily become overwhelmed by our pollution fears. Community endows its environment with credibility. Without community, unclassified rubbish mounts up, poisons fill the air and water, food is contaminated, eyesores block the skyline. Flooding in through all our senses, pollution destroys our well-being. Witches and devils ensnare us. Any tribal culture selects this and that danger to fear and sets up demarcation lines to control it. It allows people to live contentedly with a hundred other dangers which ought to terrify them out of their wits.[20]

Making Choices

By which principle ought we to live, then — economy or environment, growth or restriction, abundance or limits? Have we too little or too much money? Has time run out or is it on our side? On which side are God and nature?

The trouble about answering these questions is that the "us" is not one but many. Uneven rates of development between countries and continents, among regions and within cities, signify that what is good for "us" is not necessarily good for "them." The age of affluence that for the first time has freed large portions of society from the need to worry about material maintenance arrived just as untold others were awakening to possibilities that were being rejected by their predecessors. Just as "the pill" undermined the dangers attached to pre- or extramarital intercourse, so affluence undercut the rationale for putting up with pollution in order to promote production.

By suggesting a Nature Preservation Trust to protect "areas still relatively untouched," Ackerman and his colleagues recognize that their controls would be extremely unpopular because places not yet exploited are also poorest — mostly because unexploited areas lack development. "Thus the antidevelopment policies of the Trust may be seen by many residents of proposed nature reserves as an effort by rich urban centers to frustrate the efforts of their country cousins to develop an industrial base that will permit the newly developing to share more fully in the delights of twentieth-century life."[21]

Uneven rates of development are paralleled by unequal acceptance of heretofore prevailing paradigms. The Great Depression dealt a death blow to the "inexorable" and painful requirements of "system" in the economy. Because elements in the economic system were no longer believed to be tightly linked, governments had discretion to act to ward off suffering. Unemployment no longer was inevitable. If government could manipulate the economy at will, however, the possibility was raised of intellectually repealing economic laws, to secure the greater good without having to suffer the systematic consequences in lowered living standards.

A sense of liberation from the old limits is captured nicely in provisions of the latest amendments to the 1972 Water Quality Control Act, stating that if applying the "best available" technology does not ensure adequate wildlife, something better than the best-available technology must be used to clean up the river. "Having driven their commitment to cleanliness at any price to the point of semantic absurdity," Ackerman and company comment, environmentalists will find that "the larger social failure cannot be evaded by invoking newspeak. Billions will have been wasted in a spurious war on pollution . . . that could have been devoted to constructing a sounder relationship between industrialized society and the natural environment."[22] But how, caught between Herbert Spencer's *Social Statics* and John Maynard Keynes' *General Theory,* are we to choose? Wise men differ among themselves not only about the political economy but about the scientific validity of the sanctions — lethal explosions in atomic energy plants, erosion of money's value — invoked to justify pushing the economy or the environment beyond their customary limits.

The different perspectives that absorb us are obscured because they favor restrictiveness and expansion at different levels. Environmentalists want conservation of the resources that make up the world's interdependent and fragile ecosystem. Although natural resources must be husbanded, "unnatural" ones, presumably money, may be expended without limit, else one would be favoring the unnatural over the natural. The expansive view urges that we save to spend. Decisions are economically rational so long as they increase national income. Uneconomic decisions may be justified on other grounds, such as charity or defense, but not so far that the economy ceases to produce wealth. A government budget may be in deficit but an economy cannot run permanently at a loss. Therefore, thrift — abstention from current consumption to provide a surplus for investment — is encouraged. If the economy were socialist, the state would be advised to accumulate; in capitalist America, private persons are urged to do the same. The difference, then, is between who (government or private enterprise) is encouraged to be restrictive or expansive, and which purposes (preservation or use) are considered desirable. Even chiliastic visions of last things run in parallel: if you do violence to the principles of system, economic or ecological, time and resources will run out because God and nature will punish these pollutions.

Economists may object that they have been taken too literally. They are flexible enough to give priority to environmental values, including among them a new class of "merit wants" for which government has special responsibility. I think this would be a mistake. The essence of economics would be given up in favor of nonproductive criteria. If, like Saul Bellow's Henderson the Rain King — who spreads havoc across Africa as he cries, "I want, I want" — economics gives up its comparative advantage, flexibility can be carried so far that no discernible shape remains. Better to have an economic economics that yields to other considerations than a noneconomic economics that is not even worth displacing.

Polluting the Social Environment

Mary Douglas believes, correctly I feel, that we should "recognize each environment as a mask and support for a certain type of society. It is the value of the social form which demands our scrutiny just as clearly as the purity of milk and air and water."[23] Now we are at the nub of our dilemma: if, by environment, social relations are implied, is the goodness of environment the converse of the hatefulness of society? Is, in fact, the negative impulse — condemnation of American society — stronger than the positive principle — preference for protecting the environment?

How, otherwise, are we to interpret the accusations leveled at America's gas guzzlers, that they are sucking vital fluids from the ecosystem? The economic system signaled to us (by a low price) that oil was plentiful. Why should we not enjoy the benefits of cheap resources? Otherwise, the only rule for decision would be "abstain"! But who wants to live in a celibate society that looks but does not touch, whose guiding metaphor would be the cloister rather than the lifeboat?

The very affluence that makes possible the modern environmental movement (not merely preservation but restoration) is used to condemn ordinary Americans for enjoying the fruits of their labor. The wheat-meat vendetta — that Americans, by their gruesome gluttony, literally take food from the mouths of babes — is condemnation without cause. The implications are that in a world of limited capacity all should share equally, not merely selling what other people can afford to buy, but giving it away. If this were admitted, that would be the end of environmentalism, because ecology would be equivalent to sharing misery equally; and it is not yet clear that many Americans are prepared to take vows of perpetual poverty or, if they are, that enough would be left over to maintain, restore, and improve the natural environment.

Suspended as we are between restriction and abundance and threatened by conflicting pollutions — do, don't consume; do, don't produce; do, don't spend — the danger is nihilism. There is no virtue and no truth and it does not matter what we do. Common sense suffers because there is no common understanding to support it. Where self-hatred rules, there will be neither restriction here nor abundance there, but only flagellation everywhere.

ECONOMICS FOR ENVIRONMENTALISTS

Reconciliation between environment and economy still is possible. Each limits the other; wealth is limited by the available environment, which itself is hemmed in by economic capacity. The two systems can also integrate their perspectives. With a particular environmental goal, economic methods can be used to choose among alternative means; environment can provide limits within which economic goals may be pursued. Both systems, after all, profess a consumer bias. Economics claims to be based on (and to satisfy) consumer preference by social interaction. By intellectual cogitation, study of ecology is supposed to show what is better for humanity in relation to nature.

The condition for this accommodation is the understanding — essential to modern, self-conscious humanity — that system is a probabilistic metaphor, not a deterministic theory. System is supposed to be scientific; system virtue is not a dogma but discovery; system keeps its part in order by not trusting any part to work all the time.[24] Should system become an end in itself, it will attempt to absorb its parts. Placing too much confidence in each part of each system leads to systematic frustration, which we recognize in the ritualized hatred of actors for the imperfections of society, that is, for the error in themselves. That is why the actors find the imposed order of foreign systems an antidote to their own poison pollution.

Half a symbol may be better than none but it is not easy to cut a symbol in half. It bleeds. If symbol is system, and system is supple, it can bend; if system is rigid, it can only break. The virtue of system is that the whole may be more reliable than its parts. This presumably was the intent of our founding fathers when they consciously sought to create, by cogitation, a strong constitutional system out of weak elements — self-interested individuals and self-aggrandizing institutions would, by mutual interaction, reduce each others' errors and excesses — the larger justice of the whole, as Watergate made us aware, rising from the smaller injustices of the parts.

Environmentalism now uses technology. An instrumental device, cost-benefit analysis, appears in the service of an expressive ideology. The pure symbol will not go down, and so it is overlaid with meliorative measures, stripped of its severity, made a matter of more or less rather than all or nothing. No doubt management of impressions plays a part; the apparatus is for show, not for real. Environmentalists mean to get it all in due course. As environmentalists move up the ladder from "person-blame" to "system-blame" to "system-substitution," they raise no more hackles than strictly necessary. To appear reasonable may not be to act responsibly, but it is a start. Imitation may be instructive. Such postures may teach environmentalists more than they think. "It is de rigueur," Harrod writes in his biography of Keynes, "to pretend to understand the merits of the opposite point of view; one ends by really doing so, and thereby becomes an educated man."[25] Still, there is more than that; economics may not be a science, but neither does it need to be all dismal. Economics has its uses, even for environmentalists. For years, proponents of federal public works succeeded in imposing an absurdly low interest rate (preferring the present to the future) to support pet projects. Environmentalists just recently have realized that by fighting for an economic rate of interest (if not current market rates then at least a higher rate) they would, ipso facto, be leading government to build fewer dams, spoil less scenery, uproot fewer people, and so forth.

Economics may hold more meaning for environmentalists than they realize. Consider the controversy over direct governmental regulation of pollution versus effluent charges. The donnybrook does not decline, because the cost of staying on the current path is about to become stupendous so that the symbol of surmounting pollution will not survive. A longer look might convince environmentalists that effluent charges—by diffusing the cost of reducing pollution among consumers of products whose production produces pollution—might also permit hugely higher expenditures. Putting the central government in the position of paying for pollution all at the same time and in the same places makes the cost prohibitive. Market methods aid decentralization, which is not only more efficient economically, but likely also to prove more palatable politically. It is not necessary to raise revenues at the same time, in the same place, and in the same way.

Regulation is for the regulated. Legal orders are for lawyers. Regulation matters most to industries that have more lawyers to protect them than the public has to serve it. Regulatory agencies are training grounds for lawyers who later serve the regulated, or, as it may chance, organized environmentalists. The connection between legal training and bureaucratization is more evident in Europe because law is still the main entry-way into civil service. Lawyers are fond of regulations for the same reason that they dislike no-fault insurance or prohibition of speculative fees in medical malpractice—it is good for business. Learning (and manipulating) regulations is their chief legal stock-in-trade.

Businessmen today, of course, also are bureaucrats, not market men. Businessmen no longer believe in capitalism as competition. When put on committees to study regional problems, businessmen almost always choose hierarchy—regional government—over markets—competitive political arenas in which numerous jurisdictions compete to supply service. Corporate executives may be affected by markets, but they would rather not be. They prefer the routinized, negotiated bureaucratic order of government-sponsored oligopolistic cartels (with all of its red tape and regulation) over the relative spontaneity of the economic market in which, alas, anything might happen. Businessmen, as everyone knows, now spend their lives in large bureaucracies and come to prefer tame milieus. How regulation benefits business interests is clear; why alleged enforcers of environmental equity should prefer similar solutions is the great mystery.

To environmentalists, markets are immoral as well as impersonal. Once effluent charges were set, for instance, it would be relatively easy to monitor performance: are pollutants down to the required amounts and are affected industries paying the necessary price? Evasion, though by no means impossible, would be awkward; negotiation, though not out of the question, would be more questionable; postponement, though conceivable, would be harder to conceal.

Bureaucratic bargaining is an activity for which environmentalists are well suited by training and temperament. Public participation, moreover, meaning environmentalists' personal participation in public, goes along with revision of regulations. Setting effluent charges is not exactly a heroic public enterprises; what is worse, charges do not have to be revised continuously; worst of all, effluent charges are difficult to divide up for political bargaining. These comparative qualities—invisibility, indivisibility, and immutability — are serious disadvantages of economic (over bureaucratic) modes of decision-making about pollution.

Viewed in another way, to be sure, leaders of environmental groups have given their followers just what was wanted—symbols. And the price was right. The meaty amendments to the Water Quality Act were salted with tantalizing tastes of federal dollars for cities and sanitary engineers who—like the Army Corps of Engineers and the Bureau of Reclamation before them—believe that bigger is better and more is marvelous. Without the federal largesse to make all this possible (and if the states had to pay for the project as I suggested) there would have been no automatic agreement on the most expensive alternatives either in the Delaware River basin or elsewhere in the country.

Behavior so far does not show that economic is opposed to environmental rationality, but that both may be opposed to bureaucratic rationality, to the detriment of the lasting legitimacy of politics. At the end of their brave book, Ackerman, Ackerman, Sawyer, and Henderson strike a note of alarm:

> What is disappointing, even alarming, is the prospect of government, frustrated by the difficulty of structuring a coherent response, embarking on an urgent quest to achieve a poorly defined goal without institutions present to raise the right questions, and without the regulatory tools to achieve objectives either fairly or efficiently.[26]

Spilling seed on the ground, a form of wasting human resources, at one time was considered a kind of pollution.

Our problem is not any pollution, but which pollution. If nothing is pure, everything is polluted. System there must be, whether provided by economy, environment, or some new amalgam of both. The antithesis of order is disorder; Mary Douglas tells us, "When . . . there is no pollution and no purity and nothing edible or inedible, credible or incredible . . . there is no more meaning,"[27] nor, I should add, morality. Disagreements over degrees of environmental protection are not about relative costs and benefits but about the validity of economics itself as a form of interaction — its basis in exchange, cost, and cash — as a measure of the way we ought to relate to one another.

NOTES

1. I wish to thank Mary Douglas, William Epstein, Eugene Hammel, Helen Ingram, Jeanne Nienaber, and Jeffrey Pressman for their critical comments.
2. Bruce A. Ackerman, Susan Rose-Ackerman, James W. Sawyer, Jr., and Dale W. Henderson, *The Uncertain Search for Environmental Quality* (New York: Free Press, 1974), p. 3.
3. Ibid., p. 125.
4. Ibid., p. 143.
5. Ibid., p. 15 (footnotes omitted from table). The benefits referred to in the table are for recreation above existing use and the costs are those above the amount incurred before the study started.
6. See also ibid., pp. 167–168.
7. Ibid., p. 14.
8. Anyone who lives in a place with a view knows that the higher you go, the more you pay.
9. Ibid., p. 196.
10. Ibid., p. 206.
11. Ibid., p. 319, quoting 33 U.S. Code, 125 I(a)(I)(Supp. IV, 1974).
12. The most recent estimate is that removing all pollutants from waterborne wastes would cost $317 billion. A. Kneese and C. Schultze, *Pollution, Prices, and Public Policy* (1975), p. 78.

13. Ibid. The authors argue strongly in favor of effluent charges.
14. Ibid., p. 276.
15. Mary Douglas, "Environments at Risk," [London] *Times Literary Supplement,* October 30, 1970, pp. 1273–1275.
16. Ibid., p. 1274.
17. Ibid., p. 1275.
18. Ibid.
19. Ibid.
20. Ibid.
21. Ibid.
22. Ibid., pp. 320–321.
23. Douglas, op. cit.
24. See Martin Landau, "Redundancy, Rationality and the Problem of Duplication and Overlap," *Public Administration Review* Vol. 29, No. 4 (July-August 1969), pp. 346–358.
25. R. Harrod, *The Life of John Maynard Keynes* (New York: St. Martins Press, 1963, 1972), p. 68.
26. Ibid., p. 330.
27. Douglas, op. cit.

PART 3

DOGMA
VERSUS SKEPTICISM

In the attempt to achieve a conceptual formulation of the confusingly immense body of observational data, the scientist makes use of a whole arsenal of concepts which he imbibed practically with his mother's milk; and seldom if ever is he aware of the eternally problematic character of his concepts. He uses . . . conceptual tools of thought, as something obviously, immutably given; something having an objective value of truth which is hardly ever, and in any case not seriously, to be doubted. How could he do otherwise? How would the ascent of a mountain be possible, if the use of hands, legs, and tools had to be sanctioned step by step on the basis of the science of mechanics? And yet in the interests of science it is necessary over and over again to engage in the critique of these fundamental concepts, in order that we may not unconsciously be ruled by them. . . .

In contrast with Leibniz and Huygens, it was clear to Newton that the space concept was not sufficient to serve as the foundation for the inertia principle and the law of motion. He came to this decision even though he actively shared the uneasiness which was the cause of the opposition of the other two: space is not only introduced as an independent thing apart from material objects, but also . . . acts on all material objects, while these do not in turn exert any reaction on space.

The fruitfulness of Newton's system silenced these scruples for several centuries. . . . Today one would say about that memorable discussion: Newton's decision was, in the contemporary state of science, the only possible one, and particularly the only fruitful one. But the subsequent development of the problems, proceeding in a roundabout way which no one then could possibly foresee, has shown that the resistance of Leibniz and Huygens, intuitively well founded but supported by inadequate arguments, was actually justified.

It required a severe struggle to arrive at the concept of independent and absolute space, indispensable for the development of theory. It has required no less strenuous exertions subsequently to overcome this concept.

Albert Einstein, introduction to Max Jammer,
Concepts of Space: The History of Theories of Space in Physics
(New York: Harper & Brothers, 1969), pp. xii–xvi.

Skepticism depends on dogma; however one puts it: if most things are to be challenged, some must remain accepted; if some things are to be challenged, most must be beyond criticism. The skepticism prized in a self-conscious society must rest on a substratum of dogma. Drawing the line between dogma and skepticism, between what will be open to criticism and what not, is a primary task, even a presupposition, of policy analysis, for it involves relating our notions of desirable social relations to the values and beliefs that sustain them. Redrawing the line between dogma and skepticism is the creation of culture.

Dogma also depends on skepticism. Science is often described as organized skepticism. It is said to involve a structure of social relations in which multitudes of independent scientists, working apart from one another, are rewarded for criticizing theories by replacing them with more attractive alternatives. But were the model of skepticism fully followed, every bit of odd data and peculiar theory would have to be tested, so dissipating energies that progress would hardly be possible. Science operates within accepted professional standards of good craftsmanship and current wisdom, which may well be mistaken. Michael Polanyi says,

> Both the criteria of plausibility and of scientific value tend to enforce conformity, while the value attached to originality encourages dissent. This internal tension is essential in guiding and motivating scientific work. The professional standards of science must impose a framework of discipline and at the same time encourage rebellion against it. They must demand that, in order to be taken seriously, an investigation should largely conform to the currently predominant beliefs about the nature of things, while allowing that in order to be original it may to some extent go against these. Thus, the authority of scientific opinion enforces the teachings of science in general, for the very purpose of fostering their subversion in particular points. . . .[1]

To say that this "scientific opinion" is authoritative, that is, not ordinarily open to question, also says that it is dogmatic.

Markets are made to be skeptical. If competitive conditions prevail, no bid need be accepted merely because it is made. On the contrary, each participant is motivated to be skeptical of the other by responding to the best possible opportunities. All this skepticism, however, depends on dogma about the reliability and desirability of markets. Without an unchallenged belief that transactions made today will be valid tomorrow (witness "runs" on banks when depositors lose confidence and all demand money at once), markets would collapse. Without the belief that markets are moral, that they measure and give real value, participation in them will decline until they cannot contain enough transactions to be meaningful. Faith may not be able to move mountains, but it is indispensable for maintaining markets.

Democratic politics is also an institutional embodiment of skepticism. The rules are that there must be more than one political party, each independent of the other(s), which compete for control of government by seeking votes of citizens who are able to choose among them. This competitive redundancy (a useful duplication) is reinforced in the United States by overlap within branches (separation of powers, checks and balances) and among levels of a federal government. By requiring consent, criticism is encouraged and protected. Yet if this criticism reaches to fundamental features of government, and if the desirability of the system and hence the authority of its governors were constantly challenged, consent would give way to coercion either because of collapse from insufficient power — nobody obeys — or transformation because of excessive power — everyone has to obey. Citizens have a stake in substantive rationality, Karl Mannheim called it, in correct choice; they also have a stake in political rationality, in maintaining legitimacy so as to be able to make future decisions.

Institutional arrangements such as federalism, separation of powers, checks and balances, have been part of America's unchallengeable or at least unchallenged dogma. The function of keeping these questions relatively closed is clear. The Civil War, bloodiest of the nineteenth century, is an example of how far reopening discussion of these issues might lead. If every opinion were given equal weight or every policy, like social security, were subject to reversal, the political process could not cope. Exhaustion would be the complement of negation. With everything at stake in every throw of the political die, citizens would refuse to play the game. Deviant opinions must find it difficult to mobilize, and issues on the public agenda must be limited, to protect a political system against chaos.

Who can say when values become so divergent no bridge can span the divide? Without a substratum of trust no one need believe anyone about anything. Without agreement on primitive terms of discourse left undefined and, for a time, unexamined, communication breaks down. So extreme a situation is mirrored in more moderate moments when, in effect, we decide how much of our social relations to take for granted and how much subject to searching scrutiny. The balance we seek between dogma and skepticism reflects the paradoxical state of social self-confidence: the greater the consensus, the easier it is to examine differences, whereas the wider the gulf, the more fundamental the issues, the greater the need for self-examination, the less willingness to enter a dialogue.

At stake is resetting the conventional web of relations that enables citizens to maintain some reliability in their dealings with one another, both as rulers and as ruled. For human interactions to be understandable, they must be dependable. The totality of possible connections between actions and outcomes is staggering. People, even politicians, would go crazy if they were required to pay attention to all possible connections. Therefore selection is unavoidable. Dependability and predictability are achieved by selecting from all the varied human experiences a limited number of possible connections. Thus a web of relations that is not too complicated is generated and maintained. This is a conventional activity. We know that good arguments can be made for a different selection, but, at any time, we restrict the agenda of issues to make possible at least some kind of sensible choice.

A free society requires free men and women who know what they are doing, who can make sense of their public lives by learning how to take effective action. Of what, then, does this rational action by citizens consist? Rational choices require that the universe of public policy be seen as intelligible, with actions connected to probable outcomes, so that the citizens can habitually infuse their communal life with meaning.[2]

Social interaction in political arenas and economic markets may be thought of as continuous and cumulative testing of hypotheses about this universe with, one hopes, the most persuasive interpretation of the evidence prevailing, though only for a time. For we disagree over the meaning of meaning: who has the authority to certify what makes sense? Established regimes seek to conserve meanings, revolutionaries to destroy them, and radicals to substitute new ones. Whether larger meanings can or should last indefinitely is doubtful. Nevertheless, at any moment, citizenship implies a capacity for rational choice, which depends on a framework of intelligibility, in which some things are now taken for granted and others are open to question, in which citizens can distinguish the trivial from the important, and improve their performances. If citizens are not analysts, in this sense of rational action in a sensible context, self-government is merely self-delusion.

Trust reduces the need for anticipation. Planning, almost by definition, is a product of mistrust. After all, if social interaction were sufficient there would be no need to plan. The ordinary injunction — plan ahead — is as mistaken as can be. One should never decide earlier (unless long lead times are indispensable as in sewer systems) when one could act later with much better information. Only if one fears that social interaction will provide the wrong signals or delay them until it is too late (witness the worry that the world will suddenly run out of oil), would we wish to act so far in advance. Analysis is about activity now to affect the future. It is not necessarily making next decade's decisions in this one.

If planning is optimistic about human intellect, it is pessimistic about human relations. Planning assumes society will not be able to cope with the future so that this future must be appropriated into its past in the present. The same is true for the argument that the needs of future generations should be paramount in making current choices. Of course, if we care about our progeny, we plan to leave them better off. The usual implication, however, is that future generations will be less resourceful (the idea of progress turned on its head) so that we must take care of them in the present. Part of this pessimism is fear of failure, the feeling that one must not leave things out when one could put them in. Comprehensive calculations embody the principle of perfection: remember everything, forget nothing. Part of this principle is pure mistrust. The more social trust, the more confidently we can deal with whatever is in store for us, the less we need to wrap up all our uncertainties now for fear they will overwhelm us later.

Trusting implies relying on others' actions that one does not control or necessarily understand, or even while one does not pay attention. Macbeth violated this implicit understanding. He murdered the sleeping king who was a guest in his house. By doing so, Macbeth established a style of politics: always be alert, leave nothing to others, trust no one. This way leads to ruin. Macbeth himself can never again sleep. "Sleep no more! Macbeth does murder sleep." Equally out of step with the life-restoring rhythm of waking and sleeping is Lady Macbeth, who feels no remorse. She is pure "dogma." She cannot do anything but sleep, even while her eyes are open. Lacking self-awareness, she cannot trust herself even while sleeping. She kills herself. A viable realm is restored by the murdered king's son, Malcolm, who is oriented to tradition.

What are the manifestations of social distrust? Is its lack of respect for the competence or integrity of others among them? Do we fear that individuals will be unable to deal with the dangers and risks to which they are subjected? A prescribed first-year curriculum may be required of students who are thought incompetent to make an informed choice. Auditing is instituted to expose people who use public funds for personal purposes. But these are judgments about individuals. We face the more difficult task of locating trust and mistrust in social institutions. Our interest as students of policy analysis is that social roles will be performed so that we can count on a modicum of trustworthy and hence predictable and acceptable activity. Markets will clear transactions between buyers and sellers. Prices will signal relative scarcities so that expensive resources will be conserved and cheap resources consumed so as to increase total value. Competition among parties and politicians will produce policies that are broadly acceptable and substantially rational. Social stratification allocates statuses so as to serve society. In a word, it is social processes (interaction, we have called it) that are trusted or mistrusted, not only persons.

To the extent that social relations are deemed desirable, their products deserve approval. Interaction is acceptable. But when social relations are deemed defective, cultural change becomes imperative, and the values supporting patterns of action are challenged. Cogitation is called upon to restructure interaction. But cogitation as a mode of choice is itself suspect of intellectual hubris and social stultification; because it cannot competently replace social interaction, it enforces social conformity. Dictatorship replaces democracy. The competitive redundancy of social interaction, with its hurly-burly diversity, its upsetting almost-anarchy, is replaced by the monominded uniformity of intellectual cogitation.

Here — at the intersection between skepticism and dogma — lies a dilemma of policy analysis. Social interaction institutionalizes skepticism but depends on some palpable yet imprecise minimum of social trust. Intellectual cogitation institutionalizes dogma in finding correct solutions but depends on a real but unknown intensity of self-criticism. Interaction, whose primary principles are skeptical, needs dogma, and cogitation, whose first principles are dogmatic, needs skepticism. Answers to the question of how much dogma and how much skepticism, therefore, cannot be answered a priori but depend directly on the domain of applicability. One question, how much does it need? is countered by another, what does it lack? As we await deeper understanding of these matters, my recipe for policy analysis is: mix and season to taste.

The tension between skepticism and dogma is built into the rival needs for organizational change and organizational stability. When they try to speak truth to power, policy analysts, who perform a critical function, internalize this tension. Our ideal model of organized skepticism, "The Self-Evaluating Organization," must also learn to live with this contradiction.

One can be dogmatic about some things and skeptical about others. The combination of too little skepticism about procedures and too much about policies led President Carter into distress. Comprehensive calculations (zero-based from the ground up) did not enable him to devise coherent or acceptable solutions, across the board, to major policy problems. More calculations on fewer areas of policy should improve the product of public policy.

When citizens do their part as analysts, they subject policy dogma to scrutiny, they distinguish the more from the less important, they relate their desires to those of other citizens, and they figure out what their participation is worth not only to themselves, but to others. For citizens to be something more than ciphers, they must be able to convert their everyday activity into usable evidence for making choices about participating in public policies that connect them to other people.

NOTES

1. Michael Polanyi, "The Republic of Science: Its Political and Economic Theory," *Minerva*, Vol. 2, No. 3 (Spring 1964), pp. 58–59.
2. I am indebted to Hermann van Gunsteren's essay on "Responsibility" for this and the next paragraph.

CHAPTER 9

THE SELF-EVALUATING
ORGANIZATION

Why don't organizations evaluate their own activities? Why don't they seem to manifest rudimentary self-awareness? How long can people work in organizations without discovering their objectives or determining how well they have been carried out? I started out thinking it was bad for organizations not to evaluate, and I ended up wondering why they ever do it. Evaluation and organization, it turns out, are somewhat contradictory. Failing to understand that incompatibility, we are tempted to believe in absurdities, much in the manner of mindless bureaucrats who never wonder whether they are doing useful work. If instead we asked more intelligent questions, we would neither look so foolish nor be so surprised.

Who will evaluate and who will administer? How will power be divided among them? Which ones will bear the costs of change? Can evaluators create sufficient stability to carry on their own work in a turbulent environment? Can authority be allocated to evaluators and blame apportioned among administrators? How does one convince administrators to collect information that might help others, but can only harm them? How do we obtain support on behalf of recommendations that anger sponsors? Would the political problem be solved by creating a special organization — Evaluation Incorporated — devoted wholly to performing the analytic function? Could it obtain necessary support without abandoning its analytic mission? Can knowledge and power be joined?

EVALUATION

The ideal organization would be self-evaluating. It would continuously monitor its own activities so as to determine how well it was meeting its objectives or even whether these objectives should continue to prevail. When evaluation suggested that a change in objectives or programs to achieve them was desirable, these proposals would be taken seriously by top decision-makers who would institute the necessary changes without vested interest in continuing current activities. Instead they would steadily pursue new alternatives to better serve desired outcomes.

The ideal member of the self-evaluating organization is best conceived of as a person committed to specific modes of problem-solving. He believes in clarifying goals, relating them to different methods of achievement, creating models (sometimes quantitative) of the relationships between inputs and outputs, seeking the best-available combination. His wish is not that any specific objective be enthroned or that a particular clientele be served. Evaluative man wants to choose interesting problems and to apply maximum intelligence toward their solution.

To evaluative man the organization matters only if it meets social needs. Procedures matter only if they help accomplish objectives encompassing these needs. Efficiency is beside the point if the objective being achieved at lowest cost is inappropriate. Getting political support doesn't mean that programs devised to fulfill objectives are good; it just means that they had more votes than the others. Both objectives and resources, says evaluative man, must be modified continuously to achieve the optimal response to social need.

Evaluation should lead not only to finding better policy programs to accomplish objectives but also to altering objectives themselves. Analyzing the effectiveness of policies leads to considering alternatives that juxtapose means and ends embodied in alternative policies. Objectives as well as the means for attaining them may be deemed inappropriate. But men who have become socialized to accept set goals resist innovation so as to preserve those social objectives. The difficulties are magnified once we realize that objectives may be attached to the clientele — the poor, farmers, lumberjacks — with whom an organization's members identify. The objectives of the organization may have attracted them precisely because they see it as a means of service to people they value. They may regard changes in objectives, therefore, as proposals for "selling out" clients they wish to serve. In their eyes evaluation then becomes an enemy of the people.

Evaluative man must learn to live with contradictions. He must reduce his commitments to the organizations in which he works, the programs he carries out, and the clientele he serves. Evaluators must become agents of change acting in favor of programs as yet unborn and clienteles still unknown. Prepared to impose change on others, evaluators must have enough stability to stick to their own work. They must hang onto their own organization while preparing to abandon it. They must combine political feasibility with analytic purity. Only a brave individual would predict that these qualities can be found in one and the same person and organization.

OBSTACLES TO EVALUATION

Before the passion for formal, focused evaluation of outcomes (people in society are forever engaged in evaluative behavior), came other forms of evaluation, although it is not now common to think of them as such. One was a determination of legality. Some effort was spent to ascertain whether repetitive activities were carried on efficiently. The internal conflicts generated by these earlier modes of evaluation have received abundant documentation in the administrative literature. The legal staff considers adherence to statute and regulation a prime responsibility; violations of law are anathema to them. Yet legality may interfere with action and purpose; program personnel complain endlessly that they are hamstrung by excessive requirements for paperwork and by delays caused by matters they think of as legal niceties. The overhead units responsible for efficiency may insist that a central stenographic pool and infrequent mail service cost less to do the same amount of work. The program officials, who value responsiveness to their own needs, want service on their own schedules. These traditional organizational conflicts are magnified manyfold by efforts to evaluate the desirability of different objectives compared to the costs of achieving them.

The original cost-benefit studies in water resources were an effort to appraise the value of projects before they were undertaken, so as to select the best. Based on the doctrine of opportunity costs, cost-benefit analysis was designed to measure the alternative economic value displaced by a proposed investment. Evaluation consisted of applying the criterion (increase to national income) to alternative projects. This before-the-fact evaluation has now been supplemented, or superseded, by during-and-after studies whose purpose is either to build in evaluation as programs are initiated, or appraise them after they have been started. The change may signify that the newer social programs are considered more important, or, if one prefers, deserving of greater suspicion. But it is having profound consequences for the character of evaluation by making it coextensive with policy analysis. If evaluation takes place not only before a program is begun, and after it is finished, but during the entire life, program evaluation and prescriptive policy analysis become one and the same.

Another result of having evaluative studies that are carried on during the life of a program is that evaluators and program personnel must live (uneasily, as we shall see) side by side. The result of periodic evaluation after the program has been established is that one group of people are making statements about the worth of activities to which another group of people are devoting their lives.

Uncertain Objectives

To know whether objectives are being achieved, one must first know what they are supposed to be. Yet, the assumption that objectives are known, clear, and consistent is at variance with all experience. We know that objectives invariably may be distinguished by three outstanding qualities: they are multiple, conflicting, and vague. They mirror, in other words, the complexity and ambivalence of human social behavior. The classic case is the multiple-use concept in natural resources that posits equal value for both preservation and use. "Conservation," according to Gifford Pinchot, a father of the movement, "implies both the development and the protection of resources, the one as much as the other. . . ." Development means consumption of resources, and protection means just the opposite. You can't keep nature forever wild and still harvest the trees. You can't provide power by damming a river and still preserve the valley in its unspoiled state. Even when the dominant use is considered to be development or preservation, conflicts still arise within the categories. Should water be used for irrigating farm land, or for urban water supply? Should wilderness areas be restricted to backpacking, or should roads and trails be built to open the areas to less energetic nature lovers? The advantage of multiple and vague objectives is that attention can be shifted from one to the other as interest and opinion change without appearing to sacrifice principle. Orris Herfindahl, from whose perceptive article these examples are taken, concludes,

> this indifference to clarity of definition rests in considerable part on the existence of deep underlying conflicts among various interest groups in the area of conservation policy. . . . Clear definition might lose all the advantage to be gained from using so fine sounding a word as "conservation" or the related "develop and preserve." Clarity about real intentions might unnecessarily antagonize those who otherwise would not press home to the real meaning behind generalities.[1]

Public policies are full of similar disguised conflicts — institutional change versus political stability in community action, jobs for minorities versus economic development for its own sake, full employment versus inflation.

Evaluation cannot ordinarily proceed, then, by determining how well the unknown objectives of a program are being achieved at whatever cost. The first element of evaluation, therefore, which often proceeds simultaneously with program operations, must be a search for objectives against which to evaluate the program. Yet program personnel cannot be expected to take kindly to the suggestion that they do not know what they are doing. (If they did know, presumably they would be able to specify precisely their current objectives.)

Objectives are not just out there, like ripe fruit waiting to be plucked; they are manmade, artificial, imposed on a recalcitrant world. Inevitably, they do violence to reality by emphasizing some activities (hence organizational elements) over others. Thus the very step of defining objectives may be considered a hostile act. If they are too vague, no evaluation can be done. If they are too specific, they never encompass all the indefinable qualities that their adherents insist they have. If they are too broad, any activity may be said to contribute to them. If they are too narrow, they may favor one segment of the organization over another. Strategically located participants often refuse to accept definitions of objectives that would put them at a disadvantage or in a straightjacket should they wish to change their designation of what they do in the future. Arguments about which really, but really and truly, are the objectives of the organization may stultify all future action.

The objectives people have, the goals they seek to achieve, are a function not merely of their desirability but also of their feasibility. What we try to do depends to some degree on what we can do. If the funds for the Model Cities program evince a drastic decrease, either because Congress appropriates less or because other contributing federal agencies refuse to provide their share, the goals of the program in a city must be revised. Often the simple act of lowering one's sights will not do, because the original objectives cannot be achieved at all, and the new one might be attainable. Although both acquiring new park lands and maintaining present facilities may be pursued at higher levels of appropriations, the former may be sacrificed to the latter at lower levels.

The evaluators may first have to understand what effects a program causes before finding an objective that these causes achieve. In searching for objectives the evaluators may have the greatest difficulty in discovering precisely what difference the program has made. Failing to discover the consequences attributable to the program, evaluators cannot put dollar amounts on them. Talk of quantification is premature; no one can find causes for unknown effects.

An objective may be desirable, but no one may know how to achieve it. Evaluators must become skilled in changing objectives to those for which prevailing theory and resources are appropriate (feasibility is part of desirability), so that the organization can actually accomplish them.

The objectives used by the evaluators, furthermore, may have little to do with the ostensible purposes with which the program began, but a great deal to do with the ease of computation. Objectives must not only be related to what programs actually do, they must also fit in with the available data and the known formulas for manipulating them. The need for evaluators to imbed objectives and data in a formula modeling a solvable problem means that their own requirements place them in conflict with elements of the organization.

Different Evaluations for Different Audiences

A critical aspect of evaluation is which level within the organization might conceivably use it. There is no sense in choosing variables that allegedly contribute to success or failure of programs, however defined, unless decision-makers at some level are able to manipulate them. The moral character of backpackers may be a significant variable in determining crime rates in the wilderness, but unless park or forest-service officials can screen them in that way, the knowledge is of no use. Similarly, a department secretary might conceivably gain by learning that there are greater benefits in shifting resources from national parks to urban recreation. But the men who run the parks and forests cannot use this information; they need to know about allocation of resources within parks.

Suppose that an analysis suggests that program B is better than program A. The adherents of program A are certain to say that the evaluation is improper, not merely because they disagree with its conclusions and therefore with the operations that went into it, but also because it is, in their words, destructive, not constructive. They will argue that evaluation should tell them which elements of their program are most successful and which variables are responsible for that success. Such knowledge would enable them to transfer resources from one project or program element to another. Program administrators, if they are to look upon analysis as an aid rather than a detriment, want to be told how they might shift resources within their program and not that cancer research would be better than white-water canoeing or that boating in Kansas has higher payoff than dune buggies in Arizona. The rub comes when one realizes that every program must have some elements in it that are better than the others, however awful they may all be, and that you can always find "success" if you look for it hard enough. Evaluation can be made more welcome and relevant at the cost of vitiating its essential character.

Self-Perpetuating Policies

Suppose a policy does not appear to work. It does not seem to be accomplishing the goals set for it or it does so at excessive cost. Citizens are dissatisfied with the services they receive or they feel they are paying too much for them. Instead of the good consequences that were expected there are unexpected consequences that are bad. The obvious conclusion is that the policy has failed and should be replaced by another. But there are always competing explanations about why policies fail that may leave decision-makers uncertain over whether to abandon them. One hypothesis is that the theory behind the policy is bad and the more that is done the worse things will get. The other hypothesis is that the critical mass has not been reached. If more of the same thing were done then the policy would utimately show good results. Were these arguments applied to the American bombing of North Vietnam, it would be easy to conclude that the second explanation is self-serving. Observation reveals, however, that these alternative explanations are universal. Do poverty programs fail to achieve their objectives? The answer must be that insufficient funds have been devoted to them. Does health research fail to find the cures it is seeking? The answer must be that the critical mass has not yet been reached. Do our schools fail to show a relationship between increased resources and educational outcomes? The response is that not enough has been done. When complaints about national parks rise in proportion to increased expenditures, the reply is not that policies must be changed but that more money must be spent.

If the ostensible purpose of a policy has not been achieved or does not seem worth the cost, one can usually discover other collateral objectives that have, in fact, been accomplished. Going to the moon is not only desirable in itself, but creates technological fallout of benefit to society. The Head Start preschool nursery program for disadvantaged children may not lead to lasting improvement in their school performance, as originally predicted, but does appear to serve as a focal point for mobilizing their parents on behalf of other community goals. Should the program be abandoned or should the organization merely decide that the newly discovered goal of community organization justifies the expense and the effort? Evaluators from the national organization and local operators are likely to disagree about how the question should be answered.

Decentralization

The popularity of decentralization further deepens the potential conflict between evaluators and program managers. Decentralization, if it is more than a current slogan, means that field officers diverge considerably in their ways of implementing national programs. What is done must necessarily differ from one place to another. Imagine, then, the travail of the evaluator who discovers that the one program he is supposed to appraise turns out to be a dozen different ones, without his being certain precisely how large the differences are. Naturally he insists on standardization, and naturally local personnel do not like that.

One might think a variety of subprograms would be welcomed by evaluators who might conceive of them as natural experiments. But premature joy soon gives way to unalloyed gloom at the research programs thus created. Evaluation costs money and must itself be appraised for any benefits it might bring. The cost of evaluating a variety of sub-programs rises dramatically as the coverage of each separate subprogram requires more data and personnel, and the relationships among the programs add enormously to the complexity of the analysis.

Field personnel, in addition, are notoriously uninterested in data collection that does not serve their immediate purposes. Their task is to make things happen, not to stop and think of what forms should be filled out so that some other fellow can later make suspect use of them. Were local personnel to feel differently, they would still have trouble appreciating the need of evaluators for consistent and disaggregated data that can later be recombined to serve new purposes. The local official, who must consult his own convenience, is likely to record data periodically as time permits and to aggregate them into larger lumps so that they will be easier to collect and store. His data practices, which seem quite sensible from his perspective, are likely to drive future evaluators wild with frustration.

Time

Evaluation requires a minimum of stability; changing the program month by month makes it impossible to get a fix on it of sufficient duration to perform any study. Yet social programs, which are supposed to adapt to rapid shifts in the environment, change frequently in time and in the substance of their orientation. Therefore, evaluators become an interest group within the organization pleading for stability enough that they can learn what is going on. If evaluators want to begin soon after a program has been established, the officials in charge may plead that too little time has elapsed for the program to take hold and for its effects to be sufficiently distinctive to show up in measurements. By this time, however, evaluators have learned that if they don't get in at the start, the program will have changed and they will again be told that not enough time has elapsed to study the new orientation.

Impatience grows at the operating level because evaluators have difficulty in meeting programmatic needs at the appropriate time. Although evaluators may be pressing and operators resisting early evaluation, the tables may quickly be turned when events force a sudden program review. At that time the operators may ask for immediate analysis and evaluators may be unable to perform. Realizing the weaknesses in their analysis, evaluators are likely to ask for more and better data and much more time. But operators need information now, and not at some later date when opportunities for change may have passed them by. Thus each side is likely to accuse the other alternatively of being too fast and too slow, of wanting too much and not enough data, and of ignoring immediate problems and being too responsive to passing fancies.

The Obstacle of Dealing with Obstacles

Standing back from these experiences, evaluators may try to devise strategies for overcoming their most severe disabilities. Knowing what programs are likely to change rapidly, they may seek a broader range of data so that they will have something to go on when people change their minds. Realizing that data are not likely to occupy a high priority in the early stages, they may seek participation in determining what kinds should be collected at what intervals and in what form. They may seek outside sources of information from the Census Bureau or the Social Security Administration, so that they do not depend entirely on the response of their own organization. The price they pay is in overcollecting data that no one (including themselves) is certain they will ever use. By collecting anything and everything in sight, they can guard against the prospect that variables, unforeseen in the initial stages, will turn out to have profound importance later on. They will then have difficulty explaining why they want these data. Indeed, program personnel may begin to suspect that the data are wanted for some arcane academic purpose, such as adding to a publication record, rather than for improving operations. It will not be easy to marry evaluation and operation.

Evaluation and organization may be contradictory terms; organizational structure implies stability but evaluation suggests change. Organization generates commitment and evaluation breeds skepticism. Evaluation speaks of the relationship between action and objectives, whereas organization relates its activities to programs and clientele. No one can say for certain that self-evaluating organizations can exist, let alone become the prevailing form of administration. We can learn a good deal about the production and use of evaluation in government, nonetheless, by considering what is involved in achieving so extraordinary a state of affairs — a self-evaluating organization.

THE POLICY-ADMINISTRATION DICHOTOMY REVISITED

Organization demands the division of labor. No one person can do everything. Who, then, will carry out the evaluative activity and who will administer the programs for which the organization is responsible?

The Self-Evaluating Organization

Almost every organization has a program staff, by whatever name called, that advises top officials about policy problems. It is relatively small and conducts whatever formal evaluation does go on. Its members may exert considerable power in the organization by persuasiveness and access to the top men, or they may be merely like a benign growth that can be seen but has little effect on the body. Insofar as one wants to further analytic activities, one must think of strengthening them in relation to other elements. The idea of the self-evaluating organization, however, must mean more than this: a few men trying to force evaluation on an organization hundreds or thousands of times larger than they are. The spirit of the self-evaluating organization suggests that, in some meaningful way, the entire organization should be infused with the evaluative ethic.

Immediately we have to deal with the chain of command. How far down must the spirit of evaluation go to ensure responsiveness in the organization as a whole? If all personnel were involved there would appear to be insuperable difficulties in finding messengers, mail clerks, and secretaries to meet the criteria. If we move up one step to those who deal with the public and carry out more complex activities, the numbers still may be staggering. These tens of thousands of people certainly do not have the qualifications necessary to conduct evaluative activities, and it would be idle to pretend that they would. The forest ranger and the national-park officer may be splendid people, but they are not trained in evaluation and they are not likely to be. Yet evaluational activity appropriate to each level must be conducted if evaluation is to permeate an organization.

There has long been talk in management circles of combining accountability with decentralization. Organization subunits are given autonomy within limits for which they are held strictly accountable to their hierarchic superiors. Central power is masked but it is still there. Dividing the task so that each subunit has genuine autonomy would mean giving each a share in decisions affecting the entire organization. Decentralization is known to exist, we have learned, only so far as field units follow inconsistent and contradictory policies. One can expect the usual headquarters-field rivalries to develop, one stressing appreciation of local interests, the other fearing dissolution as the sum of its clashing units. Presumably the tension will show up in rival analyses. The center should win out because of its greater expertise, but local units always will be specialists in their own problems. They will have to be put in their place. We are back, it seems, to hierarchy. How can the center get what it wants from the periphery without overformalizing their relationship?

One model, the internalized gyroscope, is recorded in Herbert Kaufman's classic on *The Forest Ranger*. By recruitment and training, forest rangers are socialized into values that they carry wherever they go, and learn to apply in specific circumstances. Central control is achieved without apparent effort or detailed instruction because rangers have internalized the major premises from which appropriate actions generally may be deduced. The self-evaluating organization, by contrast, demands problem solving divorced from commitments to specific policies and organizational structures. The necessary skill is considerably higher and the locus of attention lies in inculcating problem-solving skills among its officers (rather than issuing predetermined instructions to them).[2] But their organizational identification is far more intense than can be expected elsewhere.

The Administration Group

Suppose that most organizational personnel are too unskilled to engage in evaluation. Suppose it is too costly to move around hundreds of thousands of officials who carry out the work of government. The next alternative is to forge the entire central administration into an evaluative unit that directs the self-evaluating organization. Several real-world models are available. Individuals in the "administration group" in Great Britain illustrate one type of central direction. Chosen for qualities of intellect that enable them to understand policy and of behavior that enable them to get along with their fellows, they move among the great departments and seek (with the political ministers) to direct activities of that vast bureaucracy. At the apex stands the Treasury, an organization with few operating commitments, whose job is to monitor activities and introduce necessary changes in the bureaucracy. Economic policy, special preserve of the Treasury, is supposed to undergo rapid movement; its personnel are used to changing tasks and objectives at short notice. Though somewhat divorced from organizations in which they share responsibility with the political ministers, top civil servants also do belong by virtue of their direct administrative interests. Complaints are heard increasingly that these men are too conservative in defense of departmental interests, too preoccupied with immediate matters, or too bound by organizational tradition to conduct serious evaluation. Hence, the Fulton Report claimed, they adapt too slowly (if at all), to changing circumstances. Steps have been taken, therefore, to establish a Central Policy Review Staff to do policy analysis for the cabinet and otherwise to encourage evaluative activity. Departments, however, remain successful in warding off outside scrutiny.

Germany and Sweden have gone considerably further in the same direction. Departments in Sweden have relatively small groups of men connected with policy questions, but administration is delegated to large public corporations set up for that purpose.[3] The state governments in Germany (the Länder) do more than 90 per cent of the administrative work, central-government departments presumably being engaged with larger questions of policy. The student of public administration in

America will at once get the picture. The policy-administration dichotomy, beloved of early American administrative theorists — thoroughly demolished, it seemed in the forties and fifties — now has reappeared with new vitality.

History of the Policy-Administration Dichotomy

The policy-administration dichotomy originated with Frank Goodnow and others in efforts to legitimate the rise of the civil service and with it the norm of neutral-competence in government. Civil servants were to be expert but not partisan. They tried to save good government from the evils of the spoils system by insulating it from partisan politics. Congress made policy; the task of the administrative apparatus was to find appropriate technical means to carry it out. Administrative actions were thought to be less general and more technical so that well-motivated administrators would be able to enact the will of the people as received from Congress or the president. Civil servants then could be chosen on technical merits, not partisan or policy politics.

An avalanche of criticism, begun in earnest by Paul Appleby's *Policy and Administration,* overwhelmed these arguments. Observation of congressional statutes showed that often they were vague, if not contradictory. There were no clear objectives to which administrators could subordinate themselves. Observation of administrative behavior showed that conflicts over the policy to be adopted continued unabated in bureaus and departments. Administrators made important decisions that deeply affected the lives of people. Choice abounded and administrators seized on it; indeed, they were often themselves divided on how to interpret statutes or how generally to frame policies under them. Interest groups made strenuous efforts to get favorable administrative enactments. Moreover, no one had sufficiently precise knowledge to determine the best way to carry out a general objective in many areas. With such large areas of uncertainty and ignorance, the values and choices of administrators counted a great deal. Taken at this level not too much could be said for maintaining the distinction between policy and administration. Nevertheless, nagging doubts remained.

Were politics and administration identical? If they were, then it was difficult to understand how we were able to talk about them separately. Or was "politics" simply a cover name for all the things that different organs of the government did? If politics and adiminstration could be separated in some way, then a division of labor might be based on them. No doubt the legislative will, if there was one, could be undermined by a series of administrative enactments. But were not these administrative decisions of a smaller and less encompassing kind than those usually made by Congress? Were there not ways in which the enactments of

Congress were (or could be) made more authoritative than the acts of administrators? Overwhelming administrative discretion did violence to democratic theory.

A New Understanding of the Policy-Administration Dichotomy

We are seeing significant efforts to rationalize the policy-administration dichotomy. The dissatisfactions of modern industrial life are being poured on the bureaucracy, and, though it seems to weigh more heavily, human satisfaction does not increase proportionally. Bureaucracy has become identified with red tape and resistance to change. Yet no one can quite imagine doing away with it because of the ever-increasing demand for services. Thus politicians who feel that the bureaucracy has become a liability,[4] clientele who think they might be better served under other arrangements, taxpayers who resent the costs, policy analysts who see organizations as barriers to the application of intelligence, will join in seeking ways to make bureaucracy more responsive. How better do this than by isolating its innovative functions from the mass of officialdom? Instead of preventing administration from being contaminated by politics, however, the purpose of the new dichotomy will be to insulate policy from the stultifying influences of bureaucracy.

WHO WILL PAY THE COSTS OF CHANGE?

Although most organizations evaluate some policies periodically, the self-evaluating organization would do so all the time. These evaluative activities would be inefficient, costing more than they are worth, unless they led to change. Indeed the self-evaluating organization is purposefully set up to encourage just that.

The self-evaluating organization will have to convince its own members to live with flux. When they first join the organization, they may think they love constant upset but experience is likely to teach them otherwise. Man's appetite for rapid change is strictly limited. People cannot bear to have their cherished beliefs challenged or their lives altered continuously. Anxiety is induced because they cannot get their bearings, and have trouble knowing exactly what they should be doing. The ensuing confusion may lead to inefficiencies in the form of hesitation or random behavior designed to cover as many bases as possible. Cynicism may grow as the wisdom of the day before yesterday gives way to some new truth, which in turn is replaced by a still more radiant one. Leaders of the self-evaluating organization will have to counter this criticism.

Building support for policies within an organization demands internal selling. Leaders of the organization must convince members that what they are doing is worthwhile. Within the self-evaluating organization the task at first may be more difficult than in more traditional bureaucracies. Personnel who evaluate are accustomed to question policy proposals and to demand persuasive arguments in their support. If the initial campaign proves successful, however, enthusiasm can be expected to reach a high pitch after all policies have been evaluated, new alternatives have been analyzed, and evidence has been induced in favor of an alternative. The danger here is overselling. Convinced that "science" is on their side, that their paper calculations are in tune with the world, evaluators are a bit too self-confident. They are set up for more disappointment than those who expect less. How much harder it is, then, when continuous evaluation suggests the need for another change in policy. Now two internal campaigns are necessary: the first involves unselling an old policy, the second, selling the new one. Past virtues have become vices and last year's goods now seem hopelessly shoddy. Perpetual change is costly.

Maintaining higher rates of change depends on the ability of those who produce it to make others pay the costs. If the change-makers themselves are forced to bear the brunt of their actions, predictably they will seek to stabilize their environment. That is the burden of almost the entire sociological literature on organizations from Weber to Crozier. The needs of members displace the organization's goals. The public purposes that the organization was supposed to serve give way to its private acts.

Rather than succumb to the diseases of bureaucracy, the self-evaluating organization will be tempted to pass them on to others. It can split itself into "evaluating" and "administering" parts, making lower levels pay the costs of change, or it can seek to impose them on other organizations in its environment. We shall deal first with difficulties encountered in trying to stabilize the evaluative top of the organization while the bottom is in continuous flux.

Let us suppose that an organization separates its evaluative head from its administrative body. People at the top do not have operating functions. They are all, in administrative jargon, staff rather than line. Their function is to appraise the consequences of policies, work out better alternatives, and have the new policies they recommend carried out by the administrative unit.

Who would bear the cost of change? One can imagine evaluators running around merrily suggesting changes without having to implement them, anxiety being absorbed by the administrators, supposedly those who should change gears and smooth out the difficulties. But administrators will not stand still for this arrangement. Because their belief about what is administratively feasible and organizationally attainable must be part of the policy that is adopted, they will bargain with evaluators.

Administrators can bring significant resources to this struggle. They deal with the public. They collect the basic information that is sent upward in one form or another. They can drag their feet, mobilize clientele, hold back information, or otherwise make cooperation difficult. Evaluators have their own advantages. They have greater authority to issue rules and regulations. They are experts in manipulating data and models to justify policies or denigrate them.

Held responsible for policy but prohibited from administering it directly, evaluators have an incentive to seek antibureaucratic delivery systems. They will, for example, prefer an income to a service strategy.[5] Evaluators can be pretty certain that clients will receive checks mailed from the central computer, whereas they cannot be sure that the services they envisage will be delivered by hordes of bureaucrats in the manner they would like. Giving people income to buy better living quarters has the great advantage of not needing a corps of officials to supervise public housing. Evaluators do not have the field personnel to supervise innumerable small undertakings; therefore they will prefer large-investment projects over smaller ones. Also they can make better use of their few people on expensive projects that justify large amounts of analytic time. Contrariwise, administrators will emphasize far-flung operations providing services that call for large numbers of people.

There are circumstances, of course, in which administrators and evaluators will reverse their normal positions. If evaluators feel there is not enough government employment, they may seek labor-intensive operations. Should administrators feel already overburdened, they may welcome policies that are easily centralized and directed by machines performing rote operations. It is more likely, however, for administrators and evaluators to expand into each other's domain. Each can reduce the bargaining powers of the other by taking unto itself some of its competitor's advantages. Thus administrators may recruit their own policy analysts to compete with the evaluators who, in turn, will seek their own contacts within the administrative apparatus to ensure a steady and reliable flow of information. If this feuding goes far enough, the result will be two organizations acting in much the same way as the one they replaced, but with additional problems of coordination.

EVALUATION, INCORPORATED

From separating evaluation and administration it is but a short step to the idea of teams of evaluators. A rough equivalent of a competitive market can be introduced by letting teams of evaluators compete for direction of policy in an area. The competition would take place in price (a specified objective accomplished at a lower cost), quality (better policies for the same money), quantity (more produced at the same cost), maintenance (we can fix things when they go wrong), experience (see our proven record), values (our policies will embody your preferences) and talent (when it comes down to it, you are buying our cleverness and we are superior). The winning team would be placed in charge until it left to go elsewhere or was successfully challenged by another team. The government might raise its price to keep a talented team or it might lower it to get rid of an incompetent one. The incentives for evaluators would be enormous — restrained, of course, by ability to perform lest they go bankrupt or lose business to competitors. The first task of the new enterprise would be to establish its own form of organization. What organizational arrangements are necessary to make competition among evaluators feasible?

Evaluators, like all consultants, must either be assured of employment somewhere, or engage in other dispensable occupations from which they can be recruited at short notice. A handful of evaluators always could be recruited by ad hoc methods. But teams of evaluators, large enough to direct major areas of policy, would be hard to assemble at short notice. They would all be doing different things instead of working together, which itself is part of the experience necessary for success. They could not even form a team unless all promised to be on the job at an arranged time if their bid were successful — yet, at the same time, they must have other jobs to fall back on if turned down.

In the previous model — evaluators generating new policies, and administrators carrying them out — these bureaucrats shouldered the major burden of uncertainty. Under the new model this imbalance is redressed because evaluators have to worry about employment security. Few people like to shift jobs all the time; fewer still enjoy the idea of periodic unemployment alternating with the anxiety of bidding to get jobs, and performing to keep them. We can be sure mechanisms will be found to reduce their uncertainty to tolerable size.

Evaluators may choose to work within administrative organizations, accepting a lower status and learning to live with disappointment in return for job stability. This pattern already is used. Evaluators may go to private industry and universities on the understanding they will be able to make occasional forays into government as part of a tiny group of advisors to leading officials; this also is done now. Both alternatives do away with the idea of competition; they merely graft a small element of evaluation onto organizations in a catch-as-catch-can way.

For self-preservation, evaluators who are in a position to compete for the direction of policy will have to form stable organizations of their own. Like the firms of management consultants they resemble, these evaluators would bid on numerous projects; the difference would be that they would do the policy work as part of the public apparatus rather than make recommendations and then disappear. Evaluation, Incorporated, as we shall call it, would include numerous possible teams, some working and others prepared to go to work. The firm would have to demand substantial overhead to provide services for the evaluators, to draw up proposals, and to compensate those members who are temporarily (they hope) out of work. Keeping Evaluation, Inc. solvent by maintaining high employment will become a major organization goal.

Evaluation, Inc. is an organization. It has managers intent on survival, members who must be induced to remain, and clients who must be served. Therefore it will constitute itself a lobby for evaluation. When the demand for services is high, it will be able to insist on the evaluative ethic; it will take services to those who are prepared to appreciate (by paying for) them. But when demands are low, Evaluation, Inc. must trim sail; it has a payroll to meet. Rather than leave a job when nonanalytical criteria prevail, it may have to swallow pride and stay on. Its managers can easily convince themselves that survival is good not only for them but for society also, which will benefit from the good Evaluation, Inc. will be able to do in better times.

If their defects stem from their insecurities, the remedy will be apparent; increase the stability of evaluators by guaranteeing them tenure of employment. Too-close identification with party or policy, in any event, proved a mixed blessing. They feasted while they were in favor and famished when they were out. Apparently they require civil service status, a government corporation, say, devoted to evaluation.

Perhaps the General Accounting Office (GAO), which is beginning to do analytic studies, will provide a model of an independent governmental organization devoted to evaluation. Because it has a steady income from its auditing work, it can afford to form, break up, and recreate teams of evaluators. Its independence from the Executive Branch (the Accountant General is responsible to Congress and serves a fifteen-year term) might facilitate objective analysis. But the independence of GAO has been maintained because it eschews involvement in controversial matters. If a new General Evaluation Office (GEO) were to issue reports that increased conflict, surely there would be a strong impulse to bring it under regular political control. The old auditing function might be compromised because objectivity about a program one has sponsored is difficult to maintain, or because public disputes lower confidence in its operations. Opponents of GEO policy positions might begin to question its impartiality in determining the legality of government expenditures. Yet protection would be difficult to arrange because the new GEO would not have a political client. By imagining the dilemma of an organization that supplies evaluation to others, we hope to illuminate the dilemmas of any organization that is serious about engaging in continuous analyses of its own activities.

Evaluation, which criticizes some programs and proposes to replace them with others, is manifestly á political activity. Though not political in the sense of party partisanship, it is political in the sense of policy advocacy. Without a steady source of political support, from somebody out there in society, it will suffer the fate of abandoned children; and the self-evaluating organization is unlikely to prosper in an orphanage.

ADJUSTING TO THE ENVIRONMENT

The self-evaluating organization uses its own programs in order to alter or abolish them. The ability to make changes when its analysis suggests they are desirable is an essential part of its capacity to make self-evaluation a living reality. Yet the ability of any organization to make self-generated changes is limited by the necessity of receiving support from its environment.

The leaders of a self-evaluating organization cannot afford to leave the results of their labors up to the fates. If their "batting average" goes 'way down, they will be in trouble. Members of the organization will lose faith because evaluation does not lead to changes in actual policy. Those attracted initially by the prospect of being powerful as well as analytical will leave to join more promising ventures, or old clients will become dissatisfied without new ones to take their place. As the true believers depart, personnel who are less motivated by the evaluative ethic will move into higher positions. Revitalization of the organization via promotion and recruitment of professing evaluators will become impossible.

In order to avoid that deadly cycle, leaders of the self-evaluating organization must seek some success. They must select organization activities, not only with an eye toward their analytic justification, but with a view toward receiving essential support. Hence they become selective evaluators. They must prohibit the massive use of organizational resources where they see little chance of success. They must seek out problems that are easy to solve, and changes that are easy to make, because they do not involve radical departures from the past. They must be prepared to hold back the results of evaluation if the times are not propitious; they must be ready to seize the proper time for change whether or not evaluations are fully prepared or wholly justified. Little by little, it seems, the behavior of the leaders will become similar to that of officials of other organizations who seek also to adapt to their environment.

The growing conservatism of the self-evaluating organization is bound to cause internal strains. Disagreements about whether the organization is being too cautious are sure to crop up. No one can prove that the leaders have correctly appraised opportunities in a rapidly shifting environment. If they try to do too much, they risk failure in the political world. If they try to do too little, they may betray their own beliefs and lose the support of their most dedicated members. Maintaining a balance between efficacy and commitment, between the instrumental and the expressive, is not easy.

Now the self-evaluating organization need not wring its collective hands. It can work to mobilize interests toward favored positions; it can seek to neutralize opposition; it can try to persuade current clientele that they will be better off, or instill a wish to be served on behalf of new beneficiaries. One fears that its reputation among clientele groups may not be the best, however, because, as a self-evaluating organization, it must be prepared to abandon (or drastically modify) programs and with them the clientele they serve. Clients will recognize such a marriage of convenience. Seeing the self-evaluating organization always eager to consider more advantageous alliances, clients will have to measure their affection according to the exact amount of service rendered. The self-evaluating organization cannot expect to receive more love than it gives. In fact, it must receive less.

Evaluation never can be fully rewarded. In the nature of things, there must be other considerations that prevail over evaluation, even if the powers that be want to follow its dictates. Preferred policies of the self-evaluating organization never are the only ones being contemplated by the government; multitudes of policies are always in being or about to be born. Some are bound to fly in the face of evaluative precepts. Consider the influence of fiscal policy upon analysis. Suppose the time has come for financial stringency; the government has decided that expenditures must be reduced. Proposals for increases may be disallowed no matter how good the justification. Reductions may be made whether indicated by analysis or not. Conversely, a political decision may be made to increase expenditure. The substantive merits of various policies clearly will have been subordinated to their immediate financial implications.

Evaluation may be wielded as a weapon in the political wars. It may be used by one faction or party against another. Government may use evaluation as a means of putting down the bureaucracy. A two-step rule for decision may be followed: the recommendations of evaluation may be accepted when they lead to reduction but rejected when they suggest increases in expenditure. Before long, members of the organization become reluctant to provide information that will be used only in a biased way. The evaluative enterprise depends on common recognition that the activity is being carried out somehow in order to secure better policies, whatever these may be, and not in support of a predetermined position. If this understanding is violated, people down the line will refuse to cooperate. They will withhold their contribution by hiding information or by not volunteering to find it. The morale of the self-evaluating organization will be threatened because its members are being asked to pervert their calling.

It's the same the whole world over: the analytically virtuous are not necessarily rewarded nor are the wicked (who do not evaluate) punished. The leaders of the self-evaluating organization, therefore, must redouble their effort to obtain political help.

JOINING KNOWLEDGE WITH POWER

To understand the requirements necessary for a self-evaluating organization is to realize why they are rarely met. The self-evaluating organization, it turns out, would be susceptible to much the same kinds of anti-evaluative tendencies as are today's organizations. It, too, must stabilize its environment, securing internal loyalty and outside support. At best, evaluation will remain only one element in administrative organizations. Yet no one can say today that it is overemphasized. No flight of fancy should lead anyone to believe that a rush to evaluation is on the horizon. We have just come back to asking how a little more rather than a little less might become part of public organizations. How might analytic integrity be combined with political efficacy?

Putting Knowledge to Work

Evaluative man does seek knowledge, but he also seeks power. His desire to do good is joined with his will to act powerfully; one is useless without the other. A critical incentive for pursuing evaluation is that the results become governmental policy. Without knowledge it would be wrong to seek power. But without power it becomes more difficult to obtain knowledge. Why should anyone supply valuable information to someone who can neither help nor harm him? Access to information may be given only on the condition that programmatic goals are altered. Evaluative man is doing well when he can pyramid resources so that greater knowledge leads to enhanced power, which in turn increases his access to information. He is in bad shape when the pursuit of power leads to the sacrifice of evaluation. His own policy problem is how to do enough of both (and not too much of either) so that knowledge and power reinforce rather than undermine one another.

The political process generates a conflict of interest within the evaluative enterprises. Evaluators see analysis as a means of deciding on better policies and selling them to others. Clients (elected officials, group leaders, top administrators) view analysis as a means of better understanding available choices with which they can control decisions. Talk of "better policies," as if it did not matter who determined them, only clouds the issues.

The evaluative group in an organization would hope that it could show political men the worth of analytic activities. Politicians, in turn, hope to learn about the desirability of the programs under evaluation. But their idea of desirability manifestly includes the support which programs generate for them and the organizations to which they belong. Hence evaluation must lead to programs that connect the interests of political leaders to the outcomes of governmental actions; otherwise, they will reject evaluation and the people who do it.

A proposed policy partly determines its own success; the support it gathers or loses in clientele is fed back into its future prospects. By its effect on the future environment of the organization, a proposed policy affects the kind of work the organization can do. Pure evaluative man, however single-minded his concentration on the intrinsic merits of programs, must consider also their interactive effects on future ability to pursue his craft. Just as he would insist on including the effect of one element in a system on another in his policy analysis, so too he must consider how present recommendations affect future ones. A proper evaluation includes the effect of a policy on the organizations responsible for it.

Consider in this organizational context the much-discussed problem of myriad government programs that may contribute to identical ends without anyone being able to control them. There may be redundancy, in which programs overlap, side by side with large areas of inattention, to which no programs are directed. More services of one kind (and less of another) are provided than might be strictly warranted. Without evaluation no one can really judge if there are too many or too few programs or whether their contents are appropriate. In any event an evaluation that did all this would get nowhere unless it did result in different institutional methods for handling the same problems.

Even on its own terms, then, evaluation should not remain apart from the organizations on which it depends for implementation. Organizational design and policy analysis are part of the same governmental process. If an organization wishes to reduce its identification with programs (and the clients who support them), for example, so that it can afford to examine different types of policy, it must adopt a political strategy geared to that end.

Diversification and Competition

The self-evaluating organization would be well advised not to depend too much on a single type of clientele. Diversification is its strategy. The more diverse its services, the more varied its clientele, the less the self-evaluating organization has to depend on any one of them, the more able it is to shift the basis of its support. Diversity creates political flexibility.

Any organization which produces one product, which engages in a limited range of activities, is unlikely to abandon them willingly. Its survival, after all, is bound up in its program. If the program goes, the organization dies. One clear implication is that the traditional wisdom about governmental organization badly needs revision.[6] If the basic principle of organization is that similar programs should be grouped together, as is now believed to be desirable, these organizations will refuse to change. On the contrary, agencies should be encouraged to differentiate their products and diversify output. If they are not faced with declining demand for all their programs, they will be more willing to abandon or modify a single one, and much more open to change.

No matter how good its internal analysis, or how persuasively an organization justifies programs to itself, something is unsatisfying about allowing this self-judgment. The ability of organizations to please themselves must ultimately (at least in a democratic society) give way to appraisal by outsiders. Critics of organizations must, therefore, recognize that their job is essential; opposition is part and parcel of evaluation. The goal would be to secure a more intelligent and analytically sophisticated level of advocacy on all sides. Diverse analyses might become, as Harry Rowen suggests, part of the mutual partisan adjustment by which creative use is made of conflicts among organized interests.

Competition itself, however, need not lead to fundamental change. Organizations may go on the offensive by growing bigger instead of better — that is, by doing more of the same. The only real change in which they are interested is magnitude. We are all familiar with the salesmanship involved in moving to new technologies or larger structures in which internal dynamism and grandiose conceptions are mistaken for new ideas. Motion may be a protection against change.

Competition, if it is to lead to desirable consequences, must take place under appropriate rules specifying who can make what kind of transaction. No one would advocate unrestrained competition among economic units without a market that makes it socially advantageous for participants to pursue private interests expecting mutual gain. Where parties are affected who are not directly represented in the market, rules may be changed to accommodate a wider range of interests. Competition among rival policies and their proponents also takes place in an arena that specifies rules for exercising power on particular decisions. Evaluators, therefore, must consider how their preferred criteria for decision will be affected by the rules for decision in political arenas within which they must operate.

The Politics of Evaluation

It appears we have returned to politics. Unless building support for policies is an integral part of designing them, their proponents are setting themselves up for disappointment. To say that one will first have a great idea and then worry about how it might be implemented is a formula for failure.[7] A good evaluation specifies not only desirable outcomes but suggests institutional mechanisms for achieving them.

If you don't know how to make an evaluation, it may make trouble for you but not anyone else. If you do know how to evaluate, it becomes a problem for others. Evaluation is an organizational problem. Although the occasional lone rider may be able to fire off an analysis now and then, eventually evaluators must institutionalize their efforts if they are to produce a steady output. Most evaluation takes place within organizations. Rejection of evaluation is done mainly by the organizations that ask for it. To create an organization that evaluates its own activities evidently demands an organizational response. If evaluation is not done at all, if it is done but not used, if used but twisted out of shape, the place to look first is not at the technical apparatus but at the organization.

Organization is first but not last. Always it is part of a larger society that conditions what it can do. Evaluation is a social problem also. So long as organizational opposition to evaluation is center front, we are not likely to become aware of the social background. Should this initial resistance be overcome, and individual organizations get to like evaluation, however, it would still face multiple defenses thrown up by social forces.

EVALUATION AS TRUST

For the self-evaluating organization all knowledge must be contingent. Change for the better is possible always though not necessarily yet attained. It is the organization par excellence that seeks knowledge. The ways in which it tries to do this, therefore, uniquely define its character.

The self-evaluating organization would be skeptical rather than committed. It would continuously be challenging its own assumptions. Not dogma but scientific doubt would be its distinguishing feature. It would seek new truth instead of defending old errors. Testing hypotheses would be its main work.

Like the model community of scholars, the self-evaluating organization would be open, truthful, and explicit. It would state its conclusions in public, show how they were determined, and give others the opportunity of refuting them. Costs and benefits of alternative programs for various groups in society would be indicated as precisely as available knowledge would permit. Everything would be above board.

Are there ways of securing the required information? Can the necessary knowledge be created? Will the truth make men free? Whatever the answer to these questions might be, each depends on trust among social groups and within organizations. Acceptance of evaluation requires a community of shared values.

The Necessity of Experimentation

An advantage of formal analysis, in which the self-evaluating organization specializes, is that it does not depend entirely on learning from experience; ordinary organizations can do that. By creating models that abstract relationships from the areas of the universe they wish to control, evaluators try to substitute manipulation of their models for events in the world. By rejecting alternatives their models tell them will work out badly (or not as well as others), analysts save scarce resources and protect the public against less worthy actions. Ultimately, however, there must be an appeal to the world of experience. No one, not even evaluators, should try theoretical notions on large populations without more tangible reasons to believe that recommended alternatives would prove efficacious.[8]

Because the defect of ordinary organizations is that they do not learn well from experience, the self-evaluating organization seeks to order that experience so that knowledge will be gained from it. The proof that a policy is good is that it works when it is tried. But because not everything can be tried, experiments lie at the heart of evaluation. They are essential for connecting alleged causes with desired effects amid limited resources.

The ability of the self-evaluating organization to perform depends on a climate of opinion that favors experimentation. If severely constrained resources make for reluctance to try new ventures, the self-evaluating organization cannot operate as advertised. Should there be strong feeling that everyone must be treated alike, experimentation would be ruled out. Take the "More Effective Schools" movement in New York City. The idea was to run an experiment to determine whether putting more resources into schools would improve the performance of deprived children. To qualify as a proper experiment, More Effective Schools had to be established in some places but not in others, so that there would be control groups. The demand for equality of treatment was so intense, however, that mass picketing took place at school sites. Favored treatment for some schools was taken as *prima facie* evidence of discrimination. It became apparent that More Effective Schools would have to be tried everywhere or nowhere. Unless groups trust each other, they will not allow experiments to be conducted, and if they are conducted anyway, will not accept the results.

The Collection and Selection of Information

Although ways of learning without experimentation may be found, no evaluation is possible without adequate information. But how much is enough? Organizational hierarchies exist in order to convert data into information. If the people at the top had to consider all the bits of data available in the far-flung reaches of the organization, they would be overwhelmed.

As data are weeded and compressed on their way through the hierarchy, however, important bits may be eliminated or distorted. One of the most often voiced criticisms of organizations is that the people at the top do not know what is going on. Information is being withheld from them or is inaccurate so that they make decisions on mistaken impressions. The desire to pass on only good news eliminates information that might put the conveyer in a bad light. Top officials, therefore, may resort to such devices as using overlapping sources of information or planting agents at lower levels. There are limits to these efforts, however, because top people have only so much time to digest what they have been told. Therefore they vacillate between fear of losing information and of being unable to struggle out from under masses of data.

How might the self-evaluating organization deal with biased information? The organization's members would have to be rewarded for passing on bad news. Those responsible for the flow of information must not, at least, be punished for telling the truth. If they are also those in charge of administering policy, it will not be possible to remove them for bad performance, because if that were done, their successors would be motivated to suppress such information. Top people must be willing to accept blame themselves, though they may not feel this is their responsibility and though their standing may be compromised. The hierarchy itself may have to give way to a system of shifting roles in which superior and subordinate positions are exchanged so that each member knows he will soon face similar difficulties. Clearly, the self-evaluating organization calls for an extraordinary amount of mutual trust.

The spread of self-evaluating organizations could enhance social trust by widening areas of agreement about the consequences of policies and the likely effects of change. Calculations as to who benefited, and to what degree, presumably would aid in political cost-benefit analysis. The legitimacy of public institutions would be enhanced if they came out of a more self-consciously analytic procedure that was increasingly recognized as such. Evaluation would be informative, meliorative, and stabilizing in the midst of change. It sounds idyllic.

Trust as the Basis of Interpretation

More information by itself does not lead unerringly to greater agreement, however, if the society is wracked by fundamental cleavages. As technology makes information more widely available, the need for interpretation will grow. Deluged by data, distrustful of others, citizens actually may grow apart as leaders collect more information about how bad things are compared to what they ought to be. The more people trust group leaders rather than governmental officials, the greater the chance that differences will be magnified rather than reconciled. Clarification of objectives may make it easier to see the social conflicts implicit in the distribution of income, or cultural preference on the environment, or differing styles of life attached to opposing views of the ideal society. Evaluation need not create agreement; perhaps it presupposes agreement that social processes are basically benevolent, and that, therefore, policy evaluation will serve their interests.

NOTES

1. Orris C. Herfindahl, "What is Conversation? Three Studies in Minerals Economics" (Washington, D.C.: Resources for the Future, 1961), p. 2, quoting from Gifford Pinchot, *Breaking New Ground* (New York: Harcourt Brace Jovanovich, 1947), p. 326.
2. Dan Horowitz, "Flexible Responsiveness and Military Strategy: The Case of the Israeli Army," *Policy Sciences*, Vol. 1, No. 2 (Summer 1970), pp. 191–205.
3. Hans Thorelli, "Overall Planning and Management in Sweden," *International Social Bulletin*, Vol. 8, No. 2 (1956).
4. The most dramatic and visible change can be found in the American presidency. Presidents have increasingly bureaucratized their operations. Within the Executive Office there are now sizable subunits, characterized by specialization and division of labor, for dealing with the media of information and communication, Congress, foreign and domestic policy, and more. At the same time, presidents seek the right to intervene at any level within the Executive Branch sporadically. Administrators are being prodded to change while the president stabilizes his environment. See Aaron Wildavsky, "Government and the People," *Commentary* Vol. 56, No. 2 (August 1973), pp. 25–32.
5. See Robert A. Levine, "Rethinking Our Social Strategies," *The Public Interest*, No. 10 (Winter 1968).
6. William A. Niskanen, *Bureaucracy and Representative Government* (Chicago: Aldine-Atherton, 1971).
7. For further discussion along these lines see Jeffrey L. Pressman and Aaron Wildavsky, *Implementation* (Berkeley and Los Angeles: University of California Press, 1973).
8. An exception of a kind is found in defense policy, where the purpose of the analytic exercises is to avoid testing critical hypotheses. Once the hypotheses on a nuclear war are tested, evaluators may not be around to revise their analyses. See Aaron Wildavsky, "Practical Consequences of the Theoretical Study of Defense Policy," *Public Administration Review*, Vol. 25, No. 1 (March 1965), pp. 90–103.

CHAPTER 10

SKEPTICISM AND DOGMA IN THE WHITE HOUSE: JIMMY CARTER'S THEORY OF GOVERNING

"Seek simplicity and distrust it."

Alfred North Whitehead

Dogma and skepticism are not necessarily universal tendencies to be applied regardless of subject. It is possible to be skeptical about some things and dogmatic about others. Indeed, unless dogma is to become utter rigidity, and skepticism sheer disbelief, there must be some combination that varies by object and degree — one trusts science more than astrology, family more than statesmen. There are contexts in which skepticism may be misplaced. Perhaps there are even experiments showing that assuming a posture of scientific skepticism toward loved ones ("How are you?" "What do you mean exactly?") is counterproductive (though some relationships may last as long as an hour under this onslaught). It is important, therefore, to differentiate the object of skepticism and the degree of dogma.

It should also prove useful to show that these special categories are relevant to daily political life. President Carter is a good subject for this purpose (Why not begin at the top?) precisely because he appears to treat some aspects of his work as variables (subject to condition and context) and others as constants, fixed firmly as guiding stars in the administrative galaxies. President Jimmy Carter, according to our hypothesis, is skeptical about the contents of public policies but dogmatic about the administrative procedures for arriving at those policies.

President Carter is not an ideologue of policy; he has flexible views on substantive policies, such as tax reform, medical care, and busing. Like most of us, as the times and conditions change, he can and does change his mind. Carter's basic beliefs are about procedures for making policy, about which he speaks with passion, determination, and consistency. He cares less about the goals than the need for goals, less about the content of policies than about their ideal form: simplicity, uniformity, predictability, hierarchy, and comprehensiveness.

Therefore, if there is a danger for President Carter, it is not that he will support unpopular *policies*, but that he will persevere with inappropriate *procedures*. The question is whether he views his procedural criteria merely as rough guidelines for formulating public policy or as immutable principles of good government. If they are hypotheses about governing, subject to refinement or abandonment in the face of contrary evidence, we have no reason for alarm; but if he does not allow his theories of governing to be refuted by experience, we all are in for hard times.

Of all the Democratic presidential candidates in the primaries, Jimmy Carter was criticized most for his alleged vagueness on policy. Actually, his campaign staff put out numerous papers outlining his proposals on issues ranging from abortion to busing to welfare.[1] The problem was not so much that he did not say specific things about issues as that he placed greater emphasis on methods, procedures, and instruments for making policy than on the content of policy itself.

The response of Stuart Eisenstat, Carter's chief "issues" advisor, to a question about which issues would dominate the campaign, will illustrate. Eisenstat grouped the issues into three types: one was the lack of long-range federal planning; a second emphasized openness; a third dealt with government reorganization.[2] The emphasis of all three was on administrative instruments, not on policy outcomes. (Long-range planning, like openness and reorganization, is not a policy but an instrument used to produce policies.) If faith in intellectual ability to put it all together is any sign, Carter on public policy is more of a planner than a politician.

In Carter's own words, a major purpose for reorganizing the federal government is to "make it simple." He favors "drastic simplification of the tax structure,"[3] "simple, workable, housing policies,"[4] "simplification of the laws and regulations to substitute education for paper-shuffling grantsmanship,"[5] simplification of the purposes of the military," and a "fighting force that is simply organized."[6] Rather than the "bewildering complexity" we now have, he wants to create a "simplified system of welfare."[7] His praise goes out to the state and local governments that have devised "simple organizational structures."[8]

How does he intend to simplify? When Carter became Governor of Georgia he reduced state agencies from 300 to 22. He proposed a similar nine-tenths reduction in the number of units at the federal level, from

1,900 down to around 200.[9] His general rationale seems to be, the fewer agencies the better. Carter, it is fair to say, does not manifest a bias toward federalism.

According to Eisenstat, another way Carter will simplify administrative structure is "to make sure that duplicating functions are not performed by one agency and that, in fact, we don't have a situation whereby duplicating programs are being administered by more than one agency."[10] Carter repeatedly has stated that one of the purposes of his proposal to introduce "zero-base budgeting" (as he did in Georgia) is "eliminating duplication and overlapping of functions."[11] In restructuring the defense establishment, Carter would like to "remove the overlapping functions and singly address the Defense Department toward the capability to fight."[12] Described by our words, Carter favors intellectual cogitation over social interaction.

UNIFORMITY

Another way in which President Carter intends to simplify policy is by uniformity. He plans to reform the welfare system by providing a uniform, national cash payment varying only according to cost of living.[13] He intends to standardize the tax structure by eliminating loopholes, treating all income the same.[14] To create uniformity, Carter would grant a direct subsidy for new housing.[15] Also he would standardize medical treatment — "We now have a wide disparity of length of stay in hospitals, a wide disparity of charges for the same services, a wide difference in the chances of one undergoing an operation" — and make criminal justice uniform by "eliminating much of the discretion that is now exercised by judges and probation officers in determining the length of sentences."[16] By now the President has learned that uniformity is almost as much a chimera as simplicity. Why? One reason is uncertainty about public policy.

PREDICTABILITY

"There's just no predictability now about government policy," Carter has complained, "no way to tell what we're going to do next in the area of housing, transportation, environmental quality, or energy."[17] He believes in "long-range planning so that government, business, labor, and other entities in our society can work together if they agree with the goals established. But at least it would be predictable."[18] And: "The major hamstring of housing development is the unpredictability of the Federal policies. . . ."[19] In agriculture, the greatest need is a "coherent, predictable, and stable government policy relating to farming and the production of food and fiber."[20] In foreign affairs, other nations are "hungry for a more predictable and mutually advantageous relationship with our country."[21] Unpredictability led Carter to condemn Henry Kissenger's policy of no permanent friends and no permanent enemies with these words: "I would . . . let our own positions be predictable."[22]

If only we agreed on long-range goals, according to Carter, we could work together to make our policies predictable. The format of his thinking is: long-range planning entails explicit delineation of goals; once goals are known (and agreed upon), policies become predictable. This predictability reduces conflict and increases cooperation. Notice that for Carter, predictability does not come from intensive interaction about continuous adjustment of policies but by intellectual agreement on original goals.

COGITATION

Carter's theory of conflict shows how he would expect to deal with a recalcitrant cabinet: "The best mechanism to minimize this problem is the establishment of long-range goals or purposes of the government and a mutual commitment to these goals by different Cabinet members. . . ." By getting early agreement, "I can't imagine a basic strategic difference developing between myself and one of my Cabinet members if the understanding were that we worked toward the long-range goals."[23] Obviously, if there were only one correct means to an agreed end, they would search together to find it. Asked how he would resolve differences with the Congress on foreign policy, Carter answered: "I hope that my normal, careful, methodical, scientific or planning approach to long-range policies . . . would serve to remove those disharmonies long before they reach the stage of actual implementation."[24] That was before he started to screen speeches so his cabinet members would not continue to contradict him.

A major Carter campaign criticism of President Ford was that Ford "allowed the nation to drift without a goal or purpose."[25] By contrast, as governor of Georgia, Carter's administration had tried to identify long-range goals: "during the first months of my term, we had 51 public meetings around the state, attended by thousands of Georgians, to formulate specific long-range goals in every realm of public life. We spelled out in writing what we hoped to accomplish at the end of two, five, or even 20 years. . . ."[26] Only if government has clearly defined goals, believes Carter, will people be prepared to "make personal sacrifices." One of his favorite quotations from the New Testament is: "If the trumpet gives an uncertain sound, who shall prepare himself for the battle?"[27] But suppose others prefer to march to different music? How would Carter contend with conflict?

Openness may not be a form of godliness for President Carter, but it must come close. He has proposed an "all-inclusive 'sunshine law' . . . [whereby] meetings of federal boards, commissions, and regulatory agencies must be opened to the public, along with those of congressional committees."[28]

In his own mind Carter connects openness with direct access to people. He favors giving the people access to governmental decision-making, and as president, to speak directly to them. Carter values openness "to let the public know what we are doing and to restore the concept in the Congress that their constituents are also my constituents. I have just as much right and responsibility to reach the people for support as a member of Congress does." Also Carter planned revival of Franklin D. Roosevelt's "fireside chat";[29] he expected to accept "special responsibility to by-pass the big shots," and to act, as it were, as the people's lobbyist.[30] Should his policies be thwarted by special interests, Carter said he would go to the people — at times identifying himself *as* the people. In reviewing experience with consumer legislation in Georgia, Carter said: "The special interest groups prevailed on about half of it. I prevailed — rather the Georgia people prevailed — on the other half."[31] Suppose all interests are special to someone: how can any President rule unless someone special supports him?

COMPREHENSIVENESS

What is consistent in these proposals? It is Carter's opposition to the intermediate groups, lobbyists who stand between government and citizen or a palace guard that stands between a president and cabinet. They fracture Carter's idea of comprehensive policy-making.

President Carter prefers to make changes comprehensively rather than "timidly or incrementally." As he says:

> Most of the controversial issues that are not routinely well-addressed can only respond to a comprehensive approach. Incremental efforts to make basic changes are often foredoomed to failure because the special interest groups can benefit from the status quo, can focus their attention on the increments that most affect themselves, and the general public can't be made either interested or aware.[32]

The same theory stands behind efforts at government reorganization:

> The most difficult thing is to reorganize incrementally. If you do it one tiny little phase at a time, then all those who see their influence threatened will combine their efforts in a sort of secretive way. They come out of the rat holes and they'll concentrate on undoing what you're trying to do. But if you can have a bold enough, comprehensive enough proposal to rally the interest and support of the general electorate, then you can overcome that special interest type lobbying pressure.[33]

In a word, "the comprehensive approach is inherently necessary to make controversial decisions."[34] That was before the President asked himself where he would get support if all he generated was controversy.

Part of Carter's political theory, then, is to change everything at once. Comprehensive change enables one both to identify the public interest by considering the merits of opposing claims and to serve that interest by making opponents fight on all fronts simultaneously, diluting their forces while concentrating one's own. The bigger the change, the greater the public attention, and the more likely it becomes that the public interest will prevail over private interests.

Primary in Carter's comprehensive reforms is their inclusiveness. A characteristic phrase of Carter is "a complete assessment of tax reform in a comprehensive way." He wants to "establish comprehensive proposals on transportation and energy and agriculture";[35] he favors a "comprehensive nationwide mandatory health-insurance program," and a "drastic reorganization of the health-care services in the U.S."[36] Although we could go on, one more foreign-affairs example must serve: because "the old international institutions no longer suffice," Carter feels, "the time has come for a new architectural effort."[37]

Because "those who prefer to work in the dark, or those whose private fiefdoms are threatened" care only about themselves, such special interests will prevent inclusive decision-making.[38] To avoid this pitfall, Carter wants to restructure the federal bureaucracy, the health system, the welfare system, the tax system, the criminal-justice system, and international institutions. Thus policy analysis, which is based on disaggregation of large into small problems, is not in favor.

According to Carter, the comprehensive approach offers a final, decisive solution to problems. From experience with government reorganization in Georgia, he has become a leading advocate of the "one-step" process.[39] Carter aims at achieving an "ultimate and final and complete resolution of New York City's problems, fiscally."[40] In the Middle East, he wanted to devise an "overall settlement rather than resuming Mr. Kissinger's step-by-step approach."[41] President Carter contends that with Soviet cooperation we can achieve "the ultimate solution" there.[42] But if the ultimate is impossible, does that also mean the proximate or merely meliorative is undesirable? Evidently not, since the hero of Camp David has sought and received acclaim essentially for trying to arrange a separate peace between Egypt and Israel.

INCOMPATIBILITY

Who can object to making governmental policy predictable so that people know what to expect? Predictability is preferable, but is it possible? To be more precise, is predictability for one agency (and its clients) compatible with predictability for others?

Is predictability consistent with uniformity, another managerial quality that President Carter seeks? One could get broad agreement on smoothing out the economic cycle by maintaining a steady low level of unemployment. A major instrument used to accomplish this objective is to vary government spending; but it becomes evident immediately that predictability in employment (assuming that it could be achieved) and predictability in expenditure policy are mutually exclusive. Similarly, predictability for recipients of government subsidies means that all who meet the qualifying conditions would receive the guaranteed sum. Predictability for governmental expenditures (and, quite possibly, for taxpayers), however, requires fixed dollar limits, not open-ended entitlements. Yet if there are limits, potential beneficiaries cannot know in advance how much they will get. All policy results cannot be predictable, and decisions about whose life will be predictable and whose won't are political as well as administrative.

The same holds true for uniformity and simplicity. Uniformity on one criterion — say, population — means diversity on other criteria, such as wealth or race or geography. Imagine that President Carter wishes to make good a promise to subsidize the arts, an intention we would like to see realized. Will money be allocated by population (which favors urban density), by area (which favors rural folk), by need (which favors those who do the least), or by past performance (which means that those who have will get more)? All these differences cannot be taken into account simultaneously with a uniform policy.

Comprehensiveness, in the sense of fundamental and inclusive change, often contradicts predictability and simplicity. Fundamental changes, precisely because they are far-reaching, are unlikely to be predictable. That is how the cost of the food-stamp program grew from an expected few hundred million dollars to more than $8 billion; and also how indexing social security against inflation had one unanticipated consequence (among others): threatening to bankrupt the system. Thus, acting inclusively, so as to consider all (or almost all) factors impinging on a problem at a specific time, is by its nature opposed to predictability, which requires that programs established in the past not be undone in the near future. But zero-base budgeting, the epitome of comprehensiveness, requires reexamining all major programs every year; this is the very opposite of predictability.

Uniformity also lives uneasily with comprehensiveness. Programs that are both uniform and comprehensive may be too expensive. If public housing must be provided everywhere by the same formula or not at all, there may be no public housing. Similarly, a desire to establish uniform benefits in all welfare programs for all eligible citizens might lead to a choice between much higher taxes or much lower benefits. "Cashing out"

all benefits from food stamps to medicaid and medicare might add up to
so large a sum that it would be voted down by Congress. Hence, the
choice might be a variety of disparate programs, or much lower benefits.
Upgrading all eligibles to the highest benefits will increase costs, and
downgrading all to the lowest will increase anger. Thus uniformity may
come at too high a price in suffering or in opposition.

A word about the relationship between uniformity and individuality.
We do not always equate fairness with being treated like everybody else;
on occasion, we would like to be treated as individuals. To be uniform,
regulations must place people in large and homogeneous categories.
Every effort to take account of special characteristics in the population
leads to further subdivision of categories and to additional provisions in
the regulations. This effort to treat people according to their individual
characteristics makes for proliferation of rules and regulations.

President Carter's desire for uniformity has led him to advocate a
principle of organization whereby administrative agencies are formed by
function or purpose.[43] Carter would have all activities involving education or health or welfare or crime, to mention but a few, in the same large
organization. As a general rule, one can say confidently that no principle
or criterion is good for every purpose. Suppose that reducing dependency
on welfare is a major purpose of the Carter administration. Should education for employment, rehabilitation in prisons, improvement of health,
mitigation of alcoholism, and Lord knows what else therefore be administered under welfare?

TOP-LIGHT AND BOTTOM-HEAVY

Carter's straining toward simplicity has led him to advocate reorganization of the federal government. Leaving aside campaign rhetoric about
the 1,900 federal agencies (a sum that equates the tiny and trivial with the
huge and important), to reduce the number of agencies at the top of the
hierarchy necessarily would increase the number at the bottom. If there
were only ten big departments, each could have 190 subunits; and if
there were ten subunits at each level, an issue would have to go through
nineteen bureaus before it was decided. The president might find this
simpler because fewer people would be reporting directly to him. But
Carter might discover also that finding out what is going on is more
difficult. Gigantic departments make it hard for anyone — Congress, secretaries, interest groups, citizens — to see inside. Conflicts between departments about overlapping responsibilities, and conflicts revealing important differences are submerged under a single departmental view.

One of the few things that can be said about organization in general
is the very thing President Carter denies — namely, that a considerable
quantity of redundancy (yes, overlap and duplication) must be built into

any enterprise.[44] When we want to make sure an activity is accomplished, as in our lunar missions, we build in alternative mechanisms for doing the same thing so that one can take over when other mechanisms fail. Efficiency, the principle of least effort, must be coupled with reliability, the probability that an act will be performed. A naive notion of efficiency would suggest that elderly and infirm persons be provided with either a visiting service or an office to which they can come or call. The more we wish to ensure actual delivery of services to the elderly, however, the more we must invest in multiple methods. Of course, there must be a limit to redundancy; but if we ever succeeded in eliminating all overlap and duplication, most things would work only once and some things not at all. It is ironic that, in the public sector, administrative reforms often aim at monopoly or concentration of power, but reforms in the private sector often aim at competition or dispersion of power.[45] Our constitutional mechanisms for coping with abuse of power, separation of powers, and checks and balances, after all, are forms of redundancy. The House and Senate and presidency overlap in jurisdiction and duplicate functions. That is why they quarrel and why we have been safe.

Carter's criteria cannot guide choice. The proverbial character of the criteria (look before you leap, but he who hesitates is lost) becomes apparent when they are paired with other equally desirable criteria: eliminating overlap and duplication detracts from reliability; predictability must go with adaptability; uniformity is worthy but so too is recognition of individual differences. President Carter's criteria for decision-making, we conclude, are individually contradictory and mutually incompatible.

The overwhelming emphasis that the president puts on procedural instruments could leave his administration vulnerable to massive displacement of goals by having success defined, at least within the administration, as degree of governmental effort rather than as degree of social accomplishment. Prisons are an example: the amount agencies spend, the number of new programs initiated, and the uniformity of procedures could replace as measures of success increase in rehabilitation or reduction in crime.

BELIEF

If our views have any credence, why, then, has Carter come to hold untenable beliefs about procedures for making policy? Perhaps they were inculcated at Annapolis; but one could just as well argue that Carter chose to go there because he wanted an instrumental approach to decision-making.[46] No doubt his father's influence was important ("My daddy . . . was a meticulous planner like me"),[47] but this could have become mere compulsiveness instead of a well-developed pattern of work. No candidate since Herbert Hoover, the Great Engineer,[48] would have thought it important to talk to the public about so arcane a subject as zero-base budgeting, going so far as to include it in five-minute television spots in 1977.

Public Confidence

Let us remove the burden from Carter and place it where it belongs, on ourselves, by asking why a highly intelligent political executive might interpret his experiences so as to reinforce his personal belief in an instrumental-cumtechnological view of public policy-making. Why, to us, does Carter seem to know worse rather than to know better?

Scientists love surprise. The more unusual a theory (the more consequences differ from cause, that is), the more surprising the conclusions, the better the theory. The further the theory leads us from what we know, the more important and promising it is considered. Good theories maximize surprise. Businessmen and politicians prefer predictability; things should be as they seem and surprises are nice if they happen to the competition. The attraction of planning (private and public) is that this element of the unexpected has been domesticated, its will subject to our own, at least in a plan on paper.

Yet as mistaken in his procedural approach as we think he is, Carter may be on solid ground in an area that we have not covered — public confidence. Our president recognizes (and has emphasized) that citizens have a right to understand their government if they are being asked to support it; simplicity and predictability of governmental activity could help achieve that support. Carter's feeling for how government looks to the people might motivate him to prefer procedures that enhance this appearance. (After Watergate, no one should look down upon efforts to improve the appearance as well as the performance of government.)

The Carter recipe for controlling conflict is to make it boil over; comprehensive change will force opposing interests into public arenas where a president can confront and overcome battling parties. But how often can this be done? Agitating some interests some of the time is not the same as upsetting most interests most of the time. Interests are lots of people who depend on government, the very same people to whom Carter must appeal for support. If Carter can space his appeals out so as not to be fighting on every front at once, there may be a chance for success; but if Carter has to fight simultaneously on many fronts, he (and the nation) are in for a difficult time.

"HE-THE-PEOPLE"

President Carter has promised to go directly to the people, both to incorporate and to transcend group interests. Incorporation works by including nearly all groups in the initial stages of policy formation. By co-optation, Carter hopes to commit most groups to support his programs (or at least not to oppose programs vigorously). Transcendence works by investing hierarchy with morality. In order to reflect the people's will, the best way to organize government is to make it democratic at the bottom and centralized at the top.[49] President Carter, then, as chief hierarch and utimate definer of the public interest, leaps over group interests by direct contact with the populace. "He-the-people" Carter would rather cogitate correctly the inchoate desires of the mass of people than bargain over who gets what the government offers.

Carter's theory of governing suggests opportunities for leadership but also obstacles to success. To reorganize the Executive Branch, the president will have to overcome both its clienteles and their elected representatives. To put through major reforms, Carter will need financial support from a Congress accustomed to making its own budget. Should presidential initiatives falter, private interests may appear to have triumphed over the public's interest. According to his own philosophy, Carter will be compelled to appeal to the people to protect his programs. But in the end, even the people may prove ungrateful; for if citizens fail the president, it will appear that people have given in to private interests instead of standing up for public duties.

The most worrisome aspect of Jimmy Carter's theory of public policy-making is his assumption that discussion will lead to agreement on long-term objectives, and that agreement will ensure support for present programs. Carter's views on conflict could survive only if all needs were compatible and past objectives were to determine future administration. This view of policy politics is untenable because interests do differ, because the price of agreement is likely to be vagueness, and because administration involves altering ends by changing means. When specific acts call for choice between how much inflation versus how much employment, or how much preservation of natural resources versus how much consumption, it becomes evident that agreement in general need not mean (and often has not meant) agreement in particular. Objectives must be related to resources, including the consent to continue.

Postscript

Observers of President Carter's first year of office agree that he has attempted to implement these procedural principles. Although he has changed course on numerous policies, from tax reform to housing, Carter has remained steadfast in attempting comprehensive solutions through hierarchic organizations; zero-base budgeting and reorganization of the Executive Branch are attempted along with comprehensive reform of energy, welfare, and a host of other policy areas.

Within the Carter administration, as Vice President Mondale says, there is general agreement that Carter has attempted to do too much too soon.[50] None of the president's proposals remains intact. Grave difficulties have come with congressmen who feel they should be doing more than implementing the president's program. There are strains with the media of information amid numerous calls for the public to punish the special interests who have been thwarting the president. Opinion polls suggest declining confidence in the president's competence, though there remains considerable approval of his personal warmth and decency. There is time to grow and to learn and to give the nation the respected and competent president it wants. Carter's apparent success in the Middle East peace talks has improved his popularity for the time being.

NOTES

1. "Jimmy Carter Presidential Campaign Issues Reference Book," July 24, 1975. Cited hereafter as "Issues Reference Book."
2. "Issues: Clearer and More Detailed," *National Journal Reports* (July 24, 1976), p. 1028.
3. "Head-to-Head on the Issues," *U.S. News and World Report* (September 13, 1976), p. 21.
4. "Issues Reference Book," p. 20.
5. "Issues Reference Book," p. 13.
6. "Interview on the Issues — What Carter Believes," *U.S. News and World Report* (May 24, 1976), p. 19; and "Issues Reference Book," p. 30.
7. "Issues Reference Book," p. 13.
8. Jimmy Carter, *Why Not the Best?* (Broadman Press, 1975), p. 147.
9. "Jimmy Carter: Not Just Peanuts," *Time* (March 8, 1976), p. 19.
10. Stated by Stuart Eisenstat, Carter's policy advisor, in *National Journal Reports* (July 24, 1976), p. 1029.
11. *The New York Times,* April 2, 1976, p. 2; and *U.S. News and World Report* (May 24, 1976), p. 19.
12. "The View from the Top of the Carter Campaign," *National Journal Reports* (July 17, 1976), p. 1002.
13. *U.S. News and World Report* (May 24, 1976), p. 23; and James P. Gannon, "The Activist: Carter, Despite Image of Outsider Favors Do-More Government," *Wall Street Journal,* April 2, 1976, p. 23.
14. "What Carter Would Do as President," *U.S. News and World Report* (July 26, 1976), p. 18.
15. "Issues Reference Book," p. 20.
16. *U.S. News and World Report* (May 24, 1976), p. 23; and July 26, 1976, p. 18.
17. *U.S. News and World Report* (May 24, 1976), p. 18.
18. "Jimmy Carter on Economics: Populist Georgia Style," *Business Week* (May 3, 1976), p. 66.
19. "Excerpts from an Interview with Jimmy Carter," *The New York Times,* March 31, 1976, p. 20.
20. "Issues Reference Book," p. 15.

21. "Carter: Seeking Clearer Goals," *Time* (May 10, 1976), p. 24.
22. *U.S. News and World Report* (May 24, 1976), p. 19.
23. *National and Journal Reports* (July 17, 1976), p. 997.
24. "Excerpts from the Interview with Carter on his Concepts in Foreign Policy," *The New York Times*, July 7, 1976, p. 12.
25. "Carter Says Ford Fails to Check Nation's 'Drift,'" *The New York Times*, August 18, 1976, p. 1.
26. Carter, *Why Not the Best?* p. 114.
27. Jimmy Carter, National Press Club. Announcement Speech for Democratic Presidential Nomination, December 12, 1974.
28. "Issues Reference Book," p. 14; and Albert R. Hunt, "Carter and Business," *Wall Street Journal*, August 12, 1976, p. 15.
29. *U.S. News and World Report* (September 13, 1976), p. 20.
30. "Carter Tells Film Stars about Poverty in the South," *The New York Times*, August 24, 1976, p. 17.
31. *National Journal Reports* (July 17, 1976), p. 998.
32. *National Journal Reports* (July 17, 1976), p. 999.
33. "State Structural Reforms," *National Journal Reports* (April 5, 1975), p. 506.
34. *National Journal Reports* (July 17, 1976), p. 999.
35. *U.S. News and World Report* (September 13, 1976), p. 21.
36. *Wall Street Journal*, April 2, 1976, p. 23.
37. Eleanor Randolf, "Carter Hits 'Lone Ranger' Foreign Policy of Kissinger," *Chicago Tribune*, June 24, 1976, p. 5.
38. Carter, Announcement Speech, December 12, 1974.
39. *National Journal Reports* (April 5, 1975), p. 506.
40. "Excerpts from an Interview with Jimmy Carter," *The New York Times*, March 31, 1976, p. 20.
41. *U.S. News and World Report* (July 26, 1976), p. 18.
42. "Where Jimmy Carter Stands on Foreign Policy," *Chicago Tribune*, May 8, 1976, p. 10.
43. This principle has had a long history, having been proposed in 1911 by the President's Commission on Economy and Efficiency: "Only by grouping services according to their character can substantial progress be made in eliminating duplication." Quoted in Peri E. Arnold, "Executive Reorganization and Administrative Theory: the Origin of the Managerial Presidency," paper presented at 1976 Annual Meeting of American Political Science Association, Chicago, Illinois, September 1976, p. 6.
44. Martin Landau, "Redundancy, Rationality, and the Problem of Duplication and Overlap," *Public Administration Review*, Vol. 29, No. 4 (July–August 1969), pp. 346–358.
45. Lewis Dexter has emphasized that modern Western society has followed the route of competition not monopoly as a means to clarify issues and procedures. He cites the example that United States antitrust laws are "deliberately designed to impose redundancy and duplication on industry." See Lewis Anthony Dexter, "The Advantages of Some Duplication and Ambiguity in Senate Committee Jurisdictions," p. 174. First staff report, Temporary Select Committee of United States Senate on Committee Jurisdiction, chairman Adlai Stevenson, issued September 1976.
46. See, for example, Vice Admiral Hyman Rickover's speech delivered in Brooklyn, N.Y. on April 9, 1958, p. 5, in which he complains about inefficiency in bureaucracy: "If overorganization lengthens our lead time we must heed Thoreau's cry of 'simplify, simplify.'"

47. Quoted in Bruce Mazlish and Edwin Diamond, "Thrice Born: A Psycho-history of Jimmy Carter's Rebirth," *New York*, No. 9, No. 35 (August 30, 1976), p. 32.
48. Hoover was an unrelenting champion of organization by "major purpose under single-headed responsibility" as a means for making agencies easier to manage and more efficient. See Peri E. Arnold, "Executive Reorganization," pp. 13–14, 20. Securing broad reorganization authority subject to Congressional veto is also the approach Carter took in Georgia and hopes to repeat in Washington. See *U.S. News and World Report* (July 26, 1976), p. 17.
49. In New York City, John Lindsay "rationalized" the city administration by consolidating and eliminating all intermediate structures, thus forming the "Office of Collective Bargaining." It soon became the sole target of public-employee union demands, thereby greatly strengthening the union's position. In Jack Douglas's apt description, the rationalization "swept away all the hedgerows behind which he [Lindsay] could have hidden." See Jack D. Douglas, "Urban Politics and Public Employee Unions," in *Public Employee Unions: A Study of the Crisis in Public Sector Labor Relations* (San Francisco: Institute for Contemporary Studies, 1976), p. 103.
50. "Mondale Says White House Overloaded Congress," *The New York Times*, December 14, 1977, p. 24A.

CHAPTER 11

CITIZENS
AS ANALYSTS

Citizenship has been studied from almost every standpoint except that of participation in public policy. The influence of citizens on the making and changing of policy, citizens' power (or the lack thereof) over public officials who make and administer policy, and the ability of the general public to hold these elites accountable, even citizens' ability to create and dissolve government itself, have been subject to scrutiny. But participation as part of policy (with the exception of Michael Lipsky's "Street Corner Bureaucrats") has been neglected.

Modern democratic theorists stress that citizens hold some power because elites must compete for citizens' favor. Free periodic elections, with the ability of citizens to switch support, has much to commend it for avoiding the worst excesses and for motivating politicians to take an interest in promoting citizens' preferences. Certainly any alternative is worse. No one claims, however, that citizens in a large state can exercise direct choice over policy or that it is usual for elections to constitute mandates in favor of specific policies. That a candidate is elected does not necessarily mean that most citizens prefer all or even most of that official's policies. Whether interest groups close the gap between citizen and government depends on whether such groups speak for their own members rather than their bureaucrats, whether those who need representation get it, and whether the balance of power among all these contenders improves upon or worsens defects in the entire system. Doubts have been expressed on all sides. To register preferences properly would require constant referenda, which would weaken government without improving representation for even the most wary citizen. Caught between infrequent elections and undesirable plebiscites, democratic theory has languished.

Would participatory democracy be an improvement? Aside from an evident elitist character (who else has the time and skill at communication to engage in endless meetings or understand the meaning of voting on this, that, and the other thing?) participatory democracy is procedural politics writ small. In no way does it differ from other politics, with its discussion about candidates, factions, and votes, except that participatory democracy is less visible to most citizens and more manipulable to the few who get to meetings or turn out for special elections. In order for citizens to participate in the operation of policy, they would have to understand what is in it for them, recognize the differences between small and large changes (so as to know whether and how much participation was worthwhile), and be involved continuously so that they could learn from experience. This chapter, therefore, is not about how citizens relate to the state, but about what it takes for citizens to participate in policy.

All the discussion of power and powerlessness — who originates, vetoes, or modifies policies — has avoided the subject of interactions within policies themselves. In everyday life, aren't postal patrons, doctors and patients, prisoners and parole boards, students, parents, and teachers involved in policies? Yet direct modes of activity have not been considered as part and parcel of public policy but as what happens after the exciting parts are over. Citizenship in public policy (after the party is over, as part of everyday life) is our subject.

CITIZENSHIP AS MORAL DEVELOPMENT

The bad reputation of citizen participation in public life is deserved. Most of us do little and know less; most people are not interested in most public issues most of the time. Why should they be? To take an interest means having to spend on politics time that might be more profitably devoted to the job or a hobby. Individuals in the United States can get wonderful jobs, marry, have happy families, and do creative work without ever taking an interest in the public realm. Primary satisfactions for most citizens do not ordinarily lie in political life; basic needs are met or thwarted on the job, in the home, among friends, and the like.

Apathy

To be interested in some issues some of the time is one thing; to be interested in most issues most of the time is quite another. If time were free and unlimited, people with an inclination to be interested might gorge themselves. But it does not happen, and even the most avid partisan of public affairs must be selective. What, then, can we say of the many who are unlikely to involve themselves, even when they are confronted with a confusing array of subjects about which they conceivably might know something?

The fact that individuals do vary enormously in the strength of their interest has profound implications for political life. If interest is a necessary condition for influence, then the uninterested cede the right to consideration and power is concentrated in the small population that does care. Yet this minority of interested citizens is large compared to the number of people who are active.

The factors that limit political activity are of cardinal importance in understanding public affairs. Activity is costly. It eats up time and energy. To be active on strategic problems in nuclear politics or on the operations of a municipal electric plant is not a matter of a few moments of reflection; many hours must be spent. One must attend meetings, listen to or participate in discussion, write letters, attempt to persuade (or be persuaded by) others, and engage in other such time-consuming labors. This means devoting less time to the job, to the children, and to hobbies. Yet these private activities are the primary interest of most people, and so the cost of participation in public affairs seems greater than the return.

Without denying the unflattering image of citizens painted in much social-science literature, I believe the implications of such portraits for public policy have not been considered with sufficient care. One response has been to rejoice that apathy keeps away those people least capable of making wise choices. So far as this position suggests that democracy remains possible even with an apathetic citizenry, one hopes it is correct. But to celebrate apathy hardly seems appropriate for a democratic society. Another view is that citizens do not participate because politics seems a sham; there is nothing in it for them. So far as people can live well without feeling compelled to participate, recognition of the right to be left alone speaks well of a society. But if citizens are left out of consideration in making important decisions, to define life as democratic would be deception.

It is not clear from critiques of citizenship whether too much or too little is expected. Citizenship also represents a problem of allocating resources for which policy analysis is appropriate. If citizenship is not to swallow citizens, demands in the public arena must be set in proportion to the rest of their lives. The question, of course, is what proportion?

Involving Citizens in Public Policymaking

None of these criticisms addresses how to make sense of citizenship in modern life. Can we differentiate types of knowledge from technical procedures (like multiple regression, which only experts know) to citizens' preferences (which only individual actors know)? By helping make what citizens learn in their daily lives part of what they need to know, analysts can improve both citizenship and public policy.

Under what conditions, then, can citizens (who know next to nothing about policy) make sensible choices? When their actions and reactions are part of policy so that they can:

1. compare efforts and results;
2. learn from personal experience;
3. distinguish more-important from less-important policies.

Though humankind may indeed be a political beast, most people prefer not to be politicians. Because general citizens' interest is limited, they must be able to tell the difference between big and little choices. How might they do so?

Many policies stand a better chance of success, I feel, if citizens have real choices and the right to choose. An exaggerated view of citizen participation — in everything, all the time — should not be countered by an exaggerated view of elites who often lack knowledge and almost never agree on objectives. Severe strain is imposed on mutual trust by the demand for heroic feats of participation from citizens and intellectual genius from elites. The demand for interaction by citizens and cogitation by elites should be diminished. To be able to bring resources and objectives together is even more important among citizens than within policies. Whatever else policy analysts may be, therefore, I believe they should be advocates of citizen participation. Being limited in influencing policy-making does not mean that citizens cannot make their will felt within policies. Designing policies that facilitate intelligent and effective participation is an essential task of policy analysis.

How we think about policy analysis depends on what is important to us. Here I propose to conceive of analysis as one way to enhance the capacity for moral development on public purposes, which I call citizenship. The first requisite of citizenship is autonomy, the ability to undertake independent action. Autonomy is a necessary (though not a sufficient) condition for giving to others. The second requisite is reciprocity, the willingness to share. The third requisite is learning, the ability to test and alter preferences (here, about public policy). In judging among alternative programs, therefore, we want to know which relate people so that each one's preferences take into account those of others who are relevant. Which policies not only allow individuals to choose but assist them in forming and changing preferences as to what is desirable? Citizenship is not only about allegiance to government but also about moral development, that is, enhancing capacity to make choices that take account of other people's preferences.

Analysts should take their moral meaning from Piaget, who defines "ethical education" much as I would describe citizenship:

We have stated that the two correlative aspects of the personality are independence and reciprocity. In contrast to the individual who has not yet reached the stage of "personality," and whose characteristics are to be oblivious of all rules and to center on himself whatever interrelations he has with his physical and social environments, the person is an individual who situates his ego in its true perspective in relation to the ego of others. He inserts it into a system of reciprocity which implies simultaneously an independent discipline, and a basic de-centering of his own activity. The two basic problems of ethical education are, therefore, to assure this de-centering and to build this discipline.[1]

When analysts cultivate citizenship, I believe, they promote better public policy.

The place to begin our discussion is a model (or caricature) of the ideal participatory citizen. We will then discuss strategies for those who wish to serve as citizens and yet survive as whole people.

MR. AND MRS. MODEL CITIZEN

What would life be like, we may ask, if citizens fulfilled even minimally the endless injunctions to be involved in public affairs? Where would they find time for family activities, for social life, for hobbies, and reading, and for just plain relaxation?

Imagine the family life of Mr. and Mrs. Model Citizen, who obey all the commands about participation. Monday and Tuesday nights they attend meetings of the local sewer-service board because it is clear that without adequate sanitation the community cannot exist. Wednesday and Thursday evenings are spent dealing with police problems; public safety, after all, is essential for the good life. Fridays are reserved for pollution, so threatening to our way of life. Saturdays go to mental health, because if people don't think straight they can't do anything else. Caucuses on lack of participation usually happen on Sunday. The week has left Mr. and Mrs. Model Citizen deeply unsatisfied, of course, because they have had to stand by while the Middle East deteriorates, national forests are cut down, and the United Nations withers away.

The next week promises to be equally hectic as mother rushes off to a meeting of the Council on Juvenile Delinquency. She had failed to notice that daughter had not been home for two days and had just been caught in a drug raid. Father was to be absent from work again, because no moral man could afford to miss the meeting at which the Welfare Council decides how to deal with indigent families. The Geratsco Fertilizer Company, however — callously indifferent to Mr. Model Citizen's public service — insists that he pay more attention to his job or consider joining the unemployment rolls himself. Father had planned to take his son on a hike, but there was too much to be done to preserve the ecological balance of his region; left to himself, the boy starts running around with a juvenile gang and gets picked up for burglary. With both children in jail, Mother and Father Model Citizen console themselves with the thought that now they will have more time (and incentive) to spend on problems of penal institutions. To sacrifice private life on the altar of citizen participation seems excessive; helping society by contributing to its social problems seems odd. No wonder there are few truly political people.

A STRATEGY OF SPECIALIZATION

Because these comments may seem sacrilegious coming from a person who devotes his life to the study of public affairs and who might be presumed to rejoice in total citizen participation, I hasten to assure the reader that I do teach and advocate citizen participation. My point thus far has been that the usual exhortations to do everything are impossible to follow. Actually, such advice inculcates guilt or a sense of futility facing the magnitude of the task. Advocates of participation are more likely than not to harm the cause they set out to advance by setting sights so high that more manageable goals are not even attempted. If we are interested not merely in the amount of participation but in its effectiveness and its reasonable relationship to the whole life of the individual, then we must suggest a goal and appropriate strategies that take into account both genuine interest and competition from other essential activities.

The goal I propose is to become a specialist and the strategy is to specialize.[2] It is vain to think that any of us can become generalists. We don't have the time, and even if we did we probably wouldn't be willing to devote those free hours solely to public life. But it is possible for most people to become effective issue-specialists. This goes for issues as far apart as disarmament and whether to sell the local electric plant. The first question is how to decide on which issue to specialize.

Choosing an Issue

All of us can find the time to read a decent newspaper and perhaps a good supplementary weekly for local affairs. If such a paper is not locally available, it is easy enough to get a subscription to a national publication such as *Christian Science Monitor* or any of the news magazines. By making a quick day-by-day survey of the news, aided now and then by news broadcasts, citizens can decide what interests them most. Soon they build up a small fund of information on a variety of issues that should better equip them to choose their specialty.

Gathering Information on an Issue

Having chosen a specialty, the next problem is how to become sufficiently informed to develop personal preferences about what needs to be done. It is not easy to learn where to begin because citizens usually do not have the background to pinpoint the literature that best meets their needs. There are, however, a number of ways to proceed that may help to cut costs of information. Citizens who are fortunate enough to know someone whom they respect and regard as informed, can ask that person for recommendations about what to read, which almost always will include additional references to other highly regarded works. Occasionally, citizens may develop a liking for a columnist or news commentator who suggests appropriate reading, or a foraging expedition to the local library may be indicated. The rule is to begin somewhere and keep at it. For there are few issues (and none of primary importance, in my opinion) that cannot be mastered once the citizen has discovered the relevant literature.

There is always the danger that our unwary citizen may feel inextricably submerged by a flood of material on a well-known issue. They will soon discover, however, that after two or three books and a half-dozen articles, the amount of repetition rises rapidly; the reader can get by more than adequately with a newspaper, a book, and a few articles every year. It is as necessary to know when to stop as when to begin.

Although it is difficult to imagine citizens doing this kind of research constantly, it is not utopian to believe that people can do it from time to time if only they will specialize. Suppose an emergency or an issue comes up requiring a decision immediately. Obviously, one should plunge right in. But a few plunges will prove tiring if not tiresome. The optimal strategy is to specialize not only in specific problems – how reading should be taught, or when police should shoot – but in the broader area, like primary education or public safety. Then one will always have a store of information by which to judge specific events when they turn up.

Sharing and Acting on Information

Specialization increases the fund of information in many ways. Citizens will meet people who share their interests, who attend the same meetings and join the same organizations, and who welcome discussion. One participant may pick up pointers from others. When some new development takes place, specialists whose interest had become established are more likely to be informed as a matter of course by public and private officials. The better acquainted with the material, the more agile the specialist is likely to become in making the required associations, increasing the efficiency of his efforts to acquire information. There can be no guarantee, of course, that the preferences of citizens who actively specialize will actually be met. Nevertheless, in political systems where the prizes go to the interested and the active, specialists have great advantages.

Granted that specialization is a useful strategy for increasing citizen influence, does this mode of operation result in a political system that meets preferences widely held in society? It does and it does not. For most citizens most of the time most public affairs are not of active interest. Such people may know that things are going well from their point of view and see no reason to participate. It is more likely that the negative is true; even citizens who have reason to believe that things are not going well may find it worth the cost in time and energy to do anything about the problem. From time to time events of great importance will occur that do lead such people to take an interest and perhaps participate sporadically. If citizens are able for the most part to bring decision-making into a responsive position on such matters, so that particular preferences are taken into account, then government may be said to be ruled mostly in accordance with the wishes that are important to those citizens. This is not majority rule in the sense that all or most community decisions accord with the preferences of a majority of citizens; it is majority rule in the special sense that the minority who feel intensely about an issue make up a majority of those who will receive consideration and some satisfaction from the outcome. In this way specialization serves citizenship by contributing to a political system that comes a little closer to meeting a wide range of preferences.

What's wrong with a strategy of specialization? Nothing for those who can use it, everything for those who cannot. Specialization has a special class bias; it works best for middle- and upper–middle-class people who have the requisite time, education, and skills in communication. For individuals who can't, or who do not want to use their skills for this purpose — categories that include most citizens on most occasions — specialization is not the answer: one might specialize but ordinarily one wouldn't. Must the choice, then, remain between sporadic acts through mechanisms of mass mobilization — political parties, labor unions, interest groups — or none at all except, possibly, voting? Having ruled out perpetual participation and even specialization (however useful for limited numbers) for most citizens, for those who want more than the act of voting every few years (however important that is), what form of participation is left?

CITIZENSHIP IN DAILY LIFE

If the citizen-analyst is hemmed in by constraints, with but one available action, there can be no citizenship because there is no choice. Only a surplus of resources can create the alternatives that might lead to correctable errors. The economic basis of citizenship consists in creating that surplus.[3] Of course, without constraints there is no citizenship, for our acts either have no consequences, because resources are limitless, or they fall upon others whose fortunes do not matter to us, because they can do nothing to or for us. Unlimited resources would signify that interactions are unnnecessary. This is Schiller's meaning: "In error only is there life and [total] knowledge death must be."

Citizenship and Interaction

The social basis of citizenship is sharing: action taken in awareness of the consequences for others. A useful shorthand definition of power is to be taken into account by others, not only because they may want to, which is nice, but because they have to, which is nicer. Citizenship is socialized, then, when choices are structured so that others are part of the action. Just as autonomy is necessary for reciprocity, the object of social policy is to make interdependence a facet of everyday individual decision-making.

For citizenship to be effective it must be part of daily life. Citizens, with resources at their command — including their understanding of the processes linking themselves to others — must be able to estimate the consequences of their actions. Otherwise, they could neither serve others, who must want what they are prepared to give, nor themselves, who must be satisfied to have done as well as possible. Our citizens must be able to make sense out of their day-to-day public lives without destroying their private existences by having to attend meetings day and night. A homely example from our common experience will illustrate.

As our choices are structured today, television repair is not amenable to the effective exercise of consumer citizenship. The consumer needs to know what is wrong with his set, how much it should cost to repair, whether the expense is worth it considering the life expectancy of the set, and whether it has in fact been repaired properly. The consumer being no technician, he is subject both to victimization by repair shops and to vicious reactions if he is wrong in blaming the serviceman for unsatisfactory work.

As I see it, the problem is that the arena of repair is badly structured in that citizens are being asked to make decisions for which they lack information, and repair shops are not making choices that they are competent to make. The solution (implied in the problem) is not to make every citizen consumer a television technician but rather to enable him to acquire appropriate data that he can convert into information. If television sets were rented instead of bought, and if all costs were covered in the rental agreement, consumers could decide which price was right — a decision they are used to making. Decisions to repair or to junk a set would be made by technicians in repair shops. Service should be superior because consumers can choose where to take their business. Potential anger is defused by comparison shopping; the shops meet unreasonable consumer demands by refusing service. Creativity consists of bringing the resources of consumers and repair shops in line with their objectives so that aggravation is replaced by negotiation, and helplessness by mastery.

Bargaining is not bad, as if it implied the sacrifice of noble principles; bargaining is beautiful because it shows that each side is comfortable enough with its own interests to interact with others who expect to gain from the transaction. It is not bargaining but hierarchy — the imposition of commands — that circumvents citizenship, because hierarchy does not leave individual units free to calculate their own interests, nor the state with the collective capacity to understand interaction. For this reason the Ministry of Finance in Germany does not use econometric models of the economy to allocate resources to operating departments. (The worst aspect of these models is not their inaccuracy — which is considerable — but their overdetermination; if there is one, and only one, correct position, then departments must accept their assigned place.) What, then, do the Finance Ministry and departments talk about? To allow for give-and-take, the budget is subdivided and decisions about individual departments are negotiated.

Citizenship of this interactive kind is exemplified in the work of Kjell Eide of Norway, who asserts, "Our task as planners is not to define people's problems for them and calculate the 'right' solution. Our task is to help increase other people's capability of handling their own problems and find their own solutions to them." In allocating state subsidies to local education bodies, he rejected a complex equation designed to take numerous variables and local variances into account, because it would rob local officials of autonomy. As he says,

> Using the formula, however, would mean that no local education authority would have a chance to calculate what subsidies they should have, or to understand why they get the amounts allocated to them. In practice, therefore, I have advocated the use of a very simple formula, according to which 450 local superintendents can easily calculate what their local authorities are due from the state, and which they can freely protest against as being inappropriate for the allocation of government money. The loss in abstract "justice" is more than compensated for by the fact that 450 superintendents have not been made just cogs in a machine.[4]

Educators who do not understand what they are getting cannot determine what they ought to give. And without reciprocity between local educators and central administrators, they cannot learn whether what they got was what they should have wanted.

Citizenship and analysis are united by the desire to bring people together so that interaction will facilitate learning. If the purpose of policy analysis — whether done directly by analysts or indirectly in the interaction among contending interests — is to perfect preferences, changes may be judged better or worse by the degree to which they allow participants to learn whether what they once thought they wanted was what they now ought to have.

An Illustration: The Problem of Primaries

An illustration is a remarkable phenomenon that occurred in 1976 during the Democratic Party's selection of a presidential candidate. As party choice converged upon a candidate, the cry went out that nobody (well, hardly anybody) knew him. Who is Jimmy Carter? That was the question. Is he competent? Is he wise? What programs does he believe in? What is he likely to do? A man about to be nominated for president by a major party, a man likely to win election, appeared to be unknown. How could that happen? Because we planned it that way.

Since the turn of the century, and with ever-increasing speed in the past decade, the proportion of convention delegates chosen by primary rather than by party caucus has increased to more than two-thirds. The idea has been to take control of conventions from party leaders (bosses, they were sometimes called) and give it to citizens by letting them choose among candidates during the nominating procedure. What, to stick to our theme, can we say about primaries as a mode of learning if they leave people wondering who it is they are about to nominate for president?

Voters in primaries know only a few other voters. What is more, none is likely to know any voter who knows the candidate personally. All must depend on the candidate's presentation of self as filtered through the media — which can't have been of much help, or voters wouldn't have been wondering what the candidate was like. Once the vote is cast, moreover, there is no opportunity to reconsider it against new information. Then the scene of action shifts to another state with a new set of voters and (depending on circumstances) a new set of candidates. The sequential staging means that voters in one have no chance to talk with those in others. For contrast, consider a deliberative convention in which delegates, from long party association, either know each other or know someone who knows delegates who know the candidates. If their hypotheses about the candidates are tested and found wanting, they can try others.

The immediate reaction is that one should prefer to participate directly in a primary instead of indirectly in a convention. The lack of trust in intermediaries, the well-known decline in support for political parties, helps explain the nomination of candidates whom nobody knows. Rather than trust people who can learn to act for us, we have chosen to act ourselves, though we cannot use this experience to improve our own performance. This dog-in-the-manger approach is not normally recommended as a basis for citizenship.

A counterargument would be that, by polling continuous cross-sections of citizens, primaries facilitate citizen choice. But does any primary represent either citizens in general or voters in the presidential election? We know they do not, skewed as each is to the better off, the highly educated, and those transiently attracted to an issue or personality. Besides, the question asked in primaries (and not asked of themselves by voters) is not who would be most attractive to a majority of voters, as politicians would ask, but which candidate among those available the citizen prefers personally. It is no wonder, then, looking back at their individual preferences, that these often fail to make sense to citizens as part of their collective choices.

I do not argue here for a different nominating system but want to show that the present one does inhibit learning. Learning ability differs between a deliberative assembly and scattered strangers voting at different places and times. Learning requires an arena in which interested parties can communicate and test hypotheses, not a ballot on which their first preference also may be the last.

Whether we want to discuss the desirability of stability or the consequences of change, our major aim should be the kind and character of relationships among people. Are these continuous or sporadic, profound or shallow, marked by ignorance or knowledge? If citizens are to establish important relationships, they must, to begin with, know which are important to them and to others.

DISTINGUISHING BIG FROM LITTLE CHANGE

Although analysis may be discussed in such abstract words as "resources," "preferences," "objectives," and even "facts," the true subjects are human beings, likely to be more interested in their own particularity than in their statistical generality. Though quantification, where appropriate, may be helpful, possibly essential, policy analysis always involves relationships among people. These interpersonal aspects do not signify merely the obvious coming together of analyst and client, but also that elements of the analyses themselves make for changes in the way people relate to each other, so that their interactions will result in different outcomes. The human side of analysis is the most important because change takes place by alteration in social interaction. My analysis of basic change is designed to show that it implies radical revision in interpersonal (or interorganizational) relations.

When we assert that a proposed change in policy is basic or fundamental or radical, we imply that we have the truth — the base, not merely the superstructure; the center, not the periphery; the essence of things, not their deceptive outer appearance. The claim is powerful — I am right, you are not — even if not always forthright. I mention this to alert readers that changes I call basic, fundamental, radical, and so forth may not be so to them.

The Traditional Criteria

The commonly proposed criteria for distinguishing fundamentally important changes from lesser ones are not always useful for policy analysis. No doubt irreversibility is a sufficient sign of basic change. But in public policy irreversibility — inability to undo a horrible mistake — is one of the least desirable qualities. How can error be corrected if changes cannot be made? Amitai Etzioni, commenting on the energy crisis, says:

> The likelihood that unexpected vectors will intervene to throw off our forecasts suggests that we should be ready to recommit our resources and efforts as we move into the future and find, alas, that we have again erred. . . . We should not permit setups that lock us in, of the sort exemplified by the Highway Trust Fund, which still pours billions into highway construction when clearly a higher priority should now go into public transit.
>
> Similarly, we ought to favor those changes in homes, offices, and factories which can be readily made and then unmade if necessary (e.g., taxes on gas and oil, which can be reduced by a stroke of a pen) rather than those which are difficult to reverse (e.g., conversion of home heating systems from gas to electricity). . . .[5]

As a criterion of basic change, the magnitude of departure from past policy also has flaws. After all, the Great Flood certainly solved the problem of human wickedness (at least for a time), but was not the sort of thing one would usually wish to recommend. Size alone, moreover, seldom serves selectivity: arming agencies with the right to withhold pensions from millions of people proved unusable in enforcing positions in disputes with states over administrative practices. Pouring money over programs has not always led to progress. Size may make waves without changing how we sail or where we go. Human behavior is (or should be) our goal. We want to locate change in human relationships that are subject to further alteration so that it is possible to learn by anticipating or living through them. A focus on human relations also permits specifying whether and how well the norms of autonomy and reciprocity have been satisfied: are choices really independent and do they relate choosers to one another?

A New Criterion: Changing Relationships (PROD)

For these purposes, I have adopted this criterion of change: altering the pattern of relationships between participants which leads to outcomes that are different. Having chosen this criterion — personal relationships whose outcomes differ (PROD) — it is then possible to judge if or when a basic (though, of course, not necessarily a better) change has taken place. When these interpersonal relationships can be specified accurately, the point at which the relationships between the participants shift to another plane (different modes of interaction leading to different outcomes) can be ascertained.

An example from budgeting, where this definition was first formulated,[6] will show why basic change is qualitative, altering interpersonal (or interorganizational) relationships. Changes that are incremental are regular repetitions of what has happened in the past. A 5 per cent increase a year from the budgetary base meets this test. If incremental changes occur with great frequency, say, once a week, their cumulative influence can also be very large, but the pattern of relationships (the agency asks for 10 per cent and Congress gives it 5) does not change. If the agency asked for a 1,000 per cent increase each year, and Congress responded by giving it 500 per cent, the financial figures would be different but the pattern still would be stable. But if the agency requests 100 per cent more and is cut 10 per cent below the previous year's base, this would be a radical change evidencing a new pattern, qualitatively different from before. Its outcome — a substantial cut from an outrageous request — also would be different.

A PROD change is not only radical but also right if new patterns of relationships increase individual autonomy and social reciprocity. The task of policy analysis is to create incentives (a structure or pattern of relationships) that generate information the people affected can use — not, to be sure, to control the decisions affecting their lives (for that would destroy the autonomy of others), but to bargain over outcomes intelligently.

Thus, by comparing what they put in to what they take out, citizens can hope to learn from their own experience. And this learning will include not only what they wish to receive but what others want them to give. Does this need for some stability signify that, for policy analysis, only small or incremental changes are possible? I think not. By conceptualizing change as patterns of interpersonal relations that alter outcomes within areas of policy, I hope to have (1) separated regular from radical changes, (2) shown how such alterations advance or hinder citizens' learning about preferences, and (3) advanced an argument against an exaggerated view of decision-making by elites in a democracy.

If objectives were indeed immutable, agreed upon or unalterably imposed, then citizens might leave public policy to technicians. But if objectives were open, as they are, if they varied with resources, as they do, then experts on preferences, namely citizens in a democracy (even prisoners in a bureaucracy), would (and do) have the most valuable expertise going. The more choices citizens make as part of ordinary activities, and the moré often they make them the better the public policy.

PROD CHANGE

To avoid bias, I shall illustrate PROD change with a private-sector, a public-sector, and a mixed-sector proposal to improve public policy.

A Private-Sector Proposal

Consider a private-sector reform of the United States Post Office. The usual complaint is that rising costs and ever-larger subsidies are accompanied by deteriorating service. The usual remedies suggested are modernization, which costs still more; exhortation, which gives you back only the hot air you put in; and re-organization (from a regular department to a quasi-autonomous corporation, and back again). The basic problem, as I understand it, is that there is little or no effective pressure for performance (1) because there are no true alternatives, and (2) because government through its taxpayers makes up the deficit. Lack of competition, fortified by government subsidy, means that one cannot tell what it should cost to mail letters.

A PROD solution would consist of abolishing the monopoly of the post office department on first-class mail. With the entry of competitors we would know at last how much mail costs, that is, the lowest price for which at least one company could deliver it. But how about the rural and remote? If government wishes to subsidize people living in these areas it can ask for competitive bids. If the subsidy appears too large, specifications of the bid could be changed to cover less frequent service or longer trips for residents to collect mail. A radical change in relationships between elements in the postal system — from subsidy by government to competition among private and public suppliers — would transform the relationships among producers and consumers.

My claim is not necessarily that everyone would get better service at lower cost. Perhaps not. Rather, I claim that producers would want to seek support from consumers who, in turn, would be motivated to decide what they were willing to pay for which sort of service. No longer would consumers think only of service, without considering (for failure to understand the relationship between taxes and subsidies) the necessary resources; no longer would producers think largely of resources without worrying about consumers (who have no place else to go). In other words, competition in mail service should lead to mutual accommodation, because producers and consumers will know what they can get compared to what they want, and not to mutual hostility, because neither has learned to relate objectives to resources. The good system lets participants, in their daily interaction, internalize an informal policy analysis; the bad system leaves them fixated at a level either of resources or of objectives, but not of both together.

A Public-Sector Proposal

Now let us look at a public-sector solution. The combination of cost inflation and decreased access to health services is caused by (see page 288) the Law of Medical Money: because the medical system absorbs all inputs, expenditures rise to the level set for insurance and subsidy. The Great Equation (medicine equals health) being false, increased inputs into medicine cause increased use and higher costs, but bring no change in the rates (morbidity and mortality) by which health is measured. The objects of health policy, therefore, ought to be limiting financial inputs consistent with equity in access. The private market has been rejected because it discriminates against poorer people, so that it has been supplemented by public subsidy for the poor and aged. But subsidy exacerbates the effects of the Law of Medical Money by increasing inputs.

A radical solution, abolishing private insurance and state action, would be to transfer all medical spending to the central government. The amount would be so large (around $180 billion at current prices) that politicians would have to compare carefully the amount devoted to medicine with such other large national purposes as environment, welfare, defense, and income left in private hands. The collective choice of the people's representatives undoubtedly would add up to less than the sum of individual choices, because the former calls for allocating limited resources and the latter does not. The connection between an individual's taxes and insurance and his use of the medical system is so remote — because it is diffused among so many policyholders and taxpayers — that possible benefits from increased use almost always seem greater than that of self-restraint. Competing with other collective purposes, however, as it has in Great Britain, medicine may seem less important, especially because it does not seem to have improved health rates. The contemporary criticisms of Britain's National Health Service — shortage of hospital beds, antiquated equipment, long queues for operations — when properly viewed from the perspective of reducing inputs by rationing services so as to limit demand, really are its best features. Because results are the same within wide limits, cost effectiveness must be improved by limiting inputs of resources.

The contrast between PROD changes and those which merely tinker with tendencies should show up in the contrast between centralization of medical service and further diffusion through the newly established local or regional Health System Agencies. The idea is to lower costs and increase access to quality medical care by giving a consortium of provider and consumer representatives the right to deny certificates of need to construct or acquire new medical facilities. The predictable result will be an even faster rate of inflation (and rate of utilization) in the most expensive medical technology. Why? Because each participant still is allowed to pass on costs to other (insurance company and governmental) parties. Services are available locally, but spending and taxing go on far away at the state and national level. Following normal political logic — cooperation is better than conflict if other parties pay — medical providers will logroll with consumer representatives; the one gains greater facilities, and the other wins more services, because there is no direct connection between their use of medical facilities and the price they pay. Were all monies paid from the same source, by contrast, medical expenditures would have to compete with others (including private incomes, by taxation). Whereas now each individual cannot see the connection between use and cost in the medical sector — which means the relationship is between atomized individuals and an amorphous collectivity — the reformed relations would be between partisans of different policies competing for shares of a public pie. If the shares of that pie are not fixed finally, they will expand only at the taxpayer's expense and, even then, will have to be divided among numerous claimants. If individuals no longer are the chief actors, they necessarily take their chances with the bureaucracy, which may or may not be benevolent. After all, I promised only to illustrate PROD change, not to abolish choice or to eliminate pain.

A Mixed-Sector Proposal

Sometimes all that can be done is to let people convince themselves they are doing their best. Because elementary and high school education now is compulsory, the chief complaints are that children (especially among the poor) do not learn, and have behavioral problems that interfere with teaching. Increasing inputs (more teachers, higher salaries, better equipment) into schooling does not appear to improve cognitive performance. Without a teaching technology to link school efforts with student achievement, no financially feasible effort is likely to help. There is no reason to believe that any of the endless alterations in the organization of teaching will have the desired effect of significantly reducing socially stratified differences in learning.

The only really radical reform in schooling therefore (save to abolish it) is the voucher plan; its main promise is parent acceptance rather than child performance. Under this plan each parent and child would be given a voucher that could be used at any school in the area. (These vouchers could vary in size, with retarded or hyperactive or other difficult children getting more resources.) Under the current system, parents cannot leave schools without leaving neighborhoods. The voucher plan would eliminate this monopoly. Because parents could switch support to other schools, teachers would have to seek their patronage; and if schools were allowed to refuse pupils, parents would have to work on problems of behavior. Thus students and schools (after the first round of "musical chairs") would have an interest in mutual accommodation. Students and their parents would learn to accept the best schools they could get and teachers and school administrators would adjust their expectations to the best students available under prevailing conditions. Parents no longer would dream of the perfect school (either because they were in one or could not hope to find one) and teachers would no longer dream of well-behaved little geniuses, because their real choice would be to have the best they could get or none. Of course, organized school personnel may resist these changes successfully, and it may take time for parents to realize they actually can exercise choice. The point is not that the voucher (or any other) proposal is perfect or costless — teachers might lose jobs because their schools lacked patronage, and minorities might do worse if vouchers were priced too low — but that this idea, unlike the plethora of proposals for the appearance without the substance of change in education, could actually alter interpersonal relations — who bargains with whom over what with how much power — in the educational system.

Choice and Change

The outcomes of bargains may be altered by changing the players as well as the rules of systemic interaction. The formation of prisoners' unions already is having that effect. Just a few years ago, prisoners did not speak; they were spoken for. The self-appointed spokesmen for prisoners supposed that prisoners wanted (because they would supposedly benefit from) group therapy. The spokesmen supposed also that prisoners preferred shorter sentences and longer probations, rather than the reverse, and that probation might assist rehabilitation. Evidence to the contrary did not lead to change; but when prisoners' unions protested against compulsory therapy and indeterminate sentencing, they found allies among prison authorities. True, the recidivism rate remains unchanged because no one knows how to change it, but human dignity (especially important when people are in prison) has been protected, and the public purse, once thought of as a public trust, has been guarded. By introducing a neglected interest, hitherto unrepresented, the information available to each participant in the penal political arena has been improved.

I have suggested that in any number of areas of policy, running from television repair to postal service to prison activities, citizenship is better served when people are freer to make more choices. These choices may come from self-interest, but interaction with others increases mutual interest. Each participant is better able to learn something no amount of study will provide: what other people prefer and are willing to give up (shorter sentences, perhaps) to get it.

It is not the motives of the actors acting alone that matter for public policy, it is the relationships among the motives of the various actors. I need not claim that the motives of prisoners to instigate unions are pure in order to judge that adding these organizations to the political process would improve it. This is true also about the motives of doctors and teachers. If teachers need students in order to work, it is not the teachers' motives (as if they were immutable), but their relationship with others that undergo change. By focusing on patterns of interpersonal relations induced by public policy, we can evaluate relationships formed in, by, and through policies. Programs (ends and instruments together) therefore, make up the unit to which moral criteria should be applied.

Yet it is commonly held that to consider objectives and resources together, as if one could know them simultaneously, violates a doctrine known as the separation of fact and value. I have been arguing not only that it is possible, indeed essential to learn about preferences, and not only that what happens to these preferences makes no sense without facts, but also that relating values to fact is at the heart of the effective intelligence I have been calling policy analysis. Examining this relationship is important because difficulties with ideas often mask disputes about action. If citizens cannot discourse intelligently about values, this inability implies either that elites (experts, analysts, the "vanguard" of the proletariat) are better able to do so or that these values must be handed down by convention or imposed by revolution.

The controversy over values and facts may be interpreted as a decline in willingness to accept as desirable that which is conventional. As more of what had been taken for granted becomes questionable, accepting current objectives becomes objectionable. Conflict in society becomes transmuted into disputes over philosophy. Both the beliefs about the world ("facts") and the norms of appropriate conduct ("values") that support social structure in the world have become problematical. When one man's convention becomes another's catastrophe, disagreement as to what are means and what are ends is only part of their lack of trust.

FACT AND VALUE: CONVENTION OR CONSTRAINT?

Philosophic disagreement over facts and values today is so strong because the differences between disputants measure how much people who take opposing positions favor social relations the way they are. The less stake people feel, the fewer facts they certify, the more they may be willing to take their chances on different future values. In the end, trust in its benevolence, are likely to prove decisive. For the present, however, we can rest on this: if objectives and preferences are screened from scrutiny, it is not possible to think interesting thoughts about policy. Being neither sluggish nor stupid, but adaptive and intelligent, citizens like us change our preferences by learning. But it is not possible to learn about preferences if preferences are values and if mankind can know only about facts. My rationale for resurrecting this ancient argument is the same as for the rest of this study: to advance analysis as moral development.

Convention vs. Constraint

The contemporary condition that gives rise to the dichotomy between fact and value is unfortunate but understandable. If all is flux, where can we stand? By separating objectives from resources in public policies, the appearance of stability is given to uncertainty; humanity can control its fate and the evidence appears in plans, national goals, and lists of objectives. Now these objectives, though part of the past — in which lies the experience from which they were conceived — point to the future, that time horizon along which they will be realized. By seeming to place objectives in front of us, the future is appropriated to the past, as if we had lived through it already, and therefore is made to look more orderly. This neatness, this apparently systematic quality, is what gives way when facts affect values and resources alter objectives. For if programs combining ends and means were subject to test by experience, they might fail, whereas objectives alone, protected from contact with the world, cannot. The "triumph of the will" occurs when all facts are reduced to values, or, in other words, the assertion of values in itself becomes the only body of facts.

I have no quarrel with those who say that, for conceptual purposes, one may wish to talk separately about "facts" and about "values." We do it all the time. It is (do I give myself away if I add "in fact?") a useful convention to avoid discussing everything at once. Karl Popper writes,

> the fundamental maxim of every critical discussion is that we should stick to our problem, and that we should subdivide it, if practicable, and try to solve no more than one problem at a time, although we may, of course, always proceed to a subsidiary problem, or replace our problem by a better one.
>
> While discussing a problem we always accept (if only temporarily) all kinds of things as unproblematic: they constitute for the time being, and for the discussion of this particular problem, what I call our background knowledge. Few parts of this background knowledge will appear to us in all contexts as absolutely unproblematic, and any particular part of it may be challenged at any time, especially if we suspect that its uncritical

acceptance may be responsible for some of our difficulties. But almost all of the vast amount of background knowledge which we constantly use in any informal discussion will, for practical reasons, necessarily remain unquestioned; and the misguided attempt to question it all — that is to say, start from scratch — can easily lead to the breakdown of a critical debate. (Were we to start the race where Adam started, I know of no reason why we should get any further than Adam did.) [7]

I agree also with those (sometimes the very same people) who say that in action (or "real life," as people who disparage thought are wont to say), fact and value are usually intertwined, so it is often difficult to disentangle them.

The confusion may arise from failure to distinguish between a convention and a constraint. In ordinary language we may speak of an objective as fixed, and discuss which of several alternatives will best achieve this objective. In itself, this practice does no harm. But if it leads to the belief that objectives or preferences are beyond argument because they comprise "values," whereas one can quarrel about resources or constraints because they are made up of "facts," I must dissent. This would mean that the most important part of learning from experience — finding out what one, under specific circumstances, ought to prefer — would be denied. Surely, when Eve ate fruit from the tree of knowledge she usurped the function of her Maker by attempting to know the difference between good and evil, not by debating over a subject that was impossible to discuss. (It was, and she lost.) If we can reason about means but not ends, if humanity is doomed to apply reasonable means to nonrational (that is, uninspectable) ends, there can be no policy analysis because the analysis involves changing preferences as well as potential actions. To commend a program means to recommend a new combination of both means and ends.

Where, then, do facts fit in? Where experience teaches us what to want. Henry Rowen says:

> In short, to many participants the analytic process will contribute to beliefs about facts and relationships and will help in the construction of value preferences. The phrase "construction of value preferences" is deliberately chosen. This reflects the view that preferences are generally built through experience and through learning about facts, about relationships, and about consequences. It is not that values are latent and only need to be "discovered" or "revealed." There is a potentially infinite number of values; they are not equally useful or valid, and part of the task of analysis is to develop ones that seem especially "right" and useful and that might become widely shared. Because value preferences are formed through a process of choice in specific cultural and institutional settings, and because, as Laurence Tribe observes, avoidance of dissonance causes us to prefer what we have chosen, the factors that influence our choices get imbedded in our values. Those that are fuzzy, fragile, not immediately useful, are

likely to be excluded and therefore are not built into the value system that we are constantly constructing and reconstructing.[8]

It is this reconstruction that makes learning part of policy analysis.

Now let us go back to what we realize we must have been saying when we agreed, for the moment, to accept an objective. No doubt we did not mean just any old objective apart from any new consideration of resources. After all, if we had only $1,000, four people, and no scientific training, we wouldn't dream of trying to go to the moon even if that had been authorized as an official government objective. No, we meant that we had entered into tacit agreements not to upset most past objectives, though we might do so if we were prepared to pay the price.

Our usage was conventional; as anyone who did not want his days clogged with disputes would see, we recognized the constraints in the situation — pathways blocked, behaviors forbidden, wealth unobtainable — by adopting the convention that most former constraints be preserved as of the present. Such a convention may be adopted for many reasons: the potential gain would not be worth the actual cost; or the one act, though small in itself, might set in motion a series of others, dependent on it, whose alteration would have incalculable consequences; or leaving these objectives undisturbed may be the understood exchange for changing others; or we might even be ruled by just plain inertia. None of these implies the immutability of the status quo. It is possible always for potential change to compete with the status quo. The "facts" to which we are so fond of referring, and the desired "values" of which so much is said, therefore, do not, in reality, exist apart from each other. They are embedded in past, present, and potential analyses, from which we learn what we prefer in part from what we'd rather not change. To be sure, in isolation we might prefer to pluck a leaf of pleasure from the tree of life, provided we didn't have to give up our whole branch for it. Paul Feyerabend says it:

> Both the relevance and the refuting character of decisive facts can be established only with the help of other theories which . . . are not in agreement with the view to be tested. This being the case, the invention and articulation of alternatives may have to precede the production of refuting facts. Empiricism, at least in some of its more sophisticated versions, demands that the empirical content of whatever knowledge we possess be increased as much as possible. Hence the invention of alternatives to the view at the centre of discussion constitutes an essential part of the empirical method.[9]

When the conventional becomes desirable, it turns into tradition; that is, it seems obligatory to do something in a particular way because it has been done that way all along. When most decisions are conventional, the remaining few can be analytical, in the sense that it is possible to know something about what one is giving up and what one is getting. If most choices are unconventional, and one can no longer assume but must predict responses, almost all become unanalytical in that neither costs nor benefits can be estimated. When the political system is under attack, so that its legitimacy varies along with all the policies it helps produce, the ability to understand what is happening, let alone to predict what is likely to follow, declines precipitously. If it is not to swallow up the life of the citizen, citizenship — learning, understanding, choosing as part of ordinary activity — requires stability.

Policy analysis is an effort to use thought to aid interaction; alternatives that might otherwise have to be experienced may be carried through in thought so that one can imagine actively how they might turn out. Even in thought, however, the few variables one can intelligently manipulate are immeasurably exceeded by those one cannot. When all or most variables vary simultaneously, thought gives way and only actions carry their own consequences. Without convention to remove most matters from contention, all facts become values and analysis as an aid to action is replaced by action. Moral development, acting to consider the consequences for others, declines and so too does citizenship.

That something (probably nearly everything) has to be taken for granted in order to apply intelligence to public policy does not mean citizens cannot discourse about values. It may mean, rather, than a smaller range of values can be discussed with greater discernment. People who are not (and do not wish to be) full-time politicians, namely most citizens most of the time, are especially vulnerable to disruption; if everything is up for grabs, they will be less likely to participate in anything. Restricting the scope of analysis, however, inevitably has a conservatizing effect; the more that is left out of analysis, evidently, the less that is subject to change. This, I contend, is a price we pay for thinking before we act; but it is a price we should consider carefully.

WHY ANALYSIS IS CONSERVATIVE

Advocates of permanent revolution believe that there should be no *terra firma*, only *terra incognita*. Stability is their enemy, flux their friend. They wish (if this is not a contradiction) to institutionalize continuous change in authority relations. Asking how we get from here to there, or whether it is the right place to go, is inappropriate for them because they reject the "here" to start with, and the "there" to end with; thus anyplace revolution stops obviously is wrong. Doubts have been expressed about whether Mao Tse-tung, the major modern exponent of permanent revolution, implicitly assumed his own permanence as repository of historical legitimacy, thus limiting the scope (rejection of communism) and hence the danger (undermining the political system) of change.[10] But it is clear that, for real radicals, meliorative moves justify the status quo; they take for granted (accept, for the moment, as "fact") the structure of social and political relations other than that implied in the substantive policy being reviewed at a particular time.

Descending from the heights of permanent revolution to more mundane matters, the radical position—that what is taken for granted is far more important than what is questioned in any analysis — undoubtedly is correct. Not only do most analyses of health or crime or education or whatever fail to consider fundamental alterations in policies, but nearly all assume the continuance of social and political relationships. Radicals, therefore, reject as conservative any analysis that does not conceive of social relationships as problematic. I shall try to illuminate the contrast between radical and conservative natures of analysis by briefly recapitulating these positions in the disputes about community power structure (inevitably unresolved) that were a staple of controversy in the sixties.[11]

Monism and Pluralism: A Misleading Controversy

To oversimplify an already simple-minded controversy, in the fifties a monistic view of political power appeared to challenge the validity of democratic institutions. C. Wright Mills seemed to imply that a single economic elite, acting outside the national political system, made all the important decisions, cumulatively heaping up resources that increasingly disadvantaged ordinary citizens. And Floyd Hunter saw the same in the city of Atlanta, Georgia. To challenge these propositions about power, Robert Dahl and his associates put forth a pluralist alternative. They claimed their studies of actual decisions in New Haven showed that different people exercised power in different areas of policy. Dahl theorized that inequalities in the distribution of resources, such as wealth, public office, and expertise, were not cumulative, so that it was at least possible for outsiders to become insiders; this made good an implied promise of democratic political life. The debate was about whether local communities, being the most numerous and easiest to study, were governed by the many or the few, were monist or pluralist. New champions, including this author,[12] entered the lists without notably enlightening a rapidly dwindling audience. The contest ended in less mutual understanding in more mutual exhaustion. Who was right? The greater wisdom is in asking what went wrong with the debate.

The question was uninteresting: it led nowhere. Pluralists did not set up their research designs to add to knowledge about political decision-making but mostly to refute monism. By studying decisions on various policies, and observing who appeared to initiate, modify, or otherwise control them, they were able to show that being in office made a big difference; the identity of powerful people, and their policy preferences, it turned out, differed from one issue to the other.

Unfortunately, the criteria for pluralism are so broad that it is difficult to imagine a community of any size not meeting them. Even the Soviet Union is likely to have factions in the Communist Party (bureaucratic and professional interests, city officials and local factory heads in contention), so that its cities might be considered pluralist. The conditions for monism are so severe — a small, cohesive, all-powerful group outside the public political process, able to control all deviations — that no one has successfully pointed to an example. If all cities are pluralist, then pluralism does not discriminate between categories of cities, so that it is impossible to inquire into the conditions for predicting pluralism compared with monism or anything else.

Reexamining the Controversy: A Question of Approach

More important than this methodological mirage, comparing a theory that is not worth challenging with one that is unchallengeable (irrefutable, therefore empty) is that monists and pluralists were trying to answer fundamentally different questions, with very different implications for public policy. And each side came up with different answers. For monists, the question was one of fundamental freedom or life-chances: why are some people poor or worse off and other people rich and better off? With this understanding, how can we improve the life-chances of the worse off so that their position in all important values — health, welfare, income, and the rest — would be the same as for the better-off? The Rousseau-like overtones of the monist question (why are some men born free and others in chains?) suggest a historical-development approach. Humankind has not reached its sorry state overnight; inequalities have accumulated over long historical periods. Thus it becomes important to find out how inequalities have persisted and who (the power elite) is responsible for maintaining these inequalities by resisting radical change. Overcoming the historical residue of inequality (or any other evil) in one stroke in one moment suggests drastic remedies. Radicals want the present to overcome, not merely modify, the past.

Pluralists, by contrast, are more interested in building on than in rejecting the past. They take a cross-sectional approach: what instruments of policy can be manipulated right now to achieve which improvements? By accepting the past, by accepting a reading of history that does not consider inequalities in resources increasing as time passes, pluralists can concentrate on policy improvements. A decisional approach, to ask about the exercise of power in various types of issues, is useful for reaching the next decision in the near future. A cross-sectional, current-decision approach is not useful for substituting wholly new methods of decision designed to produce wholesale change dramatically so as to reverse a persistent pattern of prior wrongs.

What difference would it make if policy analysis took a historical-developmental, not a cross-sectional approach? Suppose you are interested in abolishing the requirement that prisoners take therapy before being considered for parole or, as prisoners' unions desire, that indeterminate sentences give way to fixed jail terms. A cross-sectional approach, emphasizing the instruments best suited to secure that next intended effect, omits considering how prisons and prisoners became what they are, or how things might be reversed or transformed. Answers, even if they were forthcoming, would not help resolve the present problem. Theory about large-scale social change over the years, assuming that the change is knowable, cannot be transferred easily into questions about who might be moved to take the next step in prison reform. Would it be appropriate, then, for the analyst to say that if the prisoner's lot cannot be radically changed — by transforming the society and the political processes through which it acts — then nothing is worth doing? Prisoners may be excused for believing that their desires are worth achieving, even if most other things remain the same. It is certainly true that making therapy voluntary is not going to eliminate prisons or drastically alter their functions.

That most things will remain the same at any time is not incompatible with some things changing some of the time. Radical change (as when social welfare changed places with military expenditures) can result from the rapid cumulation of more modest changes. The quality of these changes, not their sheer quantity, depends on whether the interpersonal relationships of people engaged in these programs discourage or encourage citizens in daily life to act as analysts, furthering their moral development.

MORALITY AND POLICY ANALYSIS

The rationale for analysis — avoiding experience by imagining what might happen if things worked this or that way — may be its ruin. The temptation of the analyst is to treat citizens as objects. By depriving people of autonomy in thought (their consciousness is false, their experience invalid), it is possible to deny them citizenship in action. The moral role of the analyst, therefore, demands that cogitation enhance the values of interaction and (not become a substitute for) it.

Why is citizenship important for policy analysis? Because, as I have argued, without participation by citizens:

1. capacity for enhancing autonomy by learning will decline;
2. damage will be done to human dignity by denigrating reciprocity;
3. therefore, many difficulties won't improve as much and as quickly as they should, and others will get much worse, faster than necessary.

The task of analysts is stated by Martin Landau:

to probe in the interest of error prevention and to learn in the interest of error correction. This is what Kenneth Boulding calls the "institutionalization of disappointment" — a system of criticism which permits policies to be tested in such manner as to enable a self-correcting capacity.[13]

And, I should add, this testing cannot and should not be done only by policy analysts, but also (and primarily) by policy participants. The less necessary analysts make themselves, by enhancing the self-correcting characteristics of the relationships within a policy, the more they have succeeded. The moral trap of the professional, as Max Weber knew, is "living off" instead of "living for" the troubles of their clients. Doing oneself out of a job is the best way to do analysis.

Analysis must deal with individual capacity to act, and collective capacity to regulate the resulting social relationships. It is one thing to argue that citizens can be effective on the policies within which they participate; it is another to argue that the accumulation of these actions is intelligible (morally consistent) in accord with widespread preferences, and therefore rational.

NOTES

1. Jean Piaget, To Understand Is to Invent: The Future of Education (New York: Grossman, 1973), pp. 118–119.
2. This section on strategy is adapted from Aaron Wildavsky, Leadership in a Small Town (Totowa, N.J.: Bedminster Press, 1964), pp. 353–354.
3. See T. H. Marshall, Class, Citizenship and Social Development (Westport, Conn.: Greenwood Press, 1973).
4. Kjell Eide, "Assessing and Evaluating Educational Performance," Norsdick Forum, Vol. 4 (1972), p. 225.
5. Amitai Etzioni, "Future Analysis," Stop News, No. 38 (June 1976), p. 19.
6. See M. A. H. Dempster and Aaron Wildavsky, "Yes, Virginia, There Is No Magic Size for an Increment," in The Political Economy of Government Spending: Predicting U.S. Federal Appropriations (forthcoming).
7. Karl Popper, Conjectures and Refutations (New York: Basic Books, 1962), p. 238.
8. Henry S. Rowen, "Policy Analysis as Heuristic Aid: The Design of Means, Ends, and Institutions," in When Values Conflict, Laurence H. Tribe, Corinne S. Schelling, and John Voss, eds. (Cambridge, Mass.: Ballinger, 1976), p. 142.
9. Paul Feyerabend, Against Method — Outline of an Anarchistic Theory of Knowledge (London: NLB, Atlantic Highlands: Humanities Press, 1975), p. 41.
10. John B. Starr and Nancy A. Dyer, Post-Liberation Works of Mao Zedong: A Bibliography and Index (Berkeley Center for Chinese Studies, University of California, 1976).

11. C. Wright Mills, *The Power Elite* (New York: Oxford University Press, 1956); Robert A. Dahl, *Who Governs? Democracy and Power in an American City* (New Haven: Yale University Press, 1961); Nelson W. Polsby, *Community Power and Political Theory* (New Haven: Yale University Press, 1963); Raymond E. Wolfinger, *Politics of Progress* (Englewood Cliffs, N.J.: Prentice-Hall, 1974); Floyd Hunter, *Community Power Structure* (Chapel Hill: University of North Carolina Press, 1953).

12. Aaron Wildavsky, *Leadership in a Small Town* (Totowa, N.J.: Bedminster Press, 1964).

13. Martin Landau, "The Proper Domain of Policy Analysis" in "The Workshop: The Place of Policy Analysis in Political Science: Five Perspectives," *American Journal of Political Science,* Vol. 21, No. 2 (May 1977), pp. 426–427.

PART 4

POLICY ANALYSIS

The epoch that Cezanne certainly began is marked most clearly by the fact that each artist, each originator, institutes a new dimension of understanding. The apparent arbitrariness of a continuous and unending process of redefinition, on the basis of a past which is itself in a perpetual state of rediscovery and revaluation, places some values in doubt. Cezanne demonstrated, as he intended, that the process is rational and sensible nevertheless. . . . (p. 70)

Cezanne himself was well aware how problematic his standpoint would be found. He developed an uncharacteristic longing for exegesis and explanation. A preoccupation with theory and with the status of theory filled his letters and his conversation. Posterity might have made better use of the lavish clues he offered. They are certainly needed. Contemplating the seminal works on which the twentieth century has depended so greatly, we are examining what aesthetic comprehension consists of in our age. We are considering what kind of sense we can claim to make of our own culture. (p. 56)

> Laurence Gowing, "The Logic of Organized Sensations,"
> in *Cezanne: The Late Work*, by William Rubin,
> (New York: Museum of Modern Art, 1977).

There can no more be only one approved mode of policy analysis than there can be only one way of loving and learning; it all depends on "where you're at" and what you're up to. The four analyses here, chosen for their diversity from among many in which I've participated, differ in the kinds of questions they ask and the types of answers they give. Suppose, to begin at the beginning, we ask who posed the problem? Education and health are everyone's interest, widely acknowledged, open to anyone who wants to "take them on." The tax write-off for charity is also well known but only among interested elites — charitable executives, tax and budget reformers, legislators. The proverbial man on the street is probably unaware of urban outcomes. These are issues created by analysts, applying different criteria to the distribution of city services and bringing them to public notice. This is quite a range of problem posing: by everyone, by a few, by no one (except us analysts).

How about problem solving: how uniform are the solutions? The charitable scene is prescriptive and specific: the tax write-off should be replaced by a budget device subsidizing 38 per cent of contributions. Urban outcomes are prescriptive but general in that some directions are marked out — more money for books, less for library personnel, more for city streets and less for freeways — without attempting to stipulate the precise percentage of distribution. The prescription in education is even more general, calling for a change in process, which might or might not lead to a change in purpose, as parents, students, teachers, and administrators learn how to reach and keep agreements, whatever these may be. Where the purpose is to understand why problems persist, as with health policy, prescription may fade imperceptibly into description. Progressing from no prescription at all, to advising precisely what to do, with various intermediate steps is a fair range (indeed, almost all the range) of advice.

The four analyses also differ in the degree to which the difficulty is in objectives or in resources. In tax and urban services, objectives are related to resources only too well. The purpose of the analyses is to argue that objectives, such as making it easier for the rich (and harder for the poor) to contribute to charity, or the lowest cost of construction per freeway mile of traffic, lead to inequities or are otherwise inappropriate. Health and education policy present the opposite predicament; resources do not reach to objectives, which involve improving cognitive abilities or health rates. Finding problems in objectives, and finding them in resources, take up about all the space in which to locate them.

Corresponding variety occurs in calculations employed in attempting to solve problems. The proposed solution for education is procedural, replacing cogitation, which frequently fails, with interaction, which may succeed. At the other end of the spectrum, interaction that leads to inefficiencies in health policy may be followed by intervention based on cogitation (in the form of a national health service) that might at least keep costs down. Urban outcomes suggest introducing elements of cogitation because interaction over street repairs, library collections, and teacher assignments have consequences disadvantageous for poor people, sometimes unintentionally, which are no longer acceptable. Cogitation is used to restructure rules for interaction — limiting transfer of teachers, expanding repair of streets in older neighborhoods, providing books by population as well as by use — so as to produce more acceptable outcomes. Now the only way of replacing cogitation with interaction in charitable giving would be (as the slogan says) to get the government out of the business of charity by providing no subsidy whatever. Unless philanthropy is to be doubly decimated (once by inflation and once by government), only forms of cogitation involving direct governmental subsidy are left. Therefore we come up with this straightforward advice to aspiring (or expiring, as the case may be) analysts: once a problem is posed, you may attempt to solve it by replacing interaction with cogitation, cogitation with interaction, cogitation with cogitation, or interaction with . . . you guessed it.

Of what is being done now, how much should analysts take for granted and how much should they subject to criticism? In choosing between dogma and skepticism, one pays in principles. All four policies raise basic questions: should one accept the tradition of publicly provided education and, if so, is it necessary to accept a monopoly by public providers or could users be given choices among any acceptable schools? Americans are apparently unwilling to abolish private or public medicine or to go without private insurance or public subsidy, for if they had not these inhibitions, costs could be contained by relying solely on all-private or all-public medicine. If government no longer subsidized philanthropy, the difficulties of government regulation would be replaced by diminution of philanthropy worth regulating. To me (though not necessarily to you), questioning the income-tax write-off, the monopoly of public education, and the desirability of medicine against improved personal health habits is more than enough of a challenge to the status quo. Those interested in immediate change should look elsewhere, though they need go no further than the distribution of urban services, whose outcomes are subject to alteration. Is there, then, advice to give on creating or solving problems, on how to relate resources to objectives, on how to calculate by cogitation or interaction, or on how skeptical or dogmatic to be? To the extent that analysis is art, the answer is, not really, unless one considers restating the questions (benefits should exceed costs; choose the preferred solution) equivalent to an answer. So far as analysis is a craft, however, we might hope for useful rules of work. Let us first analyze the four policies and see whether they contain clues to craft.

CHAPTER 12

DOING BETTER
AND FEELING WORSE:
THE POLITICAL PATHOLOGY
OF HEALTH POLICY

According to the Great Equation, Medical Care equals Health. But the Great Equation is wrong. More available medical care does not equal better health. The best estimates are that the medical system (doctors, drugs, hospitals) affects about 10 percent of the usual indexes for measuring health: whether you live at all (infant mortality), how well you live (days lost due to sickness), how long you live (adult mortality). The remaining 90 percent are determined by factors over which doctors have little or no control, from individual life-style (smoking, exercise, worry), to social conditions (income, eating habits, physiological inheritance), to the physical environment (air and water quality). Most of the bad things that happen to people's health are at present beyond the reach of medicine.

Nobody says doctors don't help. They mend broken bones, stop infections with drugs, operate successfully on swollen appendixes. Inoculations, internal infections, and external repairs are other good reasons for keeping doctors, drugs, and hospitals around. More of the same, however, is counterproductive. Nobody needs unnecessary operations, and excessive drugs can create dependence or allergic reactions or merely enrich the nation's urine.

More money alone, then, cannot cure old complaints. In the absence of medical knowledge gained by new research, or of administrative knowledge to convert common practice into best practice, current medicine has gone as far as it can. No one is saying that medicine is good for nothing, only that it is not good for everything. Thus the marginal value of one — or one billion — dollars spent on medical care will be close to zero in improving health. And, thinking of public policy, we are not worrying about the bulk of present medical expenditures, which do have value; our main interest should be proposed future spending, which is of dubious value.

When people are polled, they are liable to say, depending on what they are asked, that they are getting good care but that there is a crisis in the medical-care system. Based on the particular survey, three-quarters to four-fifths of the population are satisfied with their doctors and the care they give; but one-third to two-thirds think the system that produces these results is in bad shape. Opinions about the family doctor, of course, are formed from personal experience. "The system," on the other hand, is an abstract entity — and here people may well imitate the attitudes of those interested and vocal elites who insist the system is in crisis.

People do have specific complaints related to their position in a class, however. The rich don't like waiting, the poor don't like high prices, and those in the middle complain about both. Everyone would like easier access to a private physician in time of need. We shall see a plausible explanation for the widespread belief that doctors are good though the system is bad. That's the trouble: everyone behaves reasonably; it is only the systemic effects of all this reasonable behavior that are unreasonable.

If most people are healthier today than people like themselves have ever been, and if access to medical care now is more evenly distributed among rich and poor, why this talk of a crisis in medical care that needs massive change? If most of the population is satisfied with its medical care, why is there so much pressure in government for change? Why, in brief, are we doing better but feeling worse? Let us try to create a theory about the political pathology of health policy.

PARADOXES, PRINCIPLES, AXIOMS, IDENTITIES, AND LAWS

The fallacy of the Great Equation is based on the Paradox of Time: past successes lead to future failures. As life expectancy increases and as formerly disabling diseases are conquered, medicine is faced with an older population whose disabilities are more difficult to defeat. The cost of cure is higher, both because the easier ills have already been dealt with, and because the patients to be treated are older. Each increment of knowledge is harder won; each improvement in health is more expensive. Thus time converts one decade's achievements into the next decade's dilemmas. Yesterday's victims of tuberculosis are today's geriatric cases. The Paradox of Time is that success lies in the past and (possibly) the future, but never in the present.

The Great Equation is rescued by the Principle of Goal Displacement, which is that any objective that cannot be attained will be replaced by one that can be approximated. Every program needs an opportunity to be successful; if a program cannot succeed in reaching its ostensible goals, sponsors may shift to goals whose achievement they can control. The process subtly becomes the purpose. And that is exactly what has happened as "health" has become equivalent to "equal access to medicine."

When government goes into public housing, it provides the actual apartments; when government goes into health, it can offer only medicine. But medicine is far from health. The government can try to equalize access to medicine, whether or not that access brings improved health. If the question is, "Does health increase with government expenditure on medicine?" the answer is likely to be "No." Just alter the question: "Has access to medicine been improved by government programs?" and the answer is most certainly, with a little qualification, "Yes."

By "access," of course, we mean quantity, not quality, of care. Access, moreover, can be measured, and progress toward an equal number of visits to doctors can be reported. But something has to be done about the distressing stickiness of health rates, which fail to keep up with access. Thus access to medical care is irrelevant to health — unless, of course, health is not the real goal but merely a cover for something more fundamental, which might be called "mental health" (reverently), or "shamanism" (irreverently), or "caring" (most accurately).

Any doctor will tell you, say sophisticates, that most patients are not sick, at least physically, and that the best medicine for them is reassurance. Tranquilizers, painkillers, and aspirin seem to be the functional equivalents, for these are the drugs most often prescribed. Wait a minute, says the medical sociologist (the student not merely of medicine's manifest, but also of its latent, functions), mental pain is just as real as physical pain. If people want to know somebody loves them, and today their preference is doctors of medicine over doctors of theology, they are entitled to get what they want.

Once "caring" has been substituted for (or made equivalent to) "doctoring," access immediately becomes a better measure of attainment. The number of times a person sees a doctor probably is a better measure of the amount of reassurance he has received than of his well-being or a decline in his disease. Therefore, what looks like a single goal substitution (access to medicine in place of better health) is actually a double displacement: caring instead of health, and access instead of caring.

This double displacement is fraught with consequences. It is hard enough to determine how much medical care is adequate but just about impossible to measure the sufficiency of "caring." The treatment of physical ills is partially subjective; the treatment of mental ills is almost entirely so. If a person is in pain, he alone can judge how much it hurts. How much caring he needs depends upon how much he wants. In the old days he was most likely to take his tension to the private sector, and there he got as much attention as he could afford. But now, with government subsidy of medicine so large, the question of how much caring he should get inevitably becomes a public worry.

By what standard should this public question be decided? One objective criterion — equality of access — inevitably stands out among the rest. For if we don't quite know what caring is or how much of it there should be, we always can say that at least it should be distributed equally. Medicaid has just about equalized the number of doctor visits per year between the poor and the rich. In fact, the upper class is showing a decrease in visits, and the life expectancy of richer males is going down somewhat. Presumably, no one is suggesting remedial action in favor of rich men. Equality, not health, is the issue.

One can always assert that even if the results of medical treatment are illusory, the poor are entitled to their share. This looks like a powerful argument, but it neglects the Axiom of Inequality, that every move to increase equality in one dimension necessarily decreases it in another. Consider space. The United States has unequal rates of development. Different geographic areas vary considerably in such matters as income, custom, and expectation. Establishing a uniform national policy disregards these differences; allowing local variation means that some areas get more unequal treatment than others. Think of time. People not only have unequal incomes, they also differ in the amount of time they are prepared to devote to medical care. In equalizing the effects of money on medical care — by removing money as a consideration — care is likely to be allocated by the distribution of available time. To the extent that the pursuit of money takes time, people with a monetary advantage will have a temporal disadvantage. You can't have it both ways, as the Axiom of Allocation makes abundantly clear.

"No system of care in the world," says David Mechanic, summing up the Axiom of Allocation, "is willing to provide as much care as people will use, and all such systems develop mechanisms that ration . . . services." Just as there is no free lunch, there is no free medicine. Rationing can be done by time (waiting lists, lines), by distance (people farther from facilities use them less than those who are closer), by complexity (forms, repeated visits, communications difficulties) by space (limiting the number of hospital beds and available doctors), or by any or all these methods in combination. But why do people want more medical service than any system is willing to provide? The answer has to do with uncertainty.

If medicine is only partially and imperfectly related to health, it follows that both doctor and patient often will be uncertain as to what is wrong or what to do about it. Otherwise — if medicine were perfectly related to health — either there would be no health problem, or it would be very different. Health rates would be on one side and health resources on the other; costs and benefits could be neatly compared. But they can't, because so often we don't know how to produce the desired benefits. Uncertainty exists because medicine is a quasi-science — more science than, say, political science; less science than civil engineering. How participants in the medical system resolve their uncertainties matters a great deal.

The Medical Uncertainty Principle states that there is always one more thing that might be done — another consultation, a new drug, a different treatment; the patient asks for more, the doctor orders more. The patient's simple rule for resolving uncertainty is to seek care up to the limit of his insurance. If everyone uses all the care he can, total costs will rise; but in this domain as in so many others the individual has so little control over the total that he does not appreciate the connection between his individual choice and the collective result. A corresponding phenomenon occurs among doctors who can resolve uncertainty by prescribing up to the limit of the patient's insurance, a rule reinforced by the high cost of malpractice. Patients bringing suit do not consider the relationship between their own success and higher medical costs for everyone. The patient is anxious, the doctor insecure; this combination is unbeatable until the irresistible force meets the immovable object — the Medical Identity.

The Medical Identity states that use is limited by availability. Only so much can be gotten out of so much. Thus, if Medical Uncertainty suggests that existing services will be used, Identity reminds us to add the words "up to the available supply." That supply is primarily doctors, who advise on the kind of care to provide and the number of hospital beds to maintain. But patients, considering only their own desires in time of need, want to maximize supply, a phenomenon that follows inexorably from the Principle of Perspective.

That principle states that social conditions and individual feelings are not the same thing. A happy social statistic may obscure a sad personal situation. A statistical equilibrium may hide a family crisis. Morbidity and mortality, in tabulating aggregate rates of disease and death, describe all of us but do not touch you and me. We do not think of ourselves as "rates." Our chances may be better or worse than the aggregate. To say that doctors are not wholly (or even mostly) successful in alleviating some symptoms is not to say that they don't help some people and that one of those people won't be me. Taking the chance that it will be me often seems to make sense, even if I have reason to believe that most people can't be helped and that some actually may be harmed. Most people, told that the same funds spent on other purposes may increase social benefits, will put personal needs first. For this reason expenditures on medical care are always larger than any estimate of the social benefit received. Now we can understand, by combining into one law the previous principle and Medical Identity, why costs rise so far and so fast.

The Law of Medical Money states that medical costs will rise to equal the sum of all private insurance and government subsidy. They do so because no one knows how much medical care ought to cost. The patient is not sure he is getting all he should, and the doctor does not want to be criticized for doing less than he might. Consider the triangular relationship among doctor, patient, and hospital. With private insurance, the doctor can use the hospital resources that are covered by the insurance while holding down his patient's own expenditures. With public subsidies, the doctor may charge his highest usual fee, abandon charitable work, and ignore the financial benefits of eliminating defaults on payments. His income rises. His patient doesn't have to pay, and his hospital expands. The patient, if he is covered by a government program or private insurance (as are about 90 percent) finds that his out-of-pocket expenses have remained the same. His insurance costs more, but either it comes out of his paycheck, looking like a fixed expense, or it is taken off his income tax as a deduction. Hospitals work on a cost-plus basis. They offer the latest and the best, pleasing both doctor and patient. They pay their help better; or, rather, they get others to pay their help. It's on the house — or at least on the insurance.

Perhaps our triangle ought to be a square: maybe we should include insurance companies. Why don't they play a cost-cutting role in medical care as they do in other industries? After all, the less the outlay, the more income for the company. The simplest explanation is that insurance companies make no difference because they are embedded in the health-care industry. The largest, Blue Cross and Blue Shield, are run by the hospital establishment on behalf of doctors. After all, hospitals do not so much have patients as they have doctors who have patients. Doctors run hospitals, not the other way around. Insurance companies unwilling to play this game have left the field. Yet Blue Cross and Blue Shield do try to limit costs. An alternative explanation is that their cost-cutting efforts are overwhelmed by trying to increase their share of the medical market; getting as many people as they can to join by offering the most comprehensive policies. If the Law of Medical Money is correct, larger numbers of policies with greater coverage, by pumping in more money, would tremendously increase medical inflation. Even if a few cost-cutting efforts are successful, therefore, they cannot compete against tens of millions of transactions whose inevitable aim is to use up the amounts made available.

What technique ultimately can limit medical costs? If the Law of Medical Money predicts that costs will increase to the limit of available funds, then that limit must be narrowed to keep costs down. Insurance may stop increasing when out-of-pocket payments exceed the growth in the standard of living; then individuals may not be willing to buy more. Subsidy may hold steady when government wants to spend more on other things or when it wants to keep down its tax take. Costs will be limited when either individuals or governments reduce the amount they put into medicine.

No doubt the Law of Medical Money is crude, even rude. No doubt it ignores individual instances of self-sacrifice. But it has the virtue of being a powerful and parsimonious predictor. Medical costs have risen (and are continuing to rise) to the limit of insurance and government subsidy.

WHY THERE IS A CRISIS

If more than three-quarters of the population are satisfied with present medical care, why is there a crisis? Surveys on this subject are inadequate, but invariably reveal two things: most people are satisfied, but (1) they wish medical care didn't cost so much, and (2) they would like to be assured of contact with their own doctor. For most people, then, the basic problems are cost and access. Why, to begin at the end, aren't doctors where patients want them to be?

To talk about physicians being maldistributed is to turn the truth upside down: it is the potential patients who are maldistributed. For doctors to be in the wrong place, they would have to be where people aren't, and yet they are accused of sticking to major population centers. If distant places with little crowding and less pollution, far away from the curses of civilization, attracted the same people who advocate their virtues, medical practitioners would live there too. Obviously, they prefer the amenities of metropolitan areas. Are doctors wrong to live where they want to live? Or are rural and remote citizens wrong to demand that physicians come where they are?

Doctors can be offered a government subsidy — more money, better facilities — on the grounds that it is a national policy for medical care to be available wherever citizens choose to live. Almost all medical students are heavily subsidized, so that it would not be entirely unjust to demand that they serve several years in places not of their own choosing. The reason such policies do not work well — from Russia to the "Ruritanias" of the world — is that people who are forced to live in places they don't like make endless efforts to escape.

Because the distribution of physicians is determined by rational choice — doctors locate where their psychic as well as economic income is highest — no special laws are needed to explain what happens. But the political pathology of health policy — the more the government spends on medicine, the less credit it gets — does require explanation.

The syndrome of "the more, the less" has to be looked at as it developed. First, we passed medicare for the elderly and medicaid for the poor. The idea was to get more people into the mainstream of good medical care. Following the Law of Medical Money, however, the immediate effect was to increase costs — not merely for the poor and elderly but for all the groups in between. You can't simply add the costs of the new coverage to the costs of the old; you have to multiply both by higher figures up to the limits of the joint coverage. This is where the Axiom of Inequality takes over. The wealthier aged, who can afford to pay, receive not merely the same benefits as the aged poor, but even more, because they are better able to negotiate the system. Class tells. Inequalities are created immediately within the same category. Worse still is the "notch effect" under medicaid, through which people just above the eligibles in income may be worse off than those below. Whatever the cutoff point, there must always be a "nearly poor" who becomes more unequal. And so too is everybody else who pays twice, first in taxes to support care for others and again in increased costs for themselves. Moreover, with increased utilization of medicine, the system becomes crowded; medical care not only is more costly but also is harder to get. So there we have the Paradox of Time — as things get better, they get worse.

The politics of medical care becomes a minus-sum game in which every institutional player leaves the table poorer than when he sat down. In the beginning, the number of new patients grows arithmetically while costs rise geometrically. The immediate crisis is cost. Medicaid throws state and federal budgets out of whack. The talk is all about chiselers, profiteers, and reductions. Forms and obstacles multiply. The Medical Identity is put in place. Uncle Sam becomes Uncle Scrooge. One would hardly gather that billions more actually are being spent on medicine for the poor. But the federal government is not the only participant who is doing better and feeling worse.

Unequal levels of development within states pit one location against another. Benefits adequate for New York City would result in coverage of half or more of the population in upstate areas as well as nearly all of Alaska's Eskimos and Arizona's Indians. The rich pay more; the poor get hassled. Patients are urged to take more of their medicine only to discover they are targets of restrictive practices. They are expected to pay deductibles before seeing a doctor and to contribute a co-payment (part of the cost) afterward. Black doctors are criticized if their practice consists predominantly of white patients, but are held up to scorn if they increase their (public) income by treating large numbers of the poor and aged in the ghettos. Doctors are urged to provide more patients with better medicine, and then are criticized for making more money. The Principle of Perspective leads each patient to want the best for himself, disregarding the social cost; at the same time, doctors are criticized for giving high-cost care to everybody who wants it. The same holds true for hospitals: keeping wages down exploits workers; raising them means taking advantage of insurance.

DOES ANYONE WIN?

Just try to abolish medicare and medicaid. Crimes against the poor and aged would be the least of the accusations. Few argue that the country would be better off without than with these programs. Yet, as the programs operate, they generate smoke so dense that their supporters are hard to find.

By now it should be clear how growing proportions of people in need of medicine can be getting it in the midst of the condition that is uni-

versally called a crisis in health care. Governments face phenomenal increases in cost. Administrators alternately fear charges of incompetence
for failing to restrain real financial abuse and charges of niggardliness
toward the needy. Patients worry about higher costs, especially as serious
or prolonged illnesses threaten them with financial catastrophe. That proportionally few people suffer this way does not decrease the worry, because medical disaster *can* happen to anyone. Physicians fear federal control, because efforts to lower costs lead to more stringent regulations. The
proliferation of forms makes the practitioners feel like bureaucrats; the
profusion of review committees threatens to keep doctors permanently
on trial. New complaints increase faster than old ones can be remedied.
Specialists in public health sing their ancient songs — you are what you
eat, as old as you feel, as good as the air you breathe — with more conviction and less effect. True but trite: what can be done isn't worth doing;
what is worth doing can't be done. The watchwords are malaise, stasis,
crisis.

If money is a barrier to medicine, the system is discriminatory. If
money is no barrier, the system gets overcrowded. If everyone is insured,
costs rise to the limit of the insurance. If many remain underinsured, their
income drops to the level of whatever medical disaster befalls them. Inability to break out of this bind has made the politics of health policy
pathological.

CURING THE SICKNESS OF HEALTH

Health policy began with a laudable effort to help people by resolving the
polarized conflict between supporters of universal, national health insurance ("socialized" medicine) and the proponents of private medicine.
Neither side believed a word uttered by the other. The issue was successfully sidestepped by implementing medical care for the aged under social
security. Agreement that the aged needed help was easier to achieve than
consensus on any overall medical system. The obvious defeat was that the
poor, who needed financial help most, were left out unless they were old
as well and covered by social security. The next move, therefore, was
medicaid for the poor, at least for those reached by state programs.

Even if one still believed that medicine equaled health, it became impossible to ignore the evidence that availability of medical services was
not the same as their delivery and use. Seeing a doctor was not the same
as doing what he prescribed. It is hard to alleviate stress in the doctor's
office when the patient goes back to the same stress at home and on the
street.

"Health delivery" became the catchword. One approach would see
services brought to the poor at neighborhood health centers. The idea was
that local control would increase sensitivity to patients' needs. But ex-

perience showed that this "sensitivity" had its price. Local "needs" encompassed a wider range of services, including employment. The costs per patient visit for seeing a public doctor or social worker were three to four times those for seeing a private practitioner. Achieving local control meant control by inside laymen rather than outside professionals, a condition doctors were loath to accept. Innovation both in medical practice and in power relationships proved an unbearable burden for distant federal sponsors who thus tried to co-opt the medical powers by getting private medicine to sponsor health centers. The price was paid — higher costs and lower local control. Amid universal complaints, programs were maintained where feasible, phased out where necessary, and forgotten where possible.

As neighborhood health centers (NHC's) were phased out, the new favorites, health-maintenance organizations (HMO's), came in. If the idea behind the NHC's was to bring services to the people, the idea behind the HMO's is to bring the people to the services. If a rationale for NHC's was to exert lay control over doctors, the rationale for HMO's is to exert medical control over costs. The idea is ancient. Doctors gather in a group facility. Individuals, or groups such as unions and universities, join the HMO at a fixed rate for specified services. By efficiencies in division of labor and features such as bonuses to doctors for less utilization, downward control is exerted on costs.

Because the main method of cutting costs is to reduce the supply of hospital beds and physician services (the Medical Identity), HMO's work by making people wait. Physicians are on salary, and must be given a quota of patients or a cost objective against which to judge their medical efforts. Both incentives may affect patients adversely. Health-maintenance patients complain about how hard it is to build up a personal relationship with a doctor who can be seen quickly if the need arises. Establishing such a relationship requires skills in communication most likely to be found among the middle class. The patient's ability to shop around for different opinions is minimized, unless he is willing to pay extra by going outside the system. Doctors are motivated to engage in preventive practices, though evidence on the efficacy of these practices is hard to come by. Doctors are motivated also to engage in bureaucratic routines to minimize patients' demands; physicians may divert patients into one another's assigned quota. In a word, HMO's are a mixed bag, with no one yet quite sure what the trade-off is between efficiency and effectiveness. Turning the Great Equation into an Identity — where Health = Health Maintenance Organization — does, however, solve a lot of problems by definition.

The HMO's may be hailed by some as an answer to the problem of distributing medical information. How is the patient-consumer to know whether he is getting proper care at reasonable cost? If it were possible to rate HMO's, and if they were in competition, people might find it easier to choose among HMO's than among myriads of private doctors. Instead of having to know whether all those tests and special consultations were necessary, or how much an operation should cost, the patients (or better still, the sponsoring organizations) might compare records of how well each HMO was able to judge. Our measures of medical quality and cost, however, still are primitive. Standards for treatment are notoriously subjective. Health rates are so tenuously connected to medicine that they are bound to be similar among similar populations so long as everyone has even limited access to care.

If health is only minimally related to care, less expertise may be about as good as more professional training.

Enter the nurse-practitioner or the medical corpsman or the old Russian *feldsher* — medical assistants trained to deal with emergencies, make simple diagnoses, and refer more complicated problems to medical doctors. These medical assistants cost less, and actually make home visits. The main disadvantage is an apparent challenge to the prestige of doctors, but it could work the other way around: doctors, who deal with the more complicated matters, might be elevated higher yet. But the success of the medical assistant nonetheless might raise questions about the mystique of medical doctors. In response, doctors might deny that anyone else can really know what needs to be done, and might agree to use assistants as additions to (but not substitutes for) physicians' services. That would mean another input into the medical system and therefore an additional cost. The politics of medicine is just as much about the power of doctors as it is about the authority of politicians.

Now we see again, but from a different angle, why the medical system seems in crisis, even though most people are satisfied with the care they get. At any one time, most people are reasonably healthy. When people do need help, they can get it; the quality of care generally is impressive; or, whatever ails the sick goes away of its own accord. But such comments apply only to the mass of patients. The elite participants — doctors, administrators, politicians — are frustrated. Anything this group turns to rebounds. Administrators are blamed for everything from malpractice by doctors to overcharges by hospitals; doctors find their professional prerogatives invaded by local activists from below, and by state and federal bureaucrats from above. From the left come charges that the system is biased against the poor because they cannot get or keep control of medical facilities, and because the rates by which health is measured are worse for the poor than for the better off; loss of health is tied to lack of power. From the right come charges that the system penalizes the professional and the productive; excessive governmental intervention leads to lower medical standards and higher costs of bureaucracy, so that costs go up but health does not. Damned if they do and cursed if they don't, the professional medical community feels that any future position is bound only to be less uncomfortable. Things can always get worse, of course, but it is not easy for doctors to see that.

Why should government pay billions for health and get back not even token tribute? If it is going to be accused of abusing the poor, neglecting the middle classes, and milking the rich; if government is to be condemned for bureaucratizing the patient and coercing the doctor, all that can be managed without spending billions. Slanders and calumnies are easier to bear when they are cost-free. Spending more for worse treatment is as bad a policy for government as it would be for any of us. The only defendant without counsel is the government. What should it do?

The Axiom of Inequality cannot be changed; it is built into the nature of things. But government can choose the kinds of inequalities with which it is prepared to live.

The Principle of Goal Displacement succeeds only in substituting access to care for health; by no means does the principle guarantee that people will value the access they get. Equal access to care will not necessarily be equated with the best care available or with all that patients believe they need. Government's task is to resolve the Paradox of Time so that, as things do get better, people will see themselves as better off. The governmental interest is not only for people to get better but to feel better. Which type of medical system would help government get gratitude, not ingrates?

ALTERNATIVE HEALTH POLICIES

In the future, this nation probably will move toward (and vacillate between) three generic types of health-care policies: (1) a mixed public and private system like the one we have now, only bigger; (2) total coverage through a national health service; and (3) income-graded catastrophic health insurance. It will be convenient to refer to these approaches as "mixed," "total," and "income."

The total and income approaches have weaknesses. The income-catastrophic approach might encourage a "sky's the limit" attitude toward large expenditures; the good side of the coin is that resources would flow to the chronically or extremely ill people who most need help. The total approach would strain the national budget, putting medical needs at the mercy of other interests, such as tax increases; on the other hand, making medicine more political might have the advantage of providing more informed judgment on its priority. The two approaches, however, are interesting more for their different strengths than for their weaknesses.

The income approach would stick with individual choice until the level of catastrophic cost was reached. Holding ability to pay relatively constant, each person would be able to decide how much (measured by what money can buy) he is willing to give up in order to purchase medical services. There would be no need to regulate the medical industry on cost and service: supply and demand would determine the price. Paperwork would be minimized. And so would bureaucracy. Under- or over-utilization could be dealt with by raising or lowering percentage limits at each level of income, rather than by dealing with tens of thousands of doctors, hospitals, pharmacies, and the like. The total approach, by contrast, could promise a kind of collective rationality in that the government would make a more direct determination of how much the nation wanted to spend on health (versus other desired) expenditures.

How might we choose between an essentially administrative and a primarily market-oriented mechanism? Would intellectual cognition provide a better bureaucratic allocation of resources than would social interaction in medical markets? Each is equally political, but they come to their politics in different ways. An income approach would be simpler to administer and easier to abandon. A total approach could promise more, because no one under current programs would be worse off (except taxpayers), and everyone with insufficient coverage would come under a comprehensive umbrella. The backers of totality fear that the income approach would preempt the health field for years to come. The proponents of income grading fear that, once a comprehensive program is begun, there will be no getting out of it — too many people would lose benefits they already have, and the medical system would have unalterably changed its character. The choice (not only now but in the future) really has to be made on fundamental grounds of a modified-market versus an almost entirely administrative approach. Which proposal would be not only proper for people but also good for government?

MARKET VERSUS ADMINISTRATIVE MECHANISMS

Going with either the market or the administrative approach consistently would be better than mixing them up. Either would give government a better chance to know what it is doing and to get credit for what it does. Expenditures on the medical system, whether too high or too low for some tastes, would be subject to overall control instead of to sudden, unpredictable increases. Patients would have a system they could understand and would therefore be able to hold government accountable for how the system was working. Under one approach patients would know that care was comprehensive, crediting government with the program but criticizing it for quality and cost. Under the other, people would know they were being encouraged to use discretion, but within boundaries guaranteeing patients protection against catastrophe. Under the present system, few can figure out what's going on, or why their coverage is inadequate, or why, because there is no effective government control, there are yet so many forms to fill out. Mixed approaches will only exacerbate these unfortunate tendencies, multiplying ambiguities about deductibles and co-payment amid startling increases in cost. If we want our future to be better than our past, let us look more closely at the bureaucratic and market models for medical care.

What do we know about medical care in a bureaucratic setting? Distressingly little. But just enough knowledge may have been collected from studies of HMO's (and of systems in other countries, especially Britain) to provide a few clues. Doctors in HMO's work fewer hours than do doctors in private practice, which is no surprise. One of the attractions of HMO's is the limit on the hours doctors can be put on call. Market physicians respond to increases in patient load by increasing the hours they see patients; physicians working in a bureaucratic context respond by spending less time with patients. Two consequences of a public system are immediately apparent: more doctors will be needed, and less time will be spent listening and examining. Patients' demands for more time with the doctor will be met by more, rather than longer, visits. But will doctors be distributed more equally over the nation? The evidence suggests not. Britain has failed to achieve this goal in the quarter-century since the National Health Service began. The reason is that not only economic but also political allocations are subject to biases — one of which, incidentally, is called majority rule. The same forces that make for medical concentration in some places are reflected in the political power necessary to supply funds to keep doctors in those places.

Surely the ratio of specialists to general practitioners could be better controlled by central direction than by centrifugal market forces. Agreed. But one should recognize the price. The much higher proportion of general practitioners in Britain is achieved by a class bias that values "consultants" (their "specialists") more highly than ordinary doctors. (Consultants are called "Mister," as if to emphasize their individual excellence, but general practitioners are given the collective title "Doctor.") The much higher proportion of specialists in America may stem in part from a desire to maintain equality among doctors — a nice illustration of the Axiom of Inequality. More equality for doctors may mean less equality for patients. One result of the British custom is the lowered quality of general practice; another is that general practitioners are denied access to hospitals. They lose control at the portal, their patients are without the comfort necessary in a stressful time and these sick people are subjected to a bewildering maze of specialists and subspecialists, none of whom may be in charge of the whole person.

Would a bureaucratic system based on fixed charges and predetermined salaries put more emphasis on cheaper prevention than on more expensive maintenance, or on outpatient rather than hospital service? Possibly. (No one knows for sure whether preventive medicine actually works.) In any event, doctors do not cease to be doctors once they start operating in a bureaucratic setting. Cure is intrinsically more interesting than prevention to doctors; it is also something they know they can achieve, whereas they cannot enforce measures such as "no smoking." If it were true, moreover, that providing ample opportunities to see doctors outside the hospital would reduce the need to use hospitals, then providing outpatient services should hold down costs. The little evidence available, however, suggests otherwise. A natural experiment for this purpose takes place when patients have generous coverage for both in- and outpatient medical services. Visits to the doctor go up, but so too does utilization of hospitals. More frequent visits generate awareness of more things wrong, for which more hospitalization is indicated. The way to limit hospital costs, if that is the objective, is to limit access by reducing the number of beds.

The great advantage of a comprehensive health service is that it keeps expenditures in line with other objectives. The Principle of Perspective works both ways: if an individual is not an aggregate, neither is an aggregate an individual. Left to our own devices, at near zero cost, you and I use as much as we and ours need. At the governmental level, however, it is a question not of personal needs and desires but of collective choice among different levels of taxation and expenditure. Hence, our collective choices should be less than the summed total of individual preferences.

At first glance it might appear strange for national health insurance (whether through private intermediaries or direct government operation) to be conceived of as a method for limiting costs; but experience in practice, as well as deduction from theory, bears out that conception. The usual complaint in Britain is that the National Health Service is being starved for funds: hospital construction has been virtually nil; the number of doctors per capita has hardly increased; long queues persist for hospitalization in all but emergency cases. Why? Because health care accounts for a sizable proportion of both government expenditure and gross national product and must compete with family allowances, housing, transportation, and all the rest. Although there are pressures to increase medical expenditures, they are counterbalanced by demands from other sectors. In times of extreme financial stringency, all too frequent as government expenditure approaches half of the GNP, it is not likely that priority will go to medicine.

The usual complaint about the market method is money; poor people are kept out of the medical system by not having enough. No one disputes it. And whatever evidence we have suggests also that the use of deductibles and co-payments exerts a disproportionate effect in deterring the poor from getting medical care. Therefore, to preserve as much of the market as possible, the response is to give additional funds to the poor that can be used for any desired purpose, including (but not limited to) medical care. This response immediately raises the issue of services in kind versus payment in cash. Enabling the poor to receive medical services without financial cost to themselves means they cannot choose alternative expenditures. A negative way of looking at this is to say that it reveals distrust of the poor: presumably the poor are not able to make rational decisions, so that government must do the deciding. A positive approach is to say that health is so important that society has an interest in ensuring that the poor receive access to care. I almost said, "whether they want it or not," but, the argument continues, the choice of seeking (or not seeking) health care is neither easy nor simple: the poor — because they are poor, because money means more to those without enough, because the poor have so many other vital needs — are under great temptation to sacrifice future health to present problems. This alleged shortsighted psychology requires that the poor be protected against themselves.

If anyone had cultural explanations for the lesser use poor people made of doctors, these have been decisively refuted. Presumably, the culture of the poor was unlike the rest of society. They didn't value good health or they lived only for the moment or were too scatterbrained to get to a doctor. The alternative hypothesis — money is a real barrier — has been tested by medicaid and medicine, and has not been found wanting: the longer these programs are available, the more often the poor see doctors.

The difficulty is not with the intellectually insubstantial (though politically potent) arguments that medical care is a right and that money should have nothing to do with medicine. The Axiom of Allocation assures us that medical care must be allocated in some way, and that if it is not done at the bottom through individual income, it will be done at the top through national income. If medicine is a right, so too are education, housing, food, employment (without which other rights can no longer be enjoyed), and so on, until we come back to the same old problems of allocating resources. The real question is whether care will be allocated by governmental mechanisms, in which one-man, one-vote is the ideal, or by the distribution of income, in which one-dollar, one-preference is the idea, modified to assist the poor.

The problem for market men is not to demonstrate scarcity of resources but to show that one of the essential conditions of buying and selling is in force. I refer to consumer information about the cost and quality of care. The same problems crop up in many other areas involving technical advice: without knowing as much as the lawyer, builder, garage mechanic, or television repairman, how can the consumer determine whether the advice is good and the work performed properly and at reasonable cost?

The image in the literature is amateur patient versus professional doctor: the patient is not sure what is wrong, who the best doctor is, and how much the treatment should cost. Worse still, doctors deliberately withhold information by making it unethical to advertise prices or criticize peers. Should the doctor be less than competent or more than usually inclined to run up a bill, the patient can do little.

This picture has elements of reality, as all of us will recognize, but it is exaggerated. People can and do ask others about their experiences with various doctors; mothers endlessly compare pediatricians, for example. The abuses we are thinking of are more likely to happen to patients who lack a stable relationship with at least one doctor, and when there is no community whose opinions the doctor values and the patient learns to consult.

Nevertheless, it is obvious that patient-consumers do lack full information about the medical services they are buying. So too, in fact, do doctors lack full knowledge of the services they are selling. How, then, improve the imperfect medical market? Would some alternative provision of medical services ensure better information?

Because all costs would be paid by taxpayers, government would have an incentive to keep the expenditures on a national health service in proportion to spending for other vital activities. The very feature that has so far made a national health service politically unpalatable (it would take over tens of billions of now private expenditures, requiring a massive tax increase) immediately would force financial responsibility on the government. Under a total governmental program, central authorities would have to determine how much should be spent and how such funds should be allocated to regional authorities. Basing the formula on numbers would put remote places at a disadvantage; basing it on area would put populous places at a disadvantage. How would regional authorities decide to divide money among hospital beds, outpatient clinics, drugs, and long-term care? There are few objective criteria. Would teams of medical specialists make the decisions? Professional boundaries would cause problems. Would administrators? Lack of medical expertise would make trouble. Administrative committees would have to decide who receives how much treatment, with the limited resources available from the central authority. Would the collective judgment of committees be better or worse than that of individuals negotiating with doctors and hospitals? No one knows. But something can be said about the trade-off between quality and cost.

Suppose the question is: under which type of system are costs likely to be highest per capita? The answer is: first, mixed public and private; second, mostly private; third, mostly public. Costs are greater under a mixed system because potential quality is valued over real cost; it pays each individual to use up his insurance and subsidy, because the quality-cost ratio is set high. Under the mostly private system, the individual is motivated to keep his costs down. Under the mostly public one, the government has an incentive to keep costs within bounds. Because each individual regards his personal worth more than his social value, however, a series of individual payments will add up to something more than the payments determined by the very same people's collective judgment. At the margins, then, the economic market, preferring quality over cost, would produce somewhat larger expenditures than would the political arena.

Who would value a public medical system? Those who want government to exert maximum control over cost. The word "cost" here may be used in two ways — financial and political. Government does more, can allocate more resources, and has more chance to give support for what it does. Citizens who care more about equality than quality of care — though, of course, people want both — also should prefer public financing, which ensures reasonably equal access, and also places medical care in the context of other pubilic needs. Doctors who value independence, and patients who value responsiveness, would be less in favor of a public system.

Who would prefer a private system, providing the effects of income were mitigated? People who want less governmental direction and more personal control over costs. These include doctors who want less governmental control, patients who want more choice, and politicians who want more leeway in allocating resources and less blame for bureaucratizing medicine.

I would prefer the income approach, because it is readily reversible: errors can be corrected. It also requires less bureaucracy and provides more choice. The total approach, however, could be infused with choice: under a single national health service, there could be three to six competitive and alternative programs, each organized differently. There could be HMO's, foundation plans (under which individual doctors contract with a central service), and other variants. Patients could use any of these programs, all of which would compete for their favor. The total sum to be spent each year would be fixed at the federal level, and each service would be paid its proportionate share according to the number and type of patients enrolled. Thus, we could take the edge off the worse features while maintaining the strengths of a bureaucratic system.

THOUGHT AND ACTION

Let us summarize. Basically there are two sites for relating cost to quality — that is, for disciplining needs, which may be infinite, by controlling resources, which are limted. One is at the level of the individual; the other, at the level of the collectivity. By comparing individuals' desires with personal resources, through the private market, the individual internalizes an informal cost-effectiveness analysis. Because incomes differ, the breakeven point differs among people. And if incomes were made more nearly equal, individuals still would differ in how much medical care they selected over other goods and services. These other valued objects would compete with medicine, leading some persons to choose lower levels of medicine and reducing the inputs into (and cost of) the system.

At the collective level there is a choice between some public services, such as medicine, and others, such as welfare, and between resources left in private hands and those devoted to the public sector. The fatal defect of the mixed system — a defect that undermines the worth of its otherwise valuable pluralism — is that the mixed system does not impose strict enough discipline at either the individual or collective level. The individual need not face the full costs, and the government need not carry the full burden.

But we-the-people don't want either a purely private or a gigantic government medical system. To our credit, no longer will we let money be the main mechanism of access to medicine. Because of our desirable devotion to freedom of choice, we will not forbid the private practice of medicine. Thus a mixed system is inevitable. Truly it reflects our willingness to embrace contradictions: more medicine at lower cost and higher quality. We-the-people call the tune, but are unwilling to pay the piper. Therefore we insist government do more, but when it does, we like it less.

What else can government do that has not yet been done? Send our medical problem children on a visit to distant relatives by turning the problem (though not, of course, the money) over to regional or local authorities. As the old joke has it, "Let his mother worry." Does this approach appear flippant? Don't worry. We have a plan.

PLANNING HEALTH-SYSTEM AGENCIES

Planning, as I have said, is being able to control the future through present acts; the more future results one controls, the more one can be said to have planned effectively.[1] Control of the future demands knowledge (understanding what one does) and power (compelling others to accomplish one's will). But to have planning does not require a plan. Any process of decision that affects behavior, whether it is a market or an administrative mechanism, may be thought of as a plan, insofar as it provides incentives for generating one sort of future behavior rather than another. Normally, the planners' problem is that they lack both power and knowledge; they cannot control the behavior of others and, if they could, the desired consequences would not ensue. When knowledge is missing and power is absent, planning becomes a word for the things we would like to do but do not know how to do or are unable to get others to do. Planning need not be a simple solution; it can be, and often is, a convoluted way of restating the problem: can we increase quantity and quality of medical services while decreasing costs? The answer is, we can't, as the National Health Planning and Resources Development Act of 1974, establishing health-system agencies (HSA's), will prove once again.

The main power of some two hundred HSA's being established is negative: by refusing to approve certificates of need (or otherwise objecting), HSA's can delay or prevent construction of regional medical services. Toward this end, HSA's are given administrative funds of their own and a local power base, in that HSA membership must comprise at least one-third medical providers and perhaps one-half consumer representatives.

The 1974 act is a plan in that it creates incentives to encourage some types of behavior. But the plan is perverse. The HSA's are mandated to reduce costs and improve delivery of health services. Actually, HSA's will increase costs and transfer ineffective delivery of service from the have-littles to the have-nots. Why? Because health-systems agencies do nothing to affect the Law of Medical Money — that expenditures and costs rise to the limit of insurance and subsidy; on the contrary, HSA's enhance the force of that law by creating incentives to increase rather than decrease use of medical resources. Every decision will be paid for elsewhere by someone else — patients, insurance companies, taxpayers. No HSA's will limit inputs into the medical system because the actors are not in charge of any fixed sum of money that would have to be allocated. All actors will continue to make internal decisions, secure in the knowledge that the costs generated ultimately will be passed on to others and that these others — because costs will diffuse over so many people — will lack requisite understanding and interest in these decisions to exert a restraining influence.

The HSA's immediately will espouse the Doctrine of the Three Increases: more professionals, more lawyers, more data. It is self-evident that establishing HSA's will lead to an enormous increase in demand for health professionals, thereby bidding up their price. As with all other major policy initiatives in recent decades, lawyers will be involved here too in greater numbers (and with enhanced authority). These lawyers will (profitably, no doubt) straighten out conflicts among previous acts and among new regulations, particularly criteria and procedural safeguards made more complex by interaction with various private and public agencies at different levels of government. The HSA lawyers will generate countervailing action on the part of providers and consumers, making more work for all. What will they produce? More data. There will be vast proliferation of data on efforts, because that is what will be produced, but not, of course, on effects, because there won't be any — at least none relating to changes in health rates. The rationality of effort will again prevail over the rationality of results. Like the Humpty Dumptys they resemble, HSA's cannot put the great equation — medical care equals health — back together again. To do that they would have to do less, whereas they are designed to do more.

In the beginning, one can imagine, various providers will be directed to join with their neighbors in combining facilites judged to be in oversupply. The HSA's will issue orders but these orders will not be obeyed. The HSA's can say "no," but they cannot mandate "yes"; they cannot command, so that they will have to bargain. What will HSA's give up to get what they want? The answer is the same as that given investors who want to reduce risks — other peoples' money. The HSA's, in effect, will levy a toll on taxpayers and holders of medical-insurance "policies"; in "real life," those persons will pay for the increased availability and use of medical goods and services by other people.

The self-evident fact that administrative expenses will increase is not the main reason for expecting a substantial rise in individual costs and total-system expenditures. For this conclusion my case rests on HSA incentives for resolving internal differences — the time-honored political method of logrolling (or, you scratch my back and I'll scratch yours). If there were a fixed sum to distribute among applicants, of course, more for one would mean less for another. But there is not, so that the interests of the main parties will lead them to resolve their differences by providing more rather than less largesse.

First the Providers

It will be hard for providers of medical services to maintain a united front if such resources as beds are taken away from providers and given to (or left with) others. A better way of solving this problem will be found by trading beds for machines and other facilities. I don't know how many CAT's (Computerized Axial Tomography) equal how many beds or kidney machines or heart units, but talented professionals will find a common currency as well as a common language. Costs will be spread around by increasing bed rates, by the usual practice of cross-subsidization (in which simpler forms of surgery pay for the more complex kinds), and by finding more treatments for which such devices can be used. Despite innumerable administrative controls, cost overruns will not be curtailed because somebody else has to pick up the tab.

Next the Consumers

Health-system agencies believe the people they represent need health services and that health delivery could certainly be improved. With this providers will agree. But consumers are not likely to have accurate cost information or know how to interpret it or, worst of all, feel its effect directly on themselves. Faced with a choice between fighting for lower costs for all, with its implication of lesser services for their clients, and agreeing to support superior services for worrying about others, consumer's representatives will invariably choose the path of least resistance. The HSA's will negotiate with providers for larger packages in which constituents can get more services, and perhaps jobs as well, in return for going along with the latest provider interests. Why should producer and consumer conflict when they can coalesce: you co-opt me and I'll co-opt you and we will all co-opt each other.

Alain Enthoven tells an instructive story:

. . . about a man who left the presidency of a medical products company to become a professor of management. One day he decided it would be fun to see some of his old associates from business days, so he organized a lunch at a nice restaurant. At the end of the meal, from habit, he reached for the check, but his successor as company president took it and said, "Let me have it; for us it's a deductible expense and the government will pay half of it through reduced corporate profits tax." But the local hospital administrator took it out of his hand saying, "No, let me take it; this will be an allowable conference expense, and we can put the whole thing in our overhead and get it back from Blue Cross and Medicare." But his neighbor took the check from him and said, "Let me have it; after all, I'm a cost-plus contractor to the government and not only will we get the cost reimbursed, but we'll get a fee on top of it." But the fifth man at the table got the check: "Look friends, I'm from a regulated industry, and we're about to go in for a rate increase. If I can put this lunch in our cost base, it will help justify a higher rate not only this year, but projected on out into the future."

The moral of the story is that regulation is taxation, taxation with representation to be sure, but still a hidden form of taxation.

Consider the HSA's combination of logrolling with barriers to entry. Naturally, HSA's will be composed of providers and consumers who are already there. They can be expected to give future providers and consumers a hard time. The most likely losers will be new proponents of health-maintenance organizations, who either will be denied certificates of need — because everything necessary ostensibly is being done by those already there — or (if HMO's cannot be resisted) who will be added onto what already exists. Every innovation that challenges existing interests either will be attached as unnecessary, or added on to keep the peace. One cannot say exactly what will happen except that we know in advance the one important thing that will not happen: old services will not give way to new ones.

The trouble with failure is that it can happen to anyone. In the past, old facilities may have died when their usefulness was outlived; this no longer will be allowed. Providers will know that their mutual interest is in insuring against failure by agreeing to bail each other out at public expense. Medical providers and their customers may not be able to improve mortality rates of the population but they certainly will work at mutual survival.

Who Wins?

It is obvious, at least in the short run. But who loses? The answer depends on which group is least able (1) to pass on costs or (2) to lobby effectively for subsidy. To no one's great surprise, the nearly poor once again will get it in the neck. The upper class will find ways to reduce taxes and the middle class will improve their insurance; the poor will get a superior subsidy. Both the top and the bottom exert influence, though in different ways. Only the nearly poor lack both a governmentally protected program and market leverage. Hence HSA's will transfer income from the nearly poor to the officially designated poor.

Presumably HSA's are designed to take the heat off the central government — don't harass your congressman; picket your local HSA instead — by adopting the time-honored methods of diffusing conflict over large areas. And, presumably, this may go on for a while if only because the confusion will be so great, the actors so numerous, the consequences so elusive, that most energies will be absorbed in figuring out whether HSA's work. When it becomes clear that they don't and won't, the conclusion is unlikely to be that collective regulation is bad but that private or pluralistic medicine has failed. By loading the medical market with the burden of regulation — capture by the interests most immediately affected, delay in adaptation to new conditions, passing the price of monopoly on to others — it will be condemned for high cost and lack of responsiveness. The lesson will be that the private market has failed and that only public administration can save us. The lesson should be that doctors should do less, and that we-the-people should do more, about our own health.

THE FUTURE

My purpose has been not to assess current political feasibility but rather to look for longer-range ways to political virtue. The proposals I believe to be the worst for sustaining government legitimacy at present are the most popular. Proposals that deserve the most zealous attention are ignored. False assumptions about the excessive cost of total care and a false belief in the inequality of the income approach have made impossible serious consideration of such proposals. Perhaps this is the way it has to be. But I am sure there remains time in which to change our ways of thinking about medical care. Medicine is by no means the only field in which how we think affects what we believe; in which what we believe is the key to how we feel; and in which how we feel determines how we act.

If politicians did not believe that greater effort makes for better health, could they justify pouring billions more into the medical system? It could be argued that faith in medicine (doctor as witchdoctor) is so deeply ingrained that no contrary evidence would be accepted. Maybe. But this argument does not touch the question of politicians as nonbelievers.

Suppose citizens were told that additional increments devoted to medicine would not improve their collective health but could give them more opportunity to express their feelings to doctors. Would people pay more for this "caring"? As much as $10 billion? Would people pay so much if the program contained no guarantee (and none do) that doctors would care more or be more available?

In any event, after the mixed approach fails, as it surely will, this country inevitably will face the same old alternatives — putting together the pieces administratively through a national health service, or dismantling what we have in favor of a modified market mechanism.

It could be, of course, that in the future, worst will turn out to be best. The three systems I have separated for analytic convenience — private, public, and mixed — in practice may not reveal such unmixed purity. A national health service, for instance, might quickly lose its putatively public character as numerous individuals opt for private care. In Scandinavian countries, even those convinced supporters of public medicine in the professional strata often prefer to use private doctors. By paying twice, once in taxes and once in fees for service, these Scandinavians raise the cost of medicine to society. Would not such a public system, actually 20 or 30 per cent private, be in reality a mixed system?

Consider an income-graded catastrophic system. To begin with, this system would have to pay all costs for those below the poverty line. As time passed, political pressure might increase the proportion of the subsidized population to 25 or 30 per cent. Costs would increase, and administrative action might be undertaken to limit coverage of expensive long-term illness. How different, then, would this presumably private system be from the mixed system it had been designed to replace?

The present as future may be replaced by the future as future only to be superseded by the future as past. First the mixed system (the present as future) will be intensified by having billions injected into it. When that fails, an income-graded catastrophic plan or a national health service (the future as future) will be tried. Efforts to make the former system wholly private will be unfeasible, because the public balks at rationing medical care solely by money. Efforts to make the latter system wholly public will fail, because a prohibition on private fees for service will appear to citizens as an intolerable restraint on liberty. Then we can expect the future as past; by the next century, we may have learned that a mixed system is bad in every respect except one — it mirrors our ambivalence. Whether we will grow up by learning to live with faults we do not wish to do without is a subject for a seer, not a social scientist,

Health policy is pathological because we are neurotic, and we insist on making our government psychotic. Our neurosis consists in knowing what is required for good health (Mother was right: Eat a good breakfast! Sleep eight hours a day! Don't drink! Don't smoke! Keep clean! And don't worry!) but not being willing to do it. Government's ambivalence consists of paying both coming and going: once for telling citizens how to be healthy, and once for paying people's bills when this goes unheeded. Psychosis appears when government persists in repeating this self-defeating play. Maybe twenty-first-century people will come to cherish their absurdities.

If the dilemma in health is that we know what to do but are not willing to do it, the difficulty with education is that we are willing to act but we do not know what to do. If the solution of health problems might lie in education, the solution to education problems lies in learning how to live with what we don't know.

NOTES

1. This section is adapted from my Davis Lecture, "Can Health Be Planned? Or, Why Doctors Should Do Less and Patients Should Do More: Forecasting the Future of Health-System Agencies," delivered at The University of Chicago, April 23, 1976 (Chicago: Center for Health Administration Studies).

CHAPTER 13

LEARNING FROM EDUCATION: IF WE'RE STILL STUCK ON THE PROBLEMS, MAYBE WE'RE TAKING THE WRONG EXAM

The Cleveland mayoral election of 1975 was fought between incumbent Mayor Ralph Perk and Arnold Pinkney, President of the School Board.[1] According to the *Oakland Tribune* of November 3, "Pinkney . . . cites what he says is a high rate of street crime under Perk and . . . Perk . . . says crime is bred in the schools where Pinkney has jurisdiction."

Not only can't the schools get Johnny to read or Mary to count, it appears, but the schools also are responsible for breeding crime. That's a long way down from the once-upon-a-time when education seemed to be the golden road leading Americans to the top.

Neither these present allegations nor those old fantasies have much substance; but something basic is bad about public education — or, at least, some very bad things seem to be happening on the sites that our schools occupy. We do not know how educators are performing; even less do we agree on any viable criteria for measuring that performance or lack of it. As far as they can be discovered, practices and policies seem inconsistent, evanescent, wishy-washy; and we want reassurance about our kids when they are out of our direct line of sight.

Also we can sense that something else is going on, that a large part of the turbulence is a function of other forces. The question, "Is education being made into, or accepting the role of, the fall guy?" should be fervently discussed.

COMPENSATION WITHOUT EDUCATION

Let me begin with Milbrey McLaughlin's excellent short book, *Evaluation and Reform*.[2] Her thesis is simple to state: The requirements of the Elementary and Secondary Education Act (ESEA), "the first major piece of social legislation to mandate project reporting," led to "little more than an annual ritualistic defense of program activities . . . used selectively to support policy positions suggested by political or economic constraints, not by new information" (pp. vii and ix). The story is both familiar and depressing. Whether it can also be made instructive remains to be seen.

Senator Robert Kennedy thought that the way for poor people to find out how well their children were doing in school was to test students in reading and mathematics periodically and compare their achievement with that of others in the same school and with children in other schools around the country. In this way, parents could hold eduators accountable for disparities in student achievement.

The trauma for Title I officials in understandable: what do you say when you have no progress to report? Their first and second annual reports therefore told about stimulating children with a new outlook on life, with vibrant and responsive classrooms, and so on. But this kind of obfuscation soon became prevarication. Professor Robert Dentler, long-term observer of the education scene in New York, wrote a piece called "Urban Eyewash" in *Urban Review* (February 1969), showing that the unpublished individual evaluations of Title I uniformly reflected failure although the glossy federal report suggested success. Everyone could agree on one thing; the data were inadequate for any analytic purpose. Neither local educational officials nor their state associations wanted to collect data that would place them in a bad light. Beyond this, *Evaluation and Reform* is about what happens when you try to persuade people to collect and report data at one level that will be used to hurt them at another.

The now-famous cost-benefit analysis of the contemporary education aspects of Title I by the TEMPO Division of the General Electric Company raised at once the question of the level at which data collected might be useful for making decisions. Senator Kennedy's idea, parents using data to hold school boards accountable, no longer applied; if the information could be used at all it would have to be by federal decision-makers in a position to decide which aspects of the program were more or less effective, or whether the program should continue at all. To serve the federal client, however, the data would have to relate inputs of Title I funds to outputs in achievement scores. But local reporting was so skimpy and sporadic that TEMPO could be certain neither that it was dealing with a Title I population nor that these schoolchildren had been subjected to a Title I program. Hence, measurements of achievement were at best debatable; and, insofar as any evidence at all appeared, there was little or no achievement to report. Why so?

Part of the answer is in our failure to discover marvelous new teaching methods in the sixties; more important, perhaps, is the suggestion, from all available evidence since the turn of the century, that school inputs have little effect on student outputs. After all, as Mc-Laughlin reminds us (p. 39), Rice showed in 1897 that the ability of students to spell hardly varied with the amount of time devoted to that subject in school; and in 1915 Merriam found a regular growth in knowledge of some school subjects despite the absence of instruction in these areas. Why expect that something so much more difficult — measurable improvement in cognitive abilities of poor children could be achieved by the mere application of money? For that was all Title I did — add money. If money would not do that job, what would? Perhaps the data base might be changed. Answers to the questions posed thus far were to be sought not in reneging on the original promise, but by designing a bigger and better survey instrument to gather baseline data against which to measure progress by compensatory activities.

By this time, the analytic staff wondered if noncompensatory activities could be justified at all. Such thoughts were profoundly disturbing to the Council of Great City Schools and the Chief State School Officers (the main lobbies on Title I programs), lobbies whose cooperation was essential for collection of data and maintenance of funds. As one chief state school officer stated, "I'll never let you into my state to draw comparisons between schools" (p. 54). Why should a state add to its already substantial data-reporting requirements if the state did not know what use might be made of the data or, even worse, if it knew exactly what would happen? Thus a compromise was arranged: the U.S. Office of Education (USOE) agreed "(1) to make no state-by-state comparisons; (2) not to aggregate pupil data by school or state; (3) to clear for release all federal reporting forms through the Chiefs" (p. 54). As a result response to the survey improved, but nevertheless "out of 180,000 questionnaires mailed, only about 8,000 to 10,000 were returned with usable achievement data, and the data that were reported were not representative of the national sample, either in terms of pupil performance or in terms of type of compensatory participation" (p. 56).

It took a year for the head of the Bureau of Elementary and Secondary Education (BESE), which sponsored the study, to find ways in which compensatory education could be made to appear either educational or compensatory. The BESE's report is, of its kind, a work of art. It contains such statements as "all disadvantaged children live in a public school district somewhere in the Nation," and that, "for participating and non-participating pupils, the rate of progress in reading skills kept pace with their historical rate of progress" (pp. 58–59). In truth, next to no progress had been made and, where it had, improved achievement clearly was related to higher socioeconomic status. That there was no Title I program, only dollars, and that the money was not always spent on the disadvantaged, may account for part of the problem but not all of it.

Another report, undertaken in 1969, was even more negative; this report showed that increased hours spent in remedial reading did not improve performance on standardized reading tests. Having failed to accomplish its main purpose for USOE — to provide positive data for Congress — "the report," McLaughlin writes, "has been, for all practical purposes, suppressed" (p. 61).

After a quixotic effort to mount a follow-up study to Professor James Coleman's report (another which showed that schools didn't have much effect), USOE's Office of Program Planning and Evaluation at last hit on the right idea and, even better, on the right slogan for its program — "It Works." Only those with a feeling for the symbolism of acronyms might have worried about hiring AIR (American Institute for Research) to do a study of exemplary programs in order to understand what went into making successful ones successful. In the "It Works" series of case studies, AIR described such successful compensatory program strategies as active involvement of parents, careful planning, material closely related to objectives, and high intensity of treatment. (As a famous student of guerrilla warfare is reported to have remarked upon seeing figures purporting to demonstrate the pacification of whole areas of the Vietnam countryside: "Interesting, if true!"). Congressmen loved the idea that "It Works," because it justified legislative investment. Alas, as McLaughlin reports, "Follow-up studies conducted by AIR . . . found that only a small portion of the original 'It Works' projects were still 'working' in following years. Whatever it is that makes a program 'work' appears to be in large part unstable or unspecified or an artifact of measurement error" (p. 88). If school districts and their teachers, parents, and administrators really knew what would work and what wouldn't, at what cost, and refused to put these successful strategies into effect, they would deserve condemnation. But because they don't know what needs to be known (nor does anyone else), these well-meaning people are reluctant to expose themselves to ridicule in return for promises that evaporate into, shall we say, air?

At first these new compensatory programs, and the information systems that supported them, had as clients the parents of poor children and local school districts; next came high USOE officials; and then Congress. The only potential client left out was Aunt BESE, which moved into the gap as soon as an administrative entrepreneur arrived on the scene. This entrepreneur's idea was to concentrate in his bureau federal programs dealing with elementary and secondary education, so that at least a stab could be made at running them; and it occurred also to this administrator that he might sponsor creation of the ultimate information system to serve all needs.

This joint (federal-state) coordinated effort at evaluation became known as Belmont (in honor of the house where officials met to work up the new management, evaluation, and reporting system). In addition to reducing overlap and duplication, Belmont's objectives included providing data for decision-making to Congress, USOE, and state and local education agencies, as well as to all state, local, and federal planners and evaluators. Finally, Belmont would supply all other federally required statistics and evaluations on elementary and secondary education. Thus, Belmont involved not only a Management Information System Project and a Master Data Analysis Plan and a Consolidated Program Information Report, as well as an Elementary School Survey, a Secondary School Survey, Anchor Test and New Cognitive Measures, and Common Status Measures, but also User's Guides and something called Preparing Evaluation Reports: A Guide for Authors. Whew!

Belmont did succeed in reducing staff in other USOE programs. In all other respects, however, this mind-boggling array of instruments, measures, and reports did not fulfill its ostensible purpose. McLaughlin calls Belmont "a very expensive flop," estimated at around $40 million, though no one knows the true cost. Moreover, she reports, no one ever has used the material. Data from the 1970 survey took the form of some 1,200 tables whose hieroglyphics could be interpreted only by those who had the rather elusive code books. It will surprise no one now to learn that otherwise valuable data on student background and condition of schools were useless because Belmont was no more effective than other groups in collecting data on student achievement.

In part, Belmont was devised as a way, at last, of winning the cooperation of state and local educational authorities. This was not achieved, however, because no one agreed on the objectives for which the data ostensibly were being collected and analyzed. The state people were too sophisticated to believe that they would never again be asked to make another report. There has been no feedback in analysis to the states, perhaps because no analysis has been done. All this explains the comment of a staff member associated with the Belmont project: "The data questionnaires were never designed with use in mind" (p. 106).

According to Milbrey McLaughlin's succinct Evaluation and Reform,

The Title I experience has shown how resistant the educational policy system is to assessment of achievements . . . and also that a number of obstacles to this confirmatory style of reporting are inherent in the system itself. The structure and control of the nation's educational system hampers all reporting, and it may preclude the accountability and impact reports reformers wanted. The obstacles to the successful implementation of evaluation policy are symptomatic of the barriers to the implementation of all categorical federal policy. In a federal system of government, and especially in education, the balance of power resides at the bottom, with special interest groups. Accordingly, the implementation of federal initiatives relies in large measure on the incentives and preferences of local authorities. . . . Thus a federal evaluation policy that conflicts in fundamental ways with local priorities is unlikely to succeed. Specifically, data on the relative effectiveness of teaching strategies or allocation of resources will be difficult to gather not only because of the unsystematic and decentralized data-collection practices existing at the local level, but also because local programs have little interest in these data and are disinclined to collect them or furnish them. Federal evaluators, then, are faced with a specifically political dilemma generated by their inability to insist upon accurate information on school effects and program impact. . . .

. . . Evaluation is just one input into a complex process that, inherently and predominantly, is not rational. . . .[3]

Is that all there is to say — that local and state school officials refuse to play the losing game of delivering achievement data that will represent them as incompetent or worse? Why label "nonrational" their efforts to stay alive? How, for instance, would analyses of data from local and state levels help in reallocating resources, or otherwise redirecting their energies? Without a technology for substantially improving the cognitive abilities of deprived children, what can schoolmen do to improve performance? How can officials in one area emulate the successes of other schools, when there are none; or if there is success, if no one knows how it was achieved? If the data at hand cannot be converted into information to improve decisions, what basis for action do educators have?

Inability to improve cognitive performance is not, however, the only blow that educators have suffered. In the past, schoolmen might have consoled themselves with the thought that schools were at least essential for certification. Graduation was required for degrees that would lead to jobs that were seen as improving the life-chances of schoolchildren. Students from high-status families could confirm their positions, and students from low-status families could move up. Formal education was the gateway to social mobility. Now, unfortunately, at the same time as educators are afraid they are not educating, that very relationship between schooling and achievement has been questioned.

EDUCATIONAL OPPORTUNITY WITHOUT SOCIAL EQUALITY

Wider access to education decreases its social and economic value. This thesis — that, without draconian measures, increasing equality of educational opportunity cannot lead to a corresponding increase in social mobility or decrease in social inequality — is enunciated in Raymond Boudon's *Education, Opportunity, and Social Inequality*.[4] Boudon creates a model that predicts these results with demonstrable support by data from both capitalist and socialist countries.

A virtue of Boudon's superb work is that his model explains the apparent paradox in the relationship between educational opportunity and social achievement. He writes:

Lower-class youngsters over time obtain more education (both absolutely and relatively). . . . But this . . . merely prevents the social expectations of the lower-class youths from declining over time; it does not make them more favorable.[5]

Comparison over time, Boudon explains, shows why a decrease in inequality of educational opportunity (IEO) cannot be expected to produce a decrease in inequality of social opportunity (ISO):

> Although the average level of educational attainment increases more rapidly in the lower than in the middle class, . . . the educational levels associated with a given structure of status expectations are simultaneously moving upward. . . . Individuals demand progressively more education over time, . . . however, the individual return tends to be zero. . . . – if we suppose a society in which middle- and higher-class people, but not lower-class people, were to demand more education over time, the status expectation of the latter would become increasingly less favorable over time.[6]

Lower class individuals must continue to obtain more education simply to stay in place. If not, they will lose ground as long as upper and middle class individuals also continue to obtain large amounts of education.

What are the policy implications of Boudon's model for education as an instrument for reducing social inequality? One conclusion Boudon draws is that "no manipulation of the educational variables is likely to have more than a moderate effect on either IEO or ISO."[7] Whereas increasing equality of income does exactly that, increasing educational opportunity does not necessarily increase economic equality because all, not just some, are made better off. Since equality is relative, only policies that make some better off than others will achieve results.

According to Boudon, even a fairly large increase in educational opportunity would not greatly affect social and economic outcomes for the least favored, but even moderate income redistribution would have a considerable effect on decreasing social and educational inequality.

Observation of most industrial societies since WWII, supports Boudon's conclusion. Although there has been an increase in equality of education, there has been little reduction in economic inequality.[8]

There is one way to make access to education equivalent to social equality: limit the supply of graduates; deny middle- and upper-class families access to higher education and allow only lower-class children to attend. This way is so drastic, however, that so far as we know, even China has not tried it, and the Soviet Union approximated it for only a few years in the thirties. Where political revolution is too weak, why should we expect educational innovation to be strong?

If Boudon's model is correct, even if presumed cultural differences in school achievement are eliminated, differences in social expectations still would eventually lead to class-biased consumption of education. Now, if schools are supposed to compensate for the negative effects of a country's social and economic structure, we may be better able to understand why schools do not succeed and why even accomplishment appears as failure.

Here is the heart of our lost hope: education cannot significantly improve the cognitive abilities of its most challenging children; and, when these children do make it through higher education, that education cannot guarantee to improve their life-chances. No one should be surprised, therefore, if educators (like others we have talked about) seek to substitute possible objectives for those which are unattainable.

THE OBJECTIVE OF HAVING OBJECTIVES

Just define the input as the output, and by definition objectives are met. If an aim of Title I of the ESEA was to redistribute income to schools with low-income students geographically, then providing and using funds does accomplish this purpose. The policy equation has become an identity, Q.E.D. Actually, according to McLaughlin, congressmen initially cared less about evaluation of pupils' achievement than about distribution and honesty. So long as the money went to the right districts and students, and was spent honestly, congressmen were satisfied. But control of expectations slipped from politicians' hands and went instead to evaluators of students' achievement.

Perhaps it is not purely fortuitous, then, that efforts have been made to substitute equality of inputs for quality of outputs as the major issue in state educational decision-making. I refer, of course, to Serrano v. Priest, in which the Supreme Court of California decided that, to the extent that educational resources are raised locally, there should be, in effect, an equal tax base behind each child; this opinion is not yet fully implemented because of the large transfers of income (higher taxes) involved. Thus, the focus shifts from what children learn to how much their school district is able to spend on them.

Leaving aside consideration of whether it is appropriate for courts to direct legislatures to allocate resources, or whether education ought to have a preferred place in constitutional interpretation, the emphasis on equality does have attractive features. Although they would not be able to guarantee achievement, educators still could show moral intent by spending more on the poor. School districts might equalize per-dollar expenditures per pupil. States might equalize resources among school districts. And the federal government might provide compensatory funds to do more for those who need it most.

If effort were accepted as a substitute for accomplishment, schools could show how hard they were trying — dollars per pupil spent, hours taught, materials used, size of class. Quality of education would be measured by educational process (which can be shown to the doubtful) rather than by educational achievement (which cannot). How, then, divert attention from test scores to educational effort?

When goals cannot be attained there is always a temptation to try more of the same. "Now that we have lost sight of our objectives," the bureaucratic folk saying goes, "we must redouble our efforts." Students in districts that spend as much as three or four times more than others, however, do little better on measures of achievement. The greatest part of new expenditures goes into teachers' salaries. Why should anyone believe that paying those same teachers more to do more of the same will lead to appreciably better results? Parents and taxpayers, who have come to believe it less and less, have become reluctant to pay more and more.

Postponement of gratification once was a time-honored norm among the middle classes. Resuscitating it and applying it to education, one might argue that present effort is supposed to lead to achievement in future generations. Because past deprivation is responsible for present disabilities, future improvement will take an equivalent amount of time; as deprivation took decades, so too will achievement. Holding the line in one generation, therefore, is essential for progress to begin in the second and to be passed on in the third. There is achievement now, this line of attack continues, that our instruments are too insensitive to capture; we need optimism about the future, to counterbalance pessimism about the present.

The delay of delight, alas, is not a strong point of our consuming culture. People may be willing to buy now and pay later, but the reverse apparently is unacceptable. The educational community — students, parents, teachers, administrators — needs visible signs, not only for its successors there and then, but for the community here and now.

The last decade, predictably, has witnessed increased emphasis on processes rather than products of education. The voucher plan, under which students and their parents are able to choose among public schools, is one example. By vesting financial support in the student rather than in the school, advocates of vouchers hope to increase choice and quality by stimulating competition. Because schools would have to compete for students, there would be an incentive to improve their teaching. Students with special problems presumably could be given more expensive vouchers to motivate schools to deal with such problems. If schools insisted on higher payments, we could learn something about the real costs of education for different kinds of students. Whether this would merely "prove" that the poor are dumb or would impel poor citizens and their schools to do better by each other is what the controversy over vouchers is about.

The objection to vouchers, other than fear of unemployment, is that simulating a private market in education will undermine public policy. The worry is that schools will be resegregated not only racially but also along class (and possibly even ethnic or religious) lines. Although devices could be invented to temper these effects, our interest lies in the "pure" voucher, because it makes public that which is otherwise private, namely, the desire of different customers for different goods at different prices.

These latent conflicts become manifest when the twin issues of decentralization and community control are raised. The initial dispute in the Ocean Hill-Brownsville area of Brooklyn was unfortunate in that the attack on teachers' prerogatives obscured the underlying effects of combining decentralization with community control. Community control in Brooklyn has differentiated primary schools according to their local clientele by class, ethnicity, race — or by whatever attributes community representatives seem to care most about. If ethnicity is given a positive value, as in the Berkeley, California schools, similar results can be achieved without neighborhood control. Under the notion "alternative schools," Berkeley students can choose among a variety of more or less academic, or more or less ethnically oriented, programs. The new rationale is different from the old tracking-by-ability-and-aspiration approach, but the results are similar. Differentiation is reintroduced into education under a different guise.

But process rather than product as solution has its pitfalls. Is there no surer way to link schooling and success? One response to the gloomy prospect of connecting education to achievement is to act directly on the economy through the polity; by assigning job quotas to biological groups, the waiting line imposed by the social structure can be cut short. By this token the only guarantee that education will not keep people down is to make who you are more important than what you know. Thus, the argument undercuts the very rationale of education.

But if, as Christopher Jencks points out, there is a general lack of correspondence between educational attainment and financial reward,[9] why should any but the students study? Because schools do not contribute much to either education or advancement, in his view, though society insists on keeping children cooped up in them, they should be prisons that are as pleasant as possible. If the true function of primary and secondary education is to keep the kiddies out of the home for most of the day and out of the job market for as long as possible (or both) schools should, on humanitarian grounds, make children happy while they are there.

But happiness can be hell. Students might feel better, initially, if they were given tasks they already did well. Presumably, students talented in athletics, music and arts, or science would be allowed to luxuriate in those subjects. If reading and arithmetic had to be taught to the unwilling, then the unwilling could learn at their own pace, which would mean a form of tracking. Such schools would be remarkably like those old-fashioned ones attacked by modern movements as segregated — biased by class and sex, inhibiting equality of opportunity, and placing students in nonacademic pigeonholes from which they cannot later escape. Education would come full circle, from forcing students into limited roles to encouraging them to create their own stereotypes.

What is most characteristic of education in our times? The very act of changing objectives. The history of contemporary education can be written of as the search for objectives that would permit educators to legitimate their function by reconciling promise with performance. Goals have been displaced. Inputs have been defined as outputs; effort has been used as an index of accomplishment. The present has been made hostage to the future, and process substituted for purpose. Goals have been misplaced. Educational objectives have been replaced by moving from achievement to filling ethnic or social quotas.

Clarification of objectives turns into confusion. The voucher plan to increase competition is discussed while districts are consolidated to decrease it; efforts to equalize expenditures coexist with compensatory funding; test scores are simultaneously emphasized and ignored. To speak of displacement of one objective by another is, in this respect, misleading. No one objective literally is lost; all are found in uneasy proximity.

By now (back to a dominant theme) it is clear why objectives, even when they are not vague, are multiple and contradictory. The causes are as narrow as individual ambivalence and as broad as social differences. Either the collective "we" want different things or, if we do agree, our individual "I's" differ on how to get those things. Vagueness or contradiction are the price of agreement. The more numerous the objectives, the more valued the objects that fall within them, the more interests those objectives encompass, and the larger the coalition that can be created to support them. And, by the way, the less important any one interest (and hence objective), the less important is any one measure. Multiplicity overcomes specificity.

Not much more can be done in education than has been done already — try anything, try everything. What, then, do educators have to offer? Change, or at least its semblance. Not knowing what else to do, educators offer change for its own sake. Everyone, in a manner of speaking, gets what he wants. Everything anyone desires is being done somewhere. Innovation becomes obfuscation as the assertion of multiple objectives becomes an excuse for failing to achieve any one. No one can accuse educators of inertia; they are always in motion. Changing objectives becomes the object of change. And the more things change. . . .

It may well be that there are not only too many but also too few objectives. Education has economic objectives, from producing job-related skills to minimizing costs. Education has social objectives, from increasing respect for various subcultures to increasing interaction among social strata. Education has ethical imperatives: equalize expenditures, compensate for past defects. Education even has educational objectives.

What is missing? Politics. Strangely enough, for an arena that has been in perpetual upheaval, education has not tried to use the consent of the governed: what will the parties give and take, school by school and district by district, so that each group will feel it has done its best and is prepared to support a common enterprise?

POLITICIZATION WITHOUT POLITICS

That which confuses observers about educational politics — its simultaneous ubiquity and elusiveness — also is its quintessential contemporary characteristic. Education is the most accessible public institution, yet also the most remote. Everything (and nothing) we want seems to go on there. Faddishness is in vogue. Excessive (almost instantaneous) responses to surface discontents stand side by side with bureaucratic procedures and deep-seated resistance to institutional change.

Elementary and secondary education, however, is more than a cacophony of contradictions; it is the example par excellence of politicizing without politics. The choice of counselors, use of materials, hiring of cafeteria help, transfer of teachers, selection of contractors, and too much more to mention have become politicized; meanwhile fleeting forces outside the schools express only intermittent, if intense, interest in the outcomes. Schools have become sites for games other people play — overemployment, ethnicity, culture, sex, equality. As the outer walls of the school system have become permeable, however, the inner sanctum has become impenetrable. Professionalization provides protection. The school loses its sense of community; it is no longer in touch with its surroundings. There is no permanent politics because there is no arena for action in which participants cannot only express but also alter their preferences in expectation of having to deal with the same people and problems in the future. For politics to be give and take, not merely hit and run, there must be a place for stable patterns of interaction, a political arena.

How can there be a local politics of education if there is no local political arena? Changes in boundaries, whether due to state-government pressure for consolidation or to federal pressure for integration, mean that the participants are constantly shifting. Boundary changes, moreover, almost always lead to increasing size. Thus, parents find that the seat of power is always moving, and usually moving farther away. Parents and students take part also in the mobility of American life, and become also a moving target for educators. Both producers and consumers of education are shifting their sites in relation to each other.

Aside from the difficulties that parents and teachers have in finding each other, both groups must contend with outsiders who affect what they do to each other. State and federal financial incentives for teaching this and doing that mean that, to maximize income, local districts must alter priorities. When a school adds an extra period of kindergarten and proposes to cut a period of high school, it does not mean that this school values one activity over the other but only that a state law offering a bonus for kindergarten but no financial loss for one less period of instruction in high school. This temptation to tinker with local education is enhanced by the fact that state and federal officials are not, in the last resort, held responsible for what happens; judges may order busing, but cannot be held accountable for the consequences. Central authorities can neither operate local education nor quite bring themselves to let the locals run it. The center cannot devise acceptable trade-offs for each school district, and the localities are inhibited from trying. Whose priorities prevail? Both, to some extent, and neither entirely. Who is ultimately responsible? The answer is the same: both and neither.

If accepting responsibility for the consequences of one's actions (or inactions) is the mark of an adult, then education has been turned over to grown-up children. Who believes that federal action and inaction in education would not change if congressmen had to send their own children to public schools in the nation's capitol? The way it works, of course, is that wealthier and more mobile parents shop around for suitable schools, leaving the poorer and less mobile to confront each other. The latter bear the brunt of race relations and of the circuses (experiments, I believe they are called) designed to divert the less advantaged from their educational bread. At once, educational politics is made more stressful (by pitting black against white, have-nots against have-littles) and less resourceful (by removing the more affluent). More and more parents who can afford to, send their children to private schools. Rich parents pay double tuition — once for public and once for private schools; and those left behind suffer a double defeat — once for their own difficulties and once for knowing they have to bear the burden of others. Now you see it, now you don't: the center wants control without responsibility, and the local district gets responsibility without control. How can the two be brought within hailing distance of each other?

The specter of community control — neighborhood schools of, by, and for neighborhood people — has obscured another questionable hypothesis, that larger schools encourage pupils' achievement. There has been a movement, in California as elsewhere, for consolidating schools. The idea is to facilitate economies of scale, push specialized services, and equalize tax resources by bringing poorer and richer districts together. The belief that bigger is better until recently has gone unchallenged. Studies of other kinds of municipal service, however — aside from water and sewers — fail to reveal any economies of scale whatsoever. Now Levy and Niskanen, in a study of school districts in California,[10] show that, beyond a minimum, increasing size goes hand in hand with decreasing pupils' performance. One possible explanation is that bureaucracy increases with size, and that having a large proportion of staff outside regular classrooms reduces the importance of good teaching. The larger the bureaucracy, the more its members deal with each other and the less interested those teachers become in pupils. Another explanation is that the smaller the district, the larger its visibility to parents and pupils, and the deeper the integration between teaching staff and the surrounding community. Social pressure substitutes for dehumanized economic incentives in motivating teachers and students to improve performance. The greater the congruence between community and school values, this hypothesis suggests, the more consistent the message to teachers and students, the more they learn together. If there were integration of school and society then the constant consent schools could receive for the good they did accomplish might overcome some unavoidable everyday evils.

How, then, assuming that a local political arena could be reestablished, would such consent be consummated between educational adults? Let us face up to the two most difficult problems — the presence of busing and the absence of achievement.[11] In effect, one set of people is taxed in hard cash to provide another group with soft symbolic support. What is in it for the providers? What do the receivers get except a longer ride? These unanswered questions swell discontent.

Suppose compensatory funding, in larger amounts than provided today, were traded for cessation of compulsory busing. Government would encourage desegregation by facilitating transportation for students who wished to go to a school they thought better in another neighborhood, for example. Government might subsidize "magnet" schools, whose special facilities would attract interested students. But government would not mandate busing. Parents would understand that their taxes go to keep neighborhood schools, and that such payments make it more worthwhile for those with lower incomes to stay in their own neighborhood schools. Quid pro quo. Alternatively, schools that contributed to desegration could be offered financial gains.[12]

Race (when class also means race) tension is at the heart of the matter. With each side acknowledging the advantages of the bargain struck, race relations might be healthier than they are now. As things stand, only a small number of whites strongly favor busing; and, again, even many of this group escape the consequences by sending their own children to private schools. The majority of whites hate busing; and most blacks hate the idea that, amid all the upset, black children do not benefit. What we need now is a mechanism to decommit people from past positions so that they can make arrangements better suited to present preferences.

CLARIFICATION OF OBJECTIVES AS A SOCIAL PROCESS

Decommitment from outrageous objectives is desirable; abandoning the essential rationale for education is not. For educators, that is now the point: What is peripheral and what is central? What is impossible and what is merely difficult?

To concentrate on busing (pro or con) is easier than to improve the cognitive abilities of children; but ease is not a sufficient reason for ignoring learning. Yet, in multiplying and diffusing objectives, educators are in danger of doing just that. Educators who continually say that they deal with the whole child apparently feel that they are not then responsible for any particular part. Yet, of course, no one can deny that the cognitive mode stands alone. There are also, at least, parts that educators call the affective mode (feelings, emotions, intuitions) and the psychomotor mode, (physical coordination and sports). There was a time when a good basketball team and the school chorus made up for a multitude of sins. But this won't work any more. Few people believe that schools are (or can be) effective in inculcating moral values or that there is always sufficient agreement on what such values should be. Also, sports generally are accepted and encouraged, but they provide avenues of mobility for only a few students. The (extracurricular) motor mode cannot substitute for education. The cognitive mode is critical, at least for those who most need it. To abandon cognition is not a displacement, but a misplacement, of objectives. How could it happen? Educators, urged to return to basics, deny ever having left the three R's. Besides, educators are quick to see that, if society's demands overwhelm the school, what teachers do doesn't matter. Apparently educators can do harm but not good. By failing to provide an atmosphere favorable to study and by slighting cognitive skills, educators may inhibit learning. But with the best intentions, schools seemingly cannot guarantee learning. So be it.

If economic class is related to educational achievement (the essential meaning of "family background" as it is used in education), it would be reasonable for educators to take this fact into account when clarifying objectives. For evaluation, educators could divide schools and classrooms into economic categories and try to achieve the highest level within each economic grouping. The only reported experiment of this kind, which took place in Atlanta, Georgia, suggested that no participant in the school system used data on relative internal achievement.[13]

Schools that paid real attention to their own potential would have better grounds for resisting imposition of unattainable objectives. To encourage this requires either structural change (institutionalizing competition among schools for students) or social stability (encouraging small schools to connect education with expectation).

As usual, it is likely that we will not so much solve our present problems as move on to future predicaments. For instance, the value orientation of schooling — from prayers to pollution to consumption and capitalism — might once again dominate the educational stage. Whether children learn respect for God, Country, Nature, and Money may matter more to a worried nation than whether Johnny can read or Mary can add. That children learn to try to satisfy more interesting wants may become more important than knowing how to satisfy current wants. Until then, however, education needs a stable political arena.

Remember that clarification of objectives is a social phenomenon that takes place in a political context. Applying analysis can help; knowing what cannot be done, à la Boudon, puts tough limits on policy proposals. Delivery of data also can aid in clarifying aims; knowing what is not being accomplished, à la McLaughlin, is essential. But converting data into information through analyses that affect choice requires being able to relate resources and objectives. The different objectives and the varying resources are attached to social forces whose participation is necessary both to legitimize and also to formulate policy. Without constraints, the number of possible combinations of resources and objectives would be too great to allow practical thinking about policy. Without patterned interaction of aims and resources it would be impossible to maintain the tension between promise and performance, between what we would like and what we can have, which makes policy acceptable to its publics. Just as prices are improper apart from markets, so settlements are strained when stable political arenas do not exist. There can be no one optimal policy; there must be a range whose acceptability is born of the ability of social forces to make and keep bargains. Inevitably, however, there are constituencies — officials at different levels, minorities, teachers' organizations, financial reformers — who will oppose reinstating a local politics of schools; these groups fear loss of gains won from state and national actions. Indeed, even parents who wish further decentralization must look to the state. The task of policy analysis in education in the years ahead will be to create incentives for building political arenas (and institutional structures, such as competition by vouchers) that participants will be encouraged to support.

If we can't learn from education or make health from medicine, what can we do? Try to convert difficulties with which we cannot deal into problems we can solve. The trouble is that past solutions quickly turn into future problems. Supporting charity via the income tax is a good example.

NOTES

1. This chapter is a revised and reduced version of a paper that originally appeared as "The Strategic Retreat on Objectives," *Policy Analysis,* Vol. 2, No. 3 (Summer 1976), pp. 499–526.
2. Milbrey Wallin McLaughlin, *Evaluation and Reform: The Elementary and Secondary Education Act of 1965/Title I,* A Rand Educational Policy Study (Cambridge, Mass.: Ballinger, 1975), p. 106.
3. Ibid., p. 119.
4. Raymond Boudon, *Education, Opportunity, and Social Inequality: Changing Prospects in Western Society* (New York: John Wiley & Sons, 1974).
5. Ibid., pp. 193–194.
6. Ibid., pp. 182–183.
7. Ibid., p. 195.
8. Ibid., p. 193.
9. Christopher Jencks et al., *Inequality: A Reassessment of the Effect of Family and Schooling in America* (New York: Basic Books, 1972).
10. Mickey Levy and William Niskanen, "Cities and Schools: A Case for Community Government in California," Working Paper No. 14 (Berkeley: Graduate School of Public Policy, University of California, 1974). Also Jonathan P. Sher and Rachel B. Tompkins, "Economy, Efficiency, and Equality: The Myths of Rural School Consolidation" (Washington, D.C.: National Institute of Education, 1976).
11. If busing actually facilitated integration, and if integration added to achievement (two big "ifs"), there would be gains to offset losses. Then it would make sense to ask how much these gains were worth. Two negatives may multiply to make a positive in the closed world of mathematics, but not in an open society.
12. See John E. Coons and Stephen D. Sugarman, "A Model Integration Incentive Act," Childhood and Government Project, Working Paper No. 44 (Berkeley-Earl Warren Legal Institute, University of California, April 1977).
13. See Bayla F. White, "The Atlanta Project: How One Large School System Responded to Performance Information," *Policy Analysis,* Vol 1 (Fall 1975), pp. 659–692. For an earlier design, with emphasis on implementation, see Aaron Wildavsky, "A Program of Accountability for Elementary Schools," *Phi Delta Kappan,* Vol. 52 (December 1970), pp. 212–216.

CHAPTER 14

A TAX BY ANY OTHER NAME:
THE DONOR-DIRECTED AUTOMATIC
PERCENTAGE-CONTRIBUTION BONUS,
A BUDGET ALTERNATIVE
FOR FINANCING GOVERNMENTAL SUPPORT
OF CHARITY

This is an analysis of the merits of four alternatives for providing governmental support to charity — the tax write-off now on the books, a tax credit, a sliding matching grant, and a percentage-contribution bonus.[1] After searching for an appropriate budget mechanism (a five-year fixed-sum authorization and appropriation), we apply some wide-ranging criteria — equity, legitimacy, efficiency, reciprocity, controllability, and others — to each of the four alternatives. In brief, the present tax write-off is grossly inequitable among donors, poorly controlled by government, and is part of a tax system that citizens increasingly feel is illegitimate. The advantages of the write-off are that it produces predictable amounts of income at low administrative cost without overtly raising questions of constitutionality. Its disadvantages would be mitigated by a tax credit in proportion to the amounts contributed by taxpayers. But the credit does not reach people who do not file returns and may significantly decrease income to charitable agencies. The sliding matching grant (under which the government pays to charity in proportion as the individual gives of his income) provides a form of equity for taxpayers but is deficient in other respects. The contribution bonus — a percentage of each dollar contributed paid to charity by government — is wholly equitable, includes all givers, sustains reciprocity with recipients, is controllable by government, and is legitimate in treating expenditures as expenditures and not as tax dodges. It also raises the possibility of increasing the government's contribution. The defects of the bonus are higher administrative costs and potential doubt about constitutionality. We conclude in favor of a percentage contribution bonus set high enough to provide marginally more income for charity and reduce financial uncertainties during the transition. Appraisal of political feasibility suggests that supporters of charity are likely to be worse off unless they come up with a more defensible approach.

When mankind was in a state of nature, clean and unspoiled, or at least there was no income tax, large fortunes, once made, were easy to retain and pass on for charitable purposes. Giving could avoid government. And so long as the same low tax was paid on all incomes, regardless of size, charities could remain innocent of favoritism. But when taxes were made progressive, it became difficult for charities to act likewise, unless government was to get most of the money. Therefore money headed in charitable directions was treated as taxable at a much lower rate. So far so good — and bad. To make more money available for charity, the rich were treated better because they were in higher tax brackets. Which evil, then, would one prefer, income-tax rates that are equal for rich and poor, or equal consideration in charitable giving?

Once government intervened to increase giving by providing a tax break, charitable causes became dependent on gifts designed with the tax advantages in mind. If tax advantages were mostly the same to all charities it wouldn't matter so much, but it happens that the poor give more to charities and the rich to universities and museums. Any effort to convert the lesser evil into the greater good by restoring equity among givers therefore runs into this hindrance: because poor and rich give to different types of charities, any change to a fairer form of government aid to charities is bound to hurt worthy causes. Fair one way is unfortunate another.

How do we undo the deleterious effects of the original intervention in policy without making things worse in order to improve them? The tax write-off, the current method for government support of charitable contributions, is profoundly inequitable and provides a limited amount to charity. Our problem is to determine if any other means would be more just, provide more revenue, and maintain the private character of charity.

BUDGET ALTERNATIVES

If government support of charitable contributions were to be financed through budget rather than tax mechanisms, which types of expenditure would be more appropriate? Each budgetary device comes with different conditions. Whether the amount of money is fixed by government or flows automatically as a consequence of action by givers, whether the money is available for one year or for many years or until the legislation is changed, all depend on the device that is used. The type of budget provision affects monetary considerations not only directly but also indirectly because of its association with a pattern of decision-making.

How the money comes determines who will be giving it. Under some provisions the money goes through appropriations committees: under others it passes only through some legislative committee. And the kind of committee considering the matter in Congress is likely also to determine which executive-branch agency will be in charge of charity. A lot is at stake in choosing the form of financing — who will get how much under what conditions.

There is more than one budgetary process. The classical types, which we usually think of as budgeting, begin with a legislative committee's authorization to spend and then getting the permission to spend from appropriations committees. Let us call this simply *appropriations budgeting.*

The second method (think of food stamps or housing allowances or agricultural price supports) begins with a mandate to spend from the Treasury (through trust funds, loans, or direct disbursements), originating with a legislative committee; it proceeds directly to the floors of the houses of Congress without stopping at the appropriations committees. Let us call this *Treasury budgeting.*

What would happen if the federal government financed its portion of charitable contributions by appropriations or treasury budgeting? Let us start with the strictest possible regimen, annual authorizations and one-year appropriations. Presumably the purpose of such a device would be to encourage frequent consideration of how much the government should give to which charitable purposes. Immediately, new political and constitutional problems would be created. To treat religious organizations in a manner different from other groups would mean running afoul of the constitutional provisions and court rulings on separation of church and state. The executive and legislative branches would have to take positions on which charities or charitable purposes were more desirable than others. Although it is not possible to say with certainty which executive departments and congressional committees would have jurisdiction, a likely result of emphasizing the substance of charitable allocation would mean lodging the task in the Department of Health, Education and Welfare, whose jurisdiction covers the largest part of philanthropic endeavor (outside of religion). Naturally the new Bureau of Charities (would "Philanthropies" sound better?), like all other bureaus would be asked to make its recommendations part of overall departmental activities. Charity might come to be looked at as a supplement to whatever was felt to be lacking in hospitals or schools or mental-health services. Federal contributions might well be seen as a lever to direct larger amounts of private money in desired directions, "freeing" other departmental funds for different purposes.

Although this "parade of horribles" might seem exaggerated, we think it is not far from the truth. The Bureau of Charities undoubtedly would wish to raise the amount of governmental contributions, but could do so only by promising programmatic results by directing the monies. Yet, if there is any principle that one would suppose particularly applicable to charitable giving — apart from allowing givers to direct money as they choose — it is that charity should operate on its own principles no matter what rules, forces, and objectives guide government policy. Otherwise, it would become evident that charities are merely a convoluted way for government to carry out activities proposed or already under way.

Predictability could be improved substantially by going to both multiyear authorizations and appropriations. However difficult the initial funding decisions might be, charitable organizations would know how much they were going to get from the government for at least three to five years. The political battle would be periodic, not continuous.

What is the likelihood, a worried charitable agency might ask, that Congress would go along with a multiyear appropriation? "Mighty slim" would have been the answer in the past. But now members of appropriations committees have expressed willingness to give up annual review in selected cases. The reason is that Treasury budgeting, promoted on grounds that stability in funding is required, threatens to undermine the appropriations process. The new budget reform is one response to this challenge. Another is to undermine the rationale of "backdoor (Treasury) spending" by providing needed stability through the front door (of appropriations).

The question of how government contribution would be dispensed remains to be answered. Charitable organizations could submit a certified total of contributions received and have the amount supplemented at the going rate; or, individuals might submit lists of their contributions of which a specified proportion would be directed to charities. Either way would result in larger administrative expenses. This increase applies especially because all individuals who make contributions — though outside the tax system, or who take standard deductions — would be included under any supplement scheme. But now we have left budgeting to go on to other criteria for judging alternatives by which to finance philanthropy. The time has come to state our criteria and apply them to alternative ways of supporting charity through government.

PROPOSALS, CRITERIA, AND CONSEQUENCES

The principal means for government support of charity is the tax write-off. Contributions to charitable organizations can be deducted from an individual's taxable income. Two proposals, one a tax expenditure and the other a budget expenditure, have been suggested as alternatives to the tax write-off. The tax expenditure takes the form of a tax credit.[2] Taxpayers receive a fixed rebate for each dollar they give to charity.

More recently, McDaniel has proposed a budget expenditure in the form of a sliding matching grant. The percentage of the federal match increases on a sliding scale as the proportion of one's income given to charity increases.[3] To these two alternatives we have added a third, a budget expenditure, in which charitable organizations receive a government supplement as a fixed proportion of the private contributions they receive. We call this alternative the "donor-directed automatic percentage-contribution bonus" (or "percentage-contribution bonus" or just "bonus" for short) because the government adds to each dollar contributed to a charity. Are these alternatives better or worse than the present tax write-off as a method for public support of private charity? No one can say because there has never been a comparative analysis of the leading alternatives.

We describe the consequences of each of the four alternative proposals — tax write-off, tax credit, contribution bonus, and the sliding matching grant — by a number of criteria that encompass critical issues related to government support of philanthropy. Though we cannot prove that our standards are better than any others, we hope to persuade the reader that these criteria are plausible and appropriate. And although people undoubtedly will differ as to which criteria deserve priority, we shall try to convince others that criteria that matter to us ought to matter to them also.

The initial criteria are those which determine whether the charitable enterprise can be carried on at all. Of these the first is targetability — the ability of private donors to give money to their chosen charity. Otherwise private charity would be public, and there would be no reason why whatever yardsticks apply to government expenditure in general should not be valid also for this class of expenditure in particular. It would be better for government to contribute nothing than to control everything. Constitutionality also is critical. If an alternative is found to contravene separation of church and state, it would not only violate deep and widely shared values, it would also be declared null and void.

Our middle-level criteria can be described by more or less, rather than all or nothing. Charity can be more or less certain or equitable and still remain charity. These standards raise questions of trade-offs — how much certainty for charitables versus how much controllability for government. Thus, we group criteria by the major interests connected with them — donors, charitables, and government.

Donors, in our view, are affected most by pluralism, equity, and reciprocity. The more donors whose contributions are subsidized by government, the more pluralistic (by including a diversity of interests) the policy alternative under which government acts. The more each donor's dollar is treated equally by government, the more equitable the policy. The less the donor's contribution is affected (or afflicted) by evident self-interest, such as tax advantages, the more the donor can expect the recipient to reciprocate.

Charitable organizations care about the total they receive, its predictability, and its distribution among them according to major purpose. The question of how each alternative for governmental support of charity affects the incentive of donors to give is subsumed under the criterion of total amount. Incentives matter only if they affect the size of the contribution.

Charity is a government matter because government money is being used to generate additional private contributions. Government watches the controllability of its subsidy to charity, the efficiency with which that money is employed, and the legitimacy of the institutional channels through which the money is distributed. Views about how much government money should go to charity undoubtedly will vary with time. But the government has a permanent interest in being able to determine what the amount will be. With regard to efficiency, government must consider two distinctly different uses of its money. One is the cost of administering the program — administrative efficiency. The other is the incentive effect government money has in encouraging private donations — allocative efficiency. Legitimacy requires further elucidation.

The government has an interest in managing its affairs so as to inspire citizen's confidence. When they feel fairly treated, that confidence is enhanced. When citizens see that governmental processes are proceeding in an open and straightforward manner, respect is maintained. Any governmental procedures may be judged, then, by how much they inspire citizens' confidence that activities are being performed in a legitimate way. People who make money, for instance, should be seen to pay taxes appropriate to their income.

Whether something can be done is an integral part of whether it will get done. An alternative must be politically feasible or the best-laid plans will come to naught. But political feasibility must not be the sole determinant of our analysis; if so, we examine only what is possible at the expense of prematurely forfeiting what might be best. An assessment of political feasibility will help us guide desirable means to productive ends.

Tax Write-off

The tax write-off decreases the charitable donor's tax bill by (depending on his tax bracket) reducing his liability. The major charge leveled is that the tax write-off leads to substantial inequities among income groups. Inequities stem from two factors. First and foremost, the write-off is worth more to the high-income than to the low-income taxpayer. Its value increases in direct proportion to the marginal tax rate. A person in the 70 per cent tax bracket can reduce his tax bill by an amount equal to 70 per cent of his contribution. This is tantamount to an individual writing a $30 check to a selected charity, and the government kicking in $70. In contrast, a person in the 14 per cent tax bracket must pay $86 to

TABLE 14.1
FOR THE AMOUNT CONTRIBUTED TO CHARITY, HIGH-INCOME PERSONS RECEIVE
A DISPROPORTIONATE SHARE OF TAX EXPENDITURES

Adjusted gross income	Number of persons taking write-off	Govern-ment tax expendi-ture ('000's)	Total contribu-tion	Aver-age tax expendi-ture per person	Aver-age contri-bution per person
		$	$	$	$
Under $5,000	3,910,667	35,000	817,610	9	209
$5,000–$10,000	10,937,788	319,000	2,739,605	29	250
$10,000–$15,000	10,206,268	503,000	3,203,956	49	313
$15,000–$20,000	4,815,864	416,000	2,000,226	86	415
$20,000–$50,000	3,297,558	771,000	2,362,016	234	716
$50,000–$100,000	339,736	426,000	748,482	1,254	2,236
Over $100,000	75,715	855,000	1,020,839	11,291	13,615
TOTAL	32,669,067	3,325,000	12,892,734		
Average per person				102	395

Estimates based on data from the United States Internal Revenue Service, Statistics of Income — 1970 Individual Tax Returns, Washington, D.C.: U.S. Government Printing Office, 1972, p. 120; and Annual Report of the Secretary of the Treasury on the State of Finances for Fiscal Year Ending June 30, 1973, "Estimated distribution of selected items of tax preferences of individuals by adjusted gross income, calendar year 1971," pp. 349–354.

his charity to get government to contribute $14. The high-income person nets, in effect, $2.23 for every dollar, whereas the low-income person receives only $0.16.

For the amount contributed to charity high-income persons get a disproportionate share of tax expenditures in the form of reduced tax bills. As Table 14.1 indicates, in 1970 people with high incomes (more than $100,000) contributed an average of slightly more than $13,600, reducing their taxes an average of more than $11,000. Low-income people (less than $5,000) contributed an average of $209, reducing their taxes an average of only $9. Although the average high-income taxpayer gave 65 times more than the average low-income person, the average high-income individual received a tax reduction 1,250 times larger than that received by the average low-income taxpayer.

Second, the tax write-off provides no benefits for those who take the standard deduction, or for those outside the tax system (who do not file returns). These people are poor or nearly poor. In 1972, 86 per cent of nonitemizers taking the $2,000 standard deduction had adjusted gross incomes below $5,000. Nonfilers also included a large proportion of low-income people, primarily those with incomes too low to be taxed.

Inequities in the opportunity to contribute to charity affect other values basic to philanthropy. Pluralism is cited as a cornerstone of philanthropy. The belief that multiple approaches are better than unitary approaches; that voluntary action, unencumbered by rigidities of government or unrestricted by the profit motive of the private sector, can lead to creative solutions to social problems; that private individuals can best direct their own assets to meet social needs — these beliefs all are vital to philanthropy. But the tax write-off is not consistent with pluralism through philanthropy. The pluralism of the tax write-off is not plural; benefits are confined mainly to upper-income groups. Worse, the write-off is part of a larger series of special provisions that have brought the tax system into disrepute.

Legitimacy is the heart of political institutions. Watergate showed that a president not only must be legitimate, but also must appear to the people to be legitimate. The tax write-off substantially reduces the appearance of (and hence erodes the basis of) legitimacy. When some people are allowed to decrease their tax bills substantially by charitable contributions, the public loses confidence in the fairness of the tax system.

In philanthropy, reciprocity is important in linking donors and recipients. If giving is not to deteriorate into either exploitation or mere market exchange between them, then there must be reciprocity. Whether and how one reciprocates is affected by how one perceives the motives of a donor.

Primarily because each donor faces different tax incentives, buried in the intricacies of provisions for deduction, the recipient has much difficulty in deciding precisely why his charity was given the gift. In philanthropy, it is not uncommon to hear the recipient asking, "Are they really trying to help me or are they more interested in getting their tax advantages?" The tax write-off obscures the donor's motives and, in so doing, discourages reciprocity.

Supporting charity through the tax system also increases government expenditures that are not controlled by Congress. The tax write-off truly is uncontrollable. The amount is not subject to annual or periodic congressional review and the tax system does not limit what a taxpayer can receive. The subsidy is concealed. Reform of neither taxation nor of budgeting is furthered by treating an expenditure as a tax deduction.

The financial inequity inherent in the tax write-off has been widely recognized:[4] its denial of a broad form of pluralism, its erosion of the legitimacy of our tax institutions, and its inhibiting effects on reciprocity are less known but equally damaging. But these formidable defects, taken alone, do not provide sufficient grounds for doing away with the present system. Perhaps, despite its deficiencies, the write-off brings benefits that cannot be obtained by other methods. What benefits are gained from inequality of opportunity to give to charity?

A possible rationale is the efficiency of, government subsidies in encouraging philanthropic contributions. If the current distribution (among various income groups) of the government tax write-off provides a substantial incentive for contributions, then this inequity may be necessary to raise funds. What does the empirical evidence reveal? For every dollar in tax expenditures (revenue foregone by the Treasury), how many additional dollars go to charity?

The evidence is far from conclusive; but four studies (by Taussig, Schwartz, Brannon, and Feldstein) are relevant.[5] As each author and his critics point out, these studies are substantially burdened with limitations that qualify the conclusions. But, as the best available, they are instructive. Taussig finds efficiency near zero, approximately 5 per cent. For every $1,000 reduction in Treasury income, charitable contributions increase by $0.05. Feldstein finds efficiency exceeds 100 per cent; the write-off increases the amount received by charities by slightly more than the reduction in revenue to the Treasury. Schwartz and Brannon find the efficiency of the write-off between the estimates of Taussig and Feldstein. If we assume the worst of all possible worlds — the tax write-off is totally inefficient — then inequities in the opportunity to contribute cannot be condoned. If we assume the best — the tax write-off is 100 per cent efficient — then such inequities may be condoned, but only if there is no other feasible alternative that does not have these inequities and is equally efficient.

The tax write-off involves only small administrative costs to the IRS and the taxpayer, none to the charitable agencies. For itemizers, contributions are listed, receipts appended, forms filed, calculations made, and tax bills reduced. For nonitemizers, standard deductions are taken, calculations made, and tax bills reduced. All is done as part of the standard operating procedures of the income-tax system. Administrative simplicity is a key virtue of the tax write-off.

Although supporting philanthropy (which inevitably includes religious organizations), the tax write-off so far has not offended the constitutional requirement for separation of church and state. Mainly because the government subsidy to philanthropy is directed to the contributor and remains concealed within the tax system, the constitutionality of the tax write-off has not been and is unlikely to be gravely challenged.

The Tax Credit

The credit works through the income-tax system by returning to each charitable donor an amount equal to a percentage of his or her contribution. The tax credit is substantially more equitable than the tax write-off. An individual's marginal tax rate no longer dictates the size of the government subsidy that he receives. Because all taxpayers itemizing contributions get a fixed percentage of charitable contribution in the form of a tax credit, the size of the donation is the only important variable. For a $100 contribution, lower-income taxpayers get the same tax credit as those with higher incomes. But those taking the standard deduction receive no tax credit. In 1972, these were two-thirds of the taxpayers, nearly all of whom had incomes below $15,000. In addition, those outside the tax system, often the very poor, of course, can receive no tax credit for their contributions. But, despite these limitations, the tax credit does eliminate inequities within the group of those itemizing charitable contributions. Thus the tax credit expands pluralism, enhances legitimacy, and strengthens reciprocity, but back-door spending through the tax system is not eliminated. Uncontrollables remain uncontrollable. Reciprocity improves as philanthropic motives for giving are not entirely obscured by differential tax advantages.

The administrative simplicity of the write-off is true also for the tax credit. Once the reimbursement rate is established, the IRS can issue tax credits as easily as it reduces taxable income. But we don't get something for nothing. What are the costs of reducing inequities? Who incurs these costs? Charities won't get more and there is reason to believe they might get considerably less. Assume the government had implemented the tax credit in 1970 and had been willing to expend the same $3.3 billion in credits as it did on tax deductions. Because tax itemizers gave $12.9 billion in that year, the average government subsidy would be about 35 percent.[6] As a result, those who received a 35 percent matching subsidy under a tax write-off would be likely to go on contributing the same amount with a tax credit. Repeal of the write-off and enactment of the tax credit *increases* the government subsidy for all those in a tax bracket below 35 percent. On the other hand, government subsidy *decreases* for all those in brackets above 35 percent. If the tax credit is to maintain a flow of charitable contributions at least equal to the write-off, then any decrease in contributions by the wealthy must be compensated by increases in contributions from the poor. This is unlikely to happen because the poor have less money.

Not only may the flow of philanthropic contributions be reduced by a tax credit, but also internal distribution of donations is likely to be affected. More will go to charities of the lower income (religion) and less to those preferred by the wealthy (education, museums, orchestras). How money is called affects who will be chosen.

Percentage-Contribution Bonus

Under the contribution bonus, the federal government makes a direct expenditure to a charitable organization at a fixed proportion of the amount voluntarily contributed by an individual. The bonus has a number of advantages over both tax write-off and tax credit because the government subsidy goes directly to the charitable organization at the initiative of the contributor.

The significance of these advantages in equity, efficiency, and total contributions illustrated by the distribution of private and public costs for the write-off versus the bonus. In 1970, the Treasury allowed taxpayers to write off $3.3 billion in taxes. Individuals made $12.9 billion in charitable contributions. Another $1.5 billion was contributed by those taking the standard deduction, making a total of $14.4 billion in individual contributions to philanthropy. Table 14.2 shows (by income class for contributors) who got how much of the government subsidy, who contributed how much of the private cost of philanthropy, and who donated how much to philanthropy.

In short, the rich as a group (more than $50,000) are about 1 per-

TABLE 14.2
THE TAX WRITE-OFF:
THE RICH (1 PERCENT OF CONTRIBUTORS) PAY 5 PERCENT OF THE PRIVATE COST ($0.5 BILLION), GIVE 14 PERCENT OF THE CHARITABLE CONTRIBUTIONS ($1.7 BILLION), BUT RECEIVE 39 PERCENT OF THE WRITE-OFF ($1.3 BILLION)

(1970 CONTRIBUTIONS, IN '000's OF DOLLARS)

Adjusted gross income group	Number in the group	Private cost of contribution[a]	Gov't subsidy (tax write-off)[b]	Total flow of contributions to charities[c]
		$	$	$
Under $5,000	3,910,667	782,610	35,000	817,610
$5,000–$10,000	10,939,788	2,420,605	319,000	2,739,605
$10,000–$15,000	10,206,268	2,700,956	503,000	3,203,956
$15,000–$20,000	4,815,864	1,584,226	416,000	2,000,226
$20,000–$50,000	3,297,558	1,591,016	771,000	2,362,016
$50,000–$100,000	339,736	322,482	426,000	748,482
Over $100,000	75,715	165,839	855,000	1,020,839
Total for tax itemizers	32,669,067	9,567,734	3,325,000	12,892,734
Total for nonitemizers				1,510,000
Total individual giving				14,402,734

[a] Private cost is calculated by subtracting the government subsidy from the total contributions for each income class.

[b] Estimates from *Annual Report of the Secretary of the Treasury on the State of Finances for Fiscal Year Ending June 30, 1973.* Washington, D.C.: Government Printing Office, 1973. See Appendix D, "Estimated distribution of selected items of tax preferences of individuals by adjusted gross income class, calendar year 1971," pp. 349–354.

[c] Based on data from the United States Internal Revenue Service, Statistics of Income — 1970 Individual Tax Returns. Washington, D.C.: U.S. Government Printing Office, 1972, p. 120.

cent of the contributors, pay 5 percent of the private costs ($0.5 billion), give 14 percent of the charitable contributions ($1.7 billion), but receive 39 percent of the government write-off ($1.3 billion).

Table 14.3 indicates the consequences of repealing the tax write-off and instituting a 35 per cent bonus. Here we assume that all contributors will give at a level equal to their private costs under the tax write-off. A wealthy person in the 70 percent tax bracket who gave $100 under the tax write-off will reduce his contribution to $30 under the contribution bonus, a person in the 14 percent tax bracket will reduce his contribution to $86; nonitemizers and those outside the tax system will contribute the same amounts. The contributions of every individual generate a 35 percent bonus. The wealthy person who gives $30 of his own money will generate a bonus of $10.50 from the government. The flow to the

TABLE 14.3
THE 35 PERCENT CONTRIBUTION BONUS: AN EQUITABLE GOVERNMENT SUBSIDY MAINTAINS THE FLOW OF CHARITABLE CONTRIBUTIONS

(1970 CONTRIBUTIONS, IN '000's OF DOLLARS)

Adjusted gross income group	Number in the group	Private cost of contribu- tion[a]	Gov't sub- sidy 35% contribu- tion bonus[b]	Total flow of contri- butions to char- itables[c]
		$	$	$
Under $5,000	3,910,667	782,610	273,913	1,056,523
$5,000–$10,000	10,939,788	2,420,605	847,211	3,267,816
$10,000–$15,000	10,206,268	2,700,956	945,332	3,646,282
$15,000–$20,000	4,815,864	1,584,226	554,479	2,138,705
$20,000–$50,000	3,297,558	1,591,016	556,856	2,147,872
$50,000–$100,000	339,736	322,482	112,868	435,350
Over $100,000	75,715	165,839	58,043	223,882
Total for itemizers	32,669,067	9,567,734	3,348,702	12,916,430
Total for nonitemizers		1,510,000	503,333	2,013,333
Total individual giving		11,067,734	3,852,035	14,929,763

[a] The private cost of the contribution for each income group is assumed to be the same under the percentage-contribution bonus as under the tax write-off.

[b] The government subsidy directed by each income group is calculated by taking 35 per cent of the private cost of the contribution for that income group.

[c] Based on data from the U.S. Internal Revenue Service, Statistics of Income, *1970 Individual Tax Returns.* Washington, D.C.: U.S. Government Printing Office, 1972, p. 120.

Assumption: It is assumed, with repeal of the tax write-off and enactment of the percentage contribution bonus, that all contributors will give at a level equal to their private costs under the tax write-off.

charity (private contributions plus government bonus) will be $40.50. The poorer person will give $86 of his own money and generate a $30 bonus from the government. The flow to the charity will be $116. Non-itemizers who gave $1.51 billion in 1970 will generate a 35 percent bonus resulting in a flow to charities of $2.01 billion. Likewise, the 35 percent bonus will increase (no one knows by how much) the contributions made by those outside the tax system.[7]

We have assumed that all individuals will reduce charitable contributions by the amount equal to the government subsidy now received under the tax write-off. This assumption is critical to our conclusions. Have we, then, loaded the dice in our favor? No, we have assumed the worst, for if the tax write-off has a 100 percent incentive effect on contributions, then the percentage contribution bonus must equal the largest amount produced by its competitor. Because repeal of the write-off might mean a decrease in charitable contributions of $3.3 billion in 1970, a contribution bonus of at least that amount should ensure that the total flow to charitables will be maintained.

It should but it might not; despite assumptions that seem safe to us analysts, people do not always behave the way we think they will. Suppose some individuals give less than their private costs and the slack is not taken up by others; or, despite current evidence, presume that the tax write-off is substantially more than 100 percent effective; or, suppose the enactment of the percentage contribution totally "turns off" a number of large contributors who then give nothing to charity. For these expected contingencies and for others that might be unanticipated in transition from the tax write-off to the contribution bonus, it is advisable to increase the percentage bonus to, say, 38 percent. The government subsidy would be $3.6 billion, costing the government and the taxpayers $0.3 billion more, but also it would guarantee at least the same flow of contributions. This inducement adds a little more to the hedge against uncertainty.

Legitimacy is enhanced and pluralism broadened by the contribution bonus. Charitable tax loopholes are driven from the tax system and back-door spending now passes through the front. Reciprocity likewise is encouraged. The donor's contribution is a clear expression of his philanthropic feeling for charity. The government subsidy is above board.

But the contribution bonus has inherent problems with (1) administration, and (2) constitutionality. The contribution bonus means higher administrative costs to government and the charitables. Although we cannot set forth a detailed administrative system, here is one possible approach: the donor would make contributions to selected charitables. Charities would report their total income to the government, and government would issue quarterly checks containing the percentage-contribution bonus. Periodic audits, of course, would be made to verify the accuracy of the reports.

Government may be unable to get the new bonus to each charitable organization at the same time as the charity received its old private contributions. But just as government makes quarterly appropriations to its agencies so that a steady flow of revenues can be maintained, the government might pay out a proportion of its past bonus to each charitable in advance of calculations. Then, after charities submitted their totals and audits were made, the rest of the money could flow in.

Although this system decreases administrative costs to donors, because they no longer have to itemize deductions and attach receipts when filling income taxes, it increases such costs to government, which must process incoming certification forms, calculate the percentage bonus, periodically issue checks to the charitables, and monitor a selected number of donor-recipient transactions to ensure that abuses do not occur. But this cost will be reduced slightly because charitable deductions are eliminated when calculating taxable income. Charitables also will incur increased administrative expenses; additional form filling will be required to ensure receipt of the federal bonus.

The contribution bonus raises a perplexing constitutional obstacle — the separation of church and state. No doubt, the form of a tax write-off is substantially different from a contribution bonus. But the write-off and the bonus have a significant and fundamental characteristic in common. Neither is initiated or directed by either state or the church. Instead, the bonus, like the write-off, can be triggered only by the donor. Bonus and write-off alike support the voluntary initiative taken by a charitable contributor. No governmental discretion on who will receive how much is required. The U.S. Supreme Court decision to uphold federal grants to church-related colleges for construction, but to forbid any grant for construction of facilities "to be used for sectarian instruction or as a place for religious worship"[8] may not be as directly relevant here.[9] For the facts in this decision indicate that the federal grant is initiated by the religious institutions and administered by a government agency. In contrast, the contribution bonus is not a grant in the normal sense of the word, for power to initiate the gift lies not with the government, or with the church, but solely and exclusively with the charitable contributor. Church and state are separate. Or so we think, but no one can guarantee the courts will uphold our logic; the percentage-contribution bonus ought to be considered constitutional, but it may not happen.

Sliding Matching Grant

To date, the only matching-grant scheme put forward in the literature calls for government to match individual contributions in proportion to the percentage of income contributed.[10] This proposal is similar to the contribution bonus in the problems it solves and the questions it raises. The sliding matching grant reduces inequity, enhances pluralism and legitimacy, and improves reciprocity. We will focus only on the most significant component, which distinguishes this proposal from the contribution bonus.

The provision that the sliding matching grant would vary according to the proportion of income contributed demands that administration of the proposal be linked to the filing of income-tax returns. Contributions as a proportion of income must be calculated by the IRS. Therefore, the initiative (for declaring the contribution to generate a government grant) rests entirely with the contributor. But contributors have little incentive to report contributions to the IRS if they no longer receive direct personal benefits in the form of a tax write-off. As a result, not all contributions will be reported, not all matching grants will be made, and charitables are likely to be shortchanged.[11]

To overcome the problem of failure to report all contributions, the charitables conceivably could report to IRS the contributions received. But donors still would have to report contributions to the IRS through the tax system so that the government's share could be calculated as a percentage of the proportion of income contributed. This approach appears to involve extremely high administrative costs and may be unworkable.

We also do not see *why* the proportion of the income devoted to charity should occupy a special place of merit in governmental policy. Equity requires that each person be treated equally by the government, not that the government discriminate against those who, for whatever reason, contribute a lower proportion of their income. If effort is to be the criterion, much more would have to be known about each taxpayer than the government could (or should) want to know.

Through our analysis of the four alternatives we have made some assumptions about the incentives each gives various classes of donors for increasing or decreasing contributions. At first blush the question may appear unworthy. Is anyone suggesting that altruism is infected with interest? Precisely. Unless people have unlimited amounts to give, the donation must be based on how much those persons can afford as well as how much they would like to contribute. Had government not entered the game, givers would need to consult only their own capacities and consciences. But once a government subsidy is available (tax write-offs have been around since 1917), any prudent person would consider how the government's contribution affected his own.

How can we calculate this subtle consideration? It is a little like children asking what would you do if. . . . Without replaying the reel of history, it is not possible to know for certain how people in different income brackets might have behaved if things had been different. Without trying various alternatives in practice, no one can say for sure; we need analysis to improve our guesswork. One way to proceed is to ask how sensitive each alternative is to different assumptions about incentives for giving.

WHAT DIFFERENCE DOES A GOVERNMENT SUBSIDY MAKE? A SENSITIVITY ANALYSIS

Four separate studies of the incentive effects of the tax write-off upon charitable contributions have led to three separate conclusions: near zero, about half, and more than 100 percent. The substantial divergence in these estimates (using a ouija board could hardly produce a wider spread) makes it difficult to draw precise conclusions about incentive effects. But precise conclusions may be unnecessary to choose among policy alternatives for supporting philanthropy. Our analysis reveals that it does not make much difference which incentive estimate is assumed for the percentage-contribution bonus, but it does make a difference for both the tax credit and the write-off.

Let us illustrate these conclusions by assessing the consequences of the percentage-contribution bonus and the tax credit, making assumptions about the incentive effects of the tax write-off. As shown in Table 14.4, a tax write-off costing the Treasury $3.4 billion resulted in total flows to charitables of $14.4 billion in 1970.[12] If the incentive effect of the write-off is 100 percent, then repeal of the write-off reduces contributions by the full $3.4 billion. Total flow will be $11.0 billion. If the contribution bonus is instituted, with the government share equal to the amount spent under the tax write-off, then the total flow is $11.0 billion plus $3.4 (the original $14.4 billion). If the incentive effect of the tax write-off is only 50 percent, then repeal of the write-off reduces contributions by one-half of the subsidy ($1.7 billion) reducing total flow to $12.7 billion. To enact the contribution bonus would increase the flow by $3.4 billion (adding $3.4 to the new base of $12.7) and result in $16.1 billion going to philanthropy. If the tax write-off has no effect on contributions, then repeal would leave contributions unchanged at $14.4 billion. Enactment of the contribution bonus increases the flow by $3.4 billion to $17.8 billion.

What about the tax credit? Table 14.4 shows that if the tax write-off has no incentive effect, then its repeal and substitution of a tax credit (also with a zero-incentive effect) leaves the flow unchanged at $14.4 billion. For each of these three assumptions we have assumed also that the bonus has no incentive effects of its own. If the bonus does induce additional giving, then repeal of the tax write-off and enactment of the bonus results in increased contributions. Therefore, we conclude — for all reasonable assumptions about the incentive effects of the tax write-

TABLE 14.4
REPEAL OF THE TAX WRITE-OFF WITH A 100 PERCENT INCENTIVE EFFECT AND
SUBSTITUTION OF THE PERCENTAGE-CONTRIBUTION BONUS WITH A 0 PERCENT
INCENTIVE EFFECT MAINTAINS TOTAL FLOWS TO CHARITABLES

Policy alternatives	Assumptions re incentive effects of government subsidy		
	Taussig 0%	Schwartz 50%	Feldstein 100%
	Total flow to charitables		
	$	$	$
Tax write-off	14.4	14.4	14.4
Eliminate tax write-off of $3.4 billion	14.4	12.7	11.0
Institute percentage contribution bonus of $3.4 billion. Assume incentive effect to be:			
0%	17.8	16.1	14.4
50%	19.5	17.8	16.1
100%	21.2	19.5	17.8
Institute tax credit of $3.4 billion. Assume incentive effect to be:			
0%	14.4	12.7	11.0
50%	16.1	14.4	12.7
100%	17.8	16.1	14.4

SOURCE. Total contribution data are for 1970. Total charitable flows are from *Giving USA, 1974 Annual Report,* a publication of the American Association of Fund-Raising Counsel, Inc. The Government subsidy is estimated from the *Annual Report of the Secretary of Treasury on the State of Finances, for Fiscal Year Ending June 30, 1973.* Washington, D.C.: U.S. Government Printing Office, 1973. Appendix D, "Estimated contribution of selected items of tax preferences of individuals by adjusted gross income class, calendar year 1971," pp. 349–354.

a Although the government subsidy in the form of a tax write-off is estimated to be $3.325 billion in 1970 we have rounded it to $3.4 billion for ease in computation. The rounding in no way affects our conclusions.

off and percentage-contribution bonus — that substituting the bonus for the tax write-off will mean the same or greater total flow to charitables.

As for the tax write-off itself, its desirability is extremely sensitive to the presumed incentive effect. For if the incentive really is near zero, many other advantages, such as low administrative expenses, become meaningless. Obviously the choice among alternatives should be decided by considering not one but many criteria.

Although a single fatal defect might be decisive, it is most likely that each of our patients suffers from several minor and major maladies. Our task is not to provide a cure-all but to determine the disease with which we are prepared to live.

HOW MUCH OF WHICH PROBLEMS ARE WE PREPARED TO LIVE WITH? AN ANALYSIS OF CRITERIA

No alternative can be all things to all people.[13] There are trade-offs on the criteria both among the groups who supply charity (the donors, the charitables, and the government) and within them. To analyze these trade-offs and their implications for selecting among alternatives, it is useful to start with what each group most desires. Meeting all the desires of one group will affect how well the desires of other groups can be met.

Perspectives: Donors, Charitables, Government

The donor wants public support for charity to be equitable, pluralistic, and encourage reciprocity. If these criteria for the donor are to be met, then the government must abandon the tax system as its means of supporting charity. Neither a tax write-off nor a tax credit is satisfactory. Donor equity, pluralism, and reciprocity are ensured if tax expenditures are replaced by budget expenditures in the form of a contribution bonus. Government legitimacy is enhanced. Because the bonus is directed to charitable organizations rather than to donors, government cares little about allocative efficiency — the incentive effect of its subsidy. The critical test of efficiency is administrative — the amount of the administrative costs that are sure to rise, with the exact level unknown. Because government subsidizes charity through a budget expenditure, we see increased government controllability in determining how much of its money should go to charity. Because government has greater leverage over the size of its subsidy, all interests of the charitables cannot be met. Although total flow to the charitables is maintained at current levels or perhaps higher, its distribution among charitable organizations is altered. Government controllability conflicts with charitable predictability.

What about the outlook for the charitable agencies and for donors? If high flows with high predictability and unaltered distribution are maintained among charitable organizations, then donors suffer in reduced equity, pluralism, and reciprocity. The tax write-off means benefits for the charitables, but levies costs on donors. For the government, legitimacy may be low, but so too are administrative costs.

What about the governmental perspective? Suppose government wants to be legitimate and efficient, and control the size of its subsidy.

TABLE 14.5
HOW MUCH OF WHICH PROBLEMS ARE WE PREPARED TO LIVE WITH? AN
ANALYSIS OF CRITERIA

	DONOR			CHARITABLES		
	Equity	Plural-ism	Reci-procity	Total flow	Predict-ability	Distri-bution
Tax write-off	low	low	low	high	high	as is
Tax credit	medium	medium	medium	medium	medium	slightly altered
Percentage-contribution bonus	high	high	high	high, perhaps higher	medium	slightly altered
Sliding matching grant	medium	medium	medium	high	medium	slightly altered

GOVERNMENT
Efficiency

	Controllability	Administrative	Allocative	Legitimacy
Tax write-off	low	high	unknown, but relevant	low
Tax credit	medium	high	unknown, but very relevant	medium
Percentage-contribution bonus	high	medium	unknown, but irrelevant	high
Sliding matching grant	high	medium	unknown, but relevant	medium

Is this possible? No. To be legitimate, government can adopt the contribution bonus that ensures controllability but reduces administrative
efficiency. To be administratively efficient, government can adopt the tax
credit but legitimacy and controllability suffer. In contrast to donors
and charitables, no alternative gives government all it wants.

Trade-offs

Let us examine how the sacrifice of one government yardstick affects
other government criteria as well as the interests of charitable organizations and donors. We will start by sacrificing controllability. If government wants to control the size of its subsidy to charity, then the
contribution bonus should be instituted. If control is sacrificed, a tax
credit can be instituted (which still means back-door tax expenditures),
but unlike the tax write-off, the size of the subsidy can be regulated by

changing the percentage rate of reimbursement. Sacrifice in control, however, affects legitimacy and efficiency; government cannot be legitimate, for the tax system conceals government expenditure and excludes nonitemizers and nonfilers from tax benefits; negative effects on donors and charitables, moreover, are substantial. Although there is equity for itemizers in the tax system, pluralism is narrow, excluding nonfilers and nonitemizers. For charitables, total flows are likely to be reduced and their predictability decreased. For donors, the system is inequitable and lacking in pluralism and reciprocity. For charitables, the flows are predictable and high, but perhaps not as high as they could be.

If government decides to give up its legitimacy the effects are similar to sacrifices in controllability. Small sacrifices in legitimacy result in a tax credit that, for charitables, reduces flows and certainty and provides equity only to tax itemizers. Large sacrifices in legitimacy result in a tax write-off, which provides predictable and high (although not the highest) flows to charitables, and penalizes donors with inequity, narrow pluralism, and little reciprocity.

And if government decides to sacrifice its efficiency by increasing administrative costs by instituting a contribution bonus? Legitimacy and controllability can be maintained at high levels. Spending on charity by back-door tax expenditures is eliminated and government has greater control over its charitable subsidy. The effects on donors are beneficial because the bonus means an equitable and pluralistic system and enhanced reciprocity. Charitables maintain high flows, increased perhaps with experience, although predictability of the flow is reduced and distribution among charitables is altered. On balance, the contribution bonus, though calling for sacrifice in administrative efficiency for government, is the preferred public means for supporting private charity.

But is it feasible? Feasibility should not preempt desirability. Feasibility should be used to guide reason in the choice of means to desired ends or of ends as closely related to the desirable as possible under the circumstances.

POLITICAL FEASIBILITY

Feasibility depends on fact: who will be helped or harmed by alternative policies? The tax write-off favors the rich over the poor and moderate income groups. The tax credit takes from the rich to extend equity to those with moderate income but not to the poor. The bonus favors the poor and nearly poor, leaves the middle income people even, and penalizes the rich. Charitables would be best off under a high-contribution bonus, next best off under the current tax write-off, and worst off under a tax credit. Governmental control of charitable contributions and the legitimacy of governmental processes works best with a contribution bonus, next best with the tax credit (under which it could at least set the rate), and worst with the write-off.

The political feasibility of the four alternatives depends on future events — strength of partisan forces, proclivities of presidents, rise and fall of inflation, importance of tax reform, mood of congressional budget committees, and much more — which no one is in a position to predict. But it is possible, in a general way, to lay out the main lines of future development that would affect government's role in assisting charitable contributions. We shall, therefore, specify three main constructs in which the impetus for tax and budget reform that relate to charitable contributions are least and most likely. Then we shall try to assess which of the four proposals would do best under each of those conditions.

It may be that the present impetus for reform will prove overwhelming. Growing disenchantment with the tax system may make all sorts of income deductions ("loopholes") suspect. Though charitable deductions may be the least venal, they yet may be caught up in a wave of wholesale change. The combination of unemployment and inflation, as well, may lead government to rationalize tax and spending activities by seeking clearer separation and greater control over each of them. The new congressional budget committees are institutions with a collective stake in seeing to it that a tax is a tax and an expenditure is an expenditure, and that they help determine what the difference will be. Under these circumstances, the precise nature of governmental contributions to charity would be up for grabs and the preferences of charitables might be buried under an avalanche of reform.

There may be reform, but moderate and mixed. The tax system, with its progressive base overburdened with numerous exceptions, may be kept but intensified. Resistance to sweeping away all deductions may be so great that the attack is selective rather than comprehensive. There may be a far more progressive income tax with fewer deductions on income, or at least different kinds of dedutions. The more progressive the tax, to be sure, the less each higher-income person actually pays toward his contribution to the national treasury, and the greater the disparities between subsidies given various income groups in the population. Incentives would be increased for wealthier individuals and decreased for those who would no longer pay taxes, or would pay only small amounts.

Perhaps the present tax system will remain essentially unchanged. Today's economic uncertainty may make various interests fight all the harder for the privileges they have. It may be not so much that the present system is considered desirable as that it is hard to find alternatives on which people and politicians can agree that would maintain the equilibrium. Undoubtedly there would be sharp attacks on some practices and attempts to modify particular ones — as has happened about every four to five years, for charity — but the result would not look very different.

If we were asked to make educated guesses about these three states of affairs, we would consider holding to the current system as least likely, with radical reform (through a flat-rate tax with elimination of deductions) as slightly more likely, and a mixed picture with emphasis on steeper tax rates (as well as selective attacks on various, but not all, deductions) as most likely. Objections to the present system are so strong, we believe, that it is only a matter of time before the system is subjected to substantial change. The question for those in charitable fields is how to accommodate that change.

Other people's assessment may differ from ours. A few may feel that radical change is just around the corner. If those persons turn out to be right, then charitables would be more strongly advised in their own interest to advocate an equitable mechanism, such as the percentage-contribution bonus, which would let charities prosper in this new era.

An alternative assessment, always worth considering because it is always plausible, is that the future will bear a remarkable resemblance to the present. Tax rates, after all, have gone down, not up in recent years. And it is anybody's guess whether loopholes are larger or smaller than they used to be. Why then should not the same forces that have lessened the severity of a nominally progressive income tax operate in the future — talk of progressivism and practice of exceptionalism. But where would this projection of the present into the future leave our charitables? Safety first would suggest going along with the write-off: inequality in return for security. We think charitables would be better off *now* in trying to combine social equity with financial opportunity. If the future is to be like the present, charitables interested in maximizing their resources still would be best off with the percentage-contribution bonus.

The distribution of income to charitables is shifted by eliminating the write-off and instituting the contribution bonus. On one hand, the effect of this shift is not as substantial as a first glance might suggest. Under reasonable assumptions, philanthropic support to higher education in 1970 would have been reduced by about $136 million (9 percent), from $1.53 billion to about $1.39 billion.[14] By raising the government bonus a couple of percentage points and by actively pursuing the broader base of potential contributors (about 71 million tax filers below the 40 percent tax bracket), the $136 million could be made up and higher education could be kept whole.

Elite institutions, which depend on big contributions for a very large part of their income, have reason to worry about the contribution bonus. Just as there are no free lunches, there is no painless way to deprive people of things they never should have had. No one, given a choice today, would choose deliberately (or would publicly defend) subsidizing the rich a lot and the poor a little or not at all. But the beneficiaries have gotten used to being benefited. Our "inequity" is their "security." The problem, then, is how to move them from a position they know to be bad to one we believe to be better without threatening their future. That is why we recommend a "buyout" of the affected interests to permit a voluntary transfer from an unjust and illegitimate method, the income-tax write-off, to a just and legitimate one, the donor-directed automatic percentage-contribution bonus. In effect, by insuring potential losers against loss, by giving them time to see if, in fact, they might not actually do better for themselves, we might facilitate an integrative solution. Virtue would become, at long last, its own reward.

It may be that our ideas as to what is desirable have affected our judgment as to what is feasible. Were a method for securing governmental support of charity being designed today, however, we do not believe that anyone would even consider the tax write-off. The choice would be between a tax credit and a contribution bonus, the former being easier to administer, the latter being more equitable. If government also had a negative income tax, so that everyone was covered by the system, tax credits would become much more desirable.

But we all live in a world we never made and must proceed from where we are rather than from where we would like to be. Even so, nothing appears in the percentage-contribution bonus to raise unmanageable political obstacles, whereas there is a great deal in the system that should call forth protest.

To get charitables to prefer the contribution bonus as the best of all feasible alternatives, it would be helpful to test its constitutionality and its effects on administrative costs. What would such a test look like? How can we experiment while leaving open the option to disregard the bonus should it be unconstitutional or ill designed to serve the requirements of charitables?

TESTING THE PERCENTAGE-CONTRIBUTION BONUS

Any test must run the gauntlet between the rigors of scientific inquiry and the realities of institutions. The test must be designed to tell us what we need to know, but not to upset institutional processes; if so, the test no longer covers what we don't know but only demonstrates what we want to prove.

The most effective way for the government to test the contribution bonus is to try it on a small scale, while leaving the tax write-off untouched. An amount of anywhere from $0.5 billion to $2.0 billion could be appropriated for each of three years. This fixed sum, directed by the contributions of private individuals, would go to charitables as a bonus, each charitable getting a share of the bonus depending upon the amount of private contributions it received — the more private contributions, the greater the bonus for that charity.

This experiment would allow the constitutionality of the bonus to be tested in the courts. If the bonus is deemed unconstitutional, the test could be dropped with the tax write-off remaining operative and undisturbed. If the bonus is deemed constitutional, then administrative costs for government to implement the percentage-contribution bonus could be determined accurately in a real-world setting. But the proposed test certainly will lead to inequities over the three-year period. Some contributors will have control over two bonuses — the tax write-off plus a percentage bonus allotted to their favorite charity. Other contributors (nonitemizers and nonfilers) will control only the percentage bonus.

But this three-year transitional inequity is the price that must be paid for more lasting equity among charitable contributors. Any test that attempts to apply the contribution bonus only to a particular group — nonitemizers, nonfilers, or both — suffers four severe problems. First, the results of the test for determining administrative costs would be applicable only to that group of contributors. We would remain uninformed about the administrative costs that would result from contributions by those now taking the tax write-off. Second, the cost of separating people who could direct the contribution bonus to charitables from those who could not would be prohibitive. Charitables would have to maintain separate lists of donations according to whether or not contributors used the write-off. Third, constitutionality would be in greater jeopardy precisely because particular groups had been singled out for special treatment. Fourth, and last, the validity of this experiment would be questioned on the grounds that it was not applied to everyone the way the percentage contribution bonus would be "in real life."

We think the percentage-contribution bonus is good enough now to become the vehicle for governmental support of charity. If others disagree, however, they can support a small-scale, time-bound test that should help all of us go from where we are to where we ought to be.

NOTES

1. This chapter was written for The Commission on Private Philanthropy and Public Needs. For their criticisms and constructive comments, including those with which we disagreed, we express our appreciation to Professors John McNulty and Lawrence Stone, Law School, and Professors Arnold Meltsner and William Niskanen, Graduate School of Public Policy, all of the University of California (Berkeley).

2. Harry C. Kahn "Philanthropic Contributions," in *Personal Deductions in the Fed-*

eral Income Tax. A study by the National Bureau of Economic Research. (Princeton: Princeton University Press, 1960), pp. 87–91.

3. Paul R. McDaniel. "Federal Matching Grants for Charitable Contributions: A Substitute for the Income Tax Deduction," *Tax Law Review*, Vol. 27, No. 3 (Spring 1972), pp. 377–413.

4. Harry C. Kahn, op. cit.; Stanley S. Surrey, "Federal Income Tax Reform; The Varied Approaches Necessary to Replace Tax Expenditures with Direct Governmental Assistance," *Harvard Law Review*, Vol. 84, No. 2 (December 1970), pp. 352–408; Paul R. McDaniel, op. cit.; Joseph A. Pechman and Benjamin A. Okner, *Individual Income Tax Erosion by Income Class*. Reprint 230 (Washington, D.C.: Brookings Institution, 1972).

5. Michael K. Taussig. "Economic Aspects of the Personal Income Tax Treatment of Charitable Contributions," *National Tax Journal*, Vol. 20, No. 1 (March 1967), pp. 1–19; Robert A. Schwartz, "Personal Philanthropic Contributions," *Journal of Political Economy*, Vol. 78, No. 6 (November/December 1970), pp. 1264–1291; Gerard M. Brannon, *The Effect of Tax Deductibility on the Level of Charitable Contributions and Variations on the Theme.* (Prepared for Fund for Public Policy Research, Washington, D.C., 1974); Martin Feldstein, *On the Effects of the Income Tax Treatment of Charitable Contributions: Some Preliminary Results*, December 20, 1973, *Research Papers*, Vol. III, Special Behavioral Studies, Foundations and Corporations, sponsored by the Commission on Private Philanthrophy and Public Needs, Department of the Treasury, 1977.

6. The total private cost for charitable contributions was $9.6 billion ($12.9 billion minus $3.3 billion). The government subsidy was $3.3 billion. Therefore, the average government subsidy is 35 percent ($3.3 billion/$9.6 billion).

7. It is not possible to calculate the amount of this bonus because no estimate has been made of the total charitable contributions made by those not filing tax returns. Attempts to estimate the total contribution by multiplying an average contribution per nonfiler by the number of nonfilers is not possible either. This is because no reliable estimate is available of the number of individuals not filing tax returns (per conversation with Joseph Pechman, The Brookings Institution, August 1974).

8. Tilton v. Richardson, 403 U.S. 672 (1971).

9. Boris I. Bittker, "Charitable Contributions: Tax Deductions or Matching Grants?" *Tax Law Review*, Vol. 28, No. 37 (1972).

10. Paul R. McDaniel, op. cit. The percentage of the federal match ranges from 5 percent for persons giving 2 percent of their incomes to charity to 50 percent for those giving more than 10 percent.

11. The necessity of a personal incentive to ensure that contributions are reported should not be underestimated. Even with the tax write-off, in which personal gains from reporting can be realized, it is unlikely that all possible contributions are itemized. Some people just forget. Certainly the Bank of America appears to recognize this: they have introduced personal checks with a tax-deduction reminder that allows the individual to check off the appropriate deduction on the front of the check.

12. As previously indicated, the actual cost to the Treasury was $3.325 billion, but for ease in calculation we have rounded ahead to $3.4 billion. This rounding in no way affects our conclusions.

13. A special word about the sliding matching grant. Table 14.5 provides a comparison of the sliding matching grant and the contribution bonus. On all criteria for each of the three groups, the sliding matching grant performs at the same level as or at a lower level than the bonus. Under the sliding matching grant, donors are worse off in equity, pluralism, and reciprocity; charitables may have smaller

total flows, government legitimacy is less, and its efficiency is reduced because of higher administrative costs. Because the sliding matching grant is constantly outperformed by the contribution bonus, it will be excluded from further analysis.

14. In 1970, higher education received about $1.53 billion in contributions. Julian Levi and Sheldon Steinbach, *Patterns of Giving to Higher Education, 1970–71* (Washington, D.C.: American Council on Education). The contribution bonus affects only about $434 million, that portion which is given by individuals in the form of cash. About 75 percent of the individual cash donations ($326 million) came from wealthy contributors (over the 38 percent tax bracket) and the remaining 25 percent ($108 million) from the middle- and lower-income groups. If about 60 percent of the flow from the wealthy is a tax subsidy then their private costs are $130 million ($326 × 40%) and for the middle- and lower-income group, if about 20 percent is a tax subsidy, then their private costs are about $86 million ($108 × 80%). Each dollar contributed gets a 38 percent bonus, hence the flow of cash contributions to higher education from the wealthy is $179 million ($130 + ($130 × 38%)) and from the middle income group $119 million ($86 + 38%)). Total flow of cash contributions is $298 million ($179 + $119). The cash reduction to higher education is about $136 million ($434−$298) and therefore the overall reduction in revenues is about 9 percent ($136/$1,530 × 100%).

CHAPTER 15

DISTRIBUTION
OF URBAN SERVICES

Are policy analysts "hired guns"? Do they sell themselves to the highest bidder, and recommend whatever their clients desire? By the very nature of the craft, this task actually is not easy to do. Analysts, when asked to help solve a problem, are likely to reformulate it: this problem cannot be solved within our limitations, but here is one like it that we can do something about. By altering the means, the ends are altered, whether that is acknowledged or not.

The client may insist on a specific solution, which a heroic analyst believes to be wrong: "Don't do it," this analyst will insist. Suppose, however, that other analysts do identify with the interests of their clientele, or that analysts believe that carrying out orders in the present will lead to good results in the future. Or suppose our analysts have families and cannot afford to be unemployed; nobody ever said life was easy.

In practice, analysts as experts are more likely to follow their own values than to have preferences imposed upon them. For one thing, analysts — usually familiar with the tendencies of clients — as often as not choose to go where values seem compatible. For another, clients often are in doubt about which policies will serve their purposes. One reason why clients may want analysis is to find out how to connect opportunities with interests.

The more productive question for us, therefore, is not how innocent analysts can be corrupted, but how their own values enter into the making of policy. Now, the difficulties the public policy is to alleviate can be found somewhere out there in society. People experience distress, which is a subjective state of individual citizens, reflecting an implied contrast between experienced reality and expectations. These difficulties usually are not defined by analysts but experienced by people, and, if the political system works well, communicated to politicians. In a democracy, citizens and not analysts define individual difficulties.

When difficulties are confronted by potential solutions, however, the connections between individual experience and social action become problematic. What is or is not a problem depends on whether it is possible to forge a link between the difficulty and the instruments available for overcoming it. Ideology enters. For actions to be considered appropriate depends both on whether those deeds are technically possible and seen as desirable. Plague indeed is a difficulty, but it is not a problem for public policy unless there are known ways of attacking it. The inequitable distribution of income is a problem only if government is able to alter it and if it is considered permissible for government to make the attempt. Deciding, then, whether a problem is or is not considered one of public policy involves not only public reaction to events but also conflict about the propriety of the government's stepping in.

Many of the most important decisions are not so much made as recorded. They are not so much individual decisions as systemic results. The results of individual choices may be added up but that is not the same as directly doing what is desired. Making something that had heretofore been a resultant, a cumulative consequence of social interaction, into a matter of conscious social choice is a major undertaking. Up till now, the difference between federal taxes imposed on citizens in various states and the federal expenditures made there has been a resultant. Either this disparity has been ignored or it has been treated as the mere addition of amounts due to population movement (old people moving to Florida to collect social security), or climate (aerospace engineers liking California), or efficiency (consolidation of services in Georgia), and so on. Now, however, senators from the Northeast and Midwest have begun to coalesce around the question of regional distribution, converting a former resultant into conscious choice. If problem finding is part of problem solution, as I have argued, analysts, at least part of the time, are in the business of creating the problems to which they then will propose solutions. Criteria can create problems. Applying yardsticks such as equity or efficiency or equality of opportunity to government programs may point up disparities between the actual and the desirable, for which remedies may then be proposed. Whether or not citizens or officials previously recognized these disparities, the gaps between actual and possible may then become problems for which solutions are sought.

The act of analysis — asking not only how things work now but how they might work better (according to criteria supplied by the analyst as well as the client) in the future — is one of creating problems as well as solving them. True enough, about some problems citizens' or officials' knowledge is so sharp that it remains only to apply clear and consistent criteria to dependable data, but naturally these are not the most important or interesting examples. For reasons that will become evident — contradictions among goals, fuzziness in formulating and applying criteria, doubts about relevance of data — analysts often become finders of their own problems, as well as solvers of other people's problems.

There is a difference between problems as presented, and as transmuted through the search for answers. My colleagues and I in the Oakland Project (I hereby introduce our illustrative analyses) did try to provide solutions for problems in libraries, education, and streets, about which Oakland officials were aware.[1] We did try to supply mechanisms through which the cost of circulating books could be decreased, the school budget increased, and street repair improved. In this attempt, however, we had to grapple with causes — unresponsive professional personnel in libraries, the unfortunate interaction of rules on external spending with internal school administration, unintended deprivation of older and poorer areas in street repair — causes with consequences that inexorably came to matter to us. Our use of different criteria, or our new approach to applying standards, or the different weights we gave to criteria all became part of the problem, because we were enmeshed in the solutions.

Consider government as a decision-making mechanism. The decisions produce outputs. Officials dispense these outputs to citizens and we define the activity as a distribution of outputs, and the pattern of distribution as allocation of resources. When anyone evaluates this distribution or pattern, we refer to outcomes. To inquire about an outcome's effect is to ask how the lives of individual citizens will be altered by governmental action in the future.

We concentrate here on the government's distribution of goods and services to the citizens of Oakland, California. We wanted to find out how such agencies as schools, libraries, and streets allocate their outputs among groups in the city, and what made any agency allocate its outputs in a particular way. We asked how the distribution of agency outputs produced outcomes that affect different kinds of people, and how to alter those outputs so as to change those outcomes. But before doing so we had to distinguish among decisions, outputs, outcomes, and influences of public organizations.

Decisions are choices among alternative courses of action. Who made a decision, and how? We can try to understand why one choice was made and others were not, by focusing on officials who made decisions and the procedures that bring about their choices. Or we may shift from decision to outputs — from organizational choice to organizational production. The question then is: what do particular choices lead an organization to produce?

This interest leads naturally to identifying outputs, that is, goods and services that the organization produces: the number of books available or taken out, students who graduate with high school degrees, miles of city streets resurfaced. Outputs, then, are the way to classify goods and services supplied by a public agency and received by (or directed at) the public. Thus one can be reasonably objective about outputs. People may disagree about which outputs are important, but agreement should be general on what an output is, how it is measured, and what the quantities are (within a reasonable margin of error).

But our investigation will go further, to the uncharted territory of outcomes, and focus instead on the citizen-consumers of goods and services.

Our evaluation of outcomes includes a subjective element because human preferences are involved. We are the evaluators, studying the distribution of outputs precisely in order to make normative judgments. Should outputs be distributed in other ways or in different proportions? Are consequences of these outputs good (or bad) for various people differently situated? Should people who are worse off be made better off? The appearance of "should" signals going beyond "facts" into "values." We will make our criteria for judgment as clear and explicit as possible, and argue for them as persuasively as we know how, but there is (and must be) plenty of room for disagreement; other yardsticks might result in different valuations. Or the applicability of several criteria to the same distribution of outputs might lead to varying appraisals of how the combined consequences of using these criteria should be evaluated.

We want to explain outcomes by their most immediate causes, at least partly because the more remote the causes, the harder they are to disentangle. Our other main interest is to suggest how outcomes might be altered. Organizational change demands that active participants be able to manipulate variables they can control. The variables should be on hand and available in the present. For the same reason, we recognize (but find irrelevant) causal factors beyond anyone's immediate control, or too "lumpy" or highly aggregated for anyone to manipulate. The idea is to make the study of outcomes relevant to potential change in public policy.

We will focus on four questions: What are the patterns of resource distribution? Why do agencies distribute resources as they do? By what criteria are agencies to be judged? How might outcomes be altered?

PATTERNS OF RESOURCE DISTRIBUTION

There is an adage that the rich get richer and the poor get poorer, but in our work we found a pattern of distribution that favored both extremes. Some mechanisms were biased toward the rich; others favored the poor. We discovered no examples of mechanisms that benefit the middle.

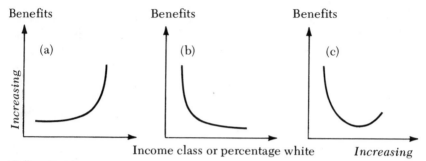

FIGURE 15.1
ALTERNATIVE DISTRIBUTIONS of BENEFITS by INCOME CLASS

The distribution of outputs follows a pattern that lends itself to graphic display. The three graphs in Figure 15.1 demonstrate.

Benefits (teachers per student, dollars of street-repaving funds per neighborhood, books per student) are placed on the vertical axis, and income class or percentage white (of the school or neighborhood or library-area residents) are placed on the horizontal axis.

Some output distributions benefit mostly the rich — the J shape of (a); some benefit primarily the poor — the L shape of (b); and some benefit both the rich and the poor but not the people between — the U shape of (c).

With specific reference to schools, in 1969 and 1970 the observed distribution of salary dollars versus neighborhood income level had a U shape. Upper-income, predominantly white schools enjoyed a relatively high level of salary dollar per student. Class sizes in these schools were average, but in experience and degrees the faculty were substantially above average. Their high qualifications resulted in high average salaries. Low-income schools also receive a high level of salary dollars per student. Teachers there had relatively little experience and degree attainment, which brought relatively low salaries. But the low salaries were outweighed by small class sizes provided through compensatory programs. Schools between these two extremes — those neither rich enough to attract teachers with long experience nor poor enough to qualify for compensatory programs — had to make do with relatively few salary dollars per student.

In 1970 and 1971 a new policy on allocating Oakland's teachers equalized salary dollars per student in all schools before compensatory resources were considered. When compensatory personnel were added, the distribution had an L shape: high salary dollars per student in the poorest schools; lower, but equal salary dollars per student in all other schools.

In searching out the allocation procedures of the street department, again we asked: do upper-income neighborhoods receive more resources than lower-income neighborhoods? Second: how does the allocation between neighborhood streets compare with the select street system of major arterial highways?

Both construction and resurfacing disbursements were analyzed. Two-thirds of Oakland's street mileage were classified local (not select), but between 1960 and 1971 these received only 6 percent of improvement expenditures. Why? Because much of the money for reconstructing streets comes from the state's apportionment of gasoline-tax revenues, which are earmarked for select streets. Besides, the professional standards of street-department engineers favor such allocation. Hence the rich hill areas received new construction money because the land was under development, and some poor areas received federal money through urban-renewal projects. Result: very little money for the rest of the city, and a U-shaped distribution curve.

The investigation into library procedures resembled the inquiry into schools: poor versus wealthy receipt of resources. And, peculiar to the library system: do branch libraries get more or less in resources than the central library?

We concluded that the library left all users worse off. Also, casual readers were disadvantaged compared with users of specialized collections; branch users in poor neighborhoods fared worst of all.

Compared with other large California cities, Oakland spent a relatively high proportion of its library budget on personnel, relatively little on acquisition of new books. In fact, after the initial work on the study was completed, a new head librarian began reallocating budget money toward books and away from overly-professionalized staffing.

The library formerly had allocated new acquisition funds by circulation. Upper-income branch libraries carried books their clients liked to read, hence high circulation and share of funding. It was the opposite for lower-income branches, which did not stock black-history books and civil-service exam manuals; hence low usage and low funding.

Indeed, the outlook of the staff itself promoted this pattern of resources. Library personnel felt their purpose was to serve the walker-in, not to promote service ("huckstering"), even less to reach out to the potential user. The resulting distribution had a J shape, favoring the well-to-do, especially the scholarly.

THREE PATTERNS: THE MORE, THE MORE; COMPENSATION; AND RESULTANTS

Three patterns of outputs became particularly noticeable. One of them David Riesman calls "the more, the more." New library acquisition funds go to those who already read. Roads go only where the cars already travel. Experienced teachers transfer to the well-to-do schools. It is as the scriptures say: "For to every one who has will more be given, and he will have abundance; but from him who has not even what he has will be taken away" (Matt. 25:29).

A second, opposite pattern is compensation. The poorest schools receive extra resources from the state and federal governments. Streets in the poorest neighborhoods are repaved as part of an urban-renewal project. A Chicano neighborhood, Fruitvale, gets funds for its own Spanish-language library.

A third pattern we shall call resultants, patterns that no one intends. We may like some of the patterns we see. We may dislike others. But many of these patterns do not represent conscious policy choices. They result from a multitude of influences that interact in unforeseen ways: bureaucrats pursuing their own immediate objectives, federal and state legislators passing special programs, local agencies chronically short of money; the list is endless. Even where straightforward discrimination is seen there often are no villains, just a number of professionals, administering other people's intentions along with their own, and unaware of the consequences of these professional actions. To examine the issue of discrimination, let us look again at the street engineers.

The broader social implications of emphasizing construction of major streets were beyond the engineers' competence. Street personnel did not object to neighborhood improvements; they just did not think it was as important as moving traffic through. So far as we can tell, the engineers did not consciously discriminate. If they turned down repair of streets in ghetto areas, they objected also to providing "frills" for Broadway merchants that did not also enhance the flow of traffic. Traffic circulation was the master for Oakland's street engineers and they served it well.

How can we explain the apparent discrimination in favor of richer dwellers in the hill areas? Hill dwellers were in a better position to benefit from the major streets favored by the street department. They got more of the limited paving funds, partly because they were better at making phone calls, partly because the street department let the utilities influence paving decisions. Individual procedures all were neutral; only the outcome was discriminatory.

The poor are not alone as objects of discrimination. How might one explain to the nearly poor or working-class parent that his children are the worst off in resources devoted to education? No one intends to disadvantage these children but it happens anyway. Children from upper-income families get experienced teachers, and parents supplement the schools' supply budget. The very poorest students receive substantial compensatory inputs from federal programs especially designated for that purpose. When the state required these funds to be concentrated, with each child receiving $300 of additional resources, the motivation was understandable. The state did not want compensatory funds dissipated by giving just a little more to each poor student. But the overall shortage of funds meant the district had to reduce the number of students in the program. Those who were needy, but not the most needy, were hurt. Restrictions on outside funds are responsible for pure anomalies. Suppose an Oakland citizen learned that the school district was increasing the length of kindergarten sessions and proposing to decrease the high school day. Suppose that person learned that the district was reducing maintenance expenditures in regular schools and simultaneously planning an elaborate rehabilitation of two dropout-prevention schools. In each situation, our citizen might reasonably conclude that these decisions represented preferences of school administrators: that an increment of time spent in kindergarten was worth more than the extra high school period, that dropout-prevention schools were in more need of repair than other schools.

Nothing of the sort would be true. The school department wanted resources to distribute; the state gave a bonus for increasing the kindergarten day and provided a restricted tax to fund dropout-prevention schools. Reduction of the high school day and cutting down general maintenance gave the district badly needed money for other purposes. Naturally, a decision once made must be defended at least partially on substantive merits. The original confusion is compounded by efforts to rationalize a decision, made to maximize income, by arguments about desirable educational policy that belong to an entirely different realm.

It would be nice to say that if these patterns do not reflect local preferences, at least they do include state and federal preferences. Yet we know that often they do not. Outside money (for agencies that can obtain it) comes from various sources. Each source dates from a different era and has different rules attached. The original motivation behind any individual program is easy to understand. The federal government or the state legislature wants to specify a result — to emphasize arterial highways, to lengthen the kindergarten day. By making incentives sufficiently advantageous, or penalties sufficiently onerous, governments can and do get their way; passionate beliefs of the moment pass into legislation. But each program interacts with others and conditions change. The result here is that the seventh- and eighth-grade tax financed high expenditures for two grades in a time of financial crisis for the rest of the system; and that restricted gas-tax revenues expanded major arterial streets in an era of interest in ecology and mass transit.

AN EXPLANATION

Our analysis of these patterns starts with the names we have given them — compensations, resultants, the more, the more — but to complete the explanation we must observe the government official. Our bureaucrat, like all of us, watches over his own welfare, and views his agency's policies as affecting that welfare. This official is interested in agency clients primarily as those clients affect the agency and, through the agency, his own welfare. Our bureaucrat cares about his profession, another aspect of the outside environment, as a source of guidance for internal conduct and as a means of furthering his mobility, thus increasing his welfare. Other people may be directly connected with distribution of an agency's resources in the city; not so our bureaucrat, to whom the shape of the resource distribution is a by-product of pursuing personal objectives.

What are this bureaucrat's goals? He wants to serve the public during a secure career free from a lot of personal conflict. This official expects a stable, perhaps advancing income for the foreseeable future and personal gratification for meeting public needs. Our bureaucrat's personal goals cannot be reconciled unless the organization is stable. If not, neither the economic nor the psychic income of this individual is likely to increase; actually, one may have to be sacrificed to the other. The bureaucrat's professional values link his own income with service to the citizen. Our bureaucratic everyman does good by acting professionally, is rewarded by promotion, and receives a portion of the surplus the organization has accumulated.

The bureaucrat must make some sense of his organizational environment, which exists to absorb, process, and reduce data to manageable form. Yet this official often must act without theory specifying relationships between inputs and outputs or criteria informing him of what is relevant. Our bureaucrat deals with this uncertainty by vastly oversimplifying his view of the environment, and by devising operational procedures that greatly decrease the need for information. This bureaucrat accordingly will limit the agency's actions to clients who present actual demands — a small portion of its potential clients.

Our bureaucrat, then, loath to stimulate his environment, will try to keep his relationships with it as quiet and as stable as possible. He will rely upon what we will call Adam Smith rules: when a customer makes a "request," take care of that client in a professional manner; otherwise, leave him alone. We place the word "request" in quotes because we use it in the sense that high book circulation is a request to libraries, and heavy traffic, a request to the street department. Adam Smith rules do not require our bureaucrat to have more contact with the public than necessary to advance objectives. Together with professional standards, Smithian rules also serve the organizational imperative to simplify decision-making and reduce uncertainty.

Now, organizations might seek to shape their environments — bureaucrats long have been accused of being empire builders. But the desired growth must be clearly understood. Is it growth that will increase the resources of the organization in step with the demands placed on it? That is good. Or does growth increase clients and services without providing corresponding resources? That is bad. Advancement within an expanded organization must not be pursued at the risk of collective impoverishment from which all members will lose.

The agencies we describe are not notably heroic. Bureaucrats often are shrinking violets who prefer to adjust to conflict with the environment.[2] Why should they struggle? Their appropriations do not, in general, depend upon the number of people they serve. Even though a bureaucrat wants his agency to grow, he does not see increasing his clientele as a means to that end. Hence that official has no particular incentive to drum up more business. At any rate, the more people agencies service, the more it costs to provide that service, and the more professional quality is threatened, the more undesirable it is to take on more customers.

Professional standards have the additional advantage of appearing to be fair. Hiring qualified librarians, moving traffic, and setting equal class sizes all seem reasonable and appropriate. Such criteria orient professionals to apparently worthy goals (quality libraries and safe roads) within their competence. The public should be well served. Yet somehow these benevolent norms and the Adam Smith rules, which ought to help everyone, end up helping some more than others.

Adam Smith rules, like so many "neutral" decision rules, are not truly neutral, but have a class bias. To understand this bias, we must recognize that the rules themselves are part of the professional and organizational norms. Professional norms set convenient standards of competence and quality performance but organizational norms provide a means for the agency to adjust to its environment. Operationally, the norms converge when the bureaucrat uses a rule to allocate the city's resources; and use of these rules encourages the pattern of "the more, the more." Now that we see the bureaucrat as a twentieth-century Adam Smith, let us reconsider the behavior of our three agencies.

ADAM SMITH IN ACTION

How would our bureaucrat function in the libraries? To secure his own career, he wanted the library to grow. But in practice this official could do little about it. The municipal budget for libraries was fixed. There was little chance for our bureaucrat to increase it either by appeals to the city council or by obtaining outside funds (which generally were unavailable). But also the budget was safe; there was no real fear the city council would cut it just because circulation was lacking.

Our bureaucrat also would want to do his job in the "right" or professional way. In fact, Oakland libraries were almost a pathological case of such professionalization. The head librarian, an aggressive personality, tried to impose professional standards by maximizing his own internal discretion. His main interest came to be hiring librarians with appropriately certified qualifications. Once in the system, those employees would apply the head librarian's own brand of professional standards to decisions such as selection of books, division of resources between central and branch libraries, and the professional qualifications of staff at branch libraries. The criteria allowed the library to keep up its specialized collections and keep out disturbing influences. Even in the branches, books of a "flighty" or temporary character were not allowed to enter the system, because branch personnel were unlikely to order them, and supervisory personnel would not have approved the requests. In any event, personnel who observed these norms imperfectly were screened out.

The library's handling of the environment is an excellent example of an Adam Smith rule: allocate new acquisition funds to the branches with the highest circulation. The initiative lies with the customer, as library patrons "vote" with their cards. The more books they take out, the more money their branch receives.

We can imagine different rules. The library could have allocated funds for new acquisitions equally per capita. Or the system could have allocated funds by circulation and unfulfilled requests. Under this system, branches in poorer neighborhoods, with many unfulfilled requests for civil-service manuals and black-history books, would have gotten better treatment. Branch libraries in poor neighborhoods might then have done more in the way of letting the neighborhood know where the library was and what it had to offer.

But all these strategies ("market research") would have gone against the professional attitudes of top staff. From the time the libraries were founded, librarians assumed that people either were — or were not — motivated to read. People who already used the library — people of quality — would benefit from the professional standards applied to book selection; librarians value what people like themselves read. Among their peers, librarians at the top no doubt took pride in their specialized collections and "quality books."

The library was able to rely so heavily on professional norms and Adam Smith rules because it was left alone. Nobody really bothered it, including its own commission of governing citizens; for many years, the library was free to be its own client, allocating resources by referring to national standards rather than to preferences of Oakland citizens, which were not strongly expressed.

How would our bureaucrat behave in the street department? He would find it easy to pursue his goal of agency growth. Unlike librarians, street engineers have access to substantial amounts of outside money on which the agency can expand. The most prominent source is the state gasoline-tax fund. Other funds include county road-building revenues and federal urban-renewal monies. The engineers also have clear professional norms that they wish to impose. These people simply want to move the largest number of cars at the highest speed possible, subject to considerations of safety.

Hypothetically, outside funds and professional norms could have clashed. In fact, they meshed. The major source of street-department monies — gasoline-tax revenues — completely coincides with professional norms. The legal restriction that limits those funds to the "select street system" ensures that the money will be spent only on streets with heavy traffic. The same reasoning holds for the way in which the county distributes its gasoline-tax funds. Only allocation of urban-renewal funds, a minor exception, runs against the engineers' norms. A good portion of those funds goes for rebuilding streets in poor urban-renewal areas where traffic will not be heavy after the renewal is completed.

Once again, Adam Smith is at work: put the money where the cars are. Traffic flow will be maximized by improving roads already heavily traveled. With this norm for justification, engineers can remain confident that they are making essentially professional decisions, and can look back to miles of physical accomplishment. Those people can point to impressive statistics about the number of vehicles moved. Moreover, that set of norms is reinforced by the restrictions placed upon the gasoline-tax money. This Adam Smith rule, too, has an allocational bias.

Maximizing traffic flow in Oakland provides well-to-do commuters (including those who live outside Oakland) with routes from their homes to their offices. The poorer citizens are left with transportation that does not improve over the years. By using this Adam Smith rule, the engineers can circumvent the question of who needs to get from one place to another. Street personnel simply take for granted that traffic already is in the right place. Citizens with the most mobility go farther and those who have least mobility get left behind.

Sometimes the poor do benefit because of Adam Smith. When a major facility, such as the airport, was located in a poor area, the more, the more principle worked for the poor. New streets were built and old ones repaired to service those facilities. The business section did not get the street modifications it wanted because downtown streets didn't have the necessary traffic. Once a neighborhood has something, for whatever reason, it gets more. The trick, apparently, is to get more earlier so that one can get more later.

The street department allocated its resurfacing resources also by using Adam Smith rules. One rule was simple: resurface streets that caused most complaints to the street department and the city council. Another rule was more involved. Because it was undesirable for a street to be resurfaced and then broken up again for utility work, the two activities had to be related in some way. The street department achieved coordination by sending the public utilities a list of possible resurfacing projects. The utilities then crossed off those projects in locations where they expected to work in the next five years. We call this an Adam Smith rule, for again the agency let someone else take the initiative for a decision.

Like other examples of Adam Smith rules, the resurfacing priorities had some allocational bias. Despite talk about organizing the poor, well-to-do neighborhood streets generated more complaints than similar streets in poor neighborhoods. Similarly, utility facilities in the poor areas were older and subject to frequent breakdown. The utility company therefore was more eager to work on those streets in the immediate future, making it unwise to resurface streets that would have to be torn up again. Giving the utilities a veto limited the resurfacing that could be done in poor areas.

We have saved the schools for last because they are our most complex story. Hiring a new school superintendent between 1969 and 1970 and 1970 and 1971 marked a change from an administration that had relied on Adam Smith rules to an administration that explicitly cared about distributing resources and designed allocation policies with such distribution in mind.

In the schools, our bureaucrat would have had ample opportunity to pursue a goal of expanding the agency. Federal compensatory funds, state compensatory funds, and numerous special programs and override taxes all provided revenue for growth without increasing the number of students. Our bureaucrat wanted also to impose specific professional norms. But these norms often were overridden through the constraints imposed by sources of funding. In the middle sixties, the Oakland school administration favored a variable class size ranging from thirty-four in high-achievement elementary schools to twenty-seven in schools with low achievement. But class sizes all were about thirty (excluding compensatory programs) shortly after the state passed its bonus regulation for class sizes. The seventh- and eighth-grade override tax set up an incentive for the city to spend substantially more on these grades while cutting back sharply on expenditures at all other levels.

Adam Smith rules were used in allocating supplies, teachers, and other personnel. If parents want to make direct contributions to the schools, let them. By the late sixties, the district's own supply budget had shrunk much; parental allocations then became important. The decision to let parents contribute to their children's schools meant that the distribution of supplies was being determined substantially not by the administration but by parental initiative. Teachers, as it were, allocated themselves. The policy of unrestricted transfers before 1970 and 1971 created a situation in which assignments were determined mostly by teachers' preferences. Like most agencies, the schools also did try to take citizens into account. Parental protest caused a number of security-guard positions to be added in the later sixties; parents also led the district to use its own funds to replace a compensatory program for Spanish-language students curtailed in 1969.

In 1970 and 1971 a new administration came in and adopted policies specifically aimed at evening out distribution of resources. The new administration substantially reduced the number of transfers approved, and adjusted the student-to-teacher ratios in poorer schools so that salary dollars per student (excluding compensatory personnel) were equal throughout the system. Distribution of supplies, however, remained unchanged.

JUDGING OUTCOMES

We have seen how Adam Smith rules work in determining patterns, such as the more, the more, but still we need a convenient handle for addressing the totality of agency performance. Where several patterns of distributing resources are followed, how should agencies be judged?

Because the issues were so complex, widespread expression of opinion by citizens about resource allocation within agencies was unlikely. The patterns of resource distribution are not self-evident to either citizen or bureaucrat; added to which, citizens' preferences are not likely to be on the same level as the allocation decisions bureaucrats make. Although citizen and bureaucrat can agree that more money should be spent on schools, the question is how much and for what specific purposes. No citizens' preference is there to serve as a criterion for judging agency allocations within those margins normally considered by decision-makers. Therefore, in our capacity as policy analysts, we will concentrate here on some standards of efficiency and equity that do permit discriminating judgments.

Efficiency

Our discussion of efficiency begins with a simple definition: an agency is inefficient if it can (but does not) produce more outputs for its budget. Are Oakland's agencies inefficient by this definition? By no means entirely, but in some areas they are, or were. Our answer depends, of course, on how we define an output. With that in mind, here are examples of allocative inefficiencies.

Consider the libraries. One output of the library system is circulation. A key to circulation is a lively, up-to-date stock of books. New books cost money, which could be found by reallocating funds in the budget. Our analysis of library staffing showed significant overqualification among the personnel. Many branch libraries had a staff of two or more professionals where one professional with a paraprofessional could have handled the work. High-salaried professionals often did clerical tasks. If staffing policies were adjusted to the actual work load, the savings in salary could be put toward new books.

The street department is another example. The department's engineers play down the use of cost information in decision-making. Costs are used as an engineering refinement after (but not before) most decisions on allocation are made. Assume that the output of the street department is as claimed by the engineers: maximizing the flow of traffic.

Implementing the goal raises a number of questions about allocation: Is it cheaper to repave a street in an early state of deterioration, or should repaving wait until deterioration is more advanced? Will traffic flow in the city be maximized by doing one large project or several smaller projects? Without heavy reliance on cost information, these questions have no answers.

So far, we have talked about inefficiency that flows from internal decisions. Inefficiencies also can be imposed from the outside, like the seventh- and eighth-grade tax and the four override taxes, which finance employees' health and pension benefits. The first tax distorts allocations among grade levels; the others distort bargaining settlements toward fringe benefits. School allocations would be improved if these monies were given to the district without restriction as to use.[3]

The definition of efficiency we have been using covers an increase in output — not recipients of that increase. That would be a question of distribution, which is contained in the economist's criterion of Pareto-optimality. For the agencies that interest us, Pareto-optimality implies allocation of resources so that nobody can be made better off without somebody else being made worse off. If there is reallocation of resources so that one person could be made better off and nobody made worse off, the agency is said to be Pareto-inefficient.

Suppose we apply Pareto-efficiency to the library and suppose we accept technological and political factors as settled. Libraries would be improved, in the sense of getting more output out of their input, if less funds went for personnel in the central library and more for new books in the branch libraries. But in each reallocation, some people — personnel or users of the central-library collection — clearly would lose. Although many arrangements may not benefit the majority of people, they are made because in each instance somebody does benefit. It is easy to talk about compensating losers but difficult to imagine how this would be done. The overall output of the library system might increase so much that the professionals who were thrown out of work could be compensated for their loss of employment. In practice, however, there are no mechanisms for accomplishing this sort of compensation.

By this reasoning, the libraries and our other agencies already are Pareto-optimal. There is no easy way out, in which no one ever gets hurt. There is little to suggest Pareto-inefficiency, meaning that some citizens could be better off and no one made worse off. If there were enough for everyone, there would be no need for allocation. Under Pareto-optimality, also, politics would have ended as soon as it had begun looking like the Polish Diet, where every member had an absolute veto. Only if we keep efficiency and distribution as simultaneous but separate criteria can we approach politics as we know it: people bargaining over expected gains and losses.

Equity

The second standard we shall apply to the distributions is one of equity. As with efficiency, equity has a number of specific meanings. In casual conversation, equity or fairness usually describes whether rich citizens get more than poor, or white citizens more than black. When we try to develop equity as a norm, the issue becomes more complex. Three possible standards of equity will illustrate our discussion.

The first standard we will call market equity. Under market equity an agency distributes resources to citizens in proportion to the taxes they pay. The agency's function is to produce services but not to engage in any redistribution. The agency's allocation resembles what would occur if the service were provided in the private market — say education produced by private schools — except that in this "market" the municipal agency may hold a monopoly position.

Figures for 1970 show that a family making from $5,000 to $15,000 pays about 6 percent of its income in property taxes, but a family making from $16,000 to $25,000 pays about 5 percent.[4] Suppose a family making $5,000 received one unit of a government service. The standard of market equity would specify that a family making $10,000 receive two units of the good, a family making $25,000 receive 4.2 units. Schools in poor neighborhoods would receive fewer dollars per student than schools in rich neighborhoods, and streets in poor neighborhoods would receive less repaving than streets in rich neighborhoods.

We will call a second equity standard equal opportunity. Here the agency distributes an equal dollar amount of resources to each citizen regardless of what he has paid in taxes.[5] Each neighborhood receives the same amount of street repaving, all schools enjoy the same expenditure per child, each library has the same staffing and new-acquisition allowance as every other in the city.

With property taxes roughly proportional to income, equal expenditure per person implies some redistribution. This redistribution is contained in the idea of equal opportunity and can be justified in a number of ways. A community may feel that education is an important socializing agency and that all children should be exposed to the same education even if upper-income families bear a disproportionate share of the cost.

The third standard is known as equal results: when the agency distributes its resources, the outcome is equal for each citizen. For libraries, equal results means dividing resources among branches so that all have equal per capita circulation. Similarly, the street department allocates its funds in such a way that all neighborhoods have streets in equal condition, and schools disperse their funds so that all children finish with the same reading ability.

Equal results involves more redistribution than does equal opportunity, because equal opportunity requires only that current inequalities be remedied, but equal results also calls for diminishing the effects of past inequalities. Equal results in education means that a child has to be compensated for his parents' inferior education (transmitted to the child in preschool years) or even for lack of parents. Equal results in streets means that the state would have to change its apportionment formulas of the gas tax so that older cities with older streets could get more money, rather than go on distributing money by population.

The conflict between equal opportunity and equal results has been prominent in the civil-rights movement.[6] When civil rights first gained national attention in the late fifties, the movement's goal was equal opportunity. Civil-rights advocates wanted everyone to be judged on ability, not on color, race, or national origin. Within this goal was the assumption that equal opportunity would produce equal results: if jobs were assigned for ability and not by criteria such as color, the proportion of blacks in any type of job would reflect their proportion in society at large.

By the middle sixties it became apparent that equal results did not flow automatically from equal opportunity. In education, children from poor families (which included most Negro families) came to school performing far below children from rich families.[7] Even when a school spent equal dollar amounts on all children throughout their education, the performance gap remained relatively constant and increased absolutely.

When those in the civil-rights movement began to realize that equal treatment did not make for equal results, demands shifted. Some demands still focused on means to an end, such as compensatory-education programs. Other demands struck directly at the ends, as in the call for hiring by racial quotas to ensure minority representation.

Equal results; the idea raises perplexing problems. Often it is not clear how the standard, even if adopted, could be enforced. It is impossible to accomplish objectives if one does not know how. If teachers knew what school inputs lead to an improvement in reading, they could calculate how much it would cost to raise the poor readers to equal the best; policy choices then could be made. The fact is, however, that the knowledge does not exist.

If equality of results in education cannot now be achieved by boosting the lower group up, it can be achieved by holding the higher group down. But who would suggest that the advantaged be held back deliberately in order to let the others catch up? Equal library circulation might be obtained by cutting down circulation (perhaps by letting the book stock become out of date) in upper-income areas. Compensatory education is one thing; preventing children from realizing their potential is quite another. Problems also are created by the way in which equal results mesh (or do not mesh) with other goals. The push for minority quotas in hiring suggests that if employers searched only for the most-qualified people, minorities would be underrepresented. Perhaps many of the best-qualified people would have been overtrained for the job so that appropriate minority employment would represent no falloff in job performance. But in many areas performance and proportional hiring conflict. Despite these difficulties, equal results has become one important standard by which to judge an agency's performance.

The equity standard a person chooses to measure is crucial in his judgment of an agency's performance. Consider two parents looking at current allocations in the Oakland school system. A well-to-do parent might look at the present allocation of funds and suggest that, if anything, it overfavored poor neighborhoods. Student-to-teacher ratios are lowest in low-income schools; these schools have specialists and extra supplies purchased with federal funds. By contrast, the richest schools have somewhat larger classes, fewer specialists, and practically no teacher aides. Any supplies they have beyond the small district allocation come through direct parental contributions. Thus the well-to-do parent concludes that the system is biased in favor of the poor.

A poor or minority citizen might come to a much different conclusion. This parent might acknowledge that dollar expenditures per pupil were higher in the poorest schools; yet he might feel that expenditures are a poor measure of outcomes. The poor citizen could argue that a more appropriate measure would be reading ability on standardized tests, claiming that as long as poor children read at lower levels than rich children (which is currently true) the allocation of resources favoring the low-income schools is insufficient.

As his standard, the rich citizen uses equality of opportunity; the poor citizen is using equality of results. By applying different yardsticks, these two parents arrive at opposite conclusions as to how the agency is performing with the same allocation.

For judging the performance of the three Oakland agencies, we summarize the three standards of equity in Table 15.1. Market equity implies the least redistribution. Equal results implies the most.

Where does each agency lie on this spectrum? The schools lie somewhere to the right of equal opportunity, and the street department to the left; the libraries lie somewhere to the left of the street department.

The rankings of the agencies in Table 15.1 reflect the influences of compensation and Adam Smith rules. The more access an agency has to restricted funds for compensatory treatment, the more its allocations will approach equal results. The more an agency relies on Adam Smith rules to distribute its resources, the more its allocations will approach market equity.

The library is least redistributive because it was extreme on both counts. The library system had less access to compensatory funds than either of the other two agencies. The library allocated its own budget by a combination of professional standards and Adam Smith rules, which clearly favored the well-to-do.

TABLE 15.1
THREE STANDARDS OF EQUITY FOR JUDGING OUTCOMES

	Market equity	Equal opportunity	Equal results
	⟶ Increasing redistribution ⟵		
Schools	The per child expenditure in each school should be proportional to the taxes paid by the neighborhood	Each child should receive equal dollar expenditure	Each child should receive enough expenditure so that all children read at the same level[a]
Libraries	The per resident expenditure in each branch should be proportional to the taxes paid by the neighborhood	Each branch should receive equal per capita expenditure	Each branch should receive enough expenditure so that circulation per capita is equal in all branches
Streets	The per resident expenditure on streets in each neighborhood should be proportional to the taxes paid by that neighborhood	Each neighborhood should receive an equal per capita (or per mile) expenditure	Each neighborhood should receive enough expenditure so that the condition of all neighborhood streets in the city is equal

[a] If not exactly the same level, at least an equal mean level for racial and income groups.

Before 1970, the school system was a kind of paradox. It had access to money for large compensatory programs, which shifted its allocations toward equal results. But the district allocated its own resources by Adam Smith rules, including rules for teacher assignments and supplies. These rules shifted the allocation back toward market equity. Beginning in 1970, a new administration eliminated these rules as they applied to teacher assignments. The result was a definite shift of the allocations toward equal results.

ALTERING OUTCOMES

Before answering our final question—how might outcomes be altered? — let us briefly review where we have been. Our argument is shown in Table 15.2, where we see that decision rules, such as Adam Smith behavior and constraints on federal and state funds, lead to decisions on allocation that favor major streets, the central library, and experienced

TABLE 15.2
OUTCOMES IN OAKLAND

Stages of government activity	Administrative behavior
Rules	Adam Smith rules Professional norms Federal and state funds Clientele requests
which lead to Decisions	Major versus minor streets Central versus branch libraries Parent contributions
analyzed as patterns of Outputs	Several distributions (U,J,L) The more, the more Compensation Resultants
to be evaluated as Outcomes	Inefficient Class bias Between market equity and equal opportunity Responsive to yesterday

teachers for some (but not other) Oakland schools. From these decisions, we discerned a number of patterns of resource distribution (particularly the more, the more), which we then evaluated as outcomes. Oakland's outcomes, we concluded were inefficient, had a class bias somewhere between the standards of market equity and equal opportunity, and were responsive to yesterday's demands. To alter outcomes, we must know first in what direction to proceed: therefore we state our preferences.

Our Preferences

Bureaucrats have to deal with the world as they find it and not as one might wish it to be. The decision-makers of today began their careers when public service meant simply doing an efficient job of handling the business that came to them. If asked why they did not seek equality of results, these decision-makers could say rightly they never had a mandate from the electorate or their administrative superiors to alter outcomes in favor of selected social groups; that is, to remake society. If some people use cars more than others or like to go to libraries, that is the way of the world; when patterns of income and reading habits change, Adam Smith rules will favor new users as much as they did the old. These rules are fair for citizens fortunate enough to have resources to make use of those rules. As society, in its mysterious ways, benefits larger numbers of citizens, citizens will then get a bonus in the shape of greater returns from municipal services.

This argument, however understandable in its time, is no longer acceptable. Oakland is a changing city. In 1940, racial minorities added up to less than 5 percent of its population. By 1970, the number had risen to 41 percent. Though some minority residents are in the middle-income group, many are poor. Poor citizens do not, in general, need libraries for scholarly research. This changing constituency should affect our agencies, and ultimately, public services have to serve the public.

Where, then, along the range from market equity to equal results, should these agencies attempt to place themselves? In offering our answer, we should remember that agencies do different things; we cannot expect the same prescription to fit each group.

The street department differs from libraries and schools in that it supplies all the output the citizen receives. Libraries and schools are supplemented by the home; the government is, for practical purposes, the sole supplier of roadways. If a neighborhood's streets are bad, it is because the department has let them deteriorate. This suggests that current department policy should be adjusted for past failures and move to something that approaches equal results. Streets, however, are an adjunct to the car, a consumer good that is bought in the market. It would not be unreasonable, therefore, for the street department to service citizens in proportion to auto ownership. To the extent that cars are unequally distributed, the street department then would favor the better off.

We have no easy way to resolve this conflict. But we can say that at least the street department should compensate poor neighborhoods for past inequality, and bring such shabby streets up to standards justified by their use. This means allocating both repaving funds and some new construction funds—judging by deterioration, not the number of complaints or the plans of the utility company. There would not be full equal results, for allocations ultimately would be based on traffic, and car users would still be favored over nonusers or lesser-users; but the street department would not be inculcating any bias that was not already present. (The irony is that as aesthetic standards change, having streets that attract traffic is fast becoming a detriment. By the time the poor get equal treatment, they may not want it.)

If the citizens of poor neighborhoods do not want improved streets for increased traffic, then the money could be spent in other ways. A number of neighborhoods in Oakland would be upgraded by sidewalks, curbs, and storm drains. Usually such situations are handled by special assessment levied on property owners, but, with absentee owners and poor tenants, such improvements are not forthcoming. With some changes in state and local law, the street department could start moving toward equal opportunity, and at the same time take these citizen's needs into account.

Securing equal results in libraries — equal circulation per citizen or size of neighborhood — is beyond anyone's present ability. The minimum requirement is to ensure equality of opportunity in access to reading material desired by different kinds of citizens. Beyond this, one can ask only for efforts to stimulate demand. If totally unsuccessful, libraries could retreat to the goal of equality of opportunity. If partially successful, libraries could push their efforts in some neighborhoods so far that services would begin to deteriorate for other citizens.

The schools are our simplest example, for current allocation there most resembles the kind of allocation we desire; this, however, calls for more substantial explanation.

To promote discrimination within a school district justified by a standard of market equity is wrong. Even if education influences life-chances less than previously thought, it should not hold people down. Letting market equity prevail would perpetuate the disadvantageous socioeconomic situation of some students.

A policy directed toward equal results presents different dilemmas. A primary problem is lack of knowledge; at this time no one knows how to improve the performance of low achievers significantly even if huge resources are made available. When we obtain this knowledge, we will face a second problem; in a world of limited resources, what we give low achievers is taken from high achievers. How do we balance this allocation? Often the question has racial overtones, but it need not. In any classroom, there is a substantial spread of abilities, typically larger than the spread between the average ability in rich schools and that in poor schools. How should a teacher allocate time in such a classroom? Is he or she to spend all the time with the poor readers and let the rich achievers fend for themselves? Is that teacher to divide time equally among all children? There are no easy answers.

If both market equity and equal results are suspect, a standard of equal opportunity probably is indicated — that is, equal expenditure per child. Equal opportunity has strong intuitive appeal as being fair on its face; it is a value shared by many citizens.

How should we resolve our uncertainty about the effect of compensatory measures: by doing less, because we see no hope of improvement? Or by doing more assuming that future evidence may provide room for more optimistic conclusions? We would do more if we thought it helpful. At least, favoring the worst off does not show that the best off are hurt by getting a little less. We can afford to chance a little more than we might if anyone obviously were being harmed.

Under conditions of risk, when a probability distribution of outcomes can be specified, we can make rational judgments relating proposed investments to likely returns. Under uncertainty, there are no such probabilities. Rather than not act at all, we need a reasonable way of hedging our bets. Experimentation immediately comes to mind. Why throw a large sum away if new knowledge could be gained by spending lesser amounts in a series of experiments? We agree; but there is more to it than that. Good experiments are not cheap, and an experiment usually requires a sizable control group. The whole idea (recall Sinclair Lewis's Arrowsmith) is that most do not get the serum or the new educational technique. Experiments impose high political costs because often they deprive people who already have less. For most of these persons, such experiments mean only that they go on not getting what they didn't have. Their usual reaction is annoyance at being guinea pigs.

Not merely the structure, but also the time horizon of these experiments works against the deprived. The idea behind each longitudinal study is to determine whether varying curriculum or class size produces lasting effects on reading or mathematical ability. The emphasis is on "lasting." Years must go by before the results, if any, are known. In the meantime, the way the deprived see it, nothing is happening. Worse still, the experiment is used as a justification for not doing more until the evidence is in and analyzed.

Despite the vogue for experimentation, some critical hypotheses cannot be tested, at least not right away or all at once. Suppose a tutorial reading program has not altered abilities over a three-to-five-year period. One hypothesis is that the theory or practice of the program leaves much to be desired. Another is that the subjects are recalcitrant. A third is that the program was not in operation long enough. A fourth is that more intensive effort — more aid or hours per student — would have paid off. Some of these hypotheses may be tested simultaneously (varying aid versus hours, for instance), but others (the longer-time theory), only by letting the process work its way into the future. How long, then, must the deprived wait?

Several kinds of experiments have been tried and others are now going on. A reasonable hedge against adversity would be to widen the distribution of resources modestly beyond equality of opportunity. In this way, as experiments go on, children who most need help will be getting some, and the other students, so far as anyone can know, will not be harmed. Maybe we ask too much of social policy too soon. Perhaps improvements will show up only over several generations.

It seems that we are back to the earlier distinction between outcomes and influences. Outcomes can be determined; we can discover whether equality of opportunity is being approximated. But compensatory action demands causal knowledge of effects — how does policy ultimately affect citizens? — that few can discover. We speak of outcomes precisely because the influence of policy is so difficult to discern. If we had to talk about influences, we could say only that we didn't know.

Another lesson is encapsulated here too. Amid the vagaries of the world it is well to do a little more than necessary now, on the off chance that it may turn out to be good policy in the future. When in doubt, as the old politicians used to say, do right. And, we now add, do a little more.

Looking at the question of equality from the vantage point of level of government, there is good reason to choose a division of labor in which the locals move to equality of opportunity and the federals move toward compensation. The obligation of local government is to afford each citizen genuine equality where local effects would be locally produced and felt. When local efforts are insufficient, it is desirable for the federal government to enhance the general equality of citizenry. That is what extra help is about.

Many advantages lie in using the federal government as a mechanism for redistribution. Disparities in relation to taxes paid and benefits received, and inequalities in expenditures per citizen, are far more evident at the local level. The greater distance between government and taxpayer, as well as the increased difficulty of connecting taxes with specific programs, make redistribution more feasible at the federal level. No citizen, unless willing to leave the country, can escape the reach of the federal government. But the citizen can move freely from one locality to another to escape conditions considered onerous or unfair. It is difficult for one city to engage in redistributive policies (which means taking resources from some citizens to give to others) unless other cities in that area do the same. The federal government, at least in theory, could take account of the anomalies among cities; no municipality could do so. Of course, it is easy to urge the federal government to redistribute; it is another matter to accomplish it.

Citizens and Bureaucrats

To alter outcomes it is necessary to change the stimuli to which bureaucratic actors respond. Bureaucratic stimuli can be changed in several areas. Work can be done to rationalize constraints on outside funding. The State of California already has relaxed some of the constraints that limit the rise of gasoline tax funds, but the state can go further in giving more discretion to local officials. Anomalous override taxes such as the seventh- and eighth-grade tax could be combined into the general fund. This would offer administrators additional flexibility in making allocative decisions, and would also make it easier to hold administrators responsible for what they have done.

Bureaucratic stimuli also can be changed by better citizens' political organization. Citizens predictably are interested in small variances that affect their immediate vicinity. When they protest against such variances, they are likely to be heard. The cost is little; the protesters are neighbors; and the demands on the city council or the board of education are couched as appeals of immediate interest to the parties. The school board (and the city council as well) likes to meet visible citizen demands that are limited both in scope and in financial commitments.

Citizens best able to understand city procedures and to organize themselves are in the best position to take advantage of this opportunity to seek redress of grievances. If every citizen adversely affected demanded special treatment, the broad line of policy might be modified enough to increase the general welfare.

Unfortunately, we know that few citizens seek and use these opportunities. Although the benefits gained are undoubtedly important to this minority, such benefits cannot change the overall patterns of allocations drastically. The street department accommodates itself to demands by altering its schedule, but not by changing basic priorities. More substantial changes might be secured if citizens were related to a major institution (such as the Redevelopment Agency) with sufficient muscle to alter allocation by its own activities. Institutions which can reduce costs by contributing funds to purchase rights-of-way or which can impose costs by increasing traffic will get their way.

Agencies are aware of public demand. Officials spend full time making decisions, collection information, finding out what other agencies are doing. The advantage of being an official appears in each of our studies. Take streets. The Federal Aviation Agency (FAA) is able to get street work done near the Oakland Airport because its people know what is happening and because FAA personnel can hint that traffic otherwise might be diverted to the rival San Jose airport. County officials, who distribute part of the gasoline-tax revenue, make their will felt by tugging on the purse strings. The Redevelopment Agency, acting through the city manager, claims additional land for new projects. It can do so only because the agency has a staff alert to the opportunity and because the city manager has an interest in helping it out. Political organization helps both by increasing the responsiveness of elected officials and by creating or supporting new agencies.

We have seen examples of citizens' protests keeping open imperiled small library branches. In schools, parents persuaded officials not to cut the sixth period out of the high school day and to retain an English-as-a-second-language program at a Chicano school even after federal funds for the program were cut. Oaklanders on Fifty-first Street, by playing the county against the city, first prevented and then expedited construction on that street as needs changed. Organizing citizens is not easy, but it does pay dividends if only because part of the course of least resistance for government is to take them into account in providing services.

Officials should be made aware of the way in which agency outputs are distributed. Calling for changes in attitude might be dismissed as utopian. Yet, we have witnessed movement in this direction. Beginning in 1970, the new school superintendent focused explicitly on distributing experienced teachers throughout the system. He cut down transfers drastically and reduced class sizes in schools that had less experienced staff. Experience was either allocated more evenly by class and race of school children, or they were compensated by lower pupil-to-teacher ratios. When the new city manager and head librarian were presented with criticisms of current allocations, these officials approved a budget that substantially increased expenditure on books while cutting back on staff. The street department engaged in discussion with the utilities, which could improve synchronization of their schedules, and reduce the likelihood of so many repaving projects being vetoed.

Professional norms are so important in determining outcomes that those of us responsible for educating these professionals may want to take a second look at the ways in which these norms are developed. Professional engineers do not have to be so single-minded about circulation of traffic, but can be educated to understand that neighborhoods are important. Both educators and librarians can be exposed to assumptions about equality that will be part of their future work. Once we understand outcomes, there is less reason to let them go on as unintended consequences.

Even if bureaucratic behavior changes, even if all Adam Smith rules are abolished, it is unrealistic to expect agencies themselves to find substantial compensatory allocations. All these city agencies are on tight budgets, and beset by demands. We have seen that minor and modest (though not unimportant) changes can be made by citizens. Yet citizens who want drastic changes in allocations for streets or education could hardly do so at the local level alone. People would have to be organized at national and state levels as well so that citizens could press for changes in the rules for distributing funds. No one can imagine such changes taking place overnight. Long years of preparation would be needed during which argument and fact were marshaled and political power mobilized to change the values officials bring to bear on these subjects. Few could predict with confidence the cumulative effect of proposed changes. No doubt each change will bring with it a train of consequences that would be evaluated for their effects; adaptation would be made using existing knowledge. Which is to say that we are not dealing with small local stuff, but with a society slowly altering fundamental notions of distributive justice.

Dilemmas of Redistribution

We have spent more time with what the government can do for the citizen as President Kennedy put it, than with what the citizen ought to do for himself. Placing the onus on government is understandable. This is, after all, a story about the activity of municipal agencies; citizens figure chiefly as they attempt to influence government, not as individuals who might wish to take personal responsibility for their affairs. Let us for a brief moment, therefore, change our focus to the citizens with civic obligations as well as civil rights.

It is wrong for any citizen to place a special burden on the state if that individual can manage alone. The state, in this respect, represents people contributing in the form of tax dollars for common purposes. The poor support their fellows along with the rich. How might our citizen take care of himself in the services provided by the three agencies we have been discussing?

The maintenance and repair functions of the street department create no difficulties for our citizens. All residents are entitled to fair distribution of available effort, and the poor have been getting proportionately less. Citizens in the hills, with higher incomes, get more and need it less; those should get less than in the past. The division of funds between arterial highways and city streets seems to rest more on general cultural change than on class divisions. Most citizens, including many poor ones, have cars and use freeways. The change that is needed is not reallocation, which would transfer advantages to different citizens, but consideration of whether most people might be better off if everyone put less emphasis on the automobile.

Libraries could put a larger burden on citizens than they have heretofore been willing to assume. Poor citizens could use libraries more extensively than they do. The advantages of education and reading have been publicized sufficiently to make library use attractive. Somewhere, however, is a point beyond which spending money to offer citizens inducements to do what is good for them anyway lacks an acceptable rationale. It is not only up to librarians to search out citizens, but also up to potential users to come forward. Librarians, whatever their defects, are trying to help, not to harm. The Adam Smith rules that help branches whose patrons read many library books also will help others if those people show initiative.

Poorer citizens who need the most help in schooling should get more. But as we are aware, schools do not know how to secure equal results in performance, much of which appears to have its roots in the home. Is it clear that all parents of poor students are doing what they can to reinforce learning in the home? Is it evident that communities from which deprived students come are mobilizing citizen self-help and making these children see that good books and good performance go together? The errors of commission by public agencies should not be overlooked, but neither should the faults of omission by citizens.

The onus, to be sure, may be aimed in the opposite direction. By what principle can inequality be justified? This profound question has agitated political philosophers from Rousseau to Rawls (indeed, long before them and no doubt long after).[8] Rousseau appears to have found the answer in elevating the idea of the community. By abdicating his sovereign will in favor of the general will expressed in the social contract,

experienced, one cannot usually have experienced and responsive teachers; insisting that the schools provide them will lead only to flight, withdrawal, or other neurotic behavior.

Another dilemma is that redistribution policies that aim at equality invariably create inequality, and are certain to set off doctrinal disputes. By compromising other values (such as equal treatment of all citizens), redistribution policies undermine the legitimacy of those political institutions which were to have been enhanced. Certainly universal application and equal treatment are prime conditions for maintaining the approval of citizens. Yet securing equal results depends precisely on not handling all people in the same way; the pipe dream of universally valid rules has to go. If the object in each area of policy is to provide special advantages for a specific minority, there will have to be a different rule for allocating resources for each group.

When we pursue redistribution policies by providing services to some and not to others, we assume that there is a foolproof way to measure progress toward equality. Certainly streets can be graded for their condition, and students can be tested for their reading achievement, but do these objective measures suffice? Even people who agree to similar measures or criteria may come to different conclusions, because programs often have differential effects. A substandard street may slow traffic for some citizens; for others, it may enhance the rustic character of the neighborhood. Equality of results, as a goal, is not clear enough to enable bureaucrats to administer programs and allocate resources.

Suppose you want to benefit citizens in poor areas by improving their streets more often. For that purpose the criterion could be that more funds go where more people live. Heavily populated poor neighborhoods should benefit. A per capita grant also would help the poor with branch libraries. The identical rule for schools, however, would leave the poor disadvantaged.

Suppose the criterion is "use." Allocating resources according to use of freeways and libraries would not help the poor. The poor would do better in education (because more of them use the schools) but not well enough, because compensatory devices are not allowed.

There is a real difference between Adam Smith rules (neutral in content if not in consequence) and other rules that are deliberately skewed to alter outcomes. The economist's idea that every benefit has associated costs must be applied also to bureaucracy. The more distributive justice for some groups becomes a bureaucratic aim, the less government will be able to manifest traditional virtues; rules that have applied equally to all citizens will have to go. Responsiveness to political leaders will be lessened by commitment to clienteles. Favoritism will be not de facto but de jure. Due process increasingly will be sacrificed to desirable outcomes. And bureaucracy will become a more dangerous and problematic element in society.

Now we can see why students of public policy in recent times increasingly have come to prefer "income" solutions. A "Karl Marx" bureaucracy might be worse than an "Adam Smith" one. If people who have more get more, if prevailing allocations of resources in specific areas are difficult to change, then increasing the income of poor people should have corresponding multiplier effects. Instead of trying directly to improve services for the poor, why not put them in a better position to make use of the Adam Smith rules, which work for those who have more to begin with? The more social interaction works in the desired direction, the less intellect will have to design direct control. We are sympathetic — but not entirely, because government will have to make choices even on income. Government will continue to provide services. There is no escape from either the empirical question — how do prevailing distributions affect citizens? — or the moral question — what should government do about methods of allocation? Assuming that we have good reason to act, of course, we would prefer to alter the incentives for interaction rather than try to figure out how every actor should be performing.

How far should government go in seeking to remedy inequalities? To say "as far as possible" is not satisfactory. Suppose it took tens of millions to secure equality of result for one individual. However much society values equality and the individual, the cost would undoubtedly be considered too great considering alternative uses to which the money could be put. The example is absurd but not entirely. So long as equality is not "priceless," so long as there is some price beyond which government ought not to go, the problem is converted from one of absolute values to one of relative costs. Government should go as far as equality of opportunity, but not far beyond that unless compensatory spending will result in greater actual equality. When government knows how much a modicum of equality will cost, officials will be able to make explicit trade-offs between the costs to some and the benefits to others — trade-offs that include the support necessary to maintain the redistributions engaged in. The question is not only one of economic rationality — which action will contribute most to national income — or of ethical rationality — which actions will best satisfy criteria of distributive justice; the problem involves political rationality too — strengthening the respect in which government is held by increasing governmental ability to act effectively with the consent of the governed. Should equality of result, then, be pushed against the intense preferences of a substantial majority of citizens? The very form of the question suggests that we would be better off thinking in a different line.

Perhaps a more modest interpretation of equal result would require only that we benefit the poor more, and keep the rich as they are. The present position of the better off would not be attached but, as a richer society generates more resources, these resources would be diverted to the worst off. Such was our position on libraries. Resources in the branches in the well-to-do neighborhoods would be maintained at current levels, and any increase of funds would be channeled to branches serving the poorest people. An attempt would be made to gain knowledge through decentralization that would encourage varied approaches.

This approach smacks of tokenism. So what if a few more streets get paved in poor areas? So what if branch libraries have (and poorer residents read) a few more books? Suppose the reading ability of poor children does go up a little? If outcomes change only a little, does a progressive reallocation of resources over the years matter?

We should not overlook the desirability of ultimately making good on the traditional American idea (no matter how often it is violated) about equality of opportunity. (There would be no need for hypocrisy if equality did not matter.) To know that substantial efforts are being made may help to build the social cohesion upon which the aspirations of a free society rest.

A free society requires free men and women who know what they are doing; that is, who can make sense out of their public lives by learning how to take effective action. Of what, then, does this rational action by citizens consist? Rational choices require that the universe of public policy be seen as intelligible, so that the citizens in it will be motivated to make it sensible to themselves and to others. Social interaction in political arenas and economic markets may be conceived as continuous and cumulative testing of hypotheses about this universe, with the most persuasive interpretation of the evidence prevailing. But only for a time. There is disagreement over the meaning of meaning: who has the right to certify what makes sense? Establishments seek to conserve meanings and revolutionaries to destroy them and possibly to substitute new ones. Whether larger meanings can (or should) last indefinitely is doubtful. Nevertheless, at any moment citizenship implies a capacity for rational choice, which itself depends on a framework of intelligibility in which this is now taken for granted and that is open to question, in which citizens can distinguish the trivial from the important, and improve their preferences. If citizens are not analysts, in this sense of national action in a sensible context, self-government is merely self-delusion.

NOTES

1. See Frank Levy, Arnold Meltsner, and Aaron Wildavsky, *Urban Outcomes* (Berkeley and Los Angeles: University of California Press, 1974).
2. See Arnold J. Meltsner, *The Politics of City Revenue* (Berkeley and Los Angeles: University of California Press, 1971), pp. 86–131, and Anthony Downs, *Inside Bureaucracy* (Boston: Little, Brown, 1967), pp. 216–217.

3. *Ibid.*
4. Each program serves a broad constituency. Removing restrictions on funding is different from removing them from, say, a compensatory-education program spending a large amount of money on a small constituency. In this first instance, recipients of benefits after reallocation will be about the same as the recipients before reallocation. In the second example, the recipients are likely to change drastically.
5. These figures would be even more pronounced if retired people — people who have no current income — were excluded from the data.
6. See, for example, Nathan Glazer, "A Breakdown of Civil Rights Enforcement," *The Public Interest* (Spring 1971), pp. 106–115.
7. Cf. James Coleman et al., *Equality of Educational Opportunity* (also known as the Coleman Report), pp. 221–277.
8. See Rousseau's *Discourse on the Origin and Foundations of Inequality Among Men*, and John Rawls, *A Theory of Justice* (Cambridge: Harvard University Press, 1971).

CHAPTER 16

ANALYSIS AS CRAFT

His mutations of color originated as much in theory as in observation. When one of his visitors was puzzled to find him painting a gray wall green, he explained that a sense of color was developed not only by work but by reasoning. . . . "He began on the shadow with a single patch, which he then overlapped with a second, and a third, until these patches, hinging one to another like screens, not only colored the object but molded its form.

. . . He deduced general laws, then drew from them principles which he applied by a kind of convention, so that he interpreted rather than copied what he saw. His vision was much more in his brain than in his eye. (pp. 57, 58, 59)

The move toward a disintegration of the object in some of the most memorable works of a painter so passionately attached to objects is the attraction and the riddle of Cezanne's last phase. The element that usurped its place, the patch of color in itself, had a history of its own in his art, one that is worth tracing. In the middle 1860's, when Cezanne for a time built pictures out of paint that was applied with a knife, in patches shaped by the knife-edge, his handling had an originality which has not always been understood. Among the Aix painters it is said to have caught on like an epidemic, and Pissarro appreciated it immediately; pictures like his still life at Toledo, painted with the knife in the following year, show how well he understood its meaning. Earlier in the century knife-painting had been the mark of an attachment to what was actual and physical in a subject. It was so for Goya and for Constable and, in particular, for Courbet who was Cezanne's inspiration. But only Cezanne realized that in the new context a picture that was touched with the knife should be painted with the knife throughout. He instinctively understood that in the new age the handling was the picture. . . .
(p. 56)

> Lawrence Gowing, "The Logic of Organized Sensations,"
> in Cezanne: The Late Work, ed. by William Rubin (New York:
> Museum of Modern Art, 1977).

A lot of "stake claiming" goes on in defining policy analysis. The landscape of our knowledge is surveyed and boundaries that delimit the domain of each discipline are drawn: "this belongs to political science, that belongs to economics." Over past centuries, the great empires of theology, geometry, and natural history have broken up, spawning a multitude of disciplinary fiefdoms. New alliances, formed on marginal lands, claim independence: econometrics, social psychology, political economy. Subdisciplinary groups coalesce, border disputes flare, while intrepid basic researchers of each discipline fan out in search of virgin territory on which to plant their flags. Explorers bearing the ensign of policy analysis seem bewildered by this scramble for territory. They expropriate lands claimed by political scientists decades ago and more recently by planners and public administrators. They skirt the edges of economics, law, organizational theory, and operations research. Some seek refuge in these disciplines. Others wait for a Moses to lead them out of the wilderness to the promised land of professionalism. Still others, being more nationalistic, want to carve out a "policy analytic" domain. But where? Establishing a discipline in the interstices of disciplines already distinct is risky; the new map is likely to reveal an impossibly gerrymandered state composed of marginal lands already contested by others.

The cartographic approach to defining policy analysis will not get us far. For one thing, the map is not the territory. And even if it were, surveyors' monuments are shifting so quickly that maps of the professions are soon outdated. Disciplinary skeptics dismiss policy analysis as nothing more than, say, "old public administration in a refurbished wardrobe."[1] It would be more fruitful to ask what these policy analysts do than where they reside. The short answer is that policy analysts create and craft problems worth solving. The long answer explains what "create and craft" means.

Economists tell you what you get for what you give up. Political scientists tell you who gets what and why. Far from being contradictory or incompatible, politics and markets are twin forms of competitive redundancy that compliment one another by learning from social interaction. By heeding much of this advice, policy analysts create conceivable solutions that enables us, as citizens, to learn what we ought to want in relation to what's available to get it with. (Of course, as life teaches us and the preceding chapters show, problems are not so much solved as alleviated, superseded, transformed, and otherwise dropped from view. "Solved" is shorthand for an activity that aims at improvement.) Because the task of analyzing policy is to try to alleviate practical problems, the analytic enterprise, Martin Landau rightly argues, "cannot recognize the limits of any field. . . . By its nature, it must follow problems wherever they go. It cannot ignore anything that may be relevant to a solution."[2] Following our metaphor, these analytic explorers must be denizens of all domains, free to cross borders and trade for the offerings of each discipline.

Landau goes on to state that "with so extensive a domain of inquiry, the enterprise is bound to be disordered. . . . No field of inquiry, no specialization can be built upon an unrestricted and indefinite domain."[3] I agree. If policy analysis is everything, then it is nothing. To tell people that all their problem-solving activity to date has actually been a form of policy analysis is just as revealing as telling them that they have been speaking prose all their lives.

Policy is a process as well as a product. It is used to refer to a process of decision-making and also to the product of that process. Policy is spoken of as what is and as what ought to be:[4] policy is perverting our priorities, and policy should serve the public interest. Each usage makes sense within its own domain but, by the same token, circumscribes what can usefully be analyzed. Limiting oneself to policy as product encourages a narrow view of rationality as presentation of results, a view that squeezes a disorderly world into the familiar procrustean formulation of objectives and alternatives.[5] Restricting oneself to process, however, may lead to the opposite evil of denigrating reason, of being unable to account for either the creation of projects or their rationalization as public arguments. Bismarck, I believe, can be credited with the notion that to have respect for politics and sausage one must not see how they are made. This quip conveys the spirit that engulfs the disorderly world of public policy, where a thin casing of policy constrains and hides the kernel of controversy inside. It is easy to describe as messy the political process that tames controversy and then to elevate the seamless casing of public representation as the epitome of reason. Rationalization of results becomes rationality.

I will state my conclusions here. As a discipline, policy analysis ("problem creation — problem solution — problem supersession") does not fit neatly into the disciplinary map. As an activity, however, policy analysis has some structure. That structure lies less in discovery (how policy analysis is created) and more in justification (how we distinguish better from worse analysis).

I find the distinction between discovery and justification useful because it permits work on the latter without worrying unduly about the former. If a book about policy analysis were to deal with the invention of new alternatives, that is with creativity, there would be little to say. Yet I am not persuaded, whatever may be said in the philosophy of science, where this distinction originated, that an impassible line separates creating and persuading. Students of public policy have reason to suspect that how policies originate affects how they are justified. We know, for example, that welfare programs that enter early, historically speaking, are, by the usual modes of incremental increase, advantaged over their successors. Just as policy may be its own cause, or agencies may alter objectives to fit better with resources, policies may take on a life of their own independent of their origins. When we take into account the impact of policies on other policies, we are *ipso facto* dealing with acts of creation. More has been said about the logic of discovery than has been admitted. Perhaps, in an activity that is supposed to be susceptible to political pressures, where social forces do not have to be smuggled in through the back door of justification, a more holistic view of change may be possible.

Problem solving for the policy analyst is as much a matter of creating a problem (1) worth solving from a social perspective and (2) capable of being solved with the resources at hand, as it is of converging to a solution when given a problem. Consider comprehensive welfare reform as an illustration. Part of the reason for replacing the myriad programs, each with its unique clientele and type of benefit, with a uniform "negative income-tax" scheme was the desire to replace problems our government knows little about — improving the welfare of its citizens — with problems about which it has come to know more — levying taxes, even "negative" ones designed to redistribute income. The parameter of the problem changed from "establishing a list of subsidized food purchases" to "calibrating the marginal tax rates so as to discover the breakeven point for maintaining a work incentive." The modes and locus of calculation also change as the policy design shifts from direct provision of services to cash payments that open up access to commercial markets. The government no longer decides the mix of food, health-care services, and housing that would benefit each recipient. Instead, the burden of calculation shifts to the recipient. Rather than one mind making the calculation, millions of minds assist in the interactions that determine the outcomes.

Two sides of analysis are in flux at the same time: defining the problem by comparison with our resources and constructing the solution to fit the problem posed. In the language of operations research, policy analysis must go beyond the task of calculating the best solution, considering the constraints and the objective, to the task of selecting the constraints in the first place and formulating a statement of the objectives. Whereas the first task requires technical competence, the second requires an equally rare composite of intelligence, judgment, and virtue. Anyone can make objectives commensurate with resources by drastically lowering expectations. Anyone can behave irresponsibly by proposing objectives incapable of being realized at least within the bounds of decency. But not just anyone can create problems more worthy of trying to solve (although perhaps failing) than the preceding problems.

That problems have the same status as solutions (neither having greater claim to performance or preference than the others) is the basis for creativity in analysis (and the cause for anomie within the profession). That analysts can say with good reason why some problems cum solutions are better than others is a basis for objectivity. What is accepted as evidence depends on how persuasive others find our analytic arguments.

In discovery, analysis as problem solving is more art than craft, more finding new ways than persuading others of their feasibility and desirability. In justification, analysis is more craft than art. Not that I prefer one to the other. Without art, analysis is doomed to repetition; without craft, analysis is unpersuasive. Shifting the frame of discourse, so that different facts become persuasive, suggests that art and craft are interdependent.

Policy analysis is creating and crafting problems worth solving. What is the clay of which recalcitrant experience is shaped into problems and how is the form of the problem determined? By understanding the material with which analysts work, we can better understand the limits and potentials of the craft.

Problems in policy are fashioned of creative tension, drawn between different poles depending on the context of discourse. If we are talking in everyday language about the government, its policies, and its organizations, the tension is drawn between our resources and our objectives. Programs mediate the two, and policy analysis compares programs, each of which is itself composed of objectives and resources.

If we switch the mode of discourse again, this time to culture, the creative tension that drives analysis arises between the historical pattern of social relationships and our evolving preferences for new patterns. The tensions between social interaction and intellectual cogitation, between asking and telling, between politics and planning, which have so much occupied us, measure the degree to which we are willing to accept what people think they want or intervene so that they will want what we think they ought to have. Policy analysis creates culture by restructuring social interaction and, consequently, the values we express by our participation as citizens in public policy.

If we switch the discourse to epistemology (what we claim to know and how we come to know it), tensions arise between our current knowledge and the experience we seek to shape to find answers to our inquiries. By testing hypotheses the analyst mediates between the two, and the essence of policy analysis is learning to recognize and correct errors. Balancing between dogma and skepticism, we continually reweave our conceptual fabric to make sense of our experience, at times explaining away the surprises, at other times revising the expectations that made us vulnerable to surprise. Just as our values, beliefs, and social structure appear malleable but not infinitely plastic, so we suspect culture is negotiable but do not know how much. It is difficult to say whether what we consider a policy problem is in us or in society. Certain events, like wars, depressions, and famines, appear to force themselves on us, whereas other happenings are highlighted because we seem to choose to focus on them.

All I can say here is that our rationalizations, once made, are just as real as our other creations.

If policy problems arise from tensions, policy solutions are the temporary and partial reduction of tension. Solutions are temporary in that the conditions producing the initial dislocation change in time, creating different tensions. Solutions often carry their own tensions with them, and acting as their own cause give rise to different problems. More and more, policies respond to past policies (as fixed sentences do to indeterminate ones or medical inflation to medical subsidy) rather than to events rooted in social life. Why, for instance, has the federal government mandated more and more forms of insurance? Not because physical risks are greater but because its own disaster programs have become so expensive that requiring insurance is a way of passing the costs back to individuals. Solutions are partial in that tension, a product of multidimensional pulls and tugs, is rarely discharged in full. To satisfy tensions in one direction fully is to exacerbate tension in the others. Predictability for one sector (say corporate taxation) is often achieved at the expense of unpredictability of others (say balanced government budgets). Problem solving is iterative. We hope, though it is not necessarily true, that our future unsatisfactory solutions will be less unsatisfactory than they were in the past.

To fragment this view, to say that changes in public policy involve neither our conceptual knowledge of the world nor the structure of social interaction, would lead to poorer rather than richer policy analysis. Suppose we conceive of the United States as a country peopled by responsible adults who are fully capable of understanding and accepting their own risks without imposing these risks on others. Social relations as they are would be sufficiently reliable to produce timely warnings of danger; future generations would act as wisely as those past, having learned to trust one another to do right. Prices would then measure real scarcities, so that when the price of oil was low this meant consumption was "okay"; should relative scarcities change, steeply higher prices would precede oil shortages in time to permit exploration for more oil or to switch to alternative sources of energy. The energy problem did not need to be problematic; we made it so by failing to follow the usual processes. This is the distrustful, shortsighted, irresponsible image of a society that produces current safety laws and regulations. First an effort was made to make seat belts mandatory; when that regulation was revised, effort went into making inflatable air bags mandatory. On-the-job safety devices worn by workers have given way to mandatory engineering controls applied to entire plants. In both cases, cheaper options exercised by individuals have given way to expensive requirements imposed by government. These new policies reveal worlds of difference about responsibility for resources, social trust, and recognition and correction of errors.

Let's examine the problems and solutions at each of these levels in more detail.

SOLUTIONS AS PROGRAMS

We are fortunate when what we should have is what we want and what we can get. For the most part, however, the spheres of wants and resources do not overlap, and these incongruities form the difficulties analysts address. With the discrepancies, we can make unilateral adjustments, such as lowering our expectations to match our resources, or redoubling our search for resources with steadfast commitment to an objective. Analysis works at both ends, and compromise amid the pulling and hauling is inherent in any solution.

Wants are often conflicting. They conflict not only at the basic level, as in economic growth versus environmental integrity, but among "second-order" characteristics of program design: we want programs that are easy to implement, inexpensive, simple, sophisticated, flexible, not arbitrary, and so forth.

It is no help to forget subjective "wants" in order to concentrate on "objective" needs. There are few absolute standards of needs, and the idea is as elusive as "benefits." Suffice it to say that a rule for decision such as "the government should allocate resources to satisfy needs" will not see us far when needs conflict.

Limited resources force compromise and choice. With a finite supply, spending resources one way means they can't be spent another. Foregone opportunity is a ubiquitous cost. Were our resources to exceed our wants, and were all our wants compatible with one another, there would be no tension, hence no need for choice, and no need for analysis of policy. If discrepancies are the problems, programs are the solutions. Policy analysis translates the choice among wants and resources into choices among programs. Something is lost in the translation, as they say, and programs as embodiments of compromises are often imprecise, arbitrary, and imperfect. Programs structure decisions as political parties structure presidential elections. In the end, we as citizens vote for candidates who result from the bargaining and brokering in their parties. Rarely does any candidate match the ideal of all citizens, because each has different conceptions of the ideal. Similarly, no program will completely resolve all the tension. We seek an Aristotelian balance among extremes; to completely resolve the tension in one direction, say devoting one-hundred times the current amount to primary education without any hope of changing pupils' performance for the better, involves producing absurd results in the others.

Programs as solutions, like candidates, come in discrete chunks. We are fortunate when program characteristics are quantifiable (the minimum level of income guarantees, the monthly medicare premium) for these programs can be continually modified, usually by splitting the difference between the high and the low. More often we are faced with an array of integral units, and selecting any one means a compromise among compromises. Programs are solutions, solutions are compromises, and compromises are more often feasible than optimal, satisfactory than perfect and tolerable than desirable.

Programs as solutions are also temporary. Resources change, along with perceptions of wants. A subtler and more interesting form of re-alignment of tensions results, not from changes in the system but by the very presence of programs within the system. Programs distort the field and "bend" objectives and resources into accommodating configurations. One evolutionary path leads to rejection of the program and a different attempt at resolution. Another path is taken when the program, imbued with life of its own, acts as its own cause. Self-protective behavior sets in. Programs retreat from objectives which could not be attained, and sub-stitute those which can. Clients who can be satisfied replace those who can't. Performance is measured by inputs instead of outcomes. Solutions in the form of programs, create problems, in the form of new tensions. Old tensions are negated rather than resolved.

This retreat on objectives is neither intrinsically desirable nor un-desirable. It can be welcomed when, faced with objectives attainable only at exorbitant political, economic, or social cost, we as citizens learn to pose better problems, obtain a more honest match between resources and objectives, and, by bumping up against constraints, increase compre-hension of our environment. Analysts should value policies by the extent to which they permit learning, the ease by which errors are identified, and the motivation produced by organizational incentives to correct error. A variety of postal letter services (both private and public) would permit recognition of error (what it should cost to mail an ordi-nary letter reliably from one place to another in a specified time) and correction of error (choosing the least expensive service). Moreover, the choice would be repetitive, experience would be more objective, and results would be reversible (by switching to another carrier), thus in-creasing the ability to learn. The capacity to propose solutions to more interesting and consequential problems that teach us about our pref-erences and our circumstances are the hallmarks of worthwhile poli-cies. Food stamps and housing allowances can be spent only for the indi-cated purposes, but a general income supplement of the same amount would allow the individual to learn about the consequences of choosing among goods and services. Solutions, like scientific theories, should be valued not only for the old difficulties they purport to end, but also for the interesting new difficulties they begin.

"Too many scientists," Robert Axelrod warns us, "tend to think in terms of what economists call 'consumer sovereignty.' This has the effect of an underemphasis on the potential of leadership, persuasion, and education."[6] This argument can be extended: past actions affect future choices. They do so, among various ways, by creating institutional arrangements. When the actions involve electoral arrangements, say proportional versus winner-take-all voting, it is immediately clear that voter preferences are shaped by such considerations as whether votes for a candidate will be wasted if that candidate has little chance of winning a majority, or, if citizens may vote for several candidates, if one's vote will count toward the final decision. The same reasoning applies to those policies which, like social security, have been established earlier and preempt resources, or, like aid to dependent children, create new relationships difficult to undo, or, like medical insurance, alter people's preferences by changing their view of who will pay how much.

Preferences do and should change. One should even concede, from universal experience, that we often do not choose wisely or act in ways that are good for us. Failure to follow healthy habits is ample testimony to that. Yet we may still hold that no one else knows enough to impose their views about what is in our own interest. Even if we ultimately come to the conclusion that someone else once knew better, that entitles them only to argue with us, not to overcome us, for then we could not learn from our mistakes. Then we would lose autonomy, because others know better, and reciprocity, because they do not have to take us into account. When we citizens are deprived of our errors we also lose our capacity for self-correction, for self-improvement by moral development.

SOLUTIONS AS HYPOTHESES

Policy analysis has its foundations for learning in pragmatism and empiricism. We value what works and we learn what works from experience, particularly experience that magnifies error and failure. The impetus for analysis flows from the clash between expectations formed from prevailing theory and our interpretation of experience. When predictions do not pan out we attempt to reimpose order on the confusion by suggesting new hypotheses about the world or by reexamining the claims to "facts." Inventing these hypotheses and discarding current theory for better theory are the learning analogues to establishing new government programs when faced with failures of current ones. We hope that new hypotheses expand into theories that better explain the world, just as we hope that new programs form better matches between resources and objectives.

Progress in public policy, however, is not inevitable; learning does not occur automatically. A new hypothesis is not always better than any old hypothesis, any more than a new program is always better than an old program. Why is learning from error so difficult to accomplish?

For one thing, error recognition and error correction are not always compatible. Without recognition, to be sure, there is unlikely to be correction. The trouble is that what facilitates recognition often inhibits correction.[7] To be readily recognized, error should be conspicuous and clear. The larger the error and the more it contrasts with its background, the easier it is to identify. Easy correction of error, however, depends on mistakes that are small in size (and hence in cost) and are necessarily close to what has gone on before. But small errors are likely to lack sharp resolution, merging imperceptibly into their backgrounds. Because they are cheap and reversible, these errors would be correctable if only they were detectable. Alternatively, big policies generate giant mistakes, which make them simple to spot but difficult to reverse, because the cost of changing past practice soars. If only big mistakes can be recognized, we would be able to detect only the errors we cannot easily correct. A combination of better detectors (to see through the bureaucratic jungle) and smaller errors (to gain experience in continuous correction) would be ideal. The conditions under which this combination is feasible remain to be studied.

Error identification means persisting with current theory (being dogmatic) because we want confirmed instances of contradiction, not anomalies that can be explained as once-in-a-lifetime quirks or paradoxes that can be resolved eventually within current theory. If dogma is the antithesis of learning, can there be virtue in dogma? The first time an anomaly appears, it is likely to be ignored. The second and third time, it may be certified as truly "paradoxical." It may take a fourth and fifth time before it is deemed a bona fide "contradiction." We ignore anomalies, live with paradoxes, and permit contradictions while retaining prevailing theory. Recognizing contradictions, we don't discard bad theory for no theory, we reject bad theory for better theory (or more accurately, bad theory for hypotheses that promise to become better theory).[8]

Learning by error correction is a gamble, and the odds favor the status quo. We weigh performance of theory that is manifestly adequate against performance of a hypothesis that is speculatively better. The burden of proof falls on the hypothesis, and all but the most sturdy sink under its weight.

It is hard to strike a balance between dogma (everything is immune from scrutiny) and skepticism (everything is up for grabs) conducive to learning. We want enough "dogma" to make crucial experiments possible. We agree to hold some things constant while we vary others so that experience is focused on one part of our conceptual web of beliefs, not on the whole network at once. Maintaining these conventions depends on trust, first that the parties to any transaction will do as they say and, second, that what they say will actually come about. When proof is demanded rather than presumed, cash in advance, capacity to produce convincing evidence is rapidly exhausted. The insistent demand (show me!) is evidence of a lack of trust. This refusal to accept conventional responses may be met either by increasing trust so that the demands diminish or by producing evidence of effectiveness.

But we also want enough skepticism to preserve the legitimacy of questioning any of our beliefs, to hold nothing immune from scrutiny. Skepticism allows us to question the integrity of supposedly crucial experiments. But when to be dogmatic and when to be skeptical ordinarily is known only after the fact. We make the decision; if it works we were right, if it does not, we were wrong. When skepticism is organized, it does not depend on the proclivities of this or that person but on social arrangements — referees for publications; incentives for catching other people's errors; rewards for new theories, which often require criticism of the old. Organized skepticism, as it is called, is the institutionalization of distrust. Trust in social interaction designed to detect and correct error reenforces reliance on individual integrity.[9]

Solutions to problems, scientific and practical alike, both reflect and create social constructs. The creative interpretation of the histories of policies involves policy analysis with social structure. Starting with public programs and treating them as social artifacts, analysts reconstruct not only a conceptual world view (that which society perceives as truth and error), they also recreate a structure of values. By proposing new programs, the policy analyst suggests new hypotheses, and hence new values that codify social relations. "Retrospection" is more than retrospective rationalization because it can help the past justify the future.

SOLUTIONS AS SOCIAL ARTIFACTS

When policy analysts propose solutions, they propose not only a mix of resources and objectives, not only an implicit causal model of a segment of reality, but also a structure of social relationships. The more the prevailing structure of social interaction shifts (Personal Relationships whose Outcomes Differ, or PROD as I called it earlier), the more radical the change. Thus we look for change by alteration in outcomes as a result of different relationships among citizens. In the winter of 1978, for example, most consumers were not aware that the federal government was actually subsidizing the price of imported oil. The lower price of domestic oil spoke louder (use me!) than exhortations about conservation. Raising the domestic price substantially to reach the international price (either by removing the subsidy or by imposing a tax as President Carter recommends) would lead to higher domestic production and lower consumption of foreign oil. By permitting people to face the real cost of oil, by changing the values they put on their transactions, their social relations would produce different outcomes. When we can specify how constraints and incentives act on individual behavior to reinforce or modify patterns of social structure, we have related policy to society through culture.

If culture is conceived as values and beliefs that bind social relationships, then policy analysis is intimately involved with culture in two ways: (1) solutions to policy problems reflect and are limited by the moral consistency of historical social relationships; (2) solutions to policy problems, by changing the structure of social relationships, alter the values and beliefs that support the social structure. As with any cycle (the chicken and the egg), causal directions are difficult to disentangle. Do we begin with deep intuitive values (such as compassion for the poor) from which we design our public programs (such as medicare, food stamps, Aid to Families with Dependent Children), and then work through the politics of implementation, or do we start with political compromises, rationalize them by imposing a grand design (such as the war on poverty), and only later internalize these norms as cultural values? The appropriate position to take on the causal role of conscious intent in the evolution of culture seems to be to accept the totality of a cycle rather than the bifurcation of "cause or effect."

The expansion of American social-welfare programs reflects a pattern of rules embodying values not immediately obvious at the political level. These include the preference to err on the side of giving to the undeserving rather than withhold from the deserving. Policies mirror changing values. Policies are the operational embodiment of what we believe when we must choose the sort of error — too much or too little consumption of food or oil or housing — we would prefer to make. Physical pollution is imbued with cultural significance, and the debate over the integrity of our physical environment complements the debate on so abstract a word as culture. I suggest a small experiment: talk to convinced environmentalists about whether there is a physical shortage of oil in the world. If there isn't, you will soon discover, there ought to be. Soon you will see that they rightly love the idea of shortage, for if the supply is running out all sorts of changes from installing solar-energy converters to outlawing large "gas guzzling" cars may be mandated. In a word, the controversy over energy policy is a dispute about how we should live.

Values, as embodied in social structure, also limit the scope of change. Policy analysis, far from being a presentation of utopian scenarios, must remain anchored in the current pattern of social relationships. History is the base; modifications in the direction of changing preferences are solutions. The conservatism implicit in treating history as the base holds not only at the organizational level, where policy analysis must acknowledge the organizational disincentives to change, but at the broader cultural level, where social disincentives to change are abundant. The analytic enterprise depends on social trust, on common recognition that the analytic activity is being carried out to secure more desirable outcomes. The limits to this common recognition are the limits to policy analysis, for it is by common consent that we distinguish facts from values. This distinction in turn is necessary before errors can be identified and subsequently corrected.

The balance struck epistemologically between dogma and skepticism must also be struck socially between convention and anarchy, and between debates over facts and values. Without temporary agreement to limit the scope of analysis (recall that this was one of the virtues of dogma), no amount of argument could settle differences, for with no "facts that matter" there is no evidence, and with no evidence, no hope for contradiction and error identification. Learning through error ceases. Negation replaces contradiction.

When programs fashion objectives after their own images, policy acts as its own cause. Theory, which acts as its own cause by dismissing new hypotheses out of hand, is called dogma. History, acting as its own justification, is called tradition. These tendencies support each other. The virtues of dogma — limiting the scope of the debate, starting with initial presumptions — are the virtues of tradition. Similarly, the vices of dogma are the vices of tradition. These include shifting the burden of proof to the challenger and inhibiting learning by preventing rectification of errors. When tradition rules, recognition of error becomes anomalous, and policy acts to perpetuate itself.

The tensions around which this book is organized have their moral sides. Relating resources to objectives so that the promise of public policy can be kept is the mark of the responsible analyst. It is irresponsible to put resources to inferior uses, depriving others of their opportunities, or to promote objectives that cannot be achieved at all or at acceptable cost. To be held responsible, as if one could control results, depends on possessing relevant resources, for otherwise accountability is a sham. Social interaction is efficacious only when autonomous individuals establish reciprocal social relationships. Individual moral development requires a balance between autonomy and reciprocity, citizen and community, which, at the public level, is the task of policy analysis.

THE CRAFT OF PROBLEM SOLVING

Good analysis compares alternative programs, neither objectives alone nor resources alone, but the assorted packages of resources and objectives, which constitute its foregone opportunities. Good analysis focuses on outcomes: what does the distribution of resources look like, how should we evaluate it, and how should we change it to comport with our notions of efficiency and equity? Good analysis is tentative. It suggests hypotheses that allow us to make better sense of our world.

Good analysis promotes learning by making errors easier to identify and by structuring incentives for their correction.

Good analysis is skeptical; by disaggregating the verifying process — evaluations should be external, independent, multiple, and continuous — no organization is required or allowed to be sole judge in its own case.

Good analysis is aware of its shortcomings and so it hedges its recommendations with margins of sensitivity to changes in underlying conditions.

Good analysis works with historical contexts so that error stands out ready for correction.

Most important, good analysis remembers people, the professionals in the bureaus who must implement the programs as well as the citizens whose participation in collective decision-making can be either enlarged or reduced by changes in the historical structure of social relationships. A focus on cognitive problem solving alone uproots man from context, viewing objectives as derived from personal experience rather than social structure. Social interaction by itself accepts rather than corrects social relations.

It would be a mistake to look at good policy analysis as if it were already here instead of what we would like it to be when it does get here. Do not ask "What is policy analysis?" as if it were apart from us. Ask rather "What can we make analysis become?" as if we were a part of this art and craft.

Craft is distinguished from technique by the use of constraints to direct rather than deflect inquiry, to liberate rather than imprison analysis within the confines of custom. Consider cost inflation in hospitals. Once it is understood that money will no longer be allowed to ration access to medicine, and that deterioration in quality is not publicly acceptable, inflation becomes rampant because we prefer it to the alternatives of relaxing constraints on access and quality. Of course no one wants inflation; it is just that when push comes to shove we want other things more. With this understanding, it becomes possible to evaluate the difficulties we have, in effect, chosen today compared to those (like grossly unequal access) we experienced yesterday and others (like providing something less than the most expensive care) we are likely to face tomorrow.

Manipulation of constraints can help make the feasible desirable. Temporary acceptance of a cognitive constraint in education — no technology for improving reading among the worst off — allows us to consider a temporary interactive solution. By facilitating bargaining in stable political arenas, parents, students, and teachers should learn to accept what they cannot change as the best they can do. Later, as technology changes, it may become possible to ask how much it is worth paying to improve cognitive accomplishment.

To recognize a constraint, to be sure, is not necessarily to accept it.

Philanthropic agencies are unable to agree on reform of the income-tax write-off, despite its acknowledged unfairness, because of its differential effect. Universities and museums depend more on the rich who use the write-off than do churches, which depend more on poorer people. Changing to a more equitable mode of governmental subsidy of charity depends on getting around this constraint by assuring one or the other type of charitable agency that their income will not be drastically reduced. Charities don't want to take a vow of poverty to help the poor. By easing the transition from a worse to a better place, "buying out" other peoples' causes — paying them off to ease the transition — has general applicability as a mechanism for increasing the feasibility of proposed policies.

The improvement of urban services requires removal of constraints. Showing that what appear to be constraints are merely customs opens up new directions for public policy. If all (or even most) library employees do not need professional skills and credentials, it becomes possible to fund additional book purchases out of savings on salary. The cumulative effect of special state funding formulas can be challenged so as to allow local school districts to spend in ways that reflect their own priorities. And "lowest cost per safe mile" need not continue to be the only rule for decision in building and maintaining streets. Preserving neighborhoods can be part of street programs, though it may take more time to reeducate professionals than to change laws. Error is most difficult to correct when it has become a way of life.

Learning from mistakes requires a criterion of correspondence separating error from accomplishment. Criteria should be sharp enough to have a cutting edge. Criteria may also conflict, so that it is useful to know when cutting one way means undercutting another. If equity and efficiency conflict (the tax write-off for charity is efficient but not equitable), one may try to find a program (treating each dollar equally by a percentage-contribution bonus) that makes the two complementary. When criteria cannot be made compatible, trade-offs among them (so much quality for so much cost in medicine, so many ineligibles for welfare let through versus so many eligibles screened out) help illuminate choice.

Suppose criteria cannot be accomplished? Then change from a criterion of correctness to one of agreement, that is, from cogitation to interaction. When one doesn't know how to accomplish what one wishes directly, one can set up procedures to search out a better result sequentially. This happened when we turned from reading scores as indicators of accomplishment to vouchers as forms of interaction designed to create a market in education. Just as we don't say that a presidential candidate is the correct but rather the popular choice, just as the market price is not virtuous but only viable, so a criterion of choice need not be correspondence with a prior standard but only agreement on the programmatic activity itself. The acceptable may not be the desirable but then we started all this to get away from educational outcomes that were neither desirable nor acceptable. Working with conflict is better than ignoring it.

For the policy analyst, which assumption is best: congruence or conflict of interests in society? Conflict is correct, analytically as well as empirically, for, by assuming conflict, analysts are led to calculate losses and gains by each major separable interest (doctors, patients, hospitals, governments, donors, charities, teachers, parents, students). Instead of lumping them all in a big blob, analysts are led to uncover interests and discover their degree of (in)compatibility. Interests may also be mutually supportive or unrelated, but that is something to learn, not assume. There is safety in assuming diversity.

Should analysts spend their time uncovering what they don't know or discovering what they do? Both, obviously, but if it is a question of priority, of allocating time (the most important personal resource), my inclination is toward self-interrogation. Analysts are themselves their most important instruments. Taking a fundamental view, making what one can of events from basic social theory, asking what Adam Smith or Karl Marx or James Madison would say, is in my experience superior to searching for all the relevant data or fantasizing that hitherto secret material will reveal all. If you wanted to know what price OPEC would be charging for oil, the hypothesis of profit maximization under monopoly (stop raising prices when a higher price constricts demand sufficiently to reduce income) would predict the current price almost exactly. Asking why it is alleged that doctors rather than patients are maldistributed, when economic theory tells us people locate to their best advantage, helps orient inquiry into what data to collect on the dispersal of doctors. Knowing that there has to be variation as well as constancy in social relations allows analysts to appraise claims about simultaneously increasing predictability for all interests, including economic stabilizers as well as agency spenders. The costs of change and who will bear them is a prime consideration in any historical period.

It is always relevant to ask how the participants in public policies resolve uncertainties because these choices probe weaknesses (no one ever knows enough) and reveal priorities by signaling the side on which error is tolerated. If doctors and patients reduce uncertainties by doing more, the consequences for cost are evident. The repeated decisions to resolve uncertainty about the size of school districts in favor of bigness suggest that ease of interaction among administrators rather than responsiveness of schools to students and parents had the highest priority. The use of professional standards in place of empirical inquiry in urban services suggests that professional presuppositions should be a major source of skepticism.

But what about analysts: how should they resolve their uncertainties? By prayer, for not all can be reduced; by theory, which may or may not be the same thing; and by studies that test the sensitivity of key variables to large changes. If a subject won't matter when giving advice on policy, then we analysts don't have to know about it. That, at least, is our excuse for ignorance. Knowing what you don't have to know can be valuable. So too is knowing what isn't known, like how to use medicine to significantly improve health or how to decrease crime or how to encourage deprived children to use libraries. Negative knowledge, knowing what doesn't work, may suggest research to overcome ignorance or encourage trial and error. Insofar as it is the task of analysis to substitute for experience (if we were willing and able to try everything there would be much less need for analysis) mental experiments have much to commend them. Could we act effectively, for example, if we decided that limiting inflation of hospital costs was our highest priority? Evidently, by nationalizing or privatizing medicine, we could. Therefore it isn't that we can't but that we won't, which, to me at least, is informative. Hypothetical history: what would happen if . . . , is another way of doing policy analysis.

SPEAKING TRUTH TO POWER

In large part, it must be admitted, knowledge is negative. It tells us what we cannot do, where we cannot go, wherein we have been wrong, but not necessarily how to loosen these constraints or correct these errors. After all, if current efforts were judged wholly satisfactory, there would be little need for analysis and less for analysts.

The truth is that this or that cannot now be done. How do we know? Craftsmen are judged by how they use their tools. Their handiwork is is done individually but judged collectively. Are the data accurate, appropriate, and manipulated according to prevailing standards? Is the evidence believable, coming from diverse sources, and tested for credibility? Are the arguments persuasive and balanced rather than one-sided? Does the analyst have a reputation for doing careful, accurate, and, if called for, imaginative work? Do other analysts with different viewpoints, and other audiences who must be persuaded, find this analyst believable? Craftsmanship is persuasive performance. Among the advantages that policy analysts yield to medical practitioners, in addition to knowledge and power, two stand out: patients take their doctors' advice as much as half the time and doctors occasionally bring good news. Like would-be prophets, analysts cry out their ill tidings in a policy wilderness.

With all the evident errors in social policy, and with the immense effort involved in correcting them, only to learn that these recent corrections lead to new errors, it hardly appears that our society suffers from a surfeit of constructive criticism. Nevertheless, it is understandable that this view — criticism is more confusing than enlightening — might gain currency.

The truth that analysts claim today is not always the same truth they will claim tomorrow. There are tides in the affairs of analysts as well as ordinary mortals. There are fashions too. The nurse who spent the first twenty years of her life walking up tenement steps to tell mothers they must under no circumstances breast-feed their children, has now spent the last twenty years advising the opposite. The people (present company included) who speak so confidently of the ineffectiveness of schooling or the irrelevance of medicine or the hopelessness of rehabilitating criminals may, for all they know now, be singing a different song in the next decade. It has happened before.

Before, though, it was possible to ignore this rabble's babble, this cacophony, these mutterings of never-satisfied intellectuals, with their stepwise regression and backward foolishness, who sow confusion among the multitudes. Now, it appears, analysts cannot be ignored, they must be taken into government. It takes one to beat one, if only to counter those who are everywhere else — in the interest groups, the congressional committees, the departments, the universities, the think tanks — ensconced in institutions mandated by law to evaluate everything and accept responsibility for nothing. Political leaders will not be believed without policy analysts and, with them, can hardly believe themselves. What happens to the simple political verities when they have to be so qualified as to be no longer so simple? What happens to social progress when it appears the bugle sounds the retreat before it sounds the charge? Isn't caution, hence conservatism, the inevitable result of knowing more about what not to do than about what to do?

Indeed it is. If you just want to rush ahead, acting beats thinking every time. Blaming the messenger for the bad news is an old story. Blaming knowledge for ignorance also has ancient antecedents. Here is Millindapanha's second-century colloquy:

> The King said: "Venerable Nagasena, will you converse with me?"
> Nagasena: "If your Majesty will speak with me as wise men converse, I will; but if your Majesty speaks with me as kings converse, I will not."
> "How then converse the wise, venerable Nagasena?"
> "The wise do not get angry when they are driven into a corner, kings do."[10]

The charge of philosophy corrupting youth is not without foundation. It is time to recognize that the Greek root from which the word "analysis" comes also means to undo or to unloose. To be knowledgeable, to be sure, is not necessarily to be wise. Wisdom and foolishness, fortunately for us analysts, are properties not only of individuals but of institutions. The rules for encouraging evaluation do not begin by directing, as intellectual cogitation might, "Appoint a wise man," but instead cover the desirability of diversity, independence, and multiplicity, which cannot be characteristics of individual's alone, but only of individuals in collectivities. And this collective consciousness has been recognized from the earliest times. The Prophet Samuel was displeased when the Israelites asked him to appoint a king over them so that they might be like other nations. But the Lord understood that this was not a rejection of Samuel, but of Israel, that is, of self-government. For the Lord had Samuel discourse on the manner of kings: "He will take your sons . . . take your daughters . . . take your fields . . . take . . . take . . . take . . . and ye shall be his servants."[11] But the Israelites were servile and the Lord let them serve. It was the institution of kingship that was defective, not merely the individual kingly manifestation, as subsequent history was to show.

To be ruled by another, paradoxical as it may appear, requires no faith, only forbearance. To be a subject requires only being an object: the rulers substitute force for faith, the ruled acquiescence for initiative. To rule oneself, however, is not only to affirm but also to subdue the self, because reciprocity as well as autonomy is required for self-government. Citizens owe allegiance to others before they receive results for themselves. Citizenship is, first, an act of faith (a willingnes to act in the absence of things seen) in political processes. These are forms of interaction, whose results must be approved before they are known; otherwise economic markets and political arenas would collapse before they got started. The skepticism inculcated in these institutions stands on a substratum of dogma. No wonder there is uneasiness over policy analysis undermining the eternal verities on which analysis itself rests without putting anything solid in its place. Skepticism is a solvent; it may corrode ideals at the expense of worshipping a false god, namely itself. In the final analysis, few will rally to skepticism as a faith.

Hence we expect to hear doubts about being doubtful. If our society is so smart, as the saying goes, why aren't we so wise? One of the latest laments comes from historian Barry Karl:

It is perhaps one of the greatest paradoxes in the history of democratic thought that, as the available methods of rational communication have expanded, faith in democratic government seems to have diminished. Greater education in the process of government and more constant perception of its daily operation produces disillusionment and cynicism. Yet those who govern today are better educated in general and better trained to govern than they have ever been. If one looks at the history of southern politics, for example, one would expect to find the hard-drinking, loud-talking Billy Carter as the successful politician in the Carter family, not Jimmy — even as recently as twenty years ago. American society is as ready for the tests of participatory democracy as any society has ever been, yet "populism" still is looked upon suspiciously in intellectual circles. Nonetheless, to argue that a highly technological society cannot be a highly

democratic one is to argue that knowledge cannot produce self-government, that knowing thyself is no longer the place to begin.[12]

Just as knowing what (which is hard) is different from knowing why
(which is harder), that differs from knowing how (which is hardest),
combining commitment with doubt is not easy.

The conditions for craftsmanship include plenty of practice at de-
tecting and correcting error. No one has said this better than Sir William
Osler:

> Begin early to make a three-fold category — clear cases, doubtful cases,
> mistakes. And learn to play the game fair, no self-deception, no shrinking
> from the truth; mercy and consideration for the other man, but none for
> yourself, upon whom you have to keep an incessant watch. You remember
> Lincoln's *mot* about the impossibility of fooling all of the people all of
> the time. It does not hold good for the individual, who can fool himself
> to his heart's content all of the time. If necessary, be cruel; use the knife
> and the cautery to cure the intumescence and moral necrosis which you
> will feel in the posterior parietal region, in Gall and Spurzheim's center of
> self-esteem, where you will find a sore spot after you have made a mistake
> in diagnosis. It is only by getting your cases grouped in this way that you
> can make any real progress in your post-collegiate education; only in this
> way can you gain wisdom with experience.[13]

In an aspiring democracy, the truth we speak is partial. There is
always more than one version of the truth and we can be most certain
that the latest statement isn't it. This is not only democracy's truth, it is
also democracy's dogma.

Error must be the engine of change. Without error there would be
one best way to achieve our objectives, which would themselves remain
unaltered and unalterable. The original sin, after all, was to eat of the
tree of knowledge so as to distinguish between good and evil. However
great our desire, however grand our design, we ordinary mortals can only
play at being God.

I have written this book to show that policy analysis is about learning
what to like; analysis is less about the realization of preferences than
about their transformation. This is my quarrel with the present paradigm
of rationality: it accepts as immutable the very order of preferences it is
our purpose to change, and it regards as perfectly plastic the recalcitrant
resources that always limit their realization. Individual analysts, to be
sure, may accept objectives as given, as not subject to modification by
them at that time. But policy analysis as a social process of relating objectives to resources by interaction as well as by cogitation, constrained
by dogma as well as criticized by skepticism, inevitably changes preferences as well as possibilities.

Public policy remains a world we never made, consciously or entirely.
Policies, acting as their own causes, drive as well as being driven. Like
ideas or theories, policies, once promulgated, exist independently of their

origins. Long after their causes fade away, their consequences carry on unless intervention alters them. Learning that it is easier to re-allocate financial resources than to reintegrate the human persona, which is roughly our common experience in the last two decades, it is only reasonable to retreat from these objectives. Whoever said wholesale changes in hearts (a negation of criminality) or minds (an affirmation of understanding) or bodies (a cultivation of health) would be simple or speedy? No one, at least not out loud. Now that the secret is out, we can perhaps proceed to perfect our preferences until old problems are superseded by new ones.

Wait! Why, if policy preferences are so important, have we spent so little time on their origin and development? In a limited way, I have tried to do exactly that: explain the development of American public policy as compromises among types of tensions. But I have not — nor, so far as I know, has anyone else — tried to locate these policy preferences in social structures and in their sustaining values and beliefs, i.e., in culture. If public policies have a life of their own, they are also an expression of who we are as public people. When it becomes clear that people (re)make their social structure much like they (re)make their policies, the next stage in the study of public policy analysis as a social process will have begun.

In the meantime, I shall end as I began by answering one question with another. What is this power to which policy analysts speak their truth? And what is this truth they seek to speak? "All power to the analysts" is not a slogan I expect to hear in the near future. Policy analysis and policy analysts in a democracy never will (and never should) be that powerful. In the United States, where the ubiquity and the influences of interest groups is matched only by ever-present hostility and efforts to undermine them, where the long-sought power of the Presidency has been enhanced only to become the problem for which it was supposed to be the solution, where the fragmentation of power has always been both a problem and a solution, pretenders to power, especially those who claim not social support but intellectual improvement, have never had an easy time. (The saga of the American Adams — John, Charles, Francis, Henry, and Brooks — shows as much.) Nor should they. For the truth they have to tell is not necessarily in them, nor in their clients, but in what these cerebral prestidigitators often profess most to despise, their give and take with others whose consent they require, not once and for all, as if the social contract were forever irrevocable, but over and over again. This policy process is certainly exhausting, hardly exhilarating, but hopefully enlightening.

If power is in pieces, which resist picking up, and truth is partial, resistant to being made whole, the reader may well ask, what is to be gained by policy analysis? Using the time-honored tools of the trade, let's turn the question around: if power were unitary and knowledge were perfect, analysis would be either supreme (appearing as the one correct policy) or superfluous (no need for error correction if there are errors to correct). Nor do I believe policy analysis is a waste of time, because no one cares about what is true and beautiful but only about what is popular and preferable. Popularity in a democracy is no mean recommendation; a policy that is marginally preferable has much to commend it compared to one that is perfectly impossible. Besides, I try to remind myself that this won't be the last time I was wrong. If, like any aspiring analyst, I have succeeded in converting conundrums that cannot be queried into questions with controvertible answers, my mission is over.

NOTES

1. Heinz Eulau, "Workshop," *American Journal of Political Science*, Vol. 21 (May 1977), p. 419.
2. Martin Landau, "The Proper Domain of Policy Analysis," in "Workshop" *American Journal of Political Science*, Vol. 21 (May 1977), p. 424.
3. *Ibid.*
4. See the preface to Jeffrey Pressman and Aaron Wildavsky, *Implementation* (Berkeley and Los Angeles: University of California Press, 1973) for the difficulties of distinguishing "policy" from its implementation.
5. For a discussion of how far policy ideas can control (or are responsible for) their implementation, see Giandomenico Majone and Aaron Wildavsky, "Implementation as Evolution: Exorcising the Ghosts in the Implementation Machine," in Howard E. Freeman (Ed.), *Policy Studies Annual Review*, Vol. 2 (Beverly Hills, Calif.: Sage Publications, 1978), pp. 103–117.
6. "The Place of Policy Analysis in Political Science: Five Perspectives," *American Journal of Political Science*, Vol. 6, No. 1 (March 1975), p. 432.
7. This idea was suggested to me by Giandomenico Majone.
8. See Imre Lakatos, "History of Science and Its Rational Reconstructions," from *Boston Studies in the Philosophy of Science*, Vol. 8 (1970–1971), pp. 91–136, 174–182.
9. On organized skepticism, see Robert K. Merton, *Sociology of Science* (Chicago: University of Chicago Press, 1973), pp. 277, 278, 311, 339; and Harriet Zuckerman, "Deviant Behavior and Social Control in Science," in Edward Sagarin, ed., *Deviance and Social Change* (Beverly Hills, Calif.: Sage Publications, 1977), especially pp. 91–93, 125–127.
10. From Johan Huizinga, *Homo Ludens* (London: Paladin, 1970).
11. I Samuel 6–8.
12. Reprinted from the *Supreme Court Review*, 1977, ed. by Philip B. Kurland and Gerhard Casper (Chicago: University of Chicago Press, 1978), p. 36.
13. Sir William Osler, *A Way of Life*, an address to Yale students (New York: Hoeber, 1937).

APPENDIX

PRINCIPLES FOR A GRADUATE SCHOOL OF PUBLIC POLICY

The early history of the Graduate School of Public Policy illustrates the twilight world of policy analysis.[1] Even if objectives are not multiple and conflicting, they are pretty sure to be vague. When I was asked to become dean in the late spring of 1969, Chancellor Roger Heyns told me what kind of school he wanted for preparing students for public service: "A good one." What was good? Finding that out, he made clear, was why he was hiring me. Although the chancellor knew what he wanted, I didn't know how to give it to him. I decided it was a good idea to think small. It should be made easy to disband the school. For that reason, prospective faculty were invited to join the school only if their talents were sufficient to guarantee them jobs elsewhere.

Our objectives were vague, and we had no information on how to achieve them; no one knew how much we might be able to get, compared to what we wanted. Pat Hayashi (later a student in our school, but then assistant to the campus budget officer) remembers that, when asked to provide figures for financing the school, he hunted for data but could find only this minute from the Board of Regents: "Berkeley campus is authorized to establish graduate schools of journalism and public affairs." Later he discovered that a Chancellor's Committee several years earlier had suggested a ceiling of one hundred master's and twenty doctoral students. "I couldn't find anything that could be used as a basis for planning," he recalled. "Fine," he was told, "why don't you just use those figures as a basis for a projection? . . . Draw on your experience as a student." Hayashi protested that he had taken "only one course in Poli Sci," but he was told that it would have to do — and it did.[2]

Vague objectives and absent information weren't the only problems; coordination was another. We knew nothing about efforts to establish schools of public policy elsewhere; no one called to tell us what they were doing, and we didn't know whom to ask. Look at it this way: after World War II, the United States, aware of other countries' difficulties, established numerous centers to study foreign areas: by the late sixties people realized the United States had problems too; thus they started schools of public policy.

In such circumstances, one is as likely to react against what has gone before as to favor something new. It seemed that schools of substantive policy had collected vast numbers of facts about general areas of interest but had run into trouble identifying solutions relevant to problems. Some schools, it appeared, had suffered from teaching courses on subjects (such as classifying personnel position) that students would learn on the job anyway, or on other subjects (such as leadership or creative management) that nobody ever had understood. A school of public policy, by contrast, would emphasize analysis of problems by constantly moving from one area of policy to another. The hope was that problem solving, rather than fact grubbing, would predominate. The school would emphasize skills that (1) could be taught and yet (2) were not easily learned on the job. The skills covered in microeconomics and quantitative modeling courses met these criteria. But they would not be enough. Informal examination of the fate of policy analyses revealed that most analytic studies had been rejected by the organizations for which they were intended. Because political feasibility tends to overwhelm analytic contributions, analysts had become embittered. Getting organizations to use policy analysis was a major part of the solution, and courses on that subject had to figure in the curriculum.

The first issue was a home for the school. To the people in charge of allocating campus space, a space was a space was a space; they wanted to give us the number of cubic feet to which we were entitled in a way that would fit in also with their plans for accommodating other units. Generously they offered us space on two floors on three levels in a recently renovated portion of a marble mausoleum in the center of the campus. To them, here was a central location, sufficient cubic feet, and modern facilities; what else could anyone want? What else, indeed — a home, a place to which students and faculty would like to come and stay. The trouble with their space was that, even when you were there, you would never know where you were. How would it be possible to create this new thing we-knew-not-what if faculty and students were insulated in egg-carton compartments without opportunities for chance encounters or even a central meeting place? It might be difficult to create whatever it was under the best of circumstances, but it would be impossible with cold space. I refused, then, to accept the deanship until the school finally got the most appropriate form of housing — an old fraternity house with lots of warm wood paneling, fireplaces, beamed ceilings, and central meeting halls.

Such minor dramas in the history of a small school may be of no interest to those who haven't lived through them; they are recalled here in their particularity and peculiarity so that the reader will know in what spirit to take the abstract statement of principles for a school of public policy that follows. The buyer sufficiently beware of the element of interest in human affairs — "every man at his best state is altogether vanity" (the 39th Psalm) — will know that nothing exactly like that actually happens, at least not in precisely the same way or in as clear-cut a manner.

STRUCTURE OF THE SCHOOL

Make direct, 100 percent-time appointments in the school, or, if you can't, hire full-time faculty for each area of the required curriculum. The main structural feature of the Graduate School of Public Policy is that no faculty members have joint appointments.

A faculty shared between two sets of students and two sets of faculty committees was a faculty shared also between two sets of quarrels. Under that arrangement, we would not have enough time to develop a new program. As Dean, I would be making requests to faculty who would be unable to fulfill them. In fields with a well-developed tradition or with clearly structured principles that can be built into a curriculum, part-time appointments might work; for fields in the stew of creation, a part-time faculty would be half-baked.

It may be, nevertheless, that on some campuses a school of public policy cannot be established without joint appointments. A full-time appointment for each area of the required curriculum would still be desirable. Why? A good job demands intense commitment. If faculty members' future prospects depend even in part on a different department (very probable with a joint appointment), this potential conflict bodes ill for the future. The dean, when recruiting, is faced with having to get two sets of approvals from two groups of people who may see the world quite differently; termination of appointments, when necessary, is no fun either. Energy is diverted from positive problems of policy (what should be taught and who should teach it) to negative notions of noninterference (what can be done with faculty hired because they raised the least difficult problems of competing constituencies).

Space should promote the interpenetration of perspectives in a program that draws necessarily from diverse disciplines. Programmatic structure will be shaped by physical space. The people you talk to may be more important than your plans in determining program content. Space may separate when it should attract. In fact, "interdisciplinary teaching and research" is usually more a slogan than a reality. Like a stamp on a letter, faculty may be only superficially stuck to each other, never really coming together. If the whole is to be greater than the sum of the parts — a major objective in schools of public policy — then opportunities for interaction must be created.

Faculty from different disciplines should be encouraged to occupy offices next to each other, to teach together, and to work on parallel projects. Barriers to effective collaboration are enormous — disciplines differ not only in content but also in modes of thought and ways of working — and success is never guaranteed.

A public-policy school should follow a single-class system: *the Master of Public Policy degree for practitioners should be the sole entryway for the Doctorate of Philosophy in Public Policy.* The chief teaching accomplishment at the Graduate School of Public Policy has been to legitimate the primary interest of top-drawer academic professionals in master's students. In some fields, such students are second-class citizens, the degree often being given as a booby prize for failing to make the doctorate, or, at best, being seen as secondary to the "real thing," the Ph.D. Were there separate entry qualifications for doctoral and master's programs, faculty might concentrate on students who would assist them in research. Because all students must take the master's program, because that's where the action is, faculty also want to get into (instead of, as so often happens, out of) the required curriculum.

The most important thing about the required curriculum in policy analysis is that there be one. Within limits, what is in a school program for the year is less important than the fact that there is a program. For that year, at least, the meaning of analysis is defined by the requirements, which signifies that there is sufficient agreement among the faculty to carry on the enterprise so that students will know what is expected of them.

Analysis should be shown, not just defined. Nothing is more stultifying than a futile search for Aristotelian essences that starts with "I don't know, either, but it must be around somewhere." Analysis is taught by teaching its components, by having the students do it, and by showing through the work of faculty members and practitioners how it can be done. By their analyses shall ye know them, the bible of Policy Analysis would undoubtedly say, if there were one. We don't have an old or a new testament, but we do have a journal, *Policy Analysis.* Its main purpose is to exemplify the best in the field.

Schools of public policy, unless they have abundant resources, *should* use *teaching time* to develop *a single series of core courses in policy analysis.* The reverse also applies: *do not engage in peripheral activities.*

FACULTY

Choose economists interested in politics, political scientists interested in economics, and sociologists, lawyers, historians, philosophers, and so on, interested in both. It is hard enough to create a common perspective — a political economy, let us say, of policy analysis — when the people already do value the work of their colleagues. Obstacles become insurmountable if economists bewail intrusion by irrational political factors; political scientists see rational choice as fit only for robots; and sociologists explain that neither group understands the latent function of its own stereotyped combat.

A useful rule of thumb is that *faculty should include people who have had practical experience in doing* (as opposed to merely talking about) *policy analysis.* Whether or not it is possible to hire a few policy analysts, *there should be an active policy of giving the faculty frequent leaves to perform policy research.* A faculty strong on theory thereby will not lose touch with practical problems.

Political scientists and organization theorists who can apply their disciplines to the analysis of policy problems are hard to find. Passive understanding will not do. Appreciation of political and organizational processes is not enough. Active manipulation of refractory political and organizational variables is required.

Hire analysts, not just economists. Economics and economists are so obviously indispensable that it is easy to get the wrong kind of faculty. Among social scientists, economists have had by far the most experience applying their theory to practical problems. The very abundance of well-trained economists — people who have done cost-benefit studies or investigated price theory — may be a snare for the unwary. The elements of microeconomics are well known; creativity lies in the ability to apply them to policy problems. It follows, therefore, that technical competence, statistical expertise, formal elegance (all desirable) are not as important as the ability to conceptualize a solution, find an appropriate model for it, develop data that suit the task, and come out with useful information or advice. For recruiting, a prospective faculty member's analysis of a problem can tell more about his or her suitability than can discussion of regression techniques.

Modeling is an art; hire an artist. The last of the indispensable positions is in quantitative modeling. Any number of people have the technical qualifications to explain quantitative models, to use statistics normally associated with them, and to run the data through them using computers. The key consideration is: Who is best at constructing the simplest model to do the job?

Do not choose people who cannot meet traditional criteria of academic excellence. If you do, the school will lose status; and with status, students; and with students, faculty; and with faculty, administrative support. There is no place for second-class citizens in a university. The faculty's work may, in some instances, be atypical in character, but whatever the work, it must be recognizable as intellectually superior.

CURRICULUM

Core courses are school courses; they belong to the school as an institution and not to the individual instructor. This is not to say that courses are formulated by committees; the faculty member who teaches the course prepares the curriculum, but in doing so he or she follows general principles formulated by the school.

Where suggestions for improving the content of ordinary courses might, by custom, be regarded as intrusive, here such comments are taken as an expected part of everyday academic life.

Don't overload the curriculum! What should be taught in a school of public policy? The answer, naturally, is AE (Almost Everything). Who is to say that history, philosophy, anthropology, law, some scientific subjects, geography, linguistics, and many other things ought not to be standard equipment for the policy analyst? Probably no one would include all these subjects, but collective choice almost guarantees that faculty members will conclude their bargains by agreeing to let the others have what they want, which means more courses. Soon enough, it becomes clear that not everything can fit, even into an enlarged curriculum. Compromise is in order. Amid much dickering, it is agreed that half of almost everything (½ AE) will have to do. The results are predictable: ½ AE = T(ex), or total exhaustion on all sides. Then comes the annual student revolt and informal bargaining to reduce the workload from 100 to something more like 60 or 70 hours a week. It is a school's task to decide not the maximum, but the minimum that must be included in the curriculum.

Seek *creative redundancy in the curriculum.* There are only a few simple questions in policy analysis: What is a problem? How is a problem distinguished from a puzzle? What are various criteria of choice? How should they be applied? How can implementation be attended to in policy design? How can estimates of political feasibility be used to guide change rather than stultify action? Cutting into these questions at different times in different ways and from different perspectives helps develop people who think of themselves not as problem avoiders but as problem solvers.

A first-year curriculum should be required. If the faculty does not know what students should be studying, it should give up its position in favor of faculty who do. Indecisiveness among the faculty is followed rapidly by anxiety among the students. If we don't know what we ought to be doing, students reason, neither will they.

Courses should stress not passive appreciation but active manipula-

tion. It is appropriate for a course in political science to convey an understanding of the political process; a related course in public policy would stress modes of intervention. We use knowledge of what is to move closer to what ought to be; the emphasis is on change.

Whereas scholars in the liberal-arts tradition want to understand their material as fully as possible (whether or not anybody can do anything about the situation), a policy analyst would rather figure out who can change what with how much effort.

One cannot overemphasize political and organizational factors, because, although students love to talk about politics, they apply economics. The theory that comes with the handy applicator is the one they will try to use. Besides, economic solutions seem more practically proportioned to the kinds of problems they think they will be asked to solve — failure of public nursery-school services, financial crisis in a local housing authority — than do estimates of the political feasibility of major programs. Students claim that no one will ever ask them to estimate political feasibility. In a literal sense, to be sure, this is true. No one is likely to call for a study by that name. But, as our graduates learn in their first jobs, the ubiquitous question — is it worth doing analysis on X or Y? — amounts to asking about feasibility. In the meantime, back at the school, it is necessary to push harder for attention to political and organizational variables, precisely because their importance is not yet matched by ease of application.

Try to inure students to disappointment, but not discourage them entirely. Out in the real world, most analyses are not accepted; and, for those which are, many factors may intervene to prevent successful implementation. A lean budget year, promotion or resignation of a key figure, fear of change, among many things, may make application of intelligence irrelevant. A person who demands continuous evidence of success cannot function as an analyst. By making students aware of the odds against them (or, rather, against their enterprise), one hopes to harden them against the considerable likelihood of failure. Telling truth to power has never been terribly popular.

Warm the curriculum! It's cold out there, and students come in to the school to warm themselves with the thought that they will go on to make useful contributions to society. It is wise, therefore, to engage them early about larger as well as smaller questions, about questions of virtue as well as questions of power.

Always take the high ground: emphasize moral aspects of public policy. Every analyst faces problems of whether to work for clients whose preferences differ, or of whether or when to quit if the work is being misused. No definitive answer can (or should) be supplied, but students need practice in identifying the relevant considerations with a balanced, tough-minded, and resilient faculty member. Also, life throws up many moral dilemmas in public policy — from the death penalty, to abortion, to police strikes, to affirmative action. Being right may well be more important than being effective, but effectiveness sometimes does increase the capacity to get rightness taken seriously. Striking a balance between the two is connected to the growth of moral consciousness. I should add that the criteria for decision embodied in many analyses (such as equity, efficiency, and equality) are essentially moral, and the ability to decide which are appropriate under different circumstances is an important part of an analyst's moral education.

Emphasize analysis, not subject matter. Keep moving from one substantive area to another — from health, to welfare, to transportation, to energy, to whatever. Analysis, of course, depends on subject matter; you can analyze only in particular. A feeling for contingency, for how particular facts alter circumstances, is important to an analyst. Learning little stories about education or welfare or transportation, however, would defeat the aim of a program dealing with general recognition and solution of problems. If our students are hired to work on health and, after two weeks or two months or two years, they are asked to work on welfare, we would be grossly disappointed if they claimed either technological or temperamental incapacity to move from one field to another.

Analysis is a stance, not a technique: no one set of operations can be taught as the essence of analysis. But there is a way of looking at things in terms of opportunity costs, or what must be given up to do whatever one wishes, or problem solving and a "can-do" view of the world. By the spring of the first year, the students' work should begin to take on analytic form. A story is told, a dilemma is outlined, and a problem stated. There is a model, a structure of resources and objectives with a criterion for choosing among alternatives. Confidence grows. Yet students can't help wondering if what they're learning to do will have any bearing on the world outside.

With one or two exceptions, our graduates are working in public policy, but in widely diverse settings and activities. Only a few work exclusively as staff analysts. Most perform in a context that includes gaining access to agency managers, fitting a recommendation to organizational dynamics, and building feeling for adoption and implementation of policy into the study itself. They help agencies define issues, identify relevant trade-offs, and negotiate with the constituencies affected by a program. Most also are involved in management: the capacity to evaluate one's own program constantly in order to correct errors may not be all a manager needs to know, but it does beat working hard to do the wrong things more efficiently. Some students do deep analysis, spending lots of time working on one problem; others will move from one problem to another with skill and, we hope, with calm. Some students will do analysis; others, who may work with a high-ranking official or legislative committee, may monitor or manage analysis, or order it or consume it, but not necessarily do the thing itself. A person who understands analysis and can interpret it to others or act as a broker of ideas is every bit as valuable as the person doing direct analytic work.

At the master's level, the program in policy analysis should be inclusive; at the doctoral level, it should be exclusive. Because so many more outstanding students apply for admission to the master's program than we can accept, a good deal of selectivity occurs at the entry point. Those we admit we try to keep, because if they go on to graduate, they will contribute much to the analytic talent so essential to the world of public policy, and we are eager to provide tutoring, counseling, and encouragement to ensure that students who persist do end up with a master's degree. We assume that our task is to help them succeed; a student resignation is also our failure. Nevertheless, there always are a few dropouts.

Because there is no point in adding to the nation's social difficulties by swelling the ranks of those who should not have doctoral degrees, we operate on the assumption that only people with unusual creativity should be admitted to the Ph.D. program. The purpose of our doctorate is to advance the field of applied policy analysis. The number of people capable of generating new knowledge is small, so that we actively try to discourage from our Ph.D. program any student who does not show both a gift and a calling. Recall that entry to the Ph.D. is possible only through the master's program: students learn much about themselves in the first year or two of that program; many who initially intended to go on for a Ph.D. find that they are attracted more to the arena of action than to a life of theory and abstraction and therefore do not go beyond the master's.

Unless a student obviously is wrong, we assume that, like the customer, *he is always right.* But we reject criticism that denies the essential nature of the program to which the student has applied. If students find the required program too restrictive; if they wish to specialize during the first year; if they find quantitative considerations dehumanizing, or resource allocation a pact with the devil, then we do not want to act on their objections. Students either must accept the best we have to offer or choose another program. For the most part, however, we assume with reason that much of whatever criticism appears is directed toward getting us to fulfill the promise of our program. The complaint that courses are insufficiently applied, for example, usually means not that the student hates discussions of fundamental principles but that the instructor — casting about in a new field without an established body of literature — is having trouble finding real examples of the principles. Although one student who does not understand how a consideration is relevant may be having a personal problem, we recognize that a complaint voiced by many students usually signals a failure on our part.

Teach students that their instructors also need to learn. Once everyone understands that we are all in this together, any feeling that the faculty is holding out on the students should dissipate. Teaching is not merely teaching but a mode of learning, because no one knows it all — or nearly enough. Education must be mutual, because policy analysis is a work of discovery and not a gold mine ready to be exploited. The mother lode has yet to be found.

ADMINISTRATION

The administrative sin of meritocratic universities is the absence of historical reciprocity. No one ever deserves to keep anything until they have proved themselves anew. Past accomplishment is what got you here, but it's not what's going to keep you here, and so we want to know why you, among our many other prima donnas, should lay claim to scarce resources. Claims may be levied only on the future.

My first month in Berkeley, in the fall of 1963, drove the point home. Curiosity impelled me to a meeting of the Faculty Senate. Sitting in the back, I overheard two men bad-mouthing another whose name I recognized as that of a Nobel laureate. Half incredulous, I wondered out loud whether this wasn't the famous scientist who had won a Nobel prize. "Yes," was the reply, "but what's he done lately?" A true story, I swear.

The administrative philosophy of the Graduate School of Public Policy is deliberately designed to counter the worst effects of this meritocratic ethos. Every effort is made to create a nurturing environment in which *students, staff, and faculty are assumed meritorious unless proved otherwise*. Between periods scheduled for appraisal of merit, members of the school are presumed to have it and are entitled to draw upon reserves of reciprocity.

A supportive environment is one in which *the administration always says "Yes" unless it has strong reason to say "No."* Before saying that something cannot be done, an effort is made to do it. Nor do we go behind (why one wants to do) anything unless it is clearly contrary to school policy. Any request to avoid teaching at least one course to undergraduates, for example, is clearly unacceptable; but requests for teaching or research assistance, for travel, for exceptions to this or that rule, and so on, are pushed to the limit of available resources. In a word, everything not specifically prohibited is permitted.

Make minimal the cost of being turned down. School members (staff, students, faculty) accustomed to rebuff may avoid bringing up matters that trouble them, or making reasonable requests unless they have little to lose. But even when rebuff is not the usual response, they are unlikely to approach a dean (their last resort) first. At our school, therefore, the associate dean maintains a completely open-door policy; he gets the word around that he is available to try things on. At worst, the members of the school get an expert explanation of why they can't (or shouldn't) have

what they want; at best — and it happens more often than not — they get
something close to what they want.

*Correcting errors when things go bad is easier if you help school
members when things are good.* Administration and staff usually meet
when one needs something from the other — a committee assignment or
exemption from a rule. It is desirable, therefore, for administrators to ask
members how things are going, and to offer assistance, outside of a specific need to ask for or grant a favor. The idea that somebody out there
cares, that administration is there to help as well as to harass, is best
reinforced when nothing evident is at stake.

Never have more rules than the number of people involved. When
we originally conceived of our Ph.D. program, we planned to do what
everyone else does, namely, to write rules defining student qualifications
for the doctoral degree in public policy. When we realized, however, that
we were likely to have no more than ten to twelve students passing
through all stages of the doctoral program at any time, it seemed fruitless
to set up a list of rules longer than the roster of students who would be
asked to conform to them. Instead, after passing the required qualifying
examination, each doctoral candidate must form a committee of three
faculty members within the school and one outside to work with on an
individual program. This is likely to include specialization in a substantive policy area, advanced work in methodology, and exploration of an
interdisciplinary field such as political economy or political sociology.
Each student's abilities and needs are the controlling factors.

Our last report to the Ford Foundation, which provided financial
support to help develop our program, for example, expressed worry about
the slow development in creating an applied subfield in public-policy
analysis. For, if knowledge of the generic aspects of policy analysis fails
to cumulate, the best minds will leave the enterprise as soon as the current fad (and it is, in part, a fad) is over. The first Ford report, written on
the heels of our initial experience with designing and implementing a
curriculum in policy analysis, bristled with complaints. There were these
from the faculty: the courses were "extremely expensive of faculty time,"
"basically bookish," requiring "a greater emphasis on . . . real problems"; "we tended to be over-general and over-abstract"; "I don't think
what we were teaching was sufficiently tested by experience or susceptible to application"; "we lack a suitable methodology"; "there was a sense
of lost momentum and discontinuity in teaching styles, methods, and substance." And these came from students: "the readings were not directly
applicable to public policy"; "the students preferred more frequent problem sets"; "the students have a desire . . . to learn the application of
various kinds of quantitative techniques as opposed to learning detailed
solutions to mathematical problems"; and there is "frustration about the
problems of addressing these questions without first having a sufficient
background in the techniques and knowledge needed to perform policy

studies." Knowing that things were tough for everyone made it easier to keep going and to have frank discussions of what could be done to improve the situation.

AFTERWORD

It would be a pity if the principles I have tried to explicate about this school, were, without consideration of controlling conditions, raised to generality. Most schools of policy that I know are more like each other than they are different, possibly because we all end up doing what we know how to do. But the beauty of the current efforts to teach policy analysis, in my opinion, lies in the diversity they do have. One school concentrates on undergraduate education, another on only doctoral candidates. Our school provides a minimum of quantitative skills, another is devoted mostly to constructing large-scale quantitative models. One school is located in a research institute, another is in a business school, and yet another is trying to integrate public and private management. There is much to be learned from these experiences about underlying conditions and their consequences. Careful comparison, not fixation on one (no doubt idiosyncratic) model, is the key to learning about schools of policy.

How much of this account is to be believed? Analysts are taught to be skeptical.

NOTES

1. The idea of a Graduate School of Public Affairs, our predecessor, appeared in the early sixties under the leadership of Professor Frederick C. Mosher. In retrospect, the School of Public Affairs appears to mark a transition between education in public administration (as evidenced by the former Master of Arts of Public Administration degree in the Political Science Department) and current instruction in policy analysis. Public Affairs, according to documents dating to the fall of 1966, was to give a year's master's degree in one of three programs — Public Administration and Public Policy; International and Comparative Administration; and Regional, Metropolitan, and Urban Affairs. The plans included mid-career training for civil servants and service courses both for students from professional schools interested in governmental careers and for recent graduates aspiring to top-level positions in public administration. The orientation was to be interdisciplinary. The flavor shows in such tentative course titles as "Public Administration," "Administrative Decision Making and Leadership," "Research in Public Affairs," and "Social Science and Administration." Reflecting the way things go in universities, the Graduate School of Public Affairs was not formally established until 1968, with its first dean appointed in the summer of 1969. In 1971 we asked the regents to change the name to Public Policy (not merely because affairs are private and policies are

public, as local wags would have it, but also because the change would better reflect the new emerging emphasis on policy analysis). We feared that a School of Policy Analysis, the most accurate name, might lead to misunderstanding, as in *psycho*analysis. This has not stopped us from calling our new journal *Policy Analysis*. The truth will out.

2. Pat Hayashi, "The Birth of the School of Public Affairs," paper submitted for a course entitled, "Policy in Higher Education," taught by Clark Kerr and Martin Trow in the Graduate School of Public Policy (Berkeley, Calif., 1971).

INDEX